W9-AZZ-029

POINT–COUNTERPOINT

Readings in American Government

Fifth Edition

Herbert M. Levine

St. Martin's Press   New York

For Albert, Louise, and Philippe Boudreau

Executive editor: Don Reisman
Manager, publishing services: Emily Berleth
Publishing services associate: Kalea Chapman
Project management: Till & Till, Inc.
Production supervisor: Joe Ford
Cover design: Marek Antoniak

Library of Congress Catalog Number: 94-65228
Copyright © 1995 by St. Martin's Press, Inc.
All rights reserved. No part of this book may be reproduced,
stored in a retrieval system, or transmitted by any form or
by any means, electronic, mechanical, photocopying, recording,
or otherwise, except as may be expressly permitted by the applicable
copyright statutes or in writing by the Publisher.
Manufactured in the United States of America.
98765
fedcba

For information, write:
St. Martin's Press, Inc.
175 Fifth Avenue
New York, NY 10010

ISBN: 0–312–09968–1

Acknowledgments

Acknowledgments and copyrights are continued at the back of the book on page 386, which constitutes an extension of the copyright page.

It is a violation of the law to reproduce these selections by any means whatsoever without the written permission of the copyright holder.

Committee on the Constitutional System. "Committee on the Constitutional System: A Bicentennial Analysis of the Constitutional Convention." Reprinted with the permission of the Committee. Requests for further reprinting should be addressed to the Committee at 1755 Massachusetts Avenue, NW, Washington, DC 20036. (Phone 202/387–8787).

Thomas O. Sargentich. "The Limits of the Parliamentary Critique of the Separation of Powers." *William and Mary Law Review*, 34, no. 3 (Spring 1993), pp. 679–682, line 5; and 707 (The Empirical Foundation . . .)–739.

Pete du Pont. "Federalism in the Twenty-First Century: Will States Exist?" 16 *Harvard Journal of Law and Public Policy*, 137–148 (1993). Copyright by the Harvard Society for Law and Public Policy, 1993. All rights reserved. Reprinted with permission. (*Note:* Footnotes have been deleted.)

Morton Keller. "State Power Needn't Be Resurrected because It Never Died." *Governing*, 2, no. 1 (October 1988), 53–57. Reprinted with permission. *Governing* Magazine, copyright 1988.

Tye Messner. "Send 'em to the Polls." *Harvard Political Review*, 19, no. 2 (January 1992), p. 16. Reprinted with permission.

Ben Sheffner. "People Are the Problem." *Harvard Political Review*, 19, no. 2 (January 1992), p. 17. Reprinted with permission.

Jonathan Yardley. "Ding-a-Ling Democracy." *Washington Post*, February 22, 1993, p. 82. © 1993, The Washington Post Writers Group. Reprinted with permission.

Diane Rehm. "Voices of America." *Washington Post*, Oct. 25, 1992, pp. C1, C4. © 1992 The Washington Post. Reprinted with permission.

Preface

NEW TO THE FIFTH EDITION

The fifth edition of *Point–Counterpoint* is heavily revised. There is a new section on civil liberties and civil rights and there are many new debate topics. Included in the 16 new debates are readings on the viability or obsolescence of the federal system (Chapter 3); democracy and the electronic media (Chapter 5); the status of feminism in the 1990s (Chapter 6); government regulation of pornography (Chapter 7); freedom of the press during wartime (Chapter 9); the death penalty (Chapter 10); politics, ideology, and the Supreme Court (Chapter 16); school choice (Chapter 17); gun control (Chapter 19); and United States foreign policy in the post-Cold War world (Chapter 21). In addition, there are updated articles on the appropriate role of the President in foreign policy (Chapter 12) and new articles on term limits (Chapter 13).

THE RATIONALE FOR *POINT–COUNTERPOINT*

The debate tradition in the United States is as old as the Republic itself. Soon after the colonists achieved independence from British rule, they debated issues as fundamental as slavery, tariffs, and the policy of the United States toward the French Revolution. Some debates in U.S. history—Lincoln-Douglas and Kennedy-Nixon—have become part of the national memory, even if misremembered or embellished.

It is with this tradition in mind that *Point–Counterpoint* has been developed. The text is a collection of readings that present contending sides of important issues in U.S. government. It is designed to contribute to a democratic tradition where vigorous controversy is regarded as both proper and desirable.

The selections deal with the basic structure of the U.S. political system, political participation, civil liberties and civil rights, the power of government policy makers, and the direction of public policy. The format of the book encourages critical thinking. Part and chapter introductions provide important background information and a synopsis of the major points in each selection. For each debate question, one "Yes" response and one "No" response are given. "Questions for Discussion" follow each debate to help students formulate their own answers to the debate question. If both conflicting views on an issue seem convincing, students can then turn to the "Suggested Readings," which provide general background information as well as pro and con arguments.

Three cautionary points are in order. First, issues can rarely be broken down into a neat classification such as liberal or conservative. In this regard, it is often the case that some of the most meaningful controversy goes on among advocates of the same political philosophy.

Second, space limitations and the format of the book dictate that only two views—"Yes" and "No"—are given for each question. More often than not, other answers could be presented, such as "Yes, but . . . ," "No, but . . . ," or even "Maybe." In the process of debate, refinements can be developed. This yes-no approach, however, should provide a start toward understanding problems of U.S. government.

Third, the book does not present a single ideological perspective. As a whole, it does not take a side on the issues but presents, instead, many views. If there is an ideological commitment, it is implicit in the nature of the format: a commitment to vigorous debate as befits the democratic tradition.

ACKNOWLEDGMENTS

I am indebted to numerous people in the academic and publishing communities who helped me at various stages in the writing and production of this edition of *Point–Counterpoint*. The editorial consultants for the book offered superb suggestions and insights, including proposals for different debate topics and stylistic changes. Specifically, I want to acknowledge the following consultants for St. Martin's Press: Vida Davoudi, Kingswood College; Kate Greene, University of Southern Mississippi; Tseggai Isaac, University of Missouri-Rolla; Nancy Kral, Tomball College; Penny Mills, Gainesville College; John M. Nickerson, University of Maine; and Aimee Shouse, Western Illinois University.

Ryan J. Barilleaux and Daniel P. Franklin, who wrote articles for previous editions, have updated their contributions. I am appreciative of their professionalism, flexibility, attention to detail, adherence to deadlines, and goodwill. As in the past, I thoroughly enjoyed working with them. I am also grateful to Jay Girotto for writing an essay for the book. I respect his talent, patience, and thoroughness.

I am indebted to Ann Hofstra Grogg, who copyedited the manuscript with her usual extraordinary skill. I also want to thank Mary Hugh Lester, associate editor at St. Martin's Press, for her help in guiding the manuscript to production.

Herbert M. Levine

Contents

the
courts
pt. 3

Dec. 6
The Budget

Part I

Foundations of the

United States Political System

I n 1987 the United States celebrated the two hundredth anniversary of the Constitution by drawing attention to the basic institutions and practices of the nation's political system. Political officials, leaders of private associations, and writers assessed anew the fundamental assumptions under which the U.S. political system was established; they examined how a system designed for a largely agrarian society consisting of thirteen eastern seaboard states had evolved over two centuries to meet the needs of a postindustrial society that spans a continent.

These observers often evaluated how well or how poorly the United States was living up to the ideas professed by the Framers of the Constitution. Whether positive or negative in their assessments, they focused on social, economic, and political institutions.

Those who looked favorably at the development of the past two centuries often drew attention to a number of features: the rise in the nation's standard of living; the integration of groups from diverse ethnic, religious, and racial backgrounds into a "melting pot" in which these groups could live in peace; the resilience of the Constitution in adapting to change; the expansion of democratic practices to include ever larger numbers of people; the competition of political parties for electoral success; the freedoms accorded to U.S. citizens in expressing ideas, protesting peacefully, and responding to accusations in the criminal justice system; and the promotion of the common defense.

Those who were critical of the developments of the past two centuries pointed to different facts to justify their negative conclusions: the great disparity in assets, in which less than 10 percent of the U.S. population controls 90 percent of the nation's wealth; the long history of discrimination against blacks, Hispanics, and native Americans; the use of the Constitution by the dominant economic groups to prevent or delay social or economic change; the practical means used by government to prevent or slow down the participation of lower-income groups in the political process; the limitation of choice resulting from a two-party rather than a multiparty political system; the use by government of infiltration and disruption tactics to undermine groups holding ideas perceived to be threatening; the failure of the criminal justice system to give all defendants an equal chance regardless of wealth and background; and the use of military force and secret operations in influencing nations abroad, such as in Indochina in the 1960s and 1970s and in Nicaragua in the 1980s.

The views of contending sides assessing the U.S. political system raise the most fundamental issues underlying that system. This part considers three of these issues: the role of the Framers in creating a "more perfect Union"—and how perfect was and is that Union; the merits of the presidential system; and the future of federalism.

Chapter 1

Has the Wisdom of the Framers of the Constitution in Promoting a "More Perfect Union" Been Overrated?

The Constitution establishes the ground rules governing the political system of the United States. What the Framers believed and how they acted at the Constitutional Convention at Philadelphia in 1787 raise questions about the effect these rules may have had on political behavior thereafter.

Historians disagree sharply about the Framers of the Constitution. Characterizations of delegates to the Constitutional Convention range from self-serving men of prominence seeking to promote the interests of their own economic class to pragmatic leaders encompassing profound differences of economic interest and political philosophy.

The basic facts about the Constitution, however, are generally accepted. The Articles of Confederation, presented in Congress in 1776 but not finally ratified by all the states until 1781, established a league of friendship among the states rather than a national government. The period under the Articles was marked by widespread debt, Shays's Rebellion (a revolt of poor Massachusetts farmers), economic decay, and an inability to negotiate commercial treaties. In 1786 a Constitutional Convention was called to revise the Articles; it met in Philadelphia from May through September 1787. Most of the delegates were young, politically experienced, financially comfortable, and afraid of the common people, whom they called "the mob." Although they shared some assumptions about government and society, they disagreed profoundly about what should and should not be included in the document they were drafting.

Despite the celebration of the Framers at many civic occasions during the Constitution's bicentennial year, some observers, like the late Supreme Court Justice Thurgood Marshall, think the wisdom of the Framers of the Constitution has been overrated. Marshall was the first black person appointed to the Supreme Court. Earlier in his career, he was an attorney with the National Association for the Advancement of Colored People (NAACP), and he argued major civil rights cases in the courts.

In a speech sparked by commemorations of the bicentennial, Marshall faults the Framers for producing a defective document that allowed for the perpetuation of slavery and denied black people and women the right to vote. He contends that developments *after* the writing of the Constitution created a more promising basis for justice and equality than did the accomplishments of the Framers. He emphasizes the adoption of the Fourteenth Amendment ensuring protection of life, liberty, and property of all persons against deprivations without due process and guaranteeing the equal protection of the laws. Credit for change, Marshall says, should go to the people who passed amendments and laws that sought to promote liberty for *all* people of the United States. Marshall celebrates the Constitution as a living document, evolving through amendments and judicial interpretation.

Marshall's speech prompted a direct response by William Bradford Reynolds, at that time the assistant attorney general in the Civil Rights Division of the Justice Department. Reynolds was a controversial figure in the Reagan administration because of his actions on civil rights matters. A number of civil rights leaders criticized him for his opposition to affirmative action and voting rights legislation. Reynold's supporters defended him as a proponent of real racial equality.

In a speech delivered at Vanderbilt University, Reynolds argues that the Framers deserve the respect accorded to them in the bicentennial celebrations. Accepting Marshall's evaluation that the original Constitution was flawed, Reynolds still asserts that the Constitution marked "the greatest advance for human liberty in the entire history of mankind, then or since." Indeed, Reynolds continues, the constitutional system of divided governmental authority and separated government power eventually allowed for blacks to secure liberty. He notes that much blame for the low status of blacks in the United States should go not to the Framers but rather to those justices who failed to follow the terms of the Constitution and the laws of the land.

☑ *YES*

Has the Wisdom of the Framers of the Constitution in Promoting a "More Perfect Union" Been Overrated?

THURGOOD MARSHALL

The Constitution: Past and Present

Nineteen eighty-seven marks the 200th anniversary of the United States Constitution. A Commission has been established to coordinate the celebration. The official meetings, essay contests, and festivities have begun.

The planned commemoration will span three years, and I am told 1987 is "dedicated to the memory of the Founders and the document they drafted in Philadelphia." We are to "recall the achievements of our Founders and the knowledge and experience that inspired them, the nature of the government they established, its origins, its character, and its ends, and the rights and privileges of citizenship, as well as its attendant responsibilities."

Like many anniversary celebrations, the plan for 1987 takes particular events and holds them up as the source of all the very best that has followed. Patriotic feelings will surely swell, prompting proud proclamations of the wisdom, foresight, and sense of justice shared by the Framers and reflected in a written document now yellowed with age. This is unfortunate—not the patriotism itself, but the tendency for the celebration to oversimplify, and overlook the many other events that have been instrumental to our achievements as a nation. The focus of this celebration invites a complacent belief that the vision of those who debated and compromised in Philadelphia yielded the "more perfect Union" it is said we now enjoy.

I cannot accept this invitation, for I do not believe that the meaning of the Constitution was forever "fixed" at the Philadelphia Convention. Nor do I find the wisdom, foresight, and sense of justice exhibited by the Framers particularly profound. To the contrary, the government they devised was defective from the start, requiring several amendments, a civil war, and momentous social transformation to attain the system of constitutional government, and its respect for the individual freedoms and human rights, we hold as fundamental today. When contemporary Americans cite "The Constitution," they invoke a concept that is vastly different from what the Framers barely began to construct two centuries ago.

For a sense of the evolving nature of the Constitution we need look no further than the first three words of the document's preamble: "We the People." When the Founding Fathers used this phrase in 1787, they did not have in mind the majority of America's citizens. "We the People" included, in the words of the Framers, "the whole Number of free Persons." On a matter so basic as the right to vote, for example, Negro slaves were excluded, although they were counted for representational purposes—at three-fifths each. Women did not gain the right to vote for over a hundred and thirty years.

These omissions were intentional. The record of the Framers' debates on the slave question is especially clear: The Southern States acceded to the demands of the New England States for giving Congress broad power to regulate commerce, in exchange for the right to continue the slave trade. The economic interests of the regions coalesced: New Englanders engaged in the "carrying trade" would profit from transporting slaves from Africa as well as goods produced in America by slave labor. The perpetuation of slavery ensured the primary source of wealth in the Southern States.

Despite this clear understanding of the role slavery would play in the new republic, use of the words "slaves" and "slavery" was carefully avoided in the original document. Political representation in the lower House of Congress was to be based on the population of "free Persons" in each State, plus three-fifths of all "other Persons." Moral principles against slavery, for those who had them, were compromised, with no explanation of the conflicting principles for which the American Revolutionary War had ostensibly been fought: the self-evident truths "that all men are created equal, that they are endowed by their Creator with certain unalienable Rights, that among these are Life, Liberty and the pursuit of Happiness."

It was not the first such compromise. Even these ringing phrases from the Declaration of Independence are filled with irony, for an early draft of what became that Declaration assailed the King of England for suppressing legislative attempts to end the slave trade and for encouraging slave rebellions. The final draft adopted in 1776 did not contain this criticism. And so again at the Constitutional Convention eloquent objections to the institution of slavery went unheeded, and its opponents eventually consented to a document which laid a foundation for the tragic events that were to follow.

Pennsylvania's Gouverneur Morris provides an example. He opposed slavery and the counting of slaves in determining the basis for representation in Congress. At the Convention he objected that

> the inhabitant of Georgia [or] South Carolina who goes to the coast of Africa, and in defiance of the most sacred laws of humanity tears away his fellow creatures from their dearest connections and damns them to the most cruel bondages, shall have more votes in a Government instituted for protection of the rights of mankind, than the Citizen of Pennsylvania or New Jersey who views with a laudable horror, so nefarious a practice.

And yet Gouverneur Morris eventually accepted the three-fifths accommodation. In fact, he wrote the final draft of the Constitution, the very document the bicentennial will commemorate.

As a result of compromise, the right of the Southern States to continue importing slaves was extended, officially, at least until 1808. We know that it actually lasted a good deal longer, as the Framers possessed no monopoly on the ability to trade moral principles for self-interest. But they nevertheless set an unfortunate example. Slaves could be imported, if the commercial interests of the North were protected. To make the compromise even more palatable, customs duties would be imposed at up to ten dollars per slave as a means of raising public revenues.

No doubt it will be said, when the unpleasant truth of the history of slavery in America is mentioned during this bicentennial year, that the Constitution was a product of its times, and embodied a compromise which, under other circumstances, would not have been made. But the effects of the Framers' compromise have remained for generations. They arose from the contradiction between guaranteeing liberty and justice to all, and denying both to Negroes.

The original intent of the phrase, "We the People," was far too clear for any ameliorating construction. Writing for the Supreme Court in 1857, Chief Justice Taney penned the following passage in the *Dred Scott* case, on the issue whether, in the eyes of the Framers, slaves were "constituent members of the sovereignty," and were to be included among "We the People":

> We think they are not, and that they are not included, and were not intended to be included. . . . They had for more than a century before been regarded as beings of an inferior order, and altogether unfit to associate with the white race . . . ; and so far inferior, that they had no

rights which the white man was bound to respect; and that the negro might justly and lawfully be reduced to slavery for his benefit. . . . [A]ccordingly, a negro of the African race was regarded . . . as an article of property, and held, and bought and sold as such. . . . [N]o one seems to have doubted the correctness of the prevailing opinion of the time.

And so, nearly seven decades after the Constitutional Convention, the Supreme Court reaffirmed the prevailing opinion of the Framers regarding the rights of Negroes in America. It took a bloody civil war before the 13th Amendment could be adopted to abolish slavery, though not the consequences slavery would have for future Americans.

While the Union survived the civil war, the Constitution did not. In its place arose a new, more promising basis for justice and equality, the 14th Amendment, ensuring protection of the life, liberty, and property of *all* persons against deprivations without due process, and guaranteeing equal protection of the laws. And yet almost another century would pass before any significant recognition was obtained of the rights of black Americans to share equally even in such basic opportunities as education, housing, and employment, and to have their votes counted, and counted equally. In the meantime, blacks joined America's military to fight its wars and invested untold hours working in its factories and on its farms, contributing to the development of this country's magnificent wealth and waiting to share in its prosperity.

What is striking is the role legal principles have played throughout America's history in determining the condition of Negroes. They were enslaved by law, emancipated by law, disenfranchised and segregated by law; and, finally,they have begun to win equality by law. Along the way, new constitutional principles have emerged to meet the challenges of a changing society. The progress has been dramatic, and it will continue.

The men who gathered in Philadelphia in 1787 could not have envisioned these changes. They could not have imagined, nor would they have accepted, that the document they were drafting would one day be construed by a Supreme Court to which had been appointed a woman and the descendent of an African slave. "We the People" no longer enslave, but the credit does not belong to the Framers. It belongs to those who refused to acquiesce in outdated notions of "liberty," "justice," and "equality," and who strived to better them.

And so we must be careful, when focusing on the events which took place in Philadelphia two centuries ago, that we not overlook the momentous events which followed, and thereby lose our proper sense of perspective. Otherwise, the odds are that for many Americans the bicentennial celebration will be little more than a blind pilgrimage to the shrine of the original document now stored in a vault in the National Archives. If we seek, instead, a sensitive understanding of the Constitution's inherent defects, and its promising evolution through 200 years of history, the celebration of the "Miracle at Philadelphia" will, in my view, be a far more meaningful and humbling experience. We will see that the true miracle was not the birth of the Constitution, but its life, a life nurtured through two turbulent centuries of our own making, and a life embodying much good fortune that was not.

Thus, in this bicentennial year, we may not all participate in the festivities with flag-waving fervor. Some may more quietly commemorate the suffering, struggle, and sacrifice that have triumphed over much of what was wrong with the original document, and observe the anniversary with hopes not realized and promises not fulfilled. I plan to celebrate the bicentennial of the Constitution as a living document, including the Bill of Rights and the other amendments protecting individual freedoms and human rights.

Has the Wisdom of the Framers of the Constitution in Promoting a "More Perfect Union" Been Overrated?

WILLIAM BRADFORD REYNOLDS
The Wisdom of the Framers

Let me start with the observation that I regard myself to be most privileged to be a public servant at a time when we celebrate the 200th Anniversary of the Constitution—a magnificent document that has, in my view, no equal in history and every reason to be feted. It is by now no revelation that the Framers would be aghast at the size and reach of government today; but they would also be enormously proud of how much of their legacy has endured. The vitality of the original Constitution, and its various amendments, is reflected by its ability to withstand spirited debate over its content and meaning, a process that thankfully has been taking place with more and more enthusiasm in town meetings and forums all around the country, involving students, public officials, and citizens of every variety in evaluating how well our Constitution has served us over the past two centuries. I find it remarkable—and an enormous tribute to the Constitution—that in every instance about which I have read, these gatherings have been hard-pressed to think of ways in which to improve it in any meaningful manner.

That is not to say that the original Constitution of 1787 was flawless. And in our celebration of the document, we must not overlook its flaws and our long and painful struggles to correct them.

If there was any tendency to do so, it was no doubt corrected a few weeks ago when Justice Thurgood Marshall spoke in Hawaii on the Constitution's Bicentennial celebration. Whatever degree of disagreement one might have with Justice Marshall's comments, he has invigorated the debate on the meaning and vitality of constitutional principles in a focused way that can only serve to underscore the importance of the document itself and why it is so deserving of this Bicentennial celebration.

In recounting his remarks, I will rely on Justice Marshall's own words. He began by warning against what he called the "tendency for the celebration to oversimplify" the adoption and meaning of the Constitution of 1787 and to "overlook the many other events that have been instrumental to our achievements as a nation"—events that, as he explains, included the Civil War and the amendments added to the Constitution in its wake. Thus, he rejected what he described as a complacent belief that the "vision of those who debated and compromised in Philadelphia yielded the 'more perfect Union' it is said we now enjoy." Justice Marshall remarked further that he does not believe—and I quote—that "the meaning of the Constitution was forever 'fixed' at the Philadelphia Convention"; nor does he find "the wisdom, foresight, and sense of justice exhibited by the Framers particularly profound." The government the Framers of 1787 devised, he declared, "was defective from the start, requiring several amendments, a civil war, and momentous social transformation to attain the system of constitutional government, and its respect for the individual freedoms and human rights, we hold as fundamental today."

More specifically, Justice Marshall faulted the original Constitution because, as he put it, the Framers "did not have in mind the majority of America's citizens." The Preamble's "We the People," the Justice said, included only whites. Justice Marshall observes that the Constitution tacitly addressed the slavery issue in two ways: in Article I, section 2, by counting "other Persons" as three-fifths of "free Persons" for purposes of Congressional representation; and in Article I, section 9, by protecting the authority of states to continue importing slaves until 1808. Because the original Constitution was defective in this manner, Justice Marshall holds that "while the Union survived the civil war, the Constitution did not." Taking its place, he said, was "a new, more promising basis for justice and equality, the 14th Amendment, ensuring protection of the life, liberty, and property of *all* persons against deprivations without due process, and guaranteeing equal protection of the laws." For Justice Marshall, it is this new Constitution that we should celebrate; not the old one, which contains "outdated notions of 'liberty,' 'justice,' and 'equality.'" Thus, Justice Marshall declines to participate in the festivities with "flag-waving fervor," but rather plans to celebrate the Bicentennial of the Constitution as a "living document, including the Bill of Rights and the other amendments protecting individual freedoms and human rights."

Justice Marshall chose to focus almost exclusively on the most tragic aspects of the American experience, but he is absolutely right to remind us of them. For the Constitution was intended to be the culmination of a great struggle for the natural rights of men—a philosophy whose cornerstone is the absolute guarantee of equality under the law. When the Framers sought to protect in the Constitution the fundamental rights of man but failed to guarantee explicitly those rights to every individual, they introduced a self-contradiction that preordained struggles and conflicts we continue to confront today.

I am concerned, however, that what Justice Marshall has encouraged is far more than a simple mid-course correction in our celebration of the Constitution. It is one thing to be reminded of the compromise on slavery during the making of the Constitution. It is quite another, however, to encourage the view that there are two constitutions, the one of 1787, the other consisting of the Bill of Rights and the 14th Amendment; that the old one is so thoroughly defective that it did not survive the Civil War, and that the new one alone is worthy of celebration. Certainly, we ought to understand and appreciate the original Constitution in light of its weaknesses as well as its considerable strengths. But in the process, we ought to respectfully decline the invitation to consign it to the dustbin of history. That is a judgment as wrong as any on the other side of the ledger that uncritically praises the document of 1787. We indeed need what Justice Marshall called for—a "proper sense of perspective."

Notwithstanding its very serious flaws, the Constitution in its original form constituted the greatest advance for human liberty in the entire history of mankind, then or since. Indeed, it was only by preserving our underlying *constitutional system*—one of divided governmental authority and separated government powers—that blacks could enjoy the fruits of liberty once that self-contradiction I alluded to was corrected.

Fresh from the experience of subjugation under the British crown on [the] one hand, and the failure of the Articles of Confederation on the other, the Framers understood that there is an interdependent relationship between fundamental rights and the structure and powers of government. Thus, they crafted a government of limited powers, grounded in natural law principles and deriving its authority from the consent of the governed. They designed a system to protect individual rights through a balance and separation of governmental powers, which would forever ensure that the new national government would not exceed its enumerated powers. Not the least of these checks against governmental invasion of individual rights was the creation in Article III of an independent judiciary as a guardian of constitutional values.

Many of the Framers were not satisfied to protect individual rights merely by limiting the power of national government; they insisted upon a Bill of Rights to safeguard explicitly those rights they deemed most fundamental. Although the Bill of Rights was separately adopted, it would be [an] error to view the original Constitution apart from the first ten amendments, for the Framers agreed from the outset that the rights enumerated in the Bill of Rights were the object of government to protect. Beyond setting forth specific rights essential to a free people, the Framers established in the Ninth and Tenth Amendments a decentralized federal structure to more fully secure the free exercise of individual rights and self-government.

This was the basic structure of government the Framers deemed necessary to vindicate the principles of the American Revolution as set forth in the Declaration of Independence; and that, in my view, is the unique and remarkable achievement we celebrate today. But in celebrating the triumph of the Constitution, I am in full agreement that we must not overlook those parts of the constitutional experiment that were not noble and which, fortunately, have long since been corrected. Indeed, the experience of the Framers' compromise on the issue of "equality under law" provides us with important lessons even today.

From our historical vantage point, there is certainly no excuse for the original Constitution's failure to repudiate slavery. In making this deal with the devil—and departing from the absolute principle of "equality under law"—the Framers undermined the moral legitimacy of the Constitution.

But we ought to recognize that on this issue the Framers were faced with a Hobson's choice. The Constitution required unanimous ratification by the states, and at least two of the states refused to consent unless the slave trade was protected. James Wilson explained the dilemma: "Under the present Confederation, the states may admit the importation of slaves as long as they please; but by this article, after the year 1808, the Congress will have power to prohibit such importation. . . . I consider this as laying the foundation for banishing slavery out of this country." We know now that this hope was far too optimistic; and indeed, it would take the Civil War to rid the nation of that evil institution.

But even as the Framers were acceding to this compromise, they were sowing the seeds for the expansion of freedom to all individuals when circumstances would permit. James Wilson, for example, emphasized that "the term *slave* was not *admitted* in this *Constitution*." Instead, the term "Person" was used, suggesting that when the slaves became "free Persons," they would be entitled to all the rights appertaining to free individuals.

Indeed, many abolitionist leaders argued that the Constitution, by its omission of any mention of slavery, did not tolerate slavery. Noting that the Constitution nowhere mentions the word "slave," Frederick Douglass declared that "[i]n that instrument, I hold there is neither warrant, license, nor sanction of the hateful thing." Yet such arguments were tragically unheeded by the United States Supreme Court in the *Dred Scott* decision, which provided succor to the notion that there are justifications for exceptions to the principle of "equality under law"—a notion that despite its sordid origins has not been totally erased to this day.

Indeed, the *Dred Scott* decision illustrates that a significant part of the responsibility for our failure to make good on the principle of "equality under law" can and should be assigned less to shortcomings in the original Constitution—as Justice Marshall would have us believe—but to those who sat where Justice Marshall now sits, charged with interpreting that document.

Justice Marshall apparently believes that the original flaws in the Constitution dictated the result in *Dred Scott*. I am more inclined toward the view of my colleagues at the Department of Justice, Charles J. Cooper and Nelson Lund, who argue that Chief Justice Taney's constitutional interpretation was "loose, disingenuous, and result-oriented." Justice Curtis' dissent sounded a warning over this type of judicial interpretation unattached to constitutional moorings that is as compelling now as it was 125 years ago:

Political reasons have not the requisite certainty to afford rules of interpretation. They are different in different men. They are different in the same men at different times. And when a strict interpretation of the Constitution, according to the fixed rules which govern the interpretation of laws, is abandoned, and the theoretical opinions of individuals are allowed to control its meaning, we no longer have a Constitution; we are under the government of individual men, who for the time being have power to declare what the Constitution is, according to their own views of what it ought to mean.

The judiciary's tragic failure to follow the terms of the Constitution did not occur in this one instance only. Indeed, the Civil War amendments and civil rights legislation passed in that era were in the next several decades emptied of meaning by the Supreme Court in decision after decision. In *Plessy v. Ferguson,* to cite but one example, the Court once again stepped in and, over the lone, brilliant dissent of the elder Justice Harlan, shamefully sacrificed the principle of "equality under law."

I daresay that had the Court fully honored its mandate under the original Constitution in *Dred Scott,* or under the Fourteenth Amendment in *Plessy* v. *Ferguson,* we could well have escaped much of the racial strife and social divisiveness that Justice Marshall lays at the doorstep of the Constitution itself. Indeed, the tragic legacy of those decisions—the deadening consequences that so regularly flow from a compromise (no matter how well intended) of the principle of "equality under law"—provides a sobering lesson for the present Court as it struggles with similar issues involving race and gender discrimination. These are issues that no less so than in an earlier era leave hanging in the balance the overarching question of whether the liberating promise of the Constitution, as originally understood and subsequently articulated in explicit terms by ratification of the Civil War amendments, will or will not be fulfilled for all Americans.

Justice Marshall, I would respectfully submit, too casually brushes so weighty a concern to one side in contending that the Constitution did not survive the Civil War. One would think that this assertion would at least invite from some quarter the obvious questions: Did separation of powers survive the Civil War? Did the executive branch and the Congress? Did, indeed, the institution of judicial review?

I must admit to quite a different reading of history, one that has an abiding appreciation of the fact that our Constitution did survive so cataclysmic an upheaval as the Civil War. In all too many instances of internal strife among a People, one form of subjugation is ultimately replaced by another. But the Civil War produced a far different (indeed unique) result: its consequence was to more perfectly secure and extend to all Americans—through the Thirteenth, Fourteenth, and Fifteenth Amendments—the blessings of liberty as set forth in the Declaration of Independence, blessings of liberty that had already been secured for other Americans in the original Constitution and Bill of Rights. It is revisionist history of the worst sort to suggest that the Fourteenth Amendment created a black constitutional slate on which judges could write their own personalized definition of equality or fundamental rights. The Civil War Amendments were a logical extension of what had come before: they represented *evolutionary,* not *revolutionary* change.

To be sure, the Fourteenth Amendment does offer support for Justice Marshall's claim that the Constitution is "a living document," but only in the sense that the Constitution itself provides a mechanism—namely, the amendment process—to reflect changing social realities. Indeed, this orderly process for constitutional "evolution" is a part of the original Constitution's genius, for it provides a mechanism to correct flaws while safeguarding the essential integrity of our constitutional structure. But the existence of this mechanism—coupled with the system of checks and balances among the three branches of the federal government and the strong endorsement of federalism principles embodied in the Tenth Amendment—makes it abundantly clear that the Framers gave no license to judges (members of the Branch regarded, to borrow from Alexander Hamilton, as the "least dangerous" of the three) to construe constitutional provisions as they see fit.

There is good reason for all this confluence of restraints on judicial activism. The Constitution is not a mass of fungible, abstract principles whose meaning varies with time; rather, it comprises a broad societal consensus on certain fundamental, absolute principles necessary for the protection of individual liberty. The Framers believed that these constitutional values should not be lightly disturbed or set aside. Accordingly, the Constitution was structured so as to require that any change reflect the broadest expression of societal consensus.

This does not leave the Supreme Court or lower federal courts unable to apply the Constitution to circumstances never contemplated by the Framers. But the Judges are not free to disengage from our constitutional moorings in furtherance of their own social agendas; they are not free to determine that the constitutional principles themselves are unwise or obsolete.

Indeed, the very premise on which rests the notion that the Constitution as originally framed has no relevance today is fatally flawed. For the fact remains that the core structure upon which the Constitution was based—a government of limited powers, federalism, separation of powers, protection of fundamental individual rights—has proven in the past two centuries far superior to any other governmental system in protecting human freedoms. And where proponents of change have successfully secured the broad consensus necessary to amend the Constitution, they have expanded and perfected those protections. But judicial activism as an illegitimate substitute for the amendment process can only jeopardize our fundamental freedoms by denigrating the structural underpinnings vital to their survival.

Justice Marshall's contrary thesis is gerry-built on a regrettable overstatement of perceived flaws in the Constitution without so much as a passing reference to the qualities that have endured for the past two hundred years: a governmental structure that has withstood the test of time, weathered turbulent conflicts, and proven itself to be the greatest engine for individual freedom in the history of mankind. That remarkable accomplishment is certainly worth the celebration it is receiving, and much, much more.

Let us not be content with less than a complete appreciation for this document on which our Republic stands. Let us accept Justice Marshall's invitation to explore fully the lessons of the past two centuries. But let us decline his invitation to break the Constitution into two, and to reject the document of 1787 and accept only that which followed the Civil War. We are under a Constitution; it is the original Constitution together with its twenty-six amendments that we must seek to understand and uphold. Let us never forget that the Constitution is in its entirety the Supreme Law of the Land, and all of the branches—the executive, legislative, and judicial—are subordinate to it. We must embrace the Constitution as a whole: not uncritically, but not unlovingly either. Our task, in this Bicentennial year, should be that of loving critics. For our Constitution has provided this great nation of ours with a charter for liberty and government that has enabled us to move ever closer to that "more perfect Union" the Framers envisioned.

In conclusion, it is fitting that I call on the words of former Chief Justice Warren Burger, the Chairman of the Bicentennial Commission. He said it best when he remarked that the Constitution "isn't perfect, but it's the best thing in the world." Our Constitution embodies the American spirit, the American Dream, and America's doctrinal commitment to civil rights—those fundamental rights we all hold equally as American citizens. For this reason, I respectfully part company with Justice Marshall in my view that it is indeed our Constitution as framed two centuries ago, and amended thereafter from time to time, that stands tall today as "the source of all the very best that has followed." Let us not hesitate to celebrate.

Questions for Discussion

1. How did the political system adopted by the United States in the late eighteenth century compare to the political systems in other countries during the same period in terms of ensuring individual freedom?
2. What would have been the consequences to the political development of the United States had the Framers included provisions outlawing slavery and granting political equality for blacks?
3. What were the assumptions of the Framers about the relationship between individuals and the government?
4. What effect did the constitutional prescription to divide power between a central government and the states and between the different branches of the central government have on the condition of black people?
5. What evidence can you supply to accept or reject the proposition that the Constitution did not survive the Civil War?
6. What impact should the intent of the Framers have on Supreme Court justices in deciding cases today? What are the reasons for your answer?

Suggested Readings

Arkes, Hadley. *Beyond the Constitution*. Princeton, N.J.: Princeton Univ. Press, 1990.

Beard, Charles A. *An Economic Interpretation of the Constitution of the United States*. New York: Free Press, 1986. [Originally published New York: Macmillan, 1913.]

Berns, Walter. *Taking the Constitution Seriously*. Lanham, Md.: Madison Books, 1991.

Currie, David P. *The Constitution in the Supreme Court: The First Hundred Years, 1789–1888*. Chicago: Univ. of Chicago Press, 1985.

———. *The Constitution in the Supreme Court: The Second Century, 1888–1986*. Chicago: Univ. of Chicago Press, 1990.

Farrand, Max, ed. *The Records of the Federal Convention of 1787*. Rev. ed. 4 vols. New Haven: Yale Univ. Press, 1966.

Goldwin, Robert A. *Why Blacks, Women, and Jews Are Not Mentioned in the Constitution and Other Unorthodox Views*. Washington, D.C.: American Enterprise Institute for Public Policy Research, 1990.

Hamilton, Alexander, James Madison, and John Jay. *The Federalist Papers*, edited by Clinton Rossiter. New York: New American Library, 1961.

Ketcham, Ralph, ed. *The Anti-Federalist Papers: and, the Constitutional Convention Debates*. New York: New American Library, 1986.

———. *Framed for Posterity: The Enduring Philosophy of the Constitution*. Lawrence: Univ. Press of Kansas, 1993.

Licht, Robert A., ed. *The Framers and Fundamental Rights*. Washington, D.C.: AEI Press, 1991.

Loury, Glenn C. "'Matters of Color': Blacks and the Constitutional Order." *Public Interest*, no. 86 (Winter 1987), 109–123.

McDonald, Forrest. *We the People: Economic Origins of the Constitution*. New Brunswick, N.J.: Transaction Publishers, 1992. [Originally published Chicago: Univ. of Chicago Press, 1958.]

Mee, Charles L., Jr. *The Genius of the People*. New York: Harper & Row, 1987.

Morris, Richard B. *Witnesses at the Creation: Hamilton, Madison, Jay and the Constitution*. New York: New American Library, 1986.

Ollman, Bertell, and Jonathan Birnbaum, eds. *The United States Constitution: 200 Years of Anti-Federalist, Abolitionist, Feminist, Muckraking, Progressive, and Especially Socialist Criticism*. New York: New York Univ. Press, 1990.

Pole, J. R. *The Pursuit of Equality in American History*. 2d ed. Berkeley: Univ. of California Press, 1993.

Chapter 2

Should the United States Pattern Its Political Institutions after the British Parliamentary System?

It is generally accepted that without compromise the Constitutional Convention would have failed. One important conflict was between the large states, which favored representation based on population, and the small states, which wanted each state to have equal representation. This conflict was resolved by establishing a House of Representatives constituted on the basis of population and a Senate represented on the principle of state equality. Another conflict involved popular participation in the political process. This division was resolved by permitting the House of Representatives to be elected by popular vote and the Senate to be elected by the state legislatures (the Seventeenth Amendment ratified in 1913 required the direct election of senators).

The Constitution provided for a stronger central government than had existed under the Articles of Confederation. That new government was to be a republic in which the president and Congress would be elected directly or indirectly by the people. The Constitution also provided for the establishment of the basic institutions of the national government: the presidency, the Congress, and the Supreme Court. Specific provisions were made for how leaders would be chosen for these offices and how their authority would be limited.

The Framers feared the concentration of power in the hands of a few, but they also wanted to avoid "mob rule" by the majority. A fundamental feature of the new Constitution was, therefore, a system of shared power. Each branch of the federal government has primary power in one area, but that power is not total. Congress, consequently, has primary legislative power; the president, primary executive power; and the Supreme Court, primary judicial power.

Each of these powers, however, is shared. The president exercises some judicial power (the nomination of judges to the Supreme Court) and some legislative power (the vetoing of legislation). Congress has some executive power (Senate confirmation of executive appointments) and some judicial power (impeachment by the House of Representatives). The Supreme Court, too, has some legislative power (the interpretation of laws) and some executive power (the administration of laws to ensure compliance with judicial decisions).

But this central feature of the Constitution is itself under debate. The Committee on the Constitutional System (CCS), a nonpartisan organization composed of present and past government officials and private citizens, argues that the system is outmoded. The CCS is chaired by Senator

Nancy Landon Kassebaum, Republican from Kansas; C. Douglas Dillon, former secretary of the treasury and undersecretary of state; and Lloyd N. Cutler, former counsel to the president. Its purpose is to study and analyze the U.S. constitutional system.

In its Report and Recommendations (1987), the CCS points to strains in the constitutional system, such as the mounting national debt, conflicts between Congress and the president over foreign policy, and malfunctions of the modern electoral system. The report places principal blame for these developments on the diffuse structure of the separation of powers and the decline in party loyalty and party cohesion at all levels of the political system. It notes the adverse effects of the system: a brief "honeymoon" between president and Congress, divided government, lack of party cohesion in Congress, loss of accountability, and lack of a mechanism for replacing failed or deadlocked government. It presents proposals adopted by the CCS and additional proposals worth considering. According to the CCS, such proposals would strengthen party cohesion, improve collaboration between the executive and legislative branches, and reduce the costs of campaigning for election.

In essence, the CCS would like the U.S. constitutional system to pattern itself after the British parliamentary system. In the British system the prime minister is a member of Parliament; the majority party or a majority coalition of parties controls the House of Commons—the chief legislative institution; and party members in the House of Commons generally vote the way the party decides. A losing vote in the House of Commons results in new elections for all members of that chamber.

In looking to the adoption of some features of the British parliamentary system in the United States, the CCS is in accord with a political literature of reverence for British institutions that began more than a century ago. In *Congressional Government: A Study in American Politics*, published in 1885, political scientist and future president Woodrow Wilson attacked the weaknesses of the separation of powers and called for reforms that would move the constitutional structure of the U.S. political system toward the British model.

Throughout the twentieth century, other critics—although differing in specific proposals—called for one or more structural reforms of the U.S. government that were borrowed from British practice. Among these critics were William MacDonald, William Yandall Elliott, Henry Hazlitt, and Thomas Finletter.

The Watergate crisis, in which the government endured a long paralysis during investigation and impeachment proceedings against President Richard Nixon, prompted renewed attention to the British model. Charles Hardin argues that Great Britain would not have had to endure such a prolonged crisis during a Watergate-type scandal. According to Hardin, the British government merely would have called for a vote of no confidence, and a special election would have replaced the head of government.

The parliamentary critique of the separation of powers is challenged by Thomas O. Sargentich, a professor at the Washington College of Law at American University in the District of Columbia. Writing in the *William and Mary Law Review,* he contends

1. It is not true that the separation of powers makes the United States inevitably prone to prolonged and debilitating stalemate. Moreover, controversy itself can be constructive in promoting fruitful negotiation.
2. The parliamentary view of effectiveness is vague.
3. Accountability in government does not require unity of governmental structure. In a separation of powers system, both the legislature and the executive are still accountable to the people.
4. The British parliamentary system is suited to Great Britain because of the character of the British people. We should not assume that a heterogeneous society, such as that of the United States, would find parliamentary institutions suitable to its character.
5. Supporters of the adoption of the parliamentary model in the United States ignore the criticisms of the parliamentary system that are being made in Great Britain. Critics of the British system argue, for example, that such institutions give unwarranted power to the administration of the moment.
6. The separation of powers system has not been inflexible but has, rather, been dynamic and responsive to change.
7. Parliamentary advocates have a highly abstract vision of the job of government as one of instrumental management. They tend to overlook the open deliberation and ongoing participation that are part of the political process.
8. Separation of powers expands political access and dialogue, an expansion beneficial to the social diversity of the United States.

Both selections in this chapter mention political parties, a political institution not mentioned in the Constitution because formal parties did not exist when the Constitution was drafted. Like some other institutions not mentioned in the Constitution—the committee system in Congress and the bureaucracy, for example—political parties have evolved to meet the needs of a changing society and have come to play an important role in the U.S. political process.

Should the United States Pattern Its Political Institutions after the British Parliamentary System?

COMMITTEE ON THE CONSTITUTIONAL SYSTEM

A Bicentennial Analysis of the American Political Structure

Two hundred years ago, the founders of the American republic decided that the governmental system that had guided them safely through the War for Independence was in need of change. They became convinced that nothing short of a new constitution would meet the demands that lay ahead.

Having reached this conclusion, they did not hesitate to take the necessary action. The result was the framing and ratification of the United States Constitution.

As we approach the bicentennial of the Constitution, Americans are eager to honor the framers' work, which is truly one of the great achievements of human history.

The system designed in 1787 has proven remarkably adaptable to the changing demands of a growing nation. Political leaders have been imaginative and bold in finding ways to adapt the system to meet evolving national responsibilities and needs. Hamilton, Jefferson and Madison themselves took the lead in creating the party system, building greater cohesion and efficiency into the lawmaking process.

As the United States shifted from an agricultural to an industrial society and the regulation of commercial and financial markets became too complex for a government of separated powers, a later generation of politicians invented the independent regulatory commission, combining rule-making, administrative and adjudicatory powers in a single governmental body.

During the 1930s, new signs of strain began to appear. In response to the Great Depression, the government embarked on a vast set of programs to manage the growth of our modern industrial economy and provide a measure of social justice for those who suffered from its malfunctions. Then dangerous challenges to American security arose in Europe and the Far East and in our own national defense, and we had to assume global military and foreign policy responsibilities. These developments, domestic and foreign, required the federal government to undertake new tasks that were unprecedented in kind or scope and could hardly have been foreseen by the framers.

Thoughtful observers soon realized that the governmental structure was straining under this enormous additional load. A series of commissions chaired by Louis Brownlow, Herbert Hoover and Roy Ash made sweeping recommendations that became the basis for extensive modernization of the executive branch. Distinguished panels in the Senate and House chaired by Mike Monroney and Robert LaFollette, Jr., Richard Bolling, Adlai Stevenson III and William Brock brought about important changes in the procedures and committee structure of Congress. Groups outside the government (such as the National Academy of Public Administration, the Committee on Political Parties of the American Political Science Association and the Committee for Economic Development), as well as individual analysts and authors, offered other suggestions for reform.

Though most of these studies confined themselves to recommending adjustments within the existing framework, many recognized that the twentieth-century problems confronting our eighteenth-century American political system might require changes in the constitutional structure. Changes in statutes and party rules are of course less difficult to make and ought to be tried before changes in the Constitution itself. Changes in the Constitution should not be shunned, however, if critical modern problems cannot be solved by other means.

In the last Federalist Paper, Alexander Hamilton urged that the Constitution be ratified despite the objections that were being raised, because there would be opportunity later to make amendments as experience revealed the need. James Madison and Gouverneur Morris likewise acknowledged imperfections in the framers' brilliant work.

For example, the same document that established the Bill of Rights also countenanced the continued practice of slavery. When that contradiction became apparent over the next century, the resulting constitutional crisis produced a terrible civil war. Abraham Lincoln called a distracted nation to attention with the words, "We must disenthrall ourselves." "The dogmas of the quiet past," he added, "are inadequate to the stormy present. . . . As our case is new, so we must think anew, and act anew." And the Constitution was amended to outlaw slavery, root and branch.

Thomas Jefferson considered the amendment process one of the Constitution's most important features. "I am certainly not an advocate for frequent and untried changes in laws and constitutions," he wrote. "But I know also that laws and institutions must go hand in hand with the progress of the human mind. As that becomes more developed, more enlightened, as new discoveries are made, new truths disclosed, and manners and opinions change with the change of circumstances, institutions must advance also and keep pace with the times."

As Jefferson foresaw, we too face unprecedented challenges. If aspects of the system framed in 1787 prevent the national government from meeting its present responsibilities, we must identify the outmoded features, separate them from the good and durable parts of the system and make the necessary modifications.

To do so is not to reject the great work of our forebears. It honors their spirit in the most sincere way: by seeking to emulate it.

SIGNS OF STRAIN

As the bicentennial draws near, the signs of strain in our governing processes are unmistakable.

Perhaps the most alarming evidence is the mounting national debt, fueled anew each year by outsized and unsustainable deficits that defy the good intentions of legislators and Presidents.

Consistency in our foreign and national security policies is also frustrated by an institutional contest of wills between Presidents and shifting, cross-party coalitions within the Congress. Over forty treaties submitted to the Senate for ratification since World War II have either been rejected or have never come to a vote. Among those that have never come to a vote are SALT [Strategic Arms Limitation Treaty] II, the 1974 and 1976 treaties on underground nuclear tests and explosions, maritime boundary treaties with Mexico and Canada, several UN [United Nations] and OAS [Organization of American States] human rights conventions, and a wide variety of bilateral trade, tax and environmental treaties. Meanwhile presidential concern over "leaks" and frustration with congressionally imposed restrictions have led Presidents and their staffs to launch important diplomatic, military and covert activities in secret and without consulting Congress.

Further problems—particularly damaging in a nation dedicated to the principle of self-government—stem from malfunctions of the modern electoral system: the high cost of running for office, the corroding influence of campaign contributions from single-interest groups, the stupefying length of campaigns (for the presidency, usually several years from initiation to inauguration), and persistently low turnout rates (among the lowest in the world for nations with competitive elections).

CAUSES

Sensing the failures and weaknesses in governmental performance, people tend to blame particular politicians or the complexity of the modern world. But our public officials are no less competent, either individually or as a group, than they used to be. Nor do our problems, as complex as they are, defy rational solutions consistent with our basic constitutional liberties. The difficulty lies mainly in the diffuse structure of the executive-legislative process and in the decline of party loyalty and cohesion at all levels of the political system.

The separation of powers, as a principle of constitutional structure, has served us well in preventing tyranny and the abuse of high office, but it has done so by encouraging confrontation, indecision and deadlock, and by diffusing accountability for the results.

Ideally our two-party system should counteract the centrifugal tendencies of the separation of powers, with each party's politicians committed to a common philosophy of government and to specific program goals for which they stand accountable at the next election. In fact, throughout most of the nineteenth century and until after the end of World War II, the loyalty of most politicians to their party was deeply felt. They ran for office on a ticket selected by the party's leaders. Once in office, they recognized a common stake in the success of their party's governance and their joint accountability as candidates of the party at the next election.

In recent decades, however, political reforms and technological changes have worked together to weaken the parties and undermine their ability to draw the separated parts of the government into coherent action. Beginning in the late nineteenth century, Congress enacted a series of measures that redistributed functions previously performed by the parties. Civil service systems stripped the parties of much of their patronage.

The rise of the welfare state took away many opportunities for service by which the parties had won and held the loyalty of their followers. The secret ballot replaced the "tickets" which had previously been prepared by the parties and handed to the voters to cast into the ballot box. The 17th Amendment (ratified in 1913), which required the direct election of Senators, dealt another blow to party cohesiveness. So did the direct primary, which came to dominate the nomination of presidential candidates, particularly after 1968.

Modern technology has enabled candidates to appeal to voters directly, through television, computer-assisted mailings and telephone campaigns, and by quick visits in jet airplanes, all of which have lessened their dependence on party organizations and leaders. The key to these technologies is money, but candidates found they could raise it directly for themselves better than through the party organization. At the same time, interest groups found they could exercise more power over legislative votes by contributing directly to selected candidates rather than to a party.

The habits of voters also changed in this new environment. Party loyalty had been the rule for most of the nineteenth century, but by the last quarter of the twentieth century, one-third of all voters were registered as independents, and even among voters registering with parties, ticket-splitting became the norm.

Many of these changes resulted from laudable reforms and were, in any case, inevitable. No one wants to roll the clock back to the time when party bosses and local "machines" dominated the political process.

Nevertheless, we need to recognize that the weakening of parties in the electoral arena has contributed to the disintegration of party cohesion among the officials we elect to public office. Members of Congress who owe their election less to their party than to their own endeavors and their own sources of funds have little incentive to cooperate with party leaders in the Congress, much less their party's incumbent in the White House. And the proliferation of congressional committees and subcommittees has increased the disarray. There are now so many that almost every member is the chairman or ranking minority member of at least one committee or subcommittee, with all the political influence, proliferating staffs, publicity and fund-raising potential needed to remain in office.

EFFECTS

Because the separation of powers encourages conflict between the branches and because the parties are weak, the capacity of the federal government to fashion, enact and administer coherent public policy has diminished and the ability of elected officials to avoid accountability for governmental failures has grown. More specifically, the problems include:

Brief Honeymoons

Only the first few months of each four-year presidential term provide an opportunity for decisive action on domestic problems. By the second year, congressional incumbents are engrossed in the mid-term election and defer difficult decisions that will offend any important interest group.

The mid-term election usually results in a setback for the President's party that weakens his leadership and increases the stalemate and deadlock in the Congress. After the mid-term election, the government comes close to immobility as the President and Congress focus their energies on the imminent presidential election.

Divided Government

We have had divided government (one party winning the White House and the other a majority in one or both houses of Congress) 60 percent of the time since 1956 and 80 percent of the time since 1968, compared to less than 25 percent of the time from the adoption of the Constitution until World War II.

This has led to inconsistency, incoherence and even stagnation in national policy. Affirmative policy decisions, as well as the *non*decisions resulting from frequent deadlocks that block any action at all, are reached by shifting majorities built out of cross-party coalitions that change from one issue to the next.

Divided government in turn reflects the decline in party loyalty and the growing practice of ticket-splitting among the electorate. In 1900 only four percent of all congressional districts were carried by one party's presidential candidate and the other party's candidate for Member of the House. By 1984, because of the growth of ticket-splitting, this happened in 44 percent of all congressional districts.

One of Woodrow Wilson's themes during the campaign of 1912—a time of divided government—was that only party government (with one party successfully bridging the separated powers by winning control of the presidency and both houses of Congress) could carry a coherent program into effect. The voters in 1912 responded by choosing party government, and Wilson's New Freedom program was successfully legislated.

Lack of Party Cohesion in Congress

Even in times of united government, disunity persists between the branches— and between and within the two houses of Congress—because many members of both the President's party and the opposition party reject the positions taken by their leaders. Legislators today have less reason to stick with their party's position and more reason to follow the urgings of non-party political action committees, which provide more of their campaign funds than the party does. The summary rejection of President Reagan's budget in 1986, even by members of his own party in the Republican-controlled Senate, dramatically illustrates the lack of party cohesion in the current political environment. This lack of cohesion induces Presidents and their staffs, as noted above, to conceal important foreign policy initiatives even from the leaders of their own party in Congress.

Loss of Accountability

Divided government and party disunity also lead to diffused accountability. No elected official defends the sum of all the inconsistent policy decisions made by so many shifting cross-party coalitions, and each successfully shifts the blame to others. Polls show the public is dissatisfied with the governmental institutions—especially Congress and the bureaucracy—that legislate and administer this hodge-podge of policies. But the public seldom holds a party accountable for these failures, and it hardly ever holds individual legislators responsible.

Since World War II, 90 percent of each party's incumbent legislators who sought another term have been reelected, even in years when their party lost the White House. In 1986 the figure was 97 percent. Benjamin Franklin's famous maxim, "We must all hang together, or assuredly we shall all hang separately," no longer applies to the Members of Congress of either party.

Lack of a Mechanism for Replacing Failed or Deadlocked Government

Presently there is no way between our fixed election dates to resolve basic disagreements between the President and Congress by referring them to the electorate. The only way to remove a failed President is by a House impeachment and Senate trial for "treason, bribery, or other high crimes and misdemeanors." And between the fixed election dates there is no way to reorient a Congress in which one or both houses obstruct an important and popular presidential program.

REMEDIES

In seeking to adjust the constitutional system to modern conditions, we must be careful to preserve its enduring virtues. We must continue to respect the Bill of Rights, protected by an independent judiciary, and we must continue to insist that elected officials be able to monitor one another's performance and call one another to account.

Consistent with these principles, it should be possible to design improvements that would encourage party cohesion and lessen the deadlock between the executive and legislative branches without sacrificing essential checks and balances. The Committee on the Constitutional System offers the following proposals as sufficiently meritorious to warrant national consideration and debate. Some of these proposals call only for adopting new party rules or statutes, while others would require amendments to the Constitution.

PROPOSALS WHICH COMMAND MAJORITY SUPPORT AMONG OUR MEMBERSHIP

Strengthening Parties as Agents of Cohesion and Accountability

1. THE PARTY PRESIDENTIAL NOMINATING CONVENTION The parties should amend their rules for the presidential nominating conventions so as to entitle all winners of the party nominations for the House and Senate, plus the holdover Senators, to seats as uncommitted voting delegates in the presidential nominating convention. This would give the congressional candidates of the party a significant voice in selecting the presidential candidate, increase the loyalties between them in the election campaign, improve cohesion between the President and the legislative incumbents of his party and tend to make them jointly accountable to the voters in the next election.

2. OPTIONAL STRAIGHT-TICKET BALLOTING Congress should enact a statute requiring all states to include a line or lever on federal election ballots enabling voters, if they so desire, to cast a straight-line party ballot for a party's candidates for all open federal offices.

A recent survey shows that nineteen states, including Illinois, New York and Pennsylvania, already have such statutes and that ticket-splitting is less common in those states. This would encourage party loyalty at the voter level and among a party's federal candidates. To the extent that it reduced ticket-splitting, it would lessen the likelihood of divided federal government, while still leaving voters free to split their tickets if they chose.

3. PUBLIC FINANCING OF CONGRESSIONAL CAMPAIGNS Congress should amend the campaign financing laws to create a Congressional Broadcast Fund similar to the existing Presidential Campaign Fund. This fund would be available to each party under a formula similar to that used for the Presidential Campaign Fund, on condition that the party and its candidates expend no other funds on campaign broadcasts. Half of each party's share would go to the nominees themselves. The other half would go to the party's Senate and House campaign committees, which could apportion the funds among candidates so as to maximize the party's chances of winning a legislative majority.

By requiring candidates to look to the party for a substantial part of their broadcast funds, this proposal would help to build party loyalty and cohesion. It would also provide a constitutional way of limiting expenditures on the largest single component of campaign financing costs.

Improving Collaboration between the Executive and Legislative Branches

1. FOUR-YEAR TERMS FOR HOUSE MEMBERS AND EIGHT-YEAR TERMS FOR SENATORS, WITH FEDERAL ELECTIONS EVERY FOURTH YEAR The present system of staggered elections has the effect of pulling the branches apart. Members of the House, who run every two years, feel a political need to demonstrate their independence from the White House, particularly in off-year elections. So do the one-third of the Senators who face an election within two years. Every other time an incumbent in either house runs for reelection, there is no presidential campaign.

The effect is to encourage legislators to distance themselves from the President and from presidential programs that may involve a difficult, short-term adjustment on the way to a worthwhile, longer-term result.

The Constitution could be amended so that the President and Members of the House would serve concurrent, four-year terms, and one Senator from each state would be elected for an eight-year term at each presidential election. This would eliminate the present House and Senate elections in the middle of the presidential term. It would lengthen and coordinate the political horizons of all incumbents. Presidents and legislators could join to enact necessary measures with the promise of longer-run benefits, without having to worry about an imminent election before the benefits were realized.

With fewer elections, the aggregate cost of campaign financing should go down, and legislators would be less frequently or immediately in thrall to the interest groups on whom they depend for funds. The honeymoon for enacting a President's program would be longer. With a four-year life for each Congress, the legislative process for the budget and other measures could be made more orderly and deliberate.

Alternatives. If the eight-year term for Senators were deemed too long, the Senate term could be shortened to four years, concurrent with the terms of the President and the House, which would also eliminate the mid-term election. Or, if the Senate would not accept a shortened term, we could keep the present six-year term. This would retain a limited mid-term election (for one-third of the Senate), permitting a partial referendum on government policy, at the cost of shortening the political horizon of one-third of the Senate.

2. PERMITTING MEMBERS OF CONGRESS TO SERVE IN THE CABINET

The Constitution now bars members of Congress from serving as heads of administrative departments or agencies or holding any other executive-branch position. This provision was intended to prevent the President from dominating Congress by offering executive positions to key legislators. But its principal effect has been to deprive the nation of administrators who would have the confidence of both the executive and legislative branches.

If the barrier were removed from the Constitution, Presidents would have the option of appointing leading legislators to cabinet positions, and legislators would have the option of accepting such offers, without being required to give up their seats in Congress. Such ties between the branches might encourage closer collaboration and help to prevent stalemates. They would broaden both the range of talent available to a President in forming his administration and the base of political leadership in the executive branch.

Under such an amendment, of course, a President would not be obliged to appoint any members of Congress to his cabinet, nor would they be obliged to accept.

Woodrow Wilson strongly favored this amendment, as a means to encourage closer collaboration between the branches. While modern legislators may have less time and incentive to join the cabinet than earlier generations, there is no longer any reason for a constitutional barrier to an experiment that has considerable promise and little risk.

3. RELAXING THE REQUIREMENTS FOR TREATY RATIFICATION

The ability to enter into formal agreements with other nations is vital to effective national government in an increasingly interdependent world. The present constitutional requirement that treaties require the approval of two-thirds of the Senate has been a major barrier to the use of treaties and has led to evasion of the treaty process by way of executive agreements.

To restore an appropriate congressional role in the making of agreements with foreign powers, this provision should be amended to require that treaties can take effect with the approving vote of a constitutional majority of both houses. If the Senate does not join in proposing such an amendment, it should at least approve an amendment reducing the present requirement of approval by two-thirds of the Senate to 60 percent.

Reducing the Costs of Campaigning for Election

The lack of any legal limit on total campaign expenditures has led to a spiraling, competitive escalation in campaign costs. In the 1986 mid-term election, the legislative candidates raised and spent $342 million, up 30 percent over 1984. The cost of campaigning has put a contested seat in Congress beyond the means of everyone who is not either personally wealthy or willing to become dependent on well-heeled special interest groups. The Supreme Court's interpretation of the First Amendment seems to prohibit Congress from limiting private campaign expenditures by legislation, although the Court has authorized public financing on the condition that candidates who accept it limit their expenditures to these federal funds.

A constitutional amendment allowing Congress to set reasonable limits on campaign expenditures would not endanger the freedom of expression guaranteed by the First Amendment. If such an amendment were adopted, many able citizens who now reject the idea of standing for election might be attracted to political office, and the divisive influence of interest group contributions might be reduced to the point where more cohesive government would again become feasible.

ADDITIONAL PROPOSALS WORTH CONSIDERING

The changes recommended in the previous section command majority support among members of the Committee on the Constitutional System. A number of other ideas have found less than majority support to date, but some members believe they are important enough to deserve further discussion. They fall into four categories.

Strengthening Party Cohesion and Party Accountability

1. ENCOURAGING PRESIDENTIAL APPEARANCES BEFORE CONGRESS

Congress and the President should work out mutually agreeable voluntary arrangements for periodic presidential appearances before major congressional committees. These appearances would be used to present presidential positions and to answer congressional questions about presidential actions and proposals. Such arrangements would be consistent with the provision in Article II that the President "shall from time to time give to the Congress information on the State of the Union." They would also encourage greater cohesion between the President and the members of his party in Congress.

2. CREATING A SHADOW CABINET FOR THE LEGISLATIVE OPPOSITION

Legislators of the party losing the presidential election should organize a "shadow cabinet." The party's leaders in each house might alternate annually as leader and spokesman of the shadow cabinet, and the party's chairman or ranking member of the major committees in each house might alternate annually as shadow spokesmen in their particular fields, with their counterparts in the other house serving as deputy spokesmen. The shadow cabinet could coordinate party positions on legislative issues and act as party spokesmen before the public.

Reducing the Likelihood of Divided Government

For 20 of the last 32 years—and for 14 out of the last 18—the White House and at least one house of Congress have been controlled by opposing parties. Some of the measures suggested above should reduce the likelihood of divided government, but they may be insufficient to eliminate it. If divided government is recognized as the preeminent cause of interbranch conflict and policy stalemate and deadlock, two stronger approaches are worth considering.

1. MANDATORY STRAIGHT TICKETS

The first approach is to make straight-ticket voting not merely easier, as suggested above, but compulsory. By constitutional amendment, each party's nominees for President, Vice President, Senate and House could be placed on the ballot as a single slate, with the voter required to cast his or her vote for one of the party slates in its entirety.

The drawback to this idea is that Americans are strongly committed to voting for the person rather than the party. They would not be easily convinced to sacrifice this freedom in the interest of party loyalty and cohesion.

2. SEQUENTIAL ELECTIONS The second approach is for Congress to enact a statute providing for sequential elections in presidential years, with the voting for President and Vice President to be conducted two to four weeks before the voting for members of Congress. Under such a proposal voters would already know, at the time they balloted for members of Congress, which party they have entrusted with the presidency. This would give the newly elected President an opportunity to persuade voters to elect a majority of the same party to Congress and thus give the party a better opportunity to carry out its program.

The drawbacks here are that in the congressional election Americans might still vote for the person rather than the party. Also, there would probably be a considerable fall-off in the number of voters in the congressional election.

Calling New Elections in the Event of Deadlock or Governmental Failure

If it were possible for a President to call new elections, or for Congress to do so, we would have a mechanism for resolving deadlocks over fundamental policy issues. Indeed, the very existence of such a mechanism would be an inducement to avoid a deadlock that could trigger new elections. It would also make it possible to reconstitute a government that had palpably failed for any other reason.

There are formidable obstacles to incorporating such a device in our present system. Should the President alone, or Congress alone, or both the President and Congress be empowered to call for new elections? How soon should they follow after the passage of the resolution calling for them? Are we prepared to vote in a month other than November? Should there be full new terms for the winners (perhaps adjusted to the regular January expiration dates), or should they fill just the unexpired terms?

These questions can probably be answered. The real questions are whether we need such a strong device for breaking deadlocks or for removing Presidents who have failed for reasons other than impeachable conduct, and whether it is likely that in a special election the electorate would break the deadlock or would simply reelect all the incumbents.

Most constitutional democracies employ such a device, and it deserves serious consideration. It is not inconsistent with separated powers, and it might well operate to encourage cooperation between the branches in order to forestall the ordeal of special elections.

Reexamining the Federal-State Relationship

The weaknesses of the federal government are in large part the result of overload. This overload could be lessened by a better division of responsibility among federal, state and local governments.

A special convocation could be held every ten years with delegates to be selected in equal numbers by federal, state and local governments in a manner to be determined by Congress, to make recommendations to achieve a more cooperative, equitable, efficient, accountable and responsive federal system, under procedures requiring Congress and the state legislatures to vote on each recommendation.

MINORITY PROPOSAL FOR A POSSIBLE PACKAGE

Further discussion of these measures, and others that may be advanced, may well produce a package offering total benefits greater than the sum of the individual parts.

Some of our members believe, for example, that the following measures could be combined into a desirable package.

1. Adopting four-year terms for House members and eight-year terms for Senators, with elections in presidential years.
2. Empowering the President (perhaps with the consent of a specified number of members of one or both houses) or the Congress (by a special or regular majority of both houses, or perhaps even by an absolute majority of the members of one house) to call for a prompt election to all federal offices for new, full terms.
3. Permitting the President to appoint members of Congress to the executive branch without requiring them to give up their seats.
4. Allowing Congress, by constitutional amendment, if necessary, to place reasonable limitations on the total that may be spent in a political campaign.
5. Holding a federal-state-local convocation every ten years to make recommendations for improving the federal system.

A WORD ABOUT PROCEDURES

Article V of the Constitution sets forth two procedures for amending the Constitution. The first is for Congress, by two-thirds majorities of both houses, to submit proposed amendments for ratification by the states. The second is for the legislatures of two-thirds of the states to petition Congress to call a convention for the purpose of proposing amendments. In either case, the proposed amendments do not become part of the Constitution until ratified by three-quarters of the states.

The former method has been used for each of the twenty-six amendments currently in the Constitution. It is a proven way to insure thoughtful consideration for proposed reforms.

The only time in American history when the alternative method may have served a useful purpose was in the drive for the 17th Amendment, which provided for the direct election of United States Senators. Resistance to passage in the Senate led backers to attempt the alternate route. Eventually, the Senate capitulated and helped to frame a congressional resolution that was subsequently ratified.

The Committee on the Constitutional System strongly favors the traditional congressional method for proposing constitutional amendments. We hope that Congress will soon initiate a study to determine whether the Constitution in its present form can provide effective, accountable government for a third century, whether perceived weaknesses in our political structure can be remedied by changes in party rule and statutes, or whether changes in the Constitution itself may be desirable. . . .

CONCLUSION

In presenting this analysis and list of proposals, the Committee wishes to stress its central conviction. The best way to honor the framers of the Constitution during this bicentennial era is to follow their example.

When the parlous state of affairs under the Continental Congress raised doubts about the fitness of the new nation's frame of government, George Washington and his associates took steps to meet the challenge. They adopted the changes necessary (in the words of the resolution that called the Convention of 1787 into being) to "render the federal constitution adequate to the exigencies of government and the preservation of the union."

Two hundred years later, we stand in awe of their achievement. We disserve their memory, however, if we ignore signs that our political system today faces challenges that it is not equipped to meet.

We need to face up to these shortcomings in the capacity of our two-hundred-year-old political structure to cope with a global economy and prevent a nuclear war. We may ultimately conclude that these shortcomings can be remedied without major structural changes, or that any major changes needed to correct them would create even greater problems. But we cannot be confident of having reached the right conclusions until we confront the problems, trace them to their roots and examine the alternatives.

It is in this spirit that we offer these proposals.

Should the United States Pattern Its Political Institutions after the British Parliamentary System?

THOMAS O. SARGENTICH

The Limits of the Parliamentary Critique of the Separation of Powers

INTRODUCTION

It is commonly asserted that the United States government is ineffective in addressing major social needs. Such criticisms have come from widely varying political perspectives and have focused on a host of problems confronting the nation—including budget deficits, unemployment, homelessness, unequal access to health care, and many more.

One prominent critique holds that the government's asserted ineffectiveness derives from its constitutional *structure*. This critique takes particular aim at the separation of powers between the legislative and executive branches. It contends that the division of authority built into our institutions interferes with efficacious governance.

A leading expression of this structural approach may be called the parliamentary critique of the separation of powers. I will use this term to refer to critics who seek to modify our constitutional structure in the direction of a parliamentary system. In particular, the critics of concern here admire the British system. They are often careful to adjust to American ears by proclaiming the need for "reform," not radical institutional change. Although calls for parliamentary reform have been with us for decades, they have become especially loud in recent years.

The parliamentary critics with whom I will deal tend to admire the strength of the British Prime Minister as compared with what they see as the relative weakness of the United States President. In particular, the British chief executive does not face an independent legislative branch that regularly pursues its own agenda. To be sure, the British Parliament can vote no confidence in the Prime Minister and thereby can force a resignation or a new election. Yet in Britain this is hardly a common occurrence. Moreover, a parliamentary system can be an extremely weak form of government if a prime minister's power depends on a shaky coalition of divergent parties. In modern Britain, however, there has been a rather strong two-party system along with a winner-take-all electoral arrangement that has tended to guarantee that one of the two leading parties—Labour or the Conservatives—will dominate Parliament.

Critics often contrast the separation of powers with what they describe as the unity, effectiveness, and accountability of the parliamentary system. On these grounds they propose amendments to the U.S. Constitution embodying the spirit of parliamentary-style arrangements. Although changes in party rules and new statutes designed to promote party cohesion also are often recommended, this Article will concentrate specifically on the critique's constitutional dimension. . . .

THE EMPIRICAL FOUNDATION OF THE PARLIAMENTARY CRITIQUE

The key empirical premise of the parliamentary critique is that the U.S. constitutional system is inevitably prone to prolonged and debilitating stalemate. There are substantial reasons for questioning this broad-scale assertion.

To begin, the critique's empirical argument assumes that whenever there is conflict between the legislative and executive branches, such conflict is a symptom of constitutional tendencies toward stalemate. The possibilities that controversy could be constructive or that fruitful negotiation could occur after some degree of impasse lie outside the parliamentarians' frame of reference. Moreover, the idea that different approaches might usefully be joined together after a process of negotiation between the branches seems to remain beyond their purview. Instead of constructive possibilities, what parliamentary critics regularly see is confusion, paralysis, and weakness.

Such a simplifying vision has considerable difficulty dealing with the subtleties of particular political conflicts. Take Henry Hazlitt: he expressed his concerns about the course of World War II in terms of a fear of deadlock between the executive and legislative branches. Take Charles Hardin: he conveyed his alarm about Watergate in terms of a critique of structural tensions in our system of government. Take contemporary critics: they often express their intense frustration with national budget deficits in terms of their laments about the separation of powers. Yet we know that World War II, Watergate, and contemporary budget realities are very different topics. Is it not evident that a critique that treats them so similarly risks overlooking important complexities and alternative explanations lying outside a preconceived frame of reference?

To elaborate, consider the World War II, Watergate, and deficit examples along with two others prominently noted in the parliamentary literature: the Senate's failure to approve the League of Nations treaty after World War I and Franklin Roosevelt's 1937 Court-packing plan.

Let us start with the League of Nations experience. Assuredly, it was an instance in which the President's policy was thwarted by the Senate. Does that show structural "stalemate" in some general sense, as Hazlitt claimed it did? Of course, the defeat would not have occurred if the Senate did not have the power to stop a treaty by refusing to give it a two-thirds vote of support. What does that prove? One needs to ask about the range of factors that actually prompted the treaty's disapproval. Consider, for example, the personalities of key political actors, public concern after World War I about continuing foreign obligations of the United States, and President Wilson's overall strategy for dealing with the Senate. Ultimately, President Wilson lost the treaty when he refused to negotiate with the Senate about the reservations it proposed for the treaty. By contrast, to cite a modern example, President Carter succeeded in obtaining ratification of the controversial Panama Canal Treaties through compromises on reservations.

In view of the complex texture of the political processes involved in the Versailles Treaty debate, it seems remarkably overstated to claim that failure to approve the agreement resulted from our governmental structure. The structure was a necessary but by no means sufficient condition for the outcome. Moreover, to focus on the result of a particular treaty process is to overlook the larger value of having the Senate participate, whatever the consequence in a specific case.

Consider also Hazlitt's point about World War II. Hazlitt suggested that the failure of the United States to ratify the League of Nations treaty led directly to Hitler's rise to power and eventually to war. What about the role played by Germany in the causation of World War II? Surely, multiple factors led to serious destabilization in that country after World War I. These observations seem so plain that one has to wonder whether Hazlitt's concern about World War II should be viewed primarily as an argumentative device for focusing attention on his structural argument. In any event, the United States helped to win World War II with the constitutional structure that Hazlitt so vehemently attacked.

Now consider Franklin Roosevelt's Court-packing plan, in which he proposed expanding the size of the Supreme Court in order to allow for the appointment of new Justices who could be expected to approve New Deal policies. Hazlitt saw this plan's failure as another confirmation of structural weakness in the U.S. government. His notion was that the President advanced a relatively extreme proposal, Congress balked, and the President carried on in other areas while dropping the Court-packing package. Hazlitt asserted that in a parliamentary system, the Court proposal would "almost certainly" not have been made. If it had been made and if a majority in Congress had been against it—as ultimately was the case in 1937—the President would have had to resign and face a special election.

As interesting as this speculation is, the Court-packing plan seems to reveal the opposite of Hazlitt's suggestion: it appears to illustrate the potential *dangers* of a parliamentary arrangement. The plan is precisely the sort of extreme administration program that could well not be stopped in a system such as Britain's. The reason is that Parliament generally rubberstamps the administration's policies, assuming that the government has a majority in the legislature. Arthur Schlesinger, Jr., has made this argument in claiming that the lesson of 1937 was not that the Court-packing plan's unpopularity should have sent the

President packing, but rather that defeat of such a plan in the first place would be unlikely in a parliamentary system. So viewed, the example pointedly confirms the importance of separation of powers and checks and balances.

The example of Watergate has been cited by Hardin as another instance of the inherent weakness of the separation of powers. The idea was that the extended period of investigation and oversight by the Senate, the House of Representatives, and the judiciary seriously weakened the governmental system. Parliamentary reformers like Hardin would have preferred the option of a vote of no confidence and a special election to save the nation from the prolonged agonies of a burdened chief executive.

A key difficulty with Hardin's story is its presupposition that, in Britain for instance, a special election would have been called. Although that is theoretically possible, the notion takes for granted that Watergate-like events would come to light in the first instance. That is problematical, however, given the British system's tendency to shy away from the kind of intense and independent investigations of government that were critical in uncovering the Watergate affair. At a minimum, a majority in Parliament would have strong incentives not to embarrass the executive unduly. After all, a new election could lead to loss of the majority's control of Parliament and the government. Moreover, a new election would require Members of Parliament to defend against electoral challenges. The Members could be expected to suppose that they have better things to do with their time. Ultimately, one has to ask whether Watergate shows that the U.S. constitutional system failed or, in the alternative, that the system worked by allowing disclosure of wrongdoing at the top of government.

Finally, consider the often-cited example of continuing national budget deficits. For contemporary parliamentary critics, the separation of powers and divided government have worked together to create what might be called a situation of hyper-stalemate in addressing the deficits. The underlying empirical assessment is traditional: it is that the U.S. constitutional system is prone to deadlock and weakness.

Yet numerous factors appear to account for the nation's budgetary situation that have little to do as such with the legislative-executive separation of powers. Of clear importance in the creation of large deficits were numerous policy decisions during the 1980s that simultaneously reduced income taxes, funded social programs, and supported a large defense build-up. *Conscious policymaking,* not structural inevitabilities, generated massive deficits.

One might respond by urging that the persistence of the deficits requires a separate explanation and that the best one is structural stalemate between the legislative and executive branches. This explanation also is extremely problematical. The fact is that national policymakers and commentators have vigorously disagreed about what to do about the deficits. Some critics have argued that the issue in general has been overblown. Others have supported a variety of steps without coming to common ground about which ones to take. Substantive policy controversies of such magnitude cannot be explained away in terms of constitutional structure.

When one backs away from the various specific examples that have been said to illustrate the failure of the separation of powers, the simplistic character of a singleminded structural explanation comes into sharp focus. History and politics are more complex than any unicausal constitutional explanation will admit. In particular, deep disagreements about the substance of policy— what people are attempting to do—are at the core of periods of confusion or conflict. It bears mention in this regard that the United States is not alone today in the manifest frustration of its people with its political process. Indeed, a number of established democracies in the contemporary period—notably including parliamentary democracies—show signs of tension between their leaders and their citizens and evidence of political disengagement, division, and doubt.

Furthermore, significant and controversial policies have continued to be adopted in modern legislation in the United States. The 1970s, a period of divided government, was a time of major growth in domestic programs through legislation. The 1980s also saw much dramatic legislative activity. These facts directly undercut the stalemate thesis. They may even suggest that the existence of power in competing branches of government could promote the proliferation of policymaking, for each institution may be able to initiate action that the other might not have initiated. However that may be, as an empirical matter the case against the separation of powers must be strenuously questioned.

One is left with the thought that the parliamentarians' claims may be less descriptive than normative in character. After all, the ultimate idea is that our government *should* be less divided and less conflict ridden. I will now turn to the critique's normative underpinnings.

THE NORMATIVE FOUNDATION OF THE PARLIAMENTARY CRITIQUE

The normative foundation of the parliamentary critique has three main aspects: a set of general standards for assessing the separation of powers; a particular picture of parliamentary institutions; and a certain view of constitutional values in the United States. I will discuss each of these matters in turn.

General Standards for Assessing the Separation of Powers

At the outset, one needs directly to confront the parliamentary critique's key arguments about the alleged ineffectiveness and unaccountability of the separation of powers. Both contentions, I will suggest, are plagued by a striking degree of vagueness and, in the end, emptiness.

THE EFFECTIVENESS ARGUMENT Everyone wants the government to be effective. Yet eventually one has to confront the fundamental question evaded by the parliamentary critique: effective for what ends? Effectiveness, after all, is concerned with the efficacy by which given goals are advanced. If I said that I was "effective" today in writing a letter, I would mean that I accomplished my letter writing. To state that I was "effective," however, is to declare nothing about whether writing a letter was the best use of my time. It also does not establish a substantive basis on which to judge the finished product. Such an evasion of substance is magnified when one speaks of an entire institution or set of institutions—indeed, an entire government—as being "effective" or "ineffective." Again, the real question is: effective for what ends?

The parliamentary critique's tendency to avoid specific substantive baselines is deep seated. The critique asserts that *whatever* one wants the U.S. government to do, it cannot do it effectively. This approach may well have been chosen to appeal to a wide range of frustrated citizens. As one parliamentary proponent has noted with frankness: "To support, constitutional reform, one must be prepared to gamble." Notably, one must gamble that the policies one deems acceptable will be implemented within the constitutional structure so earnestly sought.

Something terribly important is missing in a critique that regularly avoids the substance of political debate. From the viewpoint of people who, for example, opposed President Reagan's regulatory policies, there were significant virtues in the system of checks and balances that gave Congress the power to slow down or redirect the administration's efforts. Moreover, this virtue of checks and balances is not limited to one partisan perspective, for the basic point also applies to those who have opposed the policies of Democratic Presidents.

The existence of two different approaches to the sequence of implementing parliamentary ideas further highlights the effectiveness argument's emptiness. The first approach would simultaneously pursue constitutional *and* party-related reforms. The second would advance party-related reforms first and only thereafter would pursue constitutional change. On the former view, the constitutional system needs to be altered immediately. On the latter view, the nature of political debate in the United States, as carried out by the two major parties, needs to be transformed first, and thereafter one should consider readjusting the major institutions of government.

The latter view has been described by James MacGregor Burns, who has called for revitalizing the major parties as the initial step in strengthening the government as a whole. In particular, he has sought a reinvigorated Democratic party that would capture the energies of the left in domestic politics in order to match the Republican party that has moved to the right in recent years. From this perspective, the existence of definite and discrete party programs is an important precondition to effective governmental reform.

The key point here is that the effectiveness argument, cast as it is at such a high level of generality, does not address or resolve the basic choice that Burns notes. Once again, the argument reveals itself as a remarkably empty vessel that is ready to be given highly divergent meanings in particular contexts.

THE ACCOUNTABILITY ARGUMENT   The second major argument of the parliamentary critique—that the separation of powers is an unaccountable system of government—also confronts serious problems. The contention rests on the premise that accountability requires unity in government so that the people will know whom to hold responsible for success or failure. Yet is the public so simple minded as to be unable to assign responsibility for policy when *both* the executive and the legislative branches have an active hand in shaping policy? Joint responsibility is still responsibility. To assume that one branch needs to have overriding influence on policy in order for officials to be accountable is to bootstrap a premise about cohesive government onto the separate notion of political accountability.

Moreover, it is doubtful whether the substitution of a major check on government resulting from a special election, in place of the multiple and ongoing checks now asserted by different power centers on each other, would actually result in a net gain for accountability. After all, ongoing checks and balances between the legislative and executive branches are themselves a source of political accountability. The parliamentary critique seeks directly to undermine this source.

In addition, one must question the notion that accountability will be especially enhanced by providing for the possibility of a special election. In general, elections do provide a mechanism for holding officials accountable to the people. Yet parliamentary critics have something more specific in mind when they assail the separation of powers for being relatively less accountable than a parliamentary system. For the critics, a system that creates the possibility of a special election will allow an issue to be taken to the country so that a new, specifically tailored mandate can guide a new administration, thereby rendering it more accountable to the people.

As a practical matter, the idea of taking an issue to the country to overcome governmental deadlock raises numerous questions. If there is governmental conflict, why is it not also likely for there to be deep division in the country? Moreover, can one expect an election campaign to stay focused on a particular issue or cluster of issues? In a heterogeneous society such as the United States, debate in a campaign leading up to a special election could quickly include discussion of many divergent issues. The underlying image of a great national forum for resolving some particular question in a special election might or might not turn out to bear any resemblance to reality.

Even assuming the existence of an unproblematical mandate resulting from a special election, how does the parliamentary critique deal with the likelihood of changing attitudes and conditions after such an election? On the logic of the parliamentary position, an electoral mandate apparently lasts in undiminished form until the next election. What if the political climate significantly changes and some different matters come to the fore, yet another special or a regular election is not held?

Furthermore, the parliamentary critique's emphasis on the use of a special election to seek a national mandate to which the government is to be held accountable depends on the idea of a relatively unitary perspective adopted by the nation's voting majority. How comfortably does the notion of a sweeping national mandate on some overriding issue fit with the normative concerns of modern pluralistic politics?

One voice that is especially attentive to the diversity of American political life is that of feminist theory. Such theory is concerned that a dominant or unitary national attitude will likely mean, in present historical circumstances, a male attitude. For feminist scholars, a major goal is to preserve a sense of competing social visions in order to take account of alternative experiences and viewpoints. Whatever one thinks of the feminist critique in particular, it underscores an important general lesson. For those who feel and are marginalized, the idea of a single national will, to be somehow revealed in a special election, is likely to be threatening. It deemphasizes—many would say silences—those in a minority who have competing orientations. This point is reinforced by the fact that different groups and individuals do have diverse conceptions of the good life. To assume without doubt that a system of political interaction culminates in some unitary expression of national will to which the government must be "accountable" is to fail to grapple with the underlying societal complexity.

In fact, it seems admirable to have a governmental structure that fosters an ongoing struggle among diverse views and does not promote the lasting domination of one particular orientation. A different approach might initially lead to stronger government. If so, it would purchase strength at the expense of democratic debate. Moreover, in the long run a supposedly "strong" government as imagined by parliamentary critics might well be weakened by a tendency to disregard the diversity of Americans' views.

In important ways, the accountability argument is closely related to the effectiveness argument. Both call for a more centralized governmental structure able to pursue policies with less need for negotiation between Congress and the executive. Unsurprisingly, the problems with the two arguments are closely related. Both speak in vague generalities, and both evade substantive differences and choices in our political community.

A Picture of Parliamentary Institutions

A parliamentary critic might respond by suggesting that since we are talking about alternative constitutional systems, it is necessary only to establish that another structure has salient advantages over our own. Let us present a general picture of the British system, a proponent might urge, to understand its comparative superiority.

A key problem with this response is that it tends to rely on a caricatured version of the parliamentary system. In the first place, the parliamentary critique often overlooks that the British example is only one of innumerable modern parliamentary systems and that others differ in basic respects. It may be unsurprising that parliamentary proponents of constitutional change in the United States do not dwell on the intricacies of comparative constitutionalism, but the burden of their argument should lead them to consider main variations on parliamentary themes.

Moreover, in concentrating on the British experience, parliamentary critics often fail to take account of the important ways in which that nation's political system depends upon its unique history and culture. British commentators are not hesitant to point out such relationships. As H. R. G. Greaves noted in his classic study, the British Constitution cannot be understood "without reference to the chief characteristics of society." Such factors as the British class system and the relative ethnic homogeneity of much of the country's people—without denying the significance of nationality differences among England, Scotland, Wales, and Northern Ireland—should be contrasted to conditions in the United States.

In response, parliamentary proponents might well protest that they do not wish to transplant British institutions wholesale into this country. Yet even limited borrowing of basic ideas of another country's political structure risks overlooking that those ideas emerged in a distinct habitat. As James Ceaser has noted, the British parliamentary system functions as it does not just because it is parliamentary but because it is British.

Furthermore, admiration for British institutions should not blind us to the fact that they have been sharply criticized in that country. Many critics have argued that such institutions give unwarranted power to the administration of the moment. To be sure, if one dislikes the policies of a particular government, one might be expected to question the system. The point remains that, as a general matter, British Prime Ministers have remarkable power.

The source of contemporary concerns about the British executive's dominance is the same as the British system's singular strength: a majority in Parliament basically guarantees passage of the Prime Minister's program. As Sir Ivor Jennings observed in a leading study of the British Cabinet, "The Opposition will, almost certainly, be defeated in the House of Commons because it is a minority."

These points have not received sufficient recognition by parliamentary proponents in the United States. The justification for characterizing parliamentary government as accountable is that, in theory, the executive in a parliamentary system can be voted out of office by the legislature. A key problem with this image is that, at least in modern Britain, the legislature generally does not use the vote of no confidence as a serious or active check on the executive.

In fact, one of the most important trends in British political institutions during the present century has been the sharp growth of prime ministerial power. This development has been associated with a marked drop in the Cabinet's power and the rise of a powerful civil service with a penchant for secrecy. Notably absent from this picture is a legislature with incentives closely to review or openly to question governmental policy. This absence is not surprising. In the parliamentary system, if there is a loss of confidence in the executive, the government will resign and new elections will be held. An election obviously generates doubt about the future of each Member of Parliament. Such a prospect does create strong pressures—apart from those of the party system itself—for the majority to support the Prime Minister.

A satirical reflection of the absurdity of imagining that Members of Parliament today are free to vote their consciences, as Bagehot supposed them to be, is offered in *Yes Prime Minister,* a set of fictional "diaries" by the Right Honorable James Hacker. This book captures a sense of the strong party loyalties of British politicians. In a relevant passage, Hacker has come face to face with one Professor Marriott, whose ideas about local government reform initially had appealed to Hacker. Marriott has written a sequel to his original article, and Hacker has asked him what the party's role would be in the revised scheme. The voice is Hacker's.

> Marriott beamed. "Well, that's the marvellous thing, you see. The party organizations would be completely bypassed. MPs would become genuinely independent."
>
> I was aghast. . . .
>
> Humphrey [the Cabinet Secretary] smiled at me. "So if MPs weren't dependent on the party machine they could vote against their own government party and get away with it," he explained.
>
> "Exactly," said the Professor again. . . . "It's the end of the party machine. The end of the power of the whips."
>
> I couldn't begin to grasp how such a system could possibly work. "So . . . how would the government get its unpopular legislation through if it couldn't twist a few arms? How would it command a majority?"
>
> Marriott's answer was all too clear. "That's the whole *point.* It couldn't! A government couldn't *command* a majority! It would have to deserve it. . . . And MPs would only favor it if the voters did too. Parliament would be genuinely democratic again."
>
> I couldn't believe my ears. Who in their right mind could possibly come to the Prime Minister with such a dangerous proposal? Only some damn-fool academic. As far as I was concerned the good professor could return to the ivory tower from whence he came—and pronto!

The serious point here is fundamental: one must not overplay the idea that the British Parliament is a serious check on the Prime Minister.

A View of Constitutional Values in the United States

Parliamentary critics might respond that the separation of powers could have been well suited for an agrarian and isolated nation, but it is not suitable today.

This view conjures up an image of a constitutional straightjacket that unduly confines a world power as it seeks to address serious issues domestically and internationally. From this perspective, the constitutional framework is said to need a transfusion of energy from another model.

The central assumption underlying the straightjacket and transfusion images is that Americans are stuck with a rigid and unbending system. That assumption is wide of the mark. The institutions of United States government have evolved dramatically since the nation's founding, as shown by the tremendous growth in the power of the President and the emergence of so-called "independent" agencies. In other, not entirely consistent ways, the constitutional structure has hardly been static. However superficially appealing it may be to blame present problems on the decisions of our forbears, a thesis about the dead hand of 1787 is unduly strained.

In any event, one must consider the broader implications of a frontal assault on the separation of powers as outdated, ineffective, and unaccountable. The assault calls into question core aspects of the Constitution, and it offers in their place a vision of firm and unified governmental management. What does this approach sacrifice?

Ultimately, a number of fundamental values are threatened. At the most basic level, the argument overlooks the importance of deliberation, dialogue, and debate involving the institutions of U.S. government and the public. I will develop this theme in two parts: first, by elaborating what I will call the parliamentary critique's managerial ethos; and second, by contrasting that ethos with the principle of dialogue underlying checks and balances.

THE PARLIAMENTARY CRITIQUE'S MANAGERIAL ETHOS   The parliamentary critique's leading image of government is of an efficient machine of centralized decisionmaking that sets its goals clearly, accomplishes them smoothly, and does not engage in wrangling about ends or means. This is a highly abstract vision of the job of government as one of instrumental management.

Given the parliamentary literature's tendency to focus on management values, it is unsurprising that often it explicitly or implicitly idealizes corporate structures of governance. In fact, the literature reflects admiration for hierarchical forms of decisionmaking in general. After all, if decisions are seen to move up a chain of command with someone at the top able to say, "This is it," there should be less room for the difficulties that attend a process of broad debate about proposed policy.

This managerial ethos inevitably highlights the executive virtues at the expense of open deliberation and ongoing participation in the political process. It also directly attacks checks and balances. Even though bargaining can be expected to continue within the executive branch, the critique would have it tamed in the relations between the executive and the legislature.

Take, for instance, Lloyd Cutler's summation of the relative efficiency of our system of separation of powers as compared with that of parliamentary systems. He has contrasted the "success rates" of the two forms of government. He defined success as the executive's ability to get its program through the legislature. Under this definition, he has written, the constitutional system in the United States "is only four-fifths as efficient" as parliamentary government when both the Presidency and Congress are controlled by the same party. When there is "divided government," he has stated, the United States system is "only two-thirds as efficient" as parliamentary regimes. He has proclaimed that parliamentary regimes are "very close to one hundred percent" efficient. The reason for parliamentary success in this comparison is that the executive generally can count on the legislature's support for whatever it proposes, assuming that the executive's party has a working legislative majority.

Cutler's characterization of the relative success of the two systems is striking for a number of reasons. To speak of success without considering the content of governmental policy is to confirm the parliamentary critique's basic tendency to avoid substantive discussion of concrete public issues. Note also that in the end *the President's success* becomes the definition of success in general. It matters not at all what the Congress proposes. The underlying notion is that the government's manager—the President in our system, the Prime Minister in the British system—needs to be able to manage. This view removes from consideration the possibility that another branch of government might have something usefully different to say about public policy.

To be sure, managerialism is not a foreign set of ideas in the context of American policymaking. Its image of "getting the job done" efficiently is central to modern debates about the legitimacy of the administrative process. Managerialism also is at the root of a number of important developments in administrative law, especially including the evolution of centralized executive oversight of agency rulemaking. Yet managerialism is only an aspect of a number of competing visions of public administration, and it captures only a few of the broader normative ideas associated with contemporary ideals of administration. Moreover, it is one thing to speak of administration in managerial terms, but it is quite another to speak of the interactions between the executive *and* the legislative branches in terms of such a vision. Managerialists may be frustrated because Congress does not speak their language, but that is precisely the point: Congress speaks the language not of managers but of the democratic process, messy though it is.

The parliamentary critique's managerial ethos has profound implications in the modern age of expanded presidential power. Since the New Deal and World War II, it has been widely recognized that the President has become the initiating institution of U.S. government. The Presidency's centrality has reached such a level that the holder of that office is often seen in popular terms as the embodiment of national unity. In this context, a critique that further exalts the President by calling for the dominance of managerial values risks seriously unbalancing the relations between the two political branches.

One therefore should not be misled into thinking that parliamentary critics seek to advance the interests of the Parliament or the legislature. This misunder-

standing might be understandable given the literature's rhetoric praising Bagehot's model of government, under which independent Members of Parliament
thoughtfully voted their consciences on the great issues of the day. The modern
critique in the United States, however, is a managerially oriented, presidentially
focused approach that exalts hierarchical control of policymaking by the executive. Again, this set of commitments may have a good deal of force when one
is considering the executive branch by itself. When used as the prism through
which to view the interaction of the executive and legislative branches, however, the vision seriously undermines the role of checks and balances in general
and Congress in particular.

**THE PRINCIPLE OF DIALOGUE UNDERLYING THE CONSTITUTION'S
STRUCTURE** In turning now to the principle of dialogue underlying the Constitution's structure, it is important first to note a basic distinction. The Constitution's structural theory rests on two closely related but nevertheless separate
principles: separation of powers *and* checks and balances. The first principle
requires that the branches of government be identifiably discrete. The second
assumes that the branches are separate and then concentrates on promoting the
checking of each by the others. The task of separation summons forth a "for-
malist" analysis; it requires formal definitions of some sort to provide the base-
line for analysis. The task of checking and balancing is most closely associated
with a "functionalist" approach; it requires an awareness of the need to balance
the roles and functions of different institutions in determining their appropriate
relations.

In recent years, there has been a revival of interest among courts, lawyers,
and legal scholars in the doctrine and theory of the separation of powers and
checks and balances. It is unsurprising that attention has focused on the meth-
odological tension between formalism and functionalism in particular cases.
Yet the literature also has concentrated on the substantive values served by the
larger doctrine as a whole. Such discussions often have emphasized the singular importance of the political dialogue and interaction fostered by the Constitution's structure.

The fundamental idea is that through the separation of powers and checks
and balances, different voices—those of the President, the Senate, and the
House of Representatives—can be expected to contribute to public debate
about the ends and means of national policy. The notions are familiar: the
President speaks as the nationally elected voice of the people generally; the
Senate represents the states; and the House represents particular constituencies
that often have highly local concerns. More generally, the President speaks for
the nation, and members of Congress—while being concerned with matters of
national import—speak especially for different constituent parts of the nation.
This constitutional structure guarantees that diverse perspectives will contribute to dialogue about public policy. Such a system is in direct tension with the
top-down imperatives of the managerial ethos of parliamentarism.

Certain *caveats* are important here. First, the Constitution's structure cannot be assumed to guarantee an optimally broad dialogue among different groups in the polity. To the contrary, there are major constraints on the scope of political debate, especially including the relative powerlessness of certain groups. Much more should be done in my view to broaden political dialogue in order to include unrepresented voices. Second, separation of powers and checks and balances are designed to moderate the tendencies of a full-blown democratic regime, which could be swayed by momentary impulses of an aroused public. To that extent, the idea of dialogue in the context of the Constitution's structure needs to be distinguished from pure democratic rule. Third, other countries have evolved their own systems for achieving dialogue; my comments are directed specifically at the system in the United States.

Nevertheless, fundamental values are at stake. Foremost among them are the ideas of expanded access to power and broad dialogue in the context of our constitutional and political system. The possibilities of expanded access and dialogue follow directly from the fact that the constitutional structure is more decentralized, less unified, and thus less managerially neat than many parliamentarians would prefer. Because different institutions share power, individuals and groups may have a greater chance of winning the ear of some powerful official in their efforts to achieve representation. The significance of this fact is highlighted by taking the perspective of those who might not otherwise gain a political hearing, for instance because they do not have majority support and are not likely to achieve it in the future.

Expansion of political access and dialogue is an intelligent response to the social diversity of the United States. Having multiple pathways to power can assist in channelling social conflict in an internally riven social context. Indeed, since our nation is so diversified, it is unsurprising that people are often reluctant to embrace the idea of unity in government.

The Constitution's structure also is reassuring on the level of day-to-day partisanship, as noted earlier. For those who oppose the policies of a given administration, the value of checks on the executive is obvious. Vigorous dialogue about policymaking fostered by checks and balances also serves a number of affirmative purposes. In particular, it can promote better decisions by encouraging fuller consideration of significant alternatives.

In addition, separation of powers and checks and balances can help to prevent the dominance of particular factions or special interests. A major theme of discussions of the U.S. government has been that factions frequently gain more power than their numbers warrant. The overriding question has been how to control or limit the negative effects of special interests. Increasingly, commentators have noted that a healthy system of checks and balances, fostering debate about the impacts of governmental action as well as about competing public values, can help to ameliorate the problem of faction. This notion does not have to be cast only in terms of having certain selfish interests check other selfish interests. More generally, the contest among competing public visions, resting on larger commitments to the general good, can play out openly in a scheme of active checks and balances. To be sure, a focus on the amelioration of factional dominance should not lead one to a romanticized image of American political debate. Yet the point remains that the program of promoting checks and balances can have a moderating impact on factional control of government.

One might say in response that the broader the dialogue, the harder it will be to make any decision that sticks. One can understand the impulses for clarity that inform such a response. A system of separation of powers and checks and balances does carry with it a considerable potential for messiness and untidiness. Whatever else one might say about the Supreme Court's opinion in *INS* v. *Chadha,* the Court put well the basic point relevant here: "Convenience and efficiency are not the primary objectives—or the hallmarks—of democratic government" as envisioned in the United States Constitution.

Without meaning at all to suggest that the Constitution's system is ideal, one can say that it advances significant values and that these values are not sufficiently acknowledged by the parliamentary critique. After all, unity and effectiveness can exist in an autocratic system that is hostile to the norms of open dialogue. If we see broadened political debate in the United States as an important public aim, then we should expect—and embrace—some trade-offs in terms of managerial neatness.

CONCLUSION

For decades, parliamentary critics of the separation of powers have reproduced the same basic analysis of the structure of government in the United States. In the 1880s, Woodrow Wilson argued that the division between the legislature and the executive was a guarantee of ineffectual government. In the early 1920s, William MacDonald expressed similar concerns when claiming, rather inconsistently, that our governmental structure was the source of the public's "feeling of indifference" toward political affairs as well as of "the thinly disguised talk of revolution." During World War II, Henry Hazlitt worried about the nation's ability to win the war given the constraints of the separation of powers. At the end of World War II, Thomas Finletter feared that the United States could not lead the western alliance during peace time unless "radical improvements" were made in the federal constitutional structure. During the Watergate period, Charles Hardin expressed grave concerns about the future of our government in the absence of parliamentary-style changes. During the 1980s, other parliamentary critics attributed growing national budget deficits to weaknesses in our constitutional structure.

No doubt, tomorrow will bring other issues to prominence along with renewed attacks on the separation of powers. Yet it seems clear that no single answer can be an all-purpose response to each major challenge to our government. A one-size-fits-all approach is inappropriate given the complexity of modern society and politics.

In the end, when one looks beyond the details of parliamentary proposals to their underlying premises, one finds serious empirical and normative limits. As an empirical matter, notwithstanding predictions to the contrary, the constitutional system has neither collapsed nor proven unable to adopt innovative policies. Moreover, periods of supposed political stalemate in our history can be accounted for by a number of explanations other than one solely dealing with structural features of our constitutional arrangement. Furthermore, the managerial ethos of parliamentary reformism is in direct tension with important values associated with the dialogue that attends our system of checks and balances. The term "parliamentary reform" should not be allowed to cloud the fact that the critics advance a highly pro-executive position that would seek a strong government primarily by undercutting the independence of Congress.

The main limits of the parliamentary critique should be kept in mind as we continue to examine ways to make our government more responsive to the needs of individuals and the community. On the one hand, we should be quite wary of calls for change in the direction of a parliamentary system. On the other hand, we should be alert to the importance of a relatively open and deliberative political system that not only upholds the ideals of separation of powers and checks and balances, but also pursues reasonably efficacious responses to particular problems. It has been said that " 'we live in the description of a place and not in the place itself.' " This is as true of our vision of political possibilities as of anything else. We ultimately are responsible for developing and defending the images—the descriptions—that resonate with public values we embrace.

Questions for Discussion

1. What changes would have to be made in the Constitution for the United States to adopt a British-type parliamentary system?
2. Who would be the winners and losers of such changes?
3. To what extent has the changing character of the United States from a small agrarian society to a large postindustrial society made the presidential system outmoded?
4. Would the adoption of a parliamentary political system in 1787 have changed the course of U.S. history? If so, how?
5. Is a parliamentary system more accountable to the people than a presidential system? What are the reasons for your answer?
6. What would be the effect of the calling of a new constitutional convention to remedy the alleged defects of the U.S. political system?
7. What light do recent events, such as the amassing by the federal government of a $4 trillion debt and the U.S. response to the Iraqi invasion of Kuwait, shed on this debate? Do you think they support the arguments of CCS or Sargentich? Explain.

Suggested Readings

Cutler, Lloyd N. "To Form a Government." *Foreign Affairs*, 59, no. 1 (Fall 1980), 126–143.

Elliott, William Yandell. *The Need for Constitutional Reform: A Program for National Security.* New York: McGraw-Hill, 1935.

Esberey, Joy E. "What If There Were a Parliamentary System?" In *What If the American Political System Were Different?* edited by Herbert M. Levine, pp. 95–148. Armonk, N.Y.: M. E. Sharpe, 1992.

Finletter, Thomas K. *Can Representative Government Do the Job?* New York: Reynal & Hitchcock, 1945.

Fisher, Louis. *Constitutional Conflicts between Congress and the President.* 3d ed. Lawrence: Univ. Press of Kansas, 1991.

———. *The Politics of Shared Power: Congress and the Executive.* 3d ed. Washington, D.C.: Congressional Quarterly Press, 1993.

Goldwin, Robert A., and Art Kaufman, eds. *Separation of Powers: Does It Still Work?* Washington, D.C.: American Enterprise Institute for Public Policy Research, 1986.

Hardin, Charles M. *Constitutional Reform in America: Essays on the Separation of Powers.* Ames: Iowa State Univ. Press, 1989.

———. *Presidential Power and Accountability: Toward a New Constitution.* Chicago: Univ. of Chicago Press, 1974.

Hazlitt, Henry. *A New Constitution Now.* 2d ed. New Rochelle, N.Y.: Arlington House, 1974. [Originally published New York: McGraw-Hill, 1942.]

MacDonald, William. *A New Constitution for a New America.* New York: B. W. Huebsch, 1921.

Robinson, Donald L., ed. *Reforming American Government: The Bicentennial Papers of the Committee on the Constitutional System.* Boulder, Colo.: Westview Press, 1985.

Scarrow, Howard A. "Parliamentary and Presidential Government Compared." *Current History,* 66, no. 394 (June 1974), 264–267, 272.

Sundquist, James L. *Constitutional Reform and Effective Government.* Rev. ed. Washington, D.C.: Brookings Institution, 1992.

Thurber, James A., ed. *Divided Democracy: Cooperation and Conflict between the President and Congress.* Washington, D.C.: Congressional Quarterly Press, 1991.

U.S. Cong. *Political Economy and Constitutional Reform.* Hearings before the Joint Economic Committee, 97th Cong., 2d Sess., 1982. 2 vols.

Weaver, R. Kent. "Are Parliamentary Systems Better?" *Brookings Review,* 3, no. 4 (Summer 1985), 16–25.

Wilson, James Q. "Does the Separation of Powers Still Work?" *Public Interest,* no. 86 (Winter 1987), 36–52.

Wilson, Woodrow. *Congressional Government: A Study in American Politics.* Baltimore: Johns Hopkins Univ. Press, 1981. [Originally published Boston: Houghton Mifflin, 1885.]

Chapter 3

Is the Federal System Becoming Obsolete in the United States?

An understanding of the federal system today requires an examination of what federalism is, why it was established, and how it has evolved. Federalism is a system of government under which power is distributed between central and regional authorities in a way that provides each with important power and functions. The United States is but one of many federal systems around the world. Canada, India, and Germany are examples of nations that have federal systems. In the United States the central authority is known as the federal government, and the regional authorities are the state governments.

Federalism is a structural feature not necessarily coterminous with democracy. A federal system divides power. A unitary system, in contrast, concentrates power. In a unitary system power is controlled by the central authorities, as it is, for example, in Great Britain and France. In Great Britain, regional governing authorities are created, abolished, or rearranged by the central government at Westminster. In the federal system of the United States, however, state governments cannot be so restructured. No state boundary can be changed by the government in Washington, D.C., acting on its own authority. (An exception occurred during the Civil War when the state of West Virginia was created out of Virginia.)

A federal system was adopted in 1787 because a unitary structure would have been unacceptable to the people of the United States, who had strong loyalties to their states. In addition, the Framers of the Constitution wanted a government that would be stronger than the one existing under the Articles of Confederation, but they feared a central government that was too powerful. The federal system allowed for a compromise between those who favored a strong central government and those who supported a weak central government.

The central government was given some exclusive powers (e.g., to coin money and to establish tariffs). The states and federal government shared some powers (e.g., to tax and to spend money). The Tenth Amendment to the Constitution provides that "the powers not delegated to the United States by the Constitution, nor prohibited by it to the States, are reserved to the States respectively, or to the people."

The Constitution is not so clear, however, about where the powers of the central government end. Two centuries of conflict over this issue of states' rights have marked U.S. history. In general, the trend has been away from states' rights and toward national supremacy.

Those who argue for states' rights contend that the Constitution must be interpreted strictly. Congress should legislate only in those areas that are specifically delegated to it in the Constitution and should leave all those powers not mentioned to the states. Those who argue for national supremacy maintain, however, that the Constitution establishes a strong central government with vast authority. They support a broad interpretation of the federal government's powers.

National supremacy proponents have won victories, although they have always been under attack by states' rights advocates. In 1819, for example, in *McCulloch* v. *Maryland*, the Supreme Court upheld the power of the federal government to create a bank despite the fact that the Constitution does not grant an expressed power to the national government for this purpose. The Court held that Congress was granted broad scope through Article I, Section 8, Clause 18 of the Constitution, which gives Congress the power "to make all Laws which shall be necessary and proper" to carry out its enumerated powers.

As the character of U.S. society has changed, so, too, have the institutions of government. The relationship between the states and the national government has been influenced by these changes. With the emergence of large corporations whose activities transcend state boundaries, the role of the federal government in regulating interstate commerce has increased. Other economic problems, such as unemployment and inflation, can no longer be satisfactorily handled at the state level and require the federal government's attention.

States' rights became the slogan of groups who benefited from decentralized control—such as big business and segregationists—while national supremacy was heralded by groups that received strong support from Washington—such as labor unions and civil rights advocates. In those instances in which the states were unable or unwilling to meet the needs of a changing industrial economy and to respond to the pressures of social problems, the national government asserted its authority—often at the expense of the states. The courts have upheld the right of the federal government to move into areas previously dominated by the states— such as education, housing, commerce, and employment.

Because the issue of states' rights has become so prominent in the course of U.S. history, it would be wrong to conclude that the relationship between the federal government and the states is best categorized as a zero-sum game, that is, whatever one side gains, the other side loses. Today *cooperation* rather than *conflict* characterizes the relations between the two levels of government.

Liberals tended to support—and conservatives to oppose—the authority of the federal government over states' rights so long as racial segregation and economic regulatory matters were of central concern. But with integration and Supreme Court decisions favoring a federal government role in the economy in place, liberals have become more supportive of states' rights. Liberals appreciate that some states guarantee broader rights to citizens than are found in the Bill of Rights. Liberals also approve of the vigorous environmental and consumer protection laws that some states have enacted. Conservatives have traditionally supported states' rights. At times, however, some conservatives have preferred a federal government rather than a state government role in economic and environmental matters.

It is clear that the federal system has undergone significant changes since the late eighteenth century. But is it becoming obsolete? In an article in the *Harvard Journal of Law and Public Policy*, former Delaware Governor Pete du Pont argues that it is. Although favoring strong states in a federal system, he points to factors contributing to their weakness:

1. Federal mandates upon state governments continue to expand rapidly.
2. The Supreme Court has undermined the Tenth Amendment to the Constitution through its interpretation of the Commerce Clause.
3. The national government has taken advantage of court decisions to undermine state power in such matters as the minimum age for the legal consumption of alcoholic beverages, hazardous waste removal, zoning and building construction decisions, and public education.
4. Proposals are being put forward to further weaken state power by expanding federal government power at the expense of the states in child support and by allowing an international organization, the General Agreement on Tariffs and Trade, to make rules binding on U.S. state and local governments.

Du Pont laments the loss of state government power. He notes that the decline of federalism runs counter to the modern experience about big public and private organizations, which recognizes the perils of large, inflexible organizations and the burden they place on growth. He points to the traditional benefits that the federal system has produced for Americans and calls on the national government to avoid increasing centralization at the expense of the states.

Morton Keller, who teaches American political and legal history at Brandeis University, argues that state governments are alive and well. Writing in the magazine *Governing*, he contends

1. State governments are where much of what is important in U.S. political life is going on.
2. State governors have become presidents in recent years.
3. U.S. history shows that the power of states in the federal system follows a cyclical pattern.
4. Although the central government has grown since the New Deal

programs initiated by President Franklin D. Roosevelt, the states have taken on new powers and have established subtle but significant new complementary relationships with the federal government.

5. The regulatory apparatus that most directly impinges on the lives of modern Americans is state administered.

6. States are expanding their role in governance.

☑ YES

Is the Federal System Becoming Obsolete in the United States?

PETE DU PONT

Federalism in the Twenty-First Century: Will States Exist?

Will there be states in the twenty-first century? Perhaps you thought that was just a catchy title designed to attract you to this article. You were right, that was entirely its purpose. But the question is more than merely rhetorical. As is well-known and as this Symposium has elaborated, the power of state and local government has been continually narrowed over the years by both the federal courts and the federal Congress. This infringement, contrary to the spirit and letter of the Constitution, the Bill of Rights, and *The Federalist Papers*, must cease.

Sixteen years ago, in the first moments of my time as Governor of Delaware, I set forth the case for limiting the encroachment of the federal government: "If federalism is to survive, responsibility . . . must be shared between the state and federal governments. We must promptly end the practice of writing the rules in Washington and paying the bills in our state capitols." Unfortunately, as is usual at inaugural addresses, no one was listening—at least not in Washington. As any governor will tell you, federal mandates upon state governments continue to expand rapidly. For example, Medicare mandated services, hospital cost controls, environmental standards, welfare regulations, and wetland definitions all are enacted in Washington intentionally to limit behavior in state capitals like Dover. The sweep and reach of federal regulation seemingly knows no boundaries. As it expands, the role of state and local governments, those "laboratories of democracy," in Justice Brandeis's phrase, concurrently contracts. So the question of the role of the states in the Twenty-first Century is neither idle nor academic.

The Constitutional Convention met in Philadelphia in the summer of 1787 to revise the Articles of Confederation and increase the power of the national government. The Articles had affirmed that "each state retains its sovereignty, freedom, and independence," but they had proven too weak to sustain many of the advantages of mutual association. Separate currencies and retaliatory trade measures hobbled the nation's economy, lack of a national voice in foreign affairs caused international problems, and, most important, the national government had no effective mechanism to raise necessary revenues. So the Founders decided to seek a new system of governance.

In framing that new system, they faced a political dilemma: any national government strong enough to benefit the states and protect individual liberties is also strong enough to control the states and take those liberties away. The Founders solved this dilemma by creating a system of dual sovereignty, with some powers ceded to the national government and the others retained in the states or in the people. By 1787, federalism had already proven itself in Europe, contributing to the immense economic success of Holland in the Sixteenth and Seventeenth Centuries and of Great Britain in the Seventeenth and Eighteenth Centuries. As Barry Weingast observes, the association between federalism and economic success was "not spurious, but central to the successful economic development of each [country]." By prohibiting the national government from regulating local economies, Weingast argues, the political cost of intervention became high enough to ensure "market-preserving federalism."

Therefore, in the U.S. Constitution, the Founders sought to restrain the national government through a variety of structural devices. Among these, the most notable was the Commerce Clause, which gave Congress the limited power "to regulate commerce with foreign nations, and among the several States, and with the Indian tribes." The Bill of Rights, which soon followed the Constitution's ratification, contained further explicit restraints on the powers of the federal government; among these, the Tenth Amendment proclaimed that "[t]he powers not delegated to the United States by the Constitution, nor prohibited by it to the States, are reserved to the States respectively, or to the people." The intentions of the Framers in granting only limited powers to the national government were stated clearly by James Madison, a supporter of the new Constitution, during the ratification debates:

> The powers delegated . . . to the federal government are few and defined. . . . The powers reserved to the several States will extend to all the objects which, in the ordinary course of affairs, concern the lives, liberties, and properties of the people, and the internal order, improvement, and prosperity of the State.

But that was then, and this is now. What, in 1993, remains of the Founders' economic federalism, which they believed so crucial to the maintenance of growth and productivity? If the purpose of the written Constitution is to "define and limit" the power delegated to the national government, as Chief Justice Marshall stated in *Marbury* v. *Madison*, where are the limits on that national government today?

From the outset, the Commerce Clause served to prohibit the states from regulating any economic activity not completely local in character, while the national government regulated activities only truly interstate and commercial in scope. In the turmoil of the New Deal, however, the Supreme Court began to allow Congress to regulate activities within states, as long as Congress could show that the activity had some effect, whether direct or indirect, on interstate commerce. Of course, like the butterfly in Brazil whose motion influences, even if marginally, weather patterns in Texas, every economic activity, no matter how small, can be said to have some effect on interstate commerce.

Then came *United States* v. *Darby,* reducing the Tenth Amendment to a truism. As time passed, the Supreme Court permitted the Congress more and more latitude to regulate states' economic affairs. In a brief moment of contrition, the Court in 1976 ruled that the federal government could not regulate "traditional government functions" of the state governments themselves, but overturned even this minor limitation in 1985. In *Garcia* v. *San Antonio Metropolitan Transit Authority,* the Court held that because the Constitution granted the states a role in the selection of the executive and legislative branches of government, there was no need to fashion any "discrete limitations on the objects of federal authority." In short, the Court disavowed any judicial role in protecting the states from federal intrusion, leaving the states to fend for themselves and the national bull free to rampage through state china shops.

Needless to say, the national government has taken full advantage of its court-sanctioned strength. In the early 1980's, the federal government usurped the states' powers under the Twenty-first Amendment with respect to alcoholic beverages. Federal legislation mandated that states raise their minimum drinking age to 21 years or face the denial of road construction funds; the states, naturally, complied. In another example, when the people of New Jersey attempted to limit the importation of trash into their state, the federal courts forced New Jersey to accept garbage from states that did not want it within their own domain. States likewise have been prohibited from barring an influx of hazardous and radioactive waste. Whether the garbage be of the hazardous, medical, radioactive, or household variety, the Supreme Court has used the Commerce Clause to prevent states from maintaining a healthy and clean environment for their citizens.

Unfortunately, it doesn't stop there. Since the great constitutional compact which formed this nation was approved, the power over zoning and building decisions has been vested in the states and their localities. According to the federal courts, however, government housing should be located where the federal courts think is appropriate, rather than where local authorities may place it.

In my home state of Delaware, we know only too well about the overreaching of the federal government into our state and local affairs. For almost fifteen years now, the operations of our public schools have been micromanaged by the U.S. District Court through a series of busing orders. Federally defined racial balance has become the primary goal of the education system, ahead of reading skills, reasoning ability, knowledge, and the pursuit of excellence.

But perhaps the most outrageous act of the Supreme Court in recent history,

clearly usurping the powers of the states, is represented by a school desegregation case from Kansas City, Missouri. In that case, the federal district court
realigned the school district, finding that it was segregated, and *ordered the
school district to raise local taxes to pay for the expenses caused by the court's
decrees.* The Supreme Court upheld this action, finding that it was "plainly a
judicial act within the power of a federal court," despite the fact that it violated
the Missouri Constitution.

Liquor and garbage may seem trivial to some, but the devastation of local
schools through the quotas of federal court-ordered busing and the levying of
local taxes by federal courts are not. The power of state governments to deliver
education to their citizens and to decide upon the breadth and depth of the
taxes they will extract from their citizens go to the heart of governance.

The Founders' design of federalism, then, is effectively dead. As Michael
McConnell argues, "what the people ratified [in 1789] is something quite
different from what they got"; the erosion of state power, however, was inevitable, for "whatever the Founders' intentions, the rules they wrote are skewed in
favor of national power." And more national power we are likely to have, often
at the expense of state sovereignty, for regulation is to the federal government
as heroin is to the addict. More, always more, is needed to satisfy its craving.
Consider two recent efforts at the national and international level affecting
sensitive local issues—our families and our environment.

One proposal would federalize our child support system, an activity heretofore within the purview of the states, by turning the system over to the federal
bureaucracy. A recent proposal, advanced by the unlikely duo of conservative
Congressman Henry Hyde and liberal ex-Congressman Thomas Downey,
would subject to federal review and modification initial state child support
orders. Federal modifications could be appealed through a federal administrative process. The proposal also contains a new child support assurance program, whereby the federal government would guarantee child support payments for children whose non-custodial parents fail to pay as ordered.

Delaware Family Court Judge Battle Robinson serves on the U.S. Commission on Interstate Child Support, which recently reported to Congress that it
was far from clear that the federal government could do a better job than the
states in establishing and enforcing child support. Federalizing the system
would end state-generated creativity and innovation. Furthermore, child support is but one aspect of family law that often arises in the context of other
family issues traditionally left to states, such as divorce, custody, alimony, and
property division. Federalization would also require the U.S. government to
create and fund, at the federal level, a system parallel to one already existing at
the state level. Although these arguments weigh against the proposal, it is not
yet certain that national child support enforcement is a dead issue.

The other movement against states' power to control their own destinies will
come as a surprise, for it comes from a just and good cause: the Uruguay
Round of GATT [General Agreement on Tariffs and Trade]. It will surely surprise
most readers to learn that under GATT proposals, state consumer and environ-

mental laws and regulations that are deemed unnecessary obstacles to international trade face revocation. Yes, GATT proposals will limit states' sovereignty by imposing internationally determined norms on state conduct. Federalization of our child support system, as unwelcome as it might be, at least leaves decisions in the hands of a federal government that is *our* government. It is something else again to turn over local power to enhance product safety and environmental quality to faceless GATTeers in placid Geneva.

Under the Sanitary and Phytosanitary Standards (for foods, foodstuffs, and beverages) sections of GATT, member nations would be required to take affirmative steps to make the laws of "subfederal" governments comply with GATT. Thus, states wishing to enact consumer or environmental protection laws would be stripped of the power to do so without first obtaining the blessing of GATT members. To enact a law requiring recycling or a carcinogen-labeling law for food products, Delaware would have to notify the U.S. government, provide foreign GATT contracting parties with an opportunity to object, have the federal government consider these foreign objections without its being required to consult Delaware, and sit back while the federal government confidentially negotiates any such objections with the objecting party (again, without Delaware's participation). California's tough new auto emissions standards could be challenged, perhaps by German luxury car exporters. Oregon's prohibition on the export of unprocessed timber could be challenged, perhaps by the Japanese, the world's largest importer of old-growth raw logs. This development could profoundly change the way states do business.

Whether one personally agrees or disagrees with the wisdom of such laws or the wisdom of prohibiting the states from enacting them is not the issue. To me, the prospect of subjecting "subfederal" legislation to veto by an unelected international bureaucracy, absent the safeguards of state and U.S. constitutions, should give us pause. In this case, however, the federal Constitution clearly gives to the Congress the power "to regulate commerce with foreign nations." Outside America's borders our nation must speak with one voice, and it is a national, not a state, voice.

Within our borders, on the other hand, the opposite rule should apply. States should have the power to experiment and innovate for the very reasons set forth in 1787: smaller units of government are better able to respond to people's interests and concerns, and they are less likely to shift economic burdens from one section of the country to another, or to impose public regulation for private gain.

Regarding economic burdens, Congress regularly plays regional favorites at the expense of the nation as a whole. Amendments to energy legislation, for example, often attempt to protect high-sulfur, "dirty" eastern coal from competition with low-sulfur, "clean" western coal. The Davis-Bacon Act, which mandates union wage scales on public construction projects, and steel and automobile import quotas are examples of public laws used for private gain. Peanut and sugar subsidies give a regional spin to the same bottle. State and local governments sometimes play these costly games too, but at least they are unable to inflict their damaging consequences on an entire nation.

The costs of the erosion of federalism are not wholly economic. A federalist form of government recognizes that there are a number of fundamental values that we all share in order to exist as a nation. Our collective dedication to constitutional democracy and a republican form of government are among the things that make us all Americans. But a federalist form of government also recognizes that, beyond our shared principles, we are free to diverge. The ability of states to diverge in manners not inconsistent with the national Constitution reflects the true wisdom of federalism: not only the freedom to set a different course, but the power to do so as well.

Of all the states that should mourn the death of federalism, my own state of Delaware should grieve the most, for its people truly enjoy the blessings of the state's power to set a different course. Most obviously, Delaware has a corporate law guarded by its nearly unique Court of Chancery. Because of these constitutional and legislative creations, Delaware is America's corporate capitol. Corporate franchise fees provide over 20 percent of its state revenues, sparing poor and working poor families the ravages of a sales tax so onerous in nearly every other state. Under a federal system, Delaware may make these choices, but under a national system it might not.

Delaware enjoys a quality of justice recognized and emulated across the nation. Delaware's constitution provides for the appointment of judges and requires a political balance on its courts. A stateless America might mandate the election of local judges, as is the practice in California, Pennsylvania, and Texas.

In the 1980's, Delaware innovatively modernized its laws governing banking and financial services. Bell-shaped tax-rate curves and market-regulated credit cards blossomed the state's prosperity beyond its wildest dreams: welfare caseloads halved, individual income tax rates declined, and job opportunities exploded. Would this have been possible under national regulations? I don't believe so.

Consider, finally, the flow of history and the sum of our contemporary experience. From geopolitics to GM, the world has learned the perils of large, inflexible organizations and the burden they place on growth and opportunity. The USSR is gone, replaced by a confederation of fifteen governments, all more representative and more responsive to their peoples. General Motors and IBM are going, hobbled by their size and inflexibility. The monster mills of U.S. Steel could not compete; the flexible boutique mills of USX can both compete and win. Massive mainframe computers have been replaced by PC's, programmed for individual needs and networked to allow rapid exchange of locally developed information. Cafeteria employee benefit plans are replacing the one-size-fits-all plans of the past. By the early 1990's, it had become clear to most of us that market economies served by small, flexible entities capable of rapid innovation are the wave of the future.

It is both unfortunate and contradictory, therefore, that against this flow marches the Congress, set free by the federal judiciary, throttling federalism just as the world is recognizing its worth and centralizing authority just as decentralization is coming to be seen as the better option. Federalism is much more than a historical quirk: it is wisdom proven over 200 years and an organizational scheme crucial to success in the Twenty-first Century. America had best return to it, if it is to prosper in the future as it has in the past.

How, then, is the nation to rediscover the virtues of federalism? One would hope that the executive and legislative branches of national government would be the driving forces in our return to our constitutional roots. With rare exceptions, however, Presidents prefer accumulating power in the national government, and Congress's thirst for control is unlikely ever to be slaked. The Supreme Court, therefore, possesses a unique opportunity—even a duty—to lead America back to a more perfect union.

Both *Darby's* evisceration of the Tenth Amendment and *Garcia's* 5–4 decision that municipal mass transit systems are interstate commerce are ripe for rethinking. They are a pair of bright-line opportunities to return, in Madison's phrase, to "the sense in which the [C]onstitution was accepted and ratified by the nation" by returning to the states their Constitutional prerogative of governing local affairs. A bolder Court might disapprove federal gerrymandering of local legislative district boundaries to achieve specific racial or ethnic election outcomes, in contravention of the Constitution. In a burst of intellectual candor, the Court might even overturn *Roe* v. *Wade,* an exercise in denial of state authority as abundant in political support as it is lacking in Constitutional nexus.

But if all this is too unsettling, there exists one prospective opportunity for the Court that, in a single stroke, would send a powerful warning signal to the Congress and reinforce the Court's legitimacy in the eyes of the common citizen. Fifteen states have now, by large majorities, enacted at the ballot box legislative term limits. Litigation to void these voter-inspired limitations on federal power is already in progress. One cannot envisage a stronger statement to those members of Congress abusing federalism than to empower their victims, the citizens of the states comprising the nation, to limit their opportunity to do so.

So will there be states in the Twenty-first Century? Perhaps. I hope so, for as the governments closest to the people, the states and their local governments have historically represented the most responsive and dependable sources of protection and opportunity for individual Americans. Late in the Twentieth Century, we finally learned that uniformity is the enemy of opportunity and diversity its friend. Former West German Chancellor Konrad Adenauer is said to have observed that it was obvious God had placed limits on man's intelligence, but equally obvious that He had placed no such limits on man's foolishness. The beauty of federalism, of course, is that one state's foolishness need not be adopted by another; Congressional foolishness, however, is universal. We must choose carefully the path we wish to tread, for the path of centralization leads to frustration, calcification, and decline; the path of federalism, to the boundless opportunity our forebears saw in their new country and sought to bequeath to future generations of Americans.

Is the Federal System Becoming Obsolete in the United States?

MORTON KELLER

State Power Needn't Be Resurrected because It Never Died

Not too long ago, the experts wrote off the states as quaint remnants of the American past, all but useless in the age of the atom bomb, big federal government, a thoroughly national economy and lifestyles that seem to have less and less to do with where one lives. Typical was journalist Robert S. Allen's declaration in *Our Sovereign State* (1949): "State government is the tawdriest, most incompetent and most stultifying unit of the nation's political structure."

But suddenly the states are where much of what is vital, new, interesting and important in American politics is going on. Back in the 1940s and '50s, to be governor of a state, even to be a notable governor of a big state, was no steppingstone to the presidency, as Tom Dewey and Adlai Stevenson painfully discovered. But our presidents since 1976—first Jimmy Carter, then Ronald Reagan—went from statehouse to White House. And in 1988, Michael Dukakis of Massachusetts bids fair to follow them. [Dukakis lost, but in 1992, Bill Clinton, governor of Arkansas, was elected president.]

What is the significance of this upsurge of the states as a major setting for the drama of American public life?

Is it a quirk, an accident, a blip in the otherwise steady growth of the federal government?

Is it the first sign of a fundamental shift in American public life: the beginnings of a devolution of power to the states after decades of expanding national authority?

Or is this revival of federalism a familiar turn of the wheel, a shuffling of governmental roles between state and nation that is as old as our history? Is it a reaffirmation of Mark Twain's dictum that while history does not repeat itself, it rhymes?

The Constitution was clear enough on the respective roles of the states and the national government. The power to tax, make war, regulate commerce and provide for the general welfare rested with the federal government. Just about everything else was lodged in the states. James Madison, who more than anyone set the tone of the Constitution, explained in the *Federalist Papers:* "The powers reserved to the several states will extend to all the objects which, in the ordinary course of affairs, concern the lives, liberties and properties of the people; and the internal order, improvement and prosperity of the state."

As things turned out, the national government, not the states, was the focal point of public affairs during the nation's first quarter-century. The United States was born into a world dominated by the great, decades-long struggle between England and France. The American Revolution was fought out—and in good part determined—by the fact of that conflict. And not until the War of 1812 ended in 1815 would the new nation be free of it.

The early years of the republic were dominated by foreign-policy issues: John Jay's treaty of 1794, perceived to have given away so much to England that it set off a political firestorm which led directly to the emergence of the Jeffersonian Republicans as an opposition party; Jefferson's 1807–1809 embargo on trade overseas; and the War of 1812 with England.

The primary domestic issues of the day also were national more than state or local. They had to do with the character and survival of the government: its fiscal soundness, the role of the suddenly emergent national political parties, the no-less-sudden rise of judicial review.

The Federalist and Jeffersonian Republican parties that emerged in the 1790s were the product of the maneuverings of national figures such as Thomas Jefferson, Alexander Hamilton and James Madison. They were cadre parties spreading from the top down, not mass-based parties growing from the bottom up.

As dramatic—and as surprising—was the way in which John Marshall made judicial review by the Supreme Court an unexpectedly important part of the system of American government. Major disputes over public power and individual rights, it appeared, were to be decided by the federal judiciary.

While these national issues and institutions took form, the states were relatively minor players in the governmental game. State legislatures were distinguished not by the scale and importance of their activity, but by how little of substance came from them. A session of the Connecticut House in the early 1800s was devoted primarily to the passage of a tax on dogs; the next session with equal dedication debated its removal. Virginia planter John Campbell wrote to his son David in 1811: "I have heard with much pain that you have not recovered your health yet. Would a session in the legislature be of benefit to you?"

The conditions of American life changed dramatically after 1815, and so did the balance of power between national and state government. The years between the end of the War of 1812 and the 1850s were the high point of American federalism as a system in which the states and the federal government were at the very least co-equal partners. The basic idea of the Southern Confederacy—that a group of semisovereign states could decide to leave the Union if they chose—was a logical (if extreme) climax to this golden age of states' rights.

An exploding post-1815 American economy led to growing demands on government. There was bold talk in the wake of the War of 1812 of an "American system" of national internal improvements. "Let us bind the republic together with a perfect system of roads and canals. Let us conquer space," declared then-congressman John C. Calhoun of South Carolina in 1816. But within a few years, Calhoun was the patron saint of states' rights.

The decentralized, varied character of American society dictated that both stimulants to and regulation of economic growth came primarily from the states. Between 1815 and 1850, thousands of state laws and local ordinances provided subsidies, eased the path of incorporation, and regulated the activities of the turnpikes, land companies, canals, railroads, corporations and banks that were creating a new American economy. Social policy too—the control of slaves, the financing and the curricula of the schools, regulation of marriage and the family—was made by state legislatures and courts, local and municipal authorities. As Alexis de Tocqueville observed in the 1830s, American democracy "is allowed to follow, in the function of the laws, the natural instability of its desires."

The political parties also underwent a sea change. The top-down politics of the Federalists and the Jeffersonian Republicans gave way to a new kind of mass-based politics built from the bottom up: the politics of the Jacksonian Democrats and the Whigs. A new breed of politicians, such as New York's Democrat Martin van Buren and Whig Thurlow Weed, constructed state parties out of township committees, local newspapers, county organizations. It was from this rich, down-home political ferment that the new national political parties emerged.

Meanwhile, the federal government stagnated. Washington had only 2,199 federal employees by 1861. These were either party hacks or low-level government workers. The professional civil services taking form in 19th-century Europe had no place here.

The city itself became not the grand capital of the republic envisioned by its planners, but rather a squalid, parochial place where congressmen stayed as briefly as they could. L'Enfant's ambitious city blueprint fell into oblivion. When the new Treasury building went up in the 1830s, it was placed square in the path of what was supposed to have been a majestic Pennsylvania Avenue linking the Capitol and the White House—so far had the original scheme been forgotten.

The presidency lost its initial luster. Save for John and John Quincy Adams, chief executives from Washington through Jackson served two terms. From Jackson to Lincoln, none lasted beyond a single term.

But the emerging American national character of the early 19th century—intensely individualistic, hostile to authority, absorbed in private, local affairs—gradually eroded the capacity of the states to govern as well. Universal white male suffrage and the election of judges and other officials went hand in hand with a profound suspicion of public power.

By the 1850s, a number of state constitutions forbade subsidies for railroads or other ventures; free incorporation and banking laws made the creation of new enterprises all but automatic. The New York state constitution of 1846—the "people's constitution"—abolished "all officers for the weighing, gauging, measuring, culling or inspecting of any merchandise, produce, manufacture or commodity whatever," except for those charged with protecting the public health or ensuring honest weights and measures.

Cities and towns, too, shared in the general decline of government power. It was in this period that the courts came to define incorporated municipalities as creatures, pure and simple, of the states. So began the long saga of urban dependence on often-hostile, rural-dominated legislatures, of parochial city bosses and machines, and too-often inadequate municipal services.

Everywhere, it seemed, American freedom and individualism were leading to the decay of government. As the political scientist Walter Dean Burnham put it, "The chief distinguishing characteristic of the American political system before 1861 is that *there was no state.*"

The Civil War might have been expected to change all of this. It is conventional wisdom that the war was the great divide between an agrarian, decentralized young republic and the industrial, nationalized United States of modern times. Indeed, the Civil War may be regarded as the American version of the mid 19th-century outburst of nationalism that in the same decade led to the unification of Italy and Germany.

This war for the Union, and ultimately for the eradication of slavery, seemed to herald the coming of a strong, active national state, and even of a new conception of national citizenship transcending race. Lincoln made his presidency an impressive instrument of power. He raised and equipped the most powerful army since Napoleon, used the courts and the military to suppress dissent, and rallied public support with compelling rhetoric. Congress meanwhile enacted a protective tariff and an income tax, a national banking act, a national paper currency. And postwar civil rights acts and the 14th and 15th Amendments appeared to initiate a new era in American government, in which national authority replaced the states as the protector of the rights of citizens, regardless of color.

The Reconstruction experience made it clear, however, that neither in the structure of government nor in the realm of race relations had the Civil War wrought fundamental change. True, it ended the possibility of secession and abolished the "peculiar institution" of human slavery. But the old federalism— in particular, the states serving as the major source of social and economic policy—persisted in the new urban-industrial era.

The dominant style of party politics in the late 19th century hardly added to the capacity of the national government to cope with change. The needs of the parties themselves—highly organized, expensive to run, based primarily on regional, ethnic and religious loyalties—dictated their public policies. This was unfertile ground for the cultivation of a national state equipped to deal with complex economic and social problems.

Aside from tariff and monetary policy, the federal government of the late 19th century responded little, if at all, to the coming of an industrial, urban society. Race relations, too, rapidly disappeared from the national agenda, to be left to the none-too-tender mercies of the states and localities.

After 1900 a new generation, led by Presidents Theodore Roosevelt and Woodrow Wilson, began the slow, painful process of using the national government to deal with the problems of a modern society. The regulation of big business became a major responsibility of federal agencies and courts—though how effectively is open to debate. Laws were passed to foster the conservation of natural resources, to ensure pure foods and drugs, to prohibit child labor (although the Supreme Court of the time found this an unconstitutional use of federal power). This was a thin record. The United States badly lagged behind other major Western nations in welfare legislation. It is a revealing (and depressing) commentary on the national government of the early 20th century that its major social enactments were Prohibition and immigration restriction: policies designed more to preserve a mythical American past than to come to terms with the realities of the present.

As constitutional law expert Zechariah Chafee Jr. observed in 1920, "The health, comfort and general welfare of citizens are in the charge of the state governments and not of the United States." The half century between 1880 and 1930 saw a flood of state legislation: from corporation, labor and housing regulations to the control of prostitution, drinking and gambling. The courts upheld the vast majority of this outpouring as valid applications of the states' police power. State legislatures in 1905 alone enacted about 15,000 laws, 60 percent of them dealing with local or private matters. About the same total was produced in 1923. A 1927 estimate put the number of national, state and local laws and ordinances on the books at 10 million!

A bewildering array of state agencies, boards and commissions dealing with taxation, public health, public utilities, housing and a multitude of other concerns came into being. New York had 10 of them in 1800; 81 in 1900; and 170 in 1925. Georgia's governor complained in the mid-'20s: "We are board-ridden, commission-ridden and trustee-ridden in this state." Under the leadership of forceful governors such as Robert LaFollette of Wisconsin and Charles Evans Hughes of New York, states in the early 20th century became laboratories for experiments in legislative and administrative solutions to the problems of a complex urban-industrial society.

But as in the 19th century, effective statecraft constantly ran afoul of the machinations of vested interests and deep popular hostility to government power. Progressive reformer Frederic C. Howe gushed in 1912 that LaFollette's Wisconsin "is doing for America what Germany is doing for the world" in developing the instruments of government. But Finley Peter Dunne's comic character Mr. Dooley came closer to the prevailing national ethos when he wryly observed of the bureaucratic state: "I wisht I was a German and believed in machinery."

In money spent and results achieved, the proudest peacetime achievements of American government before the New Deal were the construction of a new highway system for the automobile age and the expansion of schooling to make public secondary education available to almost everyone (outside the South). These accomplishments, attained on a larger scale in the United States than anywhere else, were the work of the states and localities. Far from fading away, federalism in the early 20th century was as important a reality in American public life as it had been a hundred years before.

But surely this came to an end in the 1930s. Surely from the time of Franklin D. Roosevelt and the New Deal on, the states steadily, inexorably slid to a subordinate place in American government. Surely the public administration expert who announced in 1933, "The American state is finished. I do not predict that the states will go, but affirm that they are gone," knew whereof he spoke.

Surely not. Of course, from the 1930s to our own day, the federal government has taken on a vastly larger role. The benchmarks are familiar and impressive:

- The nearly 100 new agencies of the New Deal and the billions spent for relief, public works and welfare during the Depression.
- The enormous expansion of federal taxation, borrowing, expenditure— and power—during World War II, and the varying but never-again minor scale of defense spending and international engagement during the Cold War decades since.
- The constant appearance of new national enterprises large in cost and social consequence: the federal highway program; the space program; the structure of civil rights enforcement; and the welfare, medical and educational programs of the Great Society and after.

The conventional view is that this burgeoning of the American state occurred hand in hand with a shrinkage in the role and power of the American states. Certainly from the 1930s to the 1960s, state government declined in relative importance. Governors and state legislatures wallowed in mediocrity. Social and economic problems seemed to be susceptible only to national solutions. The states came to be widely regarded as historical anomalies, of no particular significance in a new, thoroughly nationalized society.

But even during this nadir of state power, federalism was far from dead—or dying. Much New Deal spending was funneled through the states rather than going directly from Washington to its recipients. This was true as well of later big-ticket programs, such as the federal highway system and Medicaid.

As Washington took on expanding tasks and powers, the states developed subtle but significant new complementary relationships to the national government. While the federal treasury came to rely more and more on personal and corporate income taxes, the states developed significant new revenue sources from sales and gasoline levies. The large number of Americans disturbed by the growth of federal power found ideological and political comfort in the rhetoric of states' rights, culminating in the opposition to the civil rights revolution. For all the growth of federal safety and health policies, much of the regulatory apparatus that most directly impinges on the lives of modern Americans— automobile registration, licensing and insurance; the harms produced by machines and crowded urban living, which are lumped together under the generic legal term of torts—remains primarily in the province of state authorities, state laws, state courts.

Now, during the final decades of the 20th century, it appears that the states if anything are expanding their place in the governance of modern America. Lyndon Johnson's block grants programs of the 1960s, Richard Nixon's state and local revenue sharing of the 1970s, Ronald Reagan's New Federalism of the 1980s have given new meaning to the concept of a federal-state partnership. Civil rights and civil liberties advocates who a generation ago depended almost entirely on national law and policy are beginning to look to state constitutional law as an underutilized resource.

Education, public health, the environment, crime: These are issues of prime and growing concern in the late 20th-century American polity. And they are areas in which state and local governments have a major, even an expanding role. Education alone is chiefly responsible for the fact that the number of state employees rose from 63 percent of the federal civilian total in 1960 to 135 percent in 1986, and local employees from 200 percent to 326 percent. In recent decades, governors and state legislatures and agencies have become notably more efficient, competent and effective. Nineteen legislatures met annually in 1962; 43 did so in 1986.

Perhaps the best way to get a grasp on what is happening is to see modern American government as an expanding balloon. Not too long ago, there was much talk of an "imperial presidency." More recently, an "imperial judiciary" aroused concern. And now attention is turning to the rise of an "imperial Congress." The fact is that the role of each branch of the national government has been changing, growing. But their overall relationship to one another has not been fundamentally altered.

This may be the case as well with the other basic structure of our government: federalism, the relationship between the states and the nation. The growth of the federal sector has been obvious for some time. It is increasingly evident that the states too are taking on new life and meaning in response to the demands of modern society.

Americans are increasingly subject to national social and economic forces. The most obvious consequence has been the growth of demands on the federal government. But the tensions and discontents of modern life have increased the need—social, even psychological—for units of government with what has been called the "geographic capability" to govern effectively, but which are not so large as to be beyond the reach and comprehension of the average citizen. Gallup found in 1936 that 56 percent of those polled favored federal over state government. But when the question was asked again in 1981, 64 percent preferred the states. In 1987, respondents were asked in which government they had "the most trust and confidence." Thirty-seven percent chose the localities, 22 percent the states, 19 percent the national government.

Finally, what of the future? It takes no great leap of the imagination to believe that the fillip to federalism provided by the Nixonian '70s and the Reagan '80s will pass, and that in the long run, the federal government will tighten its grip on the nation's public life. But it is just as easy to see Washington as a tiger long in the tooth, perhaps soon to be toothless, while new approaches to the art of governing spring up in the states and localities.

Certainly, changes in the way federalism works are both possible and desirable. Recent experience has shown that state and local obligations can often be better met when there are federal standards, and national needs can often be more flexibly and creatively met if they are spurred by federal incentives.

But if the historical record tells us anything, it is that changes in the relationship of the levels of American government are likely to be slow and piecemeal. The substance of that relationship has undergone enormous transformations in the course of 200 years. But American federalism is as meaningful at the end of the 20th century as it was at the end of the 18th. The words and music of American government have varied greatly over our history. The original rhythm—the rhyme—of our system persists.

Questions for Discussion

1. Which is closer to the people: the state or the federal government? Why?
2. What criteria can be used in evaluating whether a policy area properly belongs to the states or to the federal government?
3. What can the federal government do today to strengthen state governments?
4. Should the federal government strengthen state governments? What are the reasons for your answer?
5. What are the advantages and disadvantages of the United States becoming a unitary system?
6. Which groups would benefit and which would be hurt if the federal government gave more power to the states? What are the reasons for your answer?

Suggested Readings

Beer, Samuel H. *To Make a Nation: The Rediscovery of American Federalism.* Cambridge, Mass.: Belknap Press of the Harvard Univ. Press, 1993.

Berger, Raoul. *Federalism: The Founders' Design.* Norman: Univ. of Oklahoma Press, 1987.

Bryce, James. *The American Commonwealth.* New York: Macmillan, 1889. Vol. 1, chaps. 29–30.

Commager, Henry Steele. "Tocqueville's Mistake." *Harper's,* 269, no. 1611 (August 1984), 70–74.

Derthick, Martha. "Federal Government Mandates: Why the States Are Complaining." *Brookings Review,* 10, no. 4 (Fall 1992), 50–52.

———. "Up-to-Date in Kansas City: Reflections on American Federalism." *PS; Political Science and Politics,* 25, no. 4 (December 1992), 671–675.

Ehrenhalt, Alan. "Will the Laboratories of Democracy Ever Reopen?" *Governing,* 5, no. 8 (May 1992), 9–10.

Ornstein, Norman, and Kimberly Coursen. "As the World Turns Democratic,

Federalism Finds Favor." *American Enterprise*, 3, no. 1 (January/February 1992), 20–24.

O'Toole, Laurence J. *American Intergovernmental Relations: Foundations, Perspectives, and Issues.* 2d ed. Washington, D.C.: Congressional Quarterly Press, 1993.

Pannier, Russell. "Justifying Federalism." *William Mitchell Law Review,* 16, no. 3 (1990), 613–625.

Rivlin, Alice M. *Reviving the American Dream: The Economy, the States and the Federal Government.* Washington, D.C.: Brookings Institution, 1992.

Wise, Charles, and Rosemary O'Leary. "Is Federalism Dead or Alive in the Supreme Court? Implications for Public Administrators." *Public Administration Review,* 52, no. 6 (November/December 1992), 559–572.

Zimmerman, Joseph F. *Contemporary American Federalism: The Growth of National Power.* New York: Praeger, 1992.

Popular Participation

Democracies pride themselves on the freedom of people to participate in the political process. Such participation takes many
forms, including forming private associations known as interest
groups, getting involved in political campaigns, voting, working for political parties, and expressing ideas through speech or the mass media.

The traditional definition of an interest group is a collection of people
with common interests who work together to achieve those interests.
When a group becomes involved in the activities of government, it is
known as a political interest group.

More than a century ago, Alexis de Tocqueville observed that the
people of the United States have a propensity to form associations. This
observation has become as valid a description of the 1990s as it was of the
1830s. The United States has a large number of political interest groups—
business, labor, professional, religious, and social reform. At the same
time, many citizens do not belong to organizations other than religious
and social groups, which in some cases have no significant political role.

Interest groups engage in a variety of activities, including making financial contributions to candidates for public office and to political parties, getting their viewpoints known to the general public and to other
groups, organizing demonstrations, and influencing government officials.
Legitimate political behavior in a democracy allows for great freedom to
participate in these ways. The First Amendment of the Constitution is
often cited as the basis for such political behavior. That amendment
states:

> Congress shall make no law respecting an establishment of reli-
> gion, or prohibiting the free exercise thereof; or abridging the free-
> dom of speech, or of the press; or the right of the people peaceably to
> assemble, and to petition the government for a redress of grievances.

One form of political activity is involvement in political campaigns
and elections. In a democracy people are free to support candidates
of their choice. Such support may consist of merely voting in an election, but it may also include organizing meetings, soliciting support for
candidates, raising and spending money for candidates, and publicizing
issues.

An effective democracy requires that information be widely disseminated. The same First Amendment that protects the rights of individuals
and groups to engage in political activities also safeguards the press and

other media such as television, radio, and magazines. Television, particularly, has become the chief source of news for many people.

What people do and what they think are of vital importance to government officials. In democracies (and even in many dictatorships) government makes every effort to know what public opinion is on many issues. Sometimes government leads and sometimes it follows public opinion.

Although modern dictatorships rely on political participation, that participation is generally controlled by the ruling elite. Interest groups are not spontaneous organizations designed to be independent from government but are linked to government primarily through government-controlled leadership. And so, for example, trade unions are not free to strike or engage in protest activities—at least not legitimately. People are not free to form competitive political parties, and often there is only one political party that dominates elections. That party is regarded as having a special role in mobilizing the masses.

In many modern dictatorships elections do take place, but they are generally rigged. Where opposing candidates are permitted to compete, there is generally no significant difference between the candidates on issues. Protest movements and mass demonstrations are broken up, sometimes ruthlessly, unless those movements are controlled by the government. To be sure, protest movements and demonstrations do exist in some modern dictatorships, but government tries to control or suppress them.

In modern dictatorships, moreover, the media are not free to report the news in an objective manner. Instead, the media reflect the wishes of the ruling dictators. News is suppressed; opposition newspapers are closed down. There is only one truth—that of the government—disseminated through television, radio, magazines, and newspapers.

Many people in the world live in dictatorships. Since 1989 and 1990, however, democracy has made great gains and has replaced or diminished dictatorial rule in the former Soviet Union and in most Eastern European countries. Democracy has also made significant advances in Latin American countries. And South Africa, long under white minority rule, is experiencing change through political participation by its black community.

Although democracies are fundamentally different from dictatorships, even democracies do not always live up to the standards of freedom they cherish. In this regard, the political behavior of nongovernmental organizations in the United States poses problems for those interested in protecting democratic processes. Although it is relatively easy to discuss democracy in the abstract, actual practices in the U.S. political system raise thorny questions about the application of democracy to concrete situations. This part considers three issues pertaining to popular participation in the democratic process: compulsory voting, the role of the electronic media in political campaigns, and the status of feminism.

Chapter 4

Should Voting Be Mandatory?

A central feature of political democracy is universal suffrage. The United States today has a voting system based on universal suffrage. With the exception of people under the age of eighteen, felons, or the insane, every U.S. citizen has the right to vote. Restrictions based on registration and residence impose the only limits on this right.

Restrictions on the right to vote have existed throughout most of U.S. history. Under Article I, Section 4, of the Constitution, the states can determine the "Times, Places, and Manner" for holding elections, but Congress is permitted to alter such regulations "except as to the Places of chusing Senators." (Until 1913, senators were chosen by state legislatures.) In the early years of the Republic only white male property owners were allowed to vote in most states. The trend has been to expand the franchise to include groups previously excluded. At first property ownership as a voting requirement was eliminated. The Fifteenth Amendment to the Constitution, adopted in 1870, forbade any state to deny or abridge the right to vote "on account of race, color, or previous condition of servitude."

States, however, found ways to prevent African Americans from voting. In effect, African Americans were excluded from exercising their votes in the South through such devices as literacy tests, the white primary, and the poll tax, which required the payment of a fee to vote. Intimidation by some whites made it unlikely that African Americans would organize for the purpose of exercising the right to vote. According to the Supreme Court, political parties were considered to be "private organizations" and, consequently, not subject to the Fifteenth Amendment. Some of these restrictions also effectively disfranchised some whites. The poll tax kept poor whites from voting, and literacy tests were used to keep immigrants from voting.

The twentieth century brought major changes. The Nineteenth Amendment allowed women to vote. The Twenty-Fourth Amendment, adopted in 1964, made the payment of a poll tax or any tax illegal in federal elections, both primaries and elections. The Voting Rights Act of 1965 assured that African Americans could vote in every state. The Twenty-Sixth Amendment, adopted in 1971, established eighteen as the minimum age for voting. Supreme Court decisions and state legislation eliminated literacy tests. As a result of all these measures, the right to vote is virtually universal in the United States.

Yet many U.S. citizens do not exercise that right. In the 1992 general election, for example, the turnout rate of voters was 55.2 percent, compared to 50.2 percent in 1988, 54.4 percent in 1976, and the post–World War II high of 63.1 percent in 1960. In state and local elections the turnout is generally lower than in national elections.

Much criticism has been made of the fact that only about one out of two potential voters actually votes. In contrast, voting turnout in other Western democracies is higher. For example, in Great Britain turnout was more than 77 percent in the general elections of 1992, up from 75 percent in 1987 and the highest since February 1974.

What causes Americans not to vote is a matter of controversy. Nonvoting has been explained by the decline of political parties, the media's focus on personalities rather than political issues, the absence of perceived meaningful choices between candidates of the two major parties, widespread indifference and little faith that casting a ballot will have any meaningful effect upon the economic condition of people, and difficulties in voter registration. To address the latter, Congress passed the Motor-Voter Act in 1993, permitting registration to be automatic at the time a driver's license is renewed. When the act was passed, only twenty-five states and the District of Columbia had simplified registration procedures by adopting motor-voter legislation.

The failure to vote is sometimes described as a weakness of democracy. Throughout the twentieth century, many countries have denied the right to vote or used elections as propaganda to endorse the leadership of dictatorships. Some advocates of democracy think that there ought to be remedies for a weak turnout. One proposed remedy is mandatory voting: citizens would be legally required to vote and have to pay fines for failure to vote.

The *Harvard Political Review* published a debate on this issue. Tye Menser, a staff writer for the review, defends mandatory voting. He argues:

1. Mandatory voting would require that political information be addressed to nonvoters and, consequently, would increase political literacy.
2. Mandatory voting is no more a restriction on individual freedom than payment of taxes and school attendance. It is a civic duty.
3. Mandatory voting would strengthen democracy by increasing turnout by people with lower incomes, who historically are much less likely to vote than are more affluent citizens.

Ben Sheffner, managing editor of the review, takes the opposing view. He contends:

1. It is not true that people do not vote because they are disillusioned with government. Often they are bored with the candidates who are listed on the ballot. People vote when they

are interested enough in a campaign to become angry or disgusted.

2. Mandatory voting would not encourage citizens to be educated about politics. Rather, it would just make them cast their ballot for fear of having to pay a fine.

3. Since campaigns are directed at people who do vote, mandatory voting would encourage politicians and their political consultants to appeal to the baser emotions of a more ignorant electorate, one that is less familiar with political issues, than to people who currently cast ballots.

4. Mandatory voting is coercive and antidemocratic. People should be as free not to vote as they are to vote.

☑ YES

Should Voting Be Mandatory?

TYE MENSER

Send 'em to the Polls

Barely half of voting-age Americans made it to the polls for the most recent presidential election. Steadily declining from 64 percent in 1960, the 1988 turnout was a nadir. Congressmen were alarmed at the continuing trend of declining participation. A flurry of reform proposals flooded Congress in the wake of the election. Most recently, for example, the highly-publicized Motor Voter bill proposed to reduce registration barriers by automatically registering citizens when they obtain or renew their drivers license. These reforms, however, would have a modest impact at best. American policymakers need to take a serious look at a more substantive remedy to voter apathy: mandatory voting requirements.

Critics of this proposal usually point to the ignorance of non-voters and bemoan their effect on election outcomes. George Will, for example, argues that efforts to increase turnout merely increase the amount of ignorance brought to the political process. Others charge that the founding fathers would have included a mandatory voting provision in the Constitution if they had intended that everyone vote. Surely the Constitution was designed to provide for a government of elites—Madison's defense of election of senators by the state legislatures in the *Federalist Papers* proves it—but did the Founding Fathers intend an *electorate* of elites as well?

The increasing complexity of modern political issues leave many voters with a feeling of confusion and helplessness. Researchers have found that along with declining turnout from 1960–88 there is a declining sense of political efficacy among voters—the growing belief that one's vote doesn't matter anymore. Ignorance of issues is surely tied to this trend. Many voters, perceiving little difference between the candidates and skeptical of the importance of their vote, find it easier to stay home on election day than to sort out their position on a variety of complicated issues.

A mandatory voting scheme could combat this problem. Political information, readily available during presidential campaigns, would suddenly become an object of attention for many non-voters. Knowing they will be standing in the booth on election day, the politically apathetic will no longer be able to avoid political discussions at work or in other social situations on the grounds that they did not vote. Forcing everyone to punch the ballot, even if their choice is "none of the above," is requiring a certain level of political thought and reflection that would, in some people's lives, otherwise be lacking. Mandatory voting, then, would increase political literacy.

Critics charge that ignorant voters, oblivious to election outcomes, would merely punch a random name on the ballot or possibly support radical extremists. Research shows, however, that even the most politically ignorant non-voters are no threat to democratic processes. Study after study has indicated that non-voters value democracy just as much as voters and share opinions on most issues with voters. They are not even much different from voters in partisan identification. Mandating voting would not, therefore, lead to radically different or anti-democratic election outcomes. It would, however, increase political awareness and the sense of political efficacy in society. And while nonvoters are, indeed, more ignorant of political issues than voters, they are not much behind the generally low levels of political sophistication exhibited by all Americans.

A second criticism of mandatory voting is that it is an infringement of freedom—a use of anti-democratic means to achieve democratic ends. Though appealing on the surface, the argument crumbles under scrutiny. First, many acts are mandated by the government are much less fundamental to democracy than voting. The contract between citizen and government currently, for example, requires payment of taxes and school attendance. Voting seems much less intrusive and yet more basic than either of these duties.

Second, would requiring all people to vote be less democratic than today's exclusionary voting system? The United States is one of the only countries in which voter turnout is related to income. Registration requirements differ in all states, ranging from the burdensome to the trivial. Frances Fox Piven and Richard A. Cloward's 1988 book *Why Americans Don't Vote* describes how voting laws, poll taxes, and literacy tests have historically excluded America's low-income voters from participating in elections.

Research finds a strong commitment to democracy and strong opinions on issues (however uninformed) even among non-voters. Under a mandatory voting rule, all citizens would have the chance to air the opinions they thought were significant but unwanted.

Requiring citizens to vote would not make every American a political sophisticate. But political awareness and interest would substantially increase if each citizen was required to stand in the voting booth and make a choice on election day. The non-voters know little about politics, but they are by no means anti-democratic or radically liberal or conservative. Mandatory voting would increase American political literacy at no cost to democracy. And perhaps our electoral system would finally live up to Thomas Jefferson's political ideal— government of, by and for the people.

 NO

Should Voting Be Mandatory?

BEN SHEFFNER
People Are the Problem

In this age of frenzy about the "crisis in democracy," reformers are rushing around offering up a variety of hare-brained schemes to fix the system. Term limits, which rest on the assumption that voters are too stupid to turn incumbents out of office without being forced to, have so far gained the most attention. "Stop me before I vote again" is the battle cry of the term limiters. It won't be long before the reformers start yelping for mandatory voting. This time the refrain will be "Stop me before I *don't* vote again." Would these people please make up their minds? Making voting mandatory will not solve the perceived problem of voter apathy, will educate voters less about the candidates, and is at its core anti-democratic.

Much of the argument for mandatory voting rests on the belief that voters have stayed home in increasing numbers because they feel apathetic and disillusioned with politics. Though most in the media have accepted this assumption without question, the data collected by political scientists do not support the conventional wisdom. A major study comparing international differences in voting rates found "no relationship between political contentment and turnout." Interestingly, even if disgust with the system did predict low turnout, that would not explain low rates in the U.S. "Americans score very low on almost every item" of a scale that measures negative attitudes towards politics.

Why, then, don't Americans vote? One reasonable hypothesis is that they are bored out of their minds. Bush vs. Dukakis didn't send too many heartbeats soaring. Probably the best test of the boredom hypothesis was the recent gubernatorial election in Louisiana. Louisianians may have been disgusted by the blow-dried Nazi and the twice-indicted sleazebag, but no one accused them of being bored. In fact they were so disgusted that about 80 percent showed up to register their hearty approval for the lesser of the two evils. The message from Louisiana: the best way to get people interested in the political process is to make them angry and disgusted, not bored and happy.

Another argument in favor of mandatory voting is that if people are forced to vote, they will take the time to learn about the positions of the candidates on "the issues." Theoretically they would become ideal democratic citizens who carefully weigh all the issues before voting. There is little evidence to support this contention, and a mandatory voting scheme could have precisely the opposite effect. If people are uneducated and uninterested in politics (precisely the citizens a mandatory voting rule would affect, since they are now the least likely to vote), making them show up for 20 minutes at a polling place would not suddenly transform them into disciples of MacNeil and Lehrer [a news program on the Public Broadcasting System]. More likely they would hold onto their lack of interest in politics, develop a bit of resentment at being forced to participate against their will, and make the trek to the polling place only to avoid paying a fine, not to express a reasoned opinion.

In calling for mandatory voting, the reformers, already unhappy about what they consider the debased level of political discourse in the U.S., may only serve to worsen that problem. Political consultants may be sneaky, slimy, and amoral, but they aren't stupid. They aim their messages at those who are likely voters. Those mindless ads that reformers love to complain about actually target the more-educated members of society—those who are most likely to vote. Bringing the uneducated into the voting booth—the real effect of mandatory voting—would give consultants a new "target-rich" pool of voters to try to influence, a pool that is, quite frankly, not particularly susceptible to subtle and reasoned argument. Instead, political consultants would be tempted to appeal to the baser emotions of a more ignorant electorate that is even less likely than now to be familiar with the election's "real" issues. Imagine, a few years down the road, when Americans look back fondly on the good old days of American political campaigns, when the candidates discussed the important issues like Willie Horton and the pledge of allegiance.

The most basic problem with any mandatory voting scheme is its coercive, anti-democratic nature. Democracies should attempt to maximize the number of choices available to their citizens. Citizens should be able to vote if they want, when they want, and for whom they want. A decision not to vote is no less legitimate an option than to vote for the Democrat or Republican. The government rarely forces its citizens to take specific actions just by virtue of their citizenship. Sure, they must attend school, pay taxes, and register for the draft (men only, please), but beyond that one is hard pressed to come up with examples of cases where citizens must initiate contact with the government without expecting something in return (a driver's license, for instance). To encourage voting, the government should ease registration burdens instead of resorting to coercion that will only breed further resentment toward the state.

American democracy does have its problems, but they will not be solved by term limits, mandatory voting or most of the other wacky schemes being floated by today's reformers. Instead of complaining about defects in the process, we should concentrate on the faults of the people who make up the political élite. No process, not even one that forces citizens to take a more active role in their government, can ever guard against politicians who don't have the best interest of their constituents in mind.

Questions for Discussion

1. Why do people vote?
2. What are the socioeconomic characteristics of the people who do not vote?
3. What effect would mandatory voting have on the outcome of presidential elections? What are the reasons for your answer?
4. What effect would mandatory voting have on legislation? What are the reasons for your answer?
5. Other than mandatory voting, how can voting turnout be increased?

Suggested Readings

Avey, Michael J. *The Demobilization of American Voters: A Comprehensive Theory of Voter Turnout.* New York: Greenwood Press, 1989.

Chen, Kevin. *Political Alienation and Voting Turnout in the United States, 1960–1988.* San Francisco: Mellen Research Univ. Press, 1992.

Flanigan, William H., and Nancy H. Zingale. *Political Behavior of the American Electorate.* 8th ed. Washington, D.C.: Congressional Quarterly Press, 1994.

Krauthammer, Charles. "In Praise of Low Voter Turnout." *Time,* 135, no. 21 (May 21, 1990), 88.

Niemi, Richard G., and Herbert F. Weisberg, eds. *Classics in Voting Behavior.* Washington, D.C.: Congressional Quarterly Press, 1993.

Petrocik, John R., and Daron Shaw. "Nonvoting in America: Attitudes in Context." In *Political Participation and American Democracy,* edited by William Crotty, pp. 67–88. New York: Greenwood Press, 1991.

Piven, Frances Fox, and Richard A. Cloward. *Why Americans Don't Vote.* New York: Pantheon, 1988.

Teixeira, Ruy A. *The Disappearing American Voter.* Washington, D.C.: Brookings Institution, 1993.

———. *Why Americans Don't Vote: Turnout Decline in the United States, 1960–1984.* New York: Greenwood Press, 1987.

U.S. Cong., House of Representatives. *Voter Registration,* Hearing before the Subcommittee on Elections of the Committee on House Administration, 103d Cong., 1st Sess., 1993.

Chapter 5

Is Popular Participation in Political Matters through the Electronic Media a Threat to Democracy?

Political participation is a key element of democracy. The freedom to assemble, discuss issues of the day, and communicate with elected officials is regarded as fundamental to a democratic order.

That people have a right to participate in the political process does not mean, however, that they will exercise that right. Many Americans limit their political participation to voting, and—as we have seen in the last chapter—nearly half the American people who are eligible to vote do not vote. Relatively few Americans write their elected representatives, since to do so is time consuming and, in the minds of many people, unimportant. For many Americans, discussion about politics goes on in small groups—among family, friends, and social and economic associates. But the current electronic age of radio, television, and telephone has opened up new outlets for political expression that offer a large audience.

Today, when we want to communicate a political viewpoint, we need not talk only to our neighbors, friends, and associates. We can speak to millions of people we do not even know by using the electronic media. The electronic media command such public attention that the men and women who host national and regional talk shows have become national celebrities. Many Americans are more likely to recognize the names of hosts like Phil Donahue and Larry King than the names of their own members of Congress.

Since there are so many programs that encourage call-ins, Americans have an easy means for expressing their views before regional or national audiences. Members of Congress and state legislatures are sometimes unaware of how strongly people feel about a subject until the talk shows are besieged by irate callers with loud complaints.

When President-elect Bill Clinton nominated Zoë Baird, a corporate attorney, to be U.S. attorney general, most insiders believed that she would gain Senate approval. But on January 14, 1993, the *New York Times* reported that she and her husband had employed an illegal alien couple from Peru at their New Haven, Connecticut, home beginning in the summer of 1990. The Peruvian man and woman were hired to do household work, including child care. Employing illegal aliens is a violation of the 1986 immigration law, the story explained.

The Bairds had paid Society Security back taxes for the help before the news story broke, and they paid a fine to the Immigration and Naturalization Service (INS) for the violation shortly after the story appeared. When the story broke, they explained that they had been given legal advice that the hiring of illegal aliens for household work would not be subject to government sanctions. They also explained that they had been given incorrect advice that Social Security taxes could not be paid unless the workers had Social Security numbers.

Clinton associates and key senators seemed to indicate that Zoë Baird would still win confirmation. But the political leaders were out of touch with their constituents. People protested the nomination and called attention to the fact that the attorney general has jurisdiction over the INS. If Baird became attorney general, they said, she would not have the moral authority to deal with ordinary citizens who were guilty of a similar offense.

The talk shows were deluged with thousands of calls by people demanding the withdrawal of the nomination. The pressure became so great that Baird withdrew her name from consideration to the cabinet post on January 22.

The Baird case had continuing consequences for others in political life. There is evidence that the Clinton administration failed to nominate other figures for high government posts when it became known that they, too, had not complied with employment or immigration laws for their household help.

The influence of talk shows extended to nominees to state offices as well. When Maryland Governor William Donald Schaefer nominated John S. Arnick to be a state district court judge in 1993, he thought the nomination would proceed smoothly. Arnick was a Baltimore county Democrat and former majority leader and committee chair in the Maryland House of Delegates.

The nomination ran into trouble, however, after Judith A. Wolfer, who had been a lawyer for a Baltimore-based shelter for abused women, told the Maryland Senate Executive Nominations Committee that Arnick had made remarks offensive to women and to minorities. She referred to a meeting she had with him to discuss a domestic violence bill in 1992 when he was chair of the Maryland House Judiciary Committee.[1] A second witness later confirmed the remarks.

Although the governor and many state legislators continued to support Arnick, opposition to Arnick's confirmation surfaced in phone calls and letters to the legislators but especially as calls to the talk shows.

Talk shows on WCBM focused on the Arnick nomination. Sean Casey, director of programming and operations at the station, said, "The sentiment I hear is that people felt that the nomination was going to be rammed through [the General Assembly] when they didn't get an opportunity to voice their opposition." The station conducted a poll which said that Arnick should not be confirmed if the allegations were true.[2] Cognizant of the rising opposition to his appointment, Arnick withdrew his name from consideration.

The importance of talk shows is now well understood by politicians.

When Ross Perot appeared on the Larry King television program in 1992, he was asked whether he would run for the presidency. Perot replied that if the American people put his name on the ballot in all fifty states, he would be willing to run at his own expense. Some observers questioned whether Perot was flippantly answering a question or had cleverly used the occasion to generate a movement on his behalf. In either case, citizen committees for Perot sprouted across the nation, and the Perot presidential campaign began in earnest.

During the campaign, Bill Clinton relied on televised town meetings and call-in programs. George Bush recognized the necessity of doing so, too, and appeared on the Rush Limbaugh talk show.

Is the emergence of popular participation through the electronic media a weakness or strength of the democratic order? Jonathan Yardley, a writer for the *Washington Post*, argues in one of his regular newspaper columns that communication democracy has gone too far. He contends

1. Anger—rather than rational discourse—is at the root of protests expressed through the electronic media.
2. Government will not be able to act effectively if it must respond to popular anger.
3. Although elected representatives ought to be responsive to popular will, they should not be merely reflexive of that will. Instead, they should use their intelligence and wisdom in conducting the business of government.
4. Talk show hosts well understand that their incomes and jobs depend upon high audience ratings, and ratings depend on how much controversy and anger the programs encourage. Consequently, the talk shows do not reflect public opinion in general but opinion that is angry. They are a distortion rather than a reflection of public opinion.
5. People who call in to talk shows often do so as part of a campaign by groups with an interest in manipulating opinion. Some make more than one phone call on the same subject. In either case, what is heard is a distorted view of public opinion.

Diane Rehm, host of the *Diane Rehm Show* on WAMU-FM, defends popular participation through talk shows. She contends

1. Talks shows provide a direct link between politicians and the people, without the filter of journalists and columnists.
2. Talk shows have become a grass-roots forum for expression and exchange of ideas.
3. The ideas that callers express on the air are picked up by political pundits and made part of the political dialogue.
4. The people who call in are not "crazies" but are individuals with intelligent views who need a forum in which to be heard.

5. As politicians in the United States have become more isolated from the people, talk shows provide an opportunity for people to show good citizenship and reclaim some of their power.
6. People who call in to talk show programs feel a sense of empowerment and will be encouraged, consequently, to cast their ballots at election time.

NOTES

1. Charles Babington and Richard Tapscott, "Md. Judicial Nominee Called Unfit; Sexist and Racist Remarks Alleged," *Washington Post,* February 9, 1993, p. C1.
2. Molly Sinclair, "Airwaves Dashed Arnick; Ads, Talk Shows Withered Support," *Washington Post,* February 18, 1993, p. M1.

 YES

Is Popular Participation in Political Matters through the Electronic Media a Threat to Democracy?

JONATHAN YARDLEY

Ding-a-Ling Democracy

The good citizens of Maryland received an object lesson last week in the new civics. A nominee for the state judiciary whose confirmation had seemed a matter of routine suddenly found himself slashed to pieces by the buzz saw of irate public opinion. Within a matter of hours the call-in shows and telephone lines had delivered a *coup de grâce* to the nomination of John S. Arnick that not even the most sedulous lobbyist could hope to accomplish so speedily.

Probably this is a good thing. Arnick's qualifications for a Baltimore County District Court judgeship seem dubious at best; his nomination to the bench, and with it his removal from the State Senate, was motivated more by inside politics as played by the governor and the legislative leadership than by any passionate yearning to enrich the court with his presence. When it became clear that he harbored distinctly incorrect opinions about women and others who are infrequent presences in the corridors of power, it simultaneously became clear that certain citizens might not be able to enter his court with full confidence of fair treatment. Quite simply, Arnick had to go.

But his departure is one thing, the manner in which it was accomplished quite another. Around Maryland, as around the country itself during the late political campaign, much has been said about the voice of the people and the efficiency with which it can be heard thanks to new technology and new uses of old means of communication. By the thousands in Maryland and by the millions in the nation, Americans are patting themselves on the back for what they regard as unprecedented democratization of the political process.

To a certain self-explanatory extent this is true. As government has become isolated from those it ostensibly serves, the federal government most particularly, Americans have grown justifiably angered and frustrated by its lack of responsiveness to their needs and wants. The rise of the talk shows and the spread of voice mail have given them a degree of access to the mighty that they have not enjoyed since the nation was vastly less populous and the corridors of power were open to anyone who cared to stroll them.

Precisely how influential this access can be has already been shown twice in this still-young year, first by the Zoë Baird affair and now by that of Arnick. Nominees for important legal positions who under normal conditions would have been confirmed after little more than perfunctory testimony were asked to step down not because legislators suddenly found them incompetent but because legislators had been reduced to whimpers of terror by a noisy, emotional electorate.

There seems no safer bet in these uncertain times than that these two incidents are but the first of many. It was in the fear of inciting another such outburst that the White House made its unseemly retreat from the intended nomination of Kimba Wood, and similar fears seem to have more than a little to do with the administration's scorched-earth campaign on behalf of its economic program: Get the people on your side before they have time to start working the phones.

That emotion is central to the new civics is beyond dispute. The responses to both Baird and Arnick, though arising from matters of substance, were far more notable for emotion than for reason. Baird, whose willingness to overlook an inconvenient (and unwise) law certainly raised questions about her legal judgment, was attacked not on issues of substance but on those of style and image. People whose resources are limited were angry that, as they saw it, a privileged, overpaid yuppie thought she was above the law, and they expressed this anger in terms having far more to do with passionate class resentments than with careful analysis of a rather complex and tricky situation.

By the same token Arnick, with his insulting and remarkably insensitive comments about women, touched emotions every bit as deep and passionate. In this case they were, in addition to the familiar complaints of middle-class women caught in a culture still dominated by men, resentments against the closed, clubby, self-perpetuating character of the state government in Annapolis. The anger expressed against Baird was that of economic outsiders, while Arnick stirred the anger of political outsiders.

It is in large measure because anger is the root of these protests that we should be wary of the new egalitarianism that instant communication has forced upon us. Anger has its uses, but they do not extend to the effective or measured operation of any large institution, government most particularly. It is all well and good that the American people are more interested in affairs of state than they have been for years, but if that interest extends primarily to complaint, and if this complaint is expressed in angry, abusive terms, it is going to be very difficult for government to function even so badly as it has become accustomed to doing.

If it is important for those in power to be in touch with the people they serve, it is no less important for them to govern at a certain distance. Government in the United States is meant to be representative, but not to be merely reflexive. We elect men and women to office not to fawn but to lead, and in so doing we afford them a substantial measure of trust. To be sure, it is true that many of them have violated this trust in recent years by retreating into isolation from American realities; just as the Lowells once talked only to Cabots and the Cabots only to God, so our legislators talk only to each other and to lobbyists. But just because some people are abusing the system is not, in and of itself, reason to abandon the system.

Yet this is precisely what telephonic democracy, if allowed to operate un-checked, is certain to do. The instant, insistent and emotional expression of opinion—almost invariably negative opinion—reduces legislators to cowering lackeys, incapable of independent action. When we start screaming at them each time we see something we dislike, we make it impossible for them to legislate or administer creatively and thus we render the system itself inopera-tive.

A couple of other points should be made. One is that emotion, anger in particular, is the stock in trade of the talk show hosts. Any representations to the contrary notwithstanding, they are entertainers, not authorities on public af-fairs. Their principal job is to get high ratings that will attract big advertising. That overheated chatter rather than rational discourse produces such ratings is self-evident, so the hosts—and who can blame them?—go out of their way to provoke people into angry, bellicose calls. Many of those who fume so noisily over the airwaves are participating in talk-show theatrics at least as much as they are expressing real opinions.

The other point is that although call-in shows and telephone protests are said to be the voice of the people, this is in fact a highly debatable proposition. It is impossible to know, for example, to what extent the phone calls about Baird came from ordinary citizens who were genuinely outraged and to what extent they were orchestrated by people on the Democratic left who were infuriated by the prospect of a corporate lawyer as attorney general. By the same token, although few would dispute the depth of popular opposition to the Arnick nomination, it is equally indisputable that numerous individuals made many more than one phone call, in effect magnifying their own voices many times over and skewing the "voice of the people" beyond recognition.

Three decades ago the Supreme Court mandated one man, one vote. Should one man, one phone call be next on its docket? Don't laugh. In its insidious way, government by telephonic complaint is as hostile to representative de-mocracy as any discredited scheme from our not-so-distant past.

*Is Popular Participation in Political Matters through the
Electronic Media a Threat to Democracy?*

DIANE REHM
Voices of America

When the story of the 1992 presidential campaign is written, historians will note that it was the first one conducted, in large part, on the talk shows. As Mike Wallace put it during a recent *60 Minutes* segment about Larry King, "the nightly news is out" and the "talk shows are in." Even the president now understands that the shows present an opportunity to reach the voters in a way not possible through political ads or the evening news.

Some commentators have criticized the phenomenon. Jonathan Yardley characterized the appearances as "trivial amusements that reduce the candidates to the lowest common Hollywood denominator." Yardley went on to describe typical callers as "Americans on the margin: people with exaggerated grievances, people who have an excessive liking for the sound of their own voices, people with too much time on their hands."

I have a different view. The reason those programs have become so central to this year's campaign is that the format provides a direct connection between the politicians and the people, without the filter of a David Broder or George Will.

It is no secret by now that the voters are restless, even angry. George Bush felt it when he campaigned in New Hampshire. Congress heard voters' outrage over the House banking embarrassment long before it was expressed at the polls. And there is anger at the media. Many believe that events are being reported with biased perspectives, and people have grown weary of journalists who see themselves as stars, carrying as much authority as the officials they interrogate. In a talk-show setting, by contrast, listeners and viewers are exquisitely aware of the interaction between host and guest; they see and hear between the lines.

Above all, people are weary of one-way communication from their radios and TV sets. They're ready to talk back, and talk shows offer a two-way street. Politicians who listen—and I know they do—hear the unvarnished opinions of voters. But talk shows also give politicians a chance to talk directly with the people, in a way that's worked this year as never before. That was what happened when Ross Perot announced his intention to run for the presidency on *Larry King Live!*

Last May, Perot talked to listeners on my program. What was fascinating was his changing tone and manner during the course of the show. He was friendly and gracious with callers, while maintaining a defensive and even hostile tone with me. And listener support for Perot was wildly enthusiastic. Callers voiced respect for him, believing him when he said he would represent them rather than Washington's entrenched interests.

Increasingly, talk shows have become a grassroots forum for expression and exchange of ideas. Whether or not you're interested in making such a call yourself, the feeling you get listening to those who do is one of empowerment: the power to express an opinion publicly, to address it directly to people in high places and to have it heard by thousands of others. For anyone who listens in, the anger of the voters is nothing new.

Arbitron tells me that, on a weekly basis, 90,000 people in the Washington metropolitan area tune in Monday through Friday to hear my call-in/interview program between 10 a.m. and noon. The numbers are small when compared to national audiences listening to Larry King or Rush Limbaugh, but they are similar to those of other locally broadcast talk shows around the country.

Equally divided between men and women, nearly 40 percent of my listeners are in their offices, another 35 percent in cars. Their ages range from 18 to 80. They are doctors, lawyers, artists, people at home with children, retired persons, scientists in their labs and people out of work. They are experts on any subject, from physics to breast implants.

A small proportion of listeners actually call in—perhaps only 1 percent, and the majority of these have been men. I've asked why this is so, and women explain by saying such things as, "I'm not used to speaking out in public," or, "Growing up, my brother always did the talking," or "I'm not sure enough about my ideas."

But in the past few weeks of the campaign, women seem to have lost their reticence. Many are still angry about the manner in which Anita Hill was treated during confirmation hearings for Clarence Thomas, and angry at the behavior of members of the Senate Judiciary Committee. Recent polls indicate there's been a shift in public thinking about who was telling the truth in the Hill-Thomas confrontation, and that has been reflected in the comments of callers.

Some women didn't like Hillary Clinton's comments about an unwillingness to "stay home and bake cookies," but the attacks on her early in the campaign and after the Republican National Convention compelled many to call my program to announce, "I've never called into a talk show before, but in this case, I must." Their comments were generally supportive of the Democratic candidate's wife.

The ideas that callers express on the air have resonance. Several weeks ago, as I asked members of the press about the possibility that there might be no debates this year, a woman called to say that "candidates who accept federal matching funds should be required to debate." She went on to articulate her belief that such debates are "a job interview of the candidates by the American people." A day or two later, those same ideas were expressed on the *Mac-Neil/Lehrer Newshour,* ideas that had come not from any "expert" but from an "ordinary voter."

Once, Americans used to talk about these things over the back fence, but few people do that these days. Rather, as we travel in our cars, or work in our offices and homes, we're "tuned in" to what others are saying on talk shows. And because the guests are people in power, ranging from the local dogcatcher to the president of the United States, listeners are no longer isolated from the formerly out-of-reach bigwigs whose decisions affect our daily lives.

I suspect this all began with the protest about the 1988 congressional pay raise. Then, the airwaves were filled with rage, and people expressed their anger on the talk shows. They were moved to protest, with letters, phone calls, faxes and tea bags. These protesters were not people I would describe as "Americans on the margin" or "crazies." They were, rather, the people the nation is hearing this year as if for the first time.

As the talk shows have proliferated (in both numbers of shows and listeners), people are demanding that the moderators listen to *their* views more attentively. This has gone so far that we've seen established nontalk show programs change their formats to accommodate the candidates' unprecedented accessibility. The *CBS Morning News,* which normally does not take calls, opened its show to viewer participation for Bill Clinton and Perot. NBC's *Today* program made much the same arrangement. The talk show, in short, had arrived—so much so that the hosts themselves have become central players.

When Larry King appeared on my program the other day to talk about his latest book, a listener asked why King had raised the issue of Clinton's trip to Moscow with George Bush, when the president was his guest on CNN. Was King playing into Republican hands?

King replied that he'd had no such intention and was simply following up on several news stories he'd read. From the caller's perspective, however, King's question demanded as much scrutiny as the answer given by Bush. The chance to pin down the *questioner* is something you don't ordinarily see on *60 Minutes.*

It's been that kind of year.

I learned a valuable lesson during the controversy over Bill Clinton's troubles with the draft. After I raised the subject on the air on several different occasions, listeners became harsh in their criticism. They said I was paying too much attention to an issue most of them regarded as neither important nor relevant. Many said that continuing to talk about the draft was playing into Republican strategists' hands.

Those who didn't call wrote letters—lots of them—objecting to what they regarded as my continuing focus on something they believe has no bearing on their current concerns. They said that since they were not hearing their own views represented in the media, the media were out of touch. Again, the polls eventually reflected that view; a strong majority of those surveyed expressed a lack of interest in Clinton's draft history.

How talk show hosts handle the changing dynamic has varied. All of us seek to reach listeners by bringing people in the news to our microphones. As politicians have become more isolated, our shows provide an opportunity to flex the muscles of citizenship and return at least some of the power to the people.

The power of the people was particularly evident in the third debate, hosted by ABC's Carole Simpson. The talk-show format worked extremely well; the audience of more than 200 uncommitted voters came prepared to ask questions directly of the three candidates and those who did were thoughtful and articulate. Interestingly, the only criticisms I heard about that debate came from journalists who voiced a preference for the vice presidential "food fight," a display that left most of my callers disgusted and dismayed about our political process.

As the debates continued, the public's interest, contrary to early predictions, increased. The face-off in East Lansing drew an estimated 91 million viewers and listeners, indicating that voters are taking this election very seriously. According to the *New York Times,* record numbers of Americans are registering to vote.

There is an informed, involved, articulate citizenry out there. I want to believe that because more and more people are speaking out on the talk shows, they'll turn out at the ballot box. Their feelings of empowerment, plus the information they've gained, could well translate into a huge voter turnout. That would be the best news for the 1992 election, and, at least from my standpoint, something of a triumph for the talk show.

Questions for Discussion

1. Compare talk shows allowing call-in questions to programs devoted exclusively to commentary by political figures and pundits. What is the value for political participation by each?
2. What effect would a candidate's unwillingness to appear on a call-in show have on his or her prospects for election? What are the reasons for your answer?
3. What kinds of people are likely to call talk shows?
4. How would you detect whether there is a political bias in talk shows?
5. Could a call-in program be manipulated by advocates of a candidate or political point of view? What are the reasons for your answer?

Suggested Readings

Adams, Tom. *Grass Roots: How Ordinary People Are Changing America.* New York: Carol Publishing Group, 1991.

Elmer-Dewitt, Philip. "Dial D for Democracy." *Time,* 139, no. 23 (June 8, 1992), 44–45.

Etzioni, Amitai. "Teledemocracy." *Atlantic,* 270, no. 4 (October 1992), 34–35, 38–39.

Fineman, Howard. "The Power of Talk." *Newsweek*, 121, no. 6 (February 8, 1993), 24–29.

Frank, Reuven. "Talk, Talk, Talk." *New Leader*, 76, no. 3 (February 8–22, 1993), 20–21.

Hoyt, Michael. "Talk Radio." *Columbia Journalism Review*, 31, no. 4 (November/December 1992), 44–50.

Kinsley, Michael. "Ask a Silly Question." *New Republic*, 207, no. 2 (July 6, 1992), 6.

McClellan, Steve. "Look Who's Talking." *Broadcasting*, 122, no. 51 (December 14, 1992), 22, 24.

Roberts, James C. "The Power of Talk Radio." *American Enterprise*, 2, no. 3 (May/June 1991), 56–61.

Wolcott, James, "Rush Judgment." *New Yorker*, 69, no. 1 (February 22, 1993), 177–179.

Chapter 6

Is the Feminist Movement Dead?

The twentieth century has witnessed steady changes in the status of women. At the beginning of the century, in most states women were not permitted to vote. The Nineteenth Amendment to the Constitution, ratified in 1920, declared that the right of United States citizens to vote "shall not be denied or abridged by the United States or by any States on account of sex."

Although granted voting power, women still faced laws and practices that were discriminatory. In the decades immediately after the adoption of the Nineteenth Amendment, few women served in the Congress or in leadership positions in the executive branch of government. Women were generally denied the opportunity to reach top-level positions in the corporate world. Many professional schools, such as those in law and medicine, restricted the number of women admitted as students. The professional careers women were encouraged to pursue were concentrated in such fields as nursing and elementary school teaching. In some jobs, such as fire fighting and law enforcement, women were excluded. The pay for women was often much lower than the pay for men, even when they performed the same jobs.

World War II marked another turning point in the status of women. Since men were drafted into the armed forces, women were asked to perform jobs from which they were previously excluded, including work in heavy industry. When the war ended, however, women were called upon to give up their jobs so that the male veterans who had fought in the war could be employed.

The 1960s, with the rise of the feminist movement, marked another turning point in the status of women. The National Organization for Women (NOW) was created in 1966, largely through the inspiration of writer Betty Friedan, author of the landmark *Feminine Mystique* (1963), and other feminist activists. NOW was committed to eliminating the legal, social, political, and economic impediments to women's equality in society.

Few would question the gains women have made since the early 1960s. Women now hold posts in government, business, and professions previously denied them. In 1994, there are seven women U.S. senators, and both senators from California are women. And two women—Sandra Day O'Connor and Ruth Bader Ginsburg—are associate justices of the U.S. Supreme Court. Women hold appointed and elected posts at most political levels—national, state, and local.

Some advocates for women feel that the gains women have made have not been as great as they should be. They say that women are underrepresented in government and industry and that a "glass ceiling" prevents them from rising too high in organizations, where leadership is for the most part a male preserve. They complain about the sexism that women encounter—from brutal acts of rape and murder to sexual harassment through insulting words and jokes.

One matter that has come under discussion is whether the feminist movement, which was so forceful and gained such widespread support in the 1960s and 1970s, has any significance anymore. In an op-ed piece for the *Washington Post*, writer Sally Quinn argues that feminism as we know it is dead. She contends

1. Some of the prominent feminists are hypocrites who are not honest with women.
2. More and more women are falling away from feminism because they feel it does not represent them or their problems.
3. Feminists are arguing that women should leave their husbands to follow professions—a view that turned off mainstream women.
4. The feminist movement is perceived today as a fringe cause, often with overtones of lesbianism and man hating.

In an article appearing in *Elle* magazine, Patricia Ireland, head of NOW, answers Quinn. She says

1. Feminists actively supported Bill Clinton for president. As president, Clinton appointed many women to government posts and supported feminist issues.
2. The feminist movement is necessary to fight sexism in the United States.
3. Feminists are active in spotlighting the problems women face in the workplace.
4. Feminism remains critically important today because women know that they do not enjoy equal rights with men.

Is the Feminist Movement Dead?

SALLY QUINN
Who Killed Feminism?

There were several amazing revelations in the weeks preceding the 25th anniversary of the National Organization for Women:

- Gloria Steinem, in her new book, admits falling in love with someone who treated her badly. She had seduced him, she says, by playing down the person she was and playing up the person he wanted her to be. When he did fall in love with her, "I had to keep on not being myself."
- Jane Fonda, talking to *Time* magazine about her new husband, Ted Turner, announces that she's given up acting. "Ted is not a man that you leave to go on location," she explains. "He needs you there all the time."
- Barbra Streisand, in an interview with *Washington Post* TV critic Tom Shales, says that "even though my feminist side says people should be independent and not need to be taken care of by another person, that doesn't necessarily work that way. There's the human factor, you know."
- Washington Mayor Sharon Pratt Dixon marries a man named Kelly and, instead of reverting to Sharon Pratt, she changes her name to Sharon Pratt Kelly.
- Patricia Ireland, the new president of NOW [National Organization for Women], tells a gay magazine that, in addition to her husband, she's had a female "companion" for the last four years.

So. What are we to make of all this?

Is it possible that feminism as we have known it is dead? I think so.

Like communism in the former Soviet empire, the movement in its present form has outlasted its usefulness. There are no true feminists in the strictest sense of the word, just as there probably were never any "pure" communists.

The "feminists," and by that I mean the people who spoke for the movement, were never completely honest with women. They didn't tell the truth. They were hypocritical. Not surprisingly, when Steinem used to say, "A woman needs a man like a fish needs a bicycle," the women who believed her felt ashamed and guilty.

Like the communists who denied the existence of God and the right to worship, leaders of the feminist movement have overlooked the deepest, most fundamental needs of their constituency.

The fact is, they have never been able to separate the workplace from the bedroom.

About 15 years ago, a woman named Marabel Morgan wrote a book called *The Total Woman* which sold 3 million copies and attracted the ire of feminists all over the country.

At the time she said, to a great deal of ridicule, "I think men and women are equal in status. They're just different in function in a marriage relationship. I believe women have the edge on men with brains, but they don't have the physical strength. I also believe that one of my functions is to create a happy atmosphere in the home. I believe that falls to the woman. I can't explain it. I just know that's the way it is. My 8-year-old daughter says it's not fair. And I say, 'Honey, you've got it. It's not fair.'"

Marabel Morgan obviously touched a nerve, though in those days it was not politically correct to admit it, especially among "enlightened" women. By then, the movement was so intent on achieving the legitimate goal of equality in the office that they tried to regulate people's behavior in their personal lives.

And that's where the feminist movement ran into problems.

Many of us have made enormous strides in the past 20 years, thanks in part to NOW, the movement and women like Gloria Steinem. The question is, are these same people and groups the ones to lead the next generation?

I don't think so. Not if they continue down the same path.

Any revolution needs extremists to get it off the ground, and the women's movement was no exception. But often the people who are responsible for change outlive their effectiveness, and a new group must take over.

What's happening in this country now is that more and more women are falling away from "feminism" because it doesn't represent, or more importantly, they feel it doesn't represent, them or their problems. Feminism is defined as the "principle that women should have political, economic and social rights equal to those of men." The problems arise over the "social" rights—and nobody knows what that means.

Betty Friedan wrote *The Second Stage* several years ago, a courageous book espousing the concept of motherhood. This was something which, unbelievably, had gotten lost on many of the feminists who felt having babies was not the politically correct thing to do. She was roundly criticized by many movement women who felt her book was a distraction from the main agenda.

For most women, equality and justice are at the head of any agenda. What most women don't want, though, is being told how to live. It's still not correct to say it too loudly, but many women believe they're better understood by the Helen Gurley Browns of the world than by the Germaine Greers.

They feel betrayed and lied to because trying to live a politically correct personal life doesn't always work, as Steinem, Fonda, Streisand, Kelly and others have demonstrated. If the feminists could say they were wrong about women needing men or men needing women, what were they right about? If they were living one life and espousing another, wasn't that corrupt?

There was always the suspicion that, like the commissars who preached sacrifice to their comrades and bought their caviar at the party store, feminist leaders were publicly telling mothers of three it was great to leave their husbands and be independent—and then secretly dressing up in Fredericks of Hollywood for their guys. It was the hypocrisy that turned off the mainstream women. Trusting themselves and their own instincts, they began rejecting the notion that they had to think and feel in a way that is unnatural.

The leaders of the movement, though, never blinked. Instead of helping women fulfill their needs, helping the "total woman," they acted as if women had but one side and ignored the reality of husbands and children. *You can do it all, look at us,* was the message. The poor average woman, struggling to make it work and failing, was often hurt more than helped by these phony examples of how wonderful life could be if only they would take charge and discard the men. Women felt ashamed to be housewives, ashamed to be fulltime mothers.

Ultimately, this is what has hurt the feminist movement and, more importantly, hurt the very cause they're advocating—creating a negative reaction, the sort of thing Susan Faludi talks about in her new book, *Backlash.* Abortion rights, earning power and job promotion in the workplace are only some of the crucial issues that are being threatened today.

And people today trivialize the really important issues in the movement because the movement trivializes the important issues in peoples' personal lives. By dismissing what really goes on in the hearts and minds of women, the movement offered a target for its enemies—including the "antifeminists" who say, among other things, that they don't believe in equal pay.

The sad part is that the movement today is more and more perceived as a fringe cause, often with overtones of lesbianism and man-hating. This notion was hardly dispelled by Patricia Ireland's announcement of a "love relationship with a woman" and a declaration that she saw no reason to give up either that relationship or the one with her husband.

NOW's leader also said that she has never been anything but honest—an extremely odd choice of language. What are we talking about here? We are not just talking about open relationships or honesty or even lesbianism for that matter. Rather, what Ms. Ireland is talking about is, to my mind, adultery.

Most women I know are turned off by her boastful revelation, though they're reluctant to admit it. You can be absolutely sure that if she were having an affair with a man, we would never hear about it. But what kind of standards is she espousing? Would we elect anyone to a political office who announced they were having an affair? Can you imagine George Bush telling the world that he was having a homosexual relationship with another man and it was just swell with Barbara?

It is impossible to read the Ireland declaration and argue that the movement she leads is still in touch with the majority of women. How many women are going to tell their daughters that Patricia Ireland is a role model? The truth is that many women have come to see the feminist movement as anti-male, anti-child, anti-family, anti-feminine. And therefore it has nothing to do with us.

Today, 25 years after the birth of NOW, the legacy of the feminist movement —beyond its vision and agenda—is a lot of confusion. So many women, and men too, are confused about what their roles are. For so long, they have been taught to pretend, to hide, to conceal their real feelings and their real beliefs about each other. You were either a good feminist or sexist, and the demands were rigid.

But life is more complicated than that, as the nation saw during the William Kennedy Smith rape trial and the debate over whether Clarence Thomas ever sexually harassed Anita Hill. The women who believed Hill were outraged at her treatment by the Senate Judiciary Committee. But they were not without doubts. For a "pure" feminist, though, it was not politically correct to express them. The same kind of problem arose with the Smith trial, where, if you believed Smith's version, you were judged to have betrayed the movement.

All of these sexual issues are especially confusing to men. It's good for them, says the party line. But most women are confused too. Beyond the obvious cases (and everybody knows what they are), there's no simple test of what sexual harassment is. As one extremely liberated and politically sensitive male friend of mine said to me, "If you work for me and I ask you out, and you say no, that's sexual harassment, and if you say yes, it isn't."

The point is that such issues fall out of the strict confines of the workplace. And once in the bedroom, things can get very murky, even among the most clear-thinking.

Most of us have husbands and sons and brothers and fathers that we love. We don't want them to be chauvinist pigs or wimps. We want them to be people who care about justice and equality as much as we do. And we don't need somebody else to tell us who should do the dishes.

We need leaders, like Betty Friedan, who will speak to those needs as well as the other issues that are so important. A friend of mine asked her college-age daughter the other day about feminism. Her daughter said she wasn't really a feminist but truly believed that there was no job she couldn't have, no profession she couldn't aspire to. For that alone, the feminist movement should be proud.

But that's not enough.

Whoever the new leaders are, whoever emerges to speak to the real issues confronting most women, will not succeed unless they are willing and able to acknowledge and address the basic question—the "human factor."

Is the Feminist Movement Dead?

PATRICIA IRELAND
Feminism Is Not Dead

Whenever I hear someone argue that feminism is dead, dying, irrelevant, or elitist, I assume they've either been living on a desert island or have been spending too much time at Georgetown parties with the rich and famous.

Think about the events of only the last 18 months. In the fall of 1991, the nation was transfixed by the Clarence Thomas–Anita Hill confrontation, which galvanized women into a new wave of activism. Feminists had been leading the fight against sexual harassment in the workplace for years, getting only yawns or condescending smiles from the men in power. But in the 1992 elections, by tapping into the anger over the arrogant and sexist treatment of Hill, women candidates ran—and won—in record numbers: In the Congress our representation grew from 5 to 10 percent.

Even so, the scandals seem to keep on coming. Take the case of Senator Bob Packwood. The Senate went ahead and allowed Packwood to be seated even though as many as 23 women, at last count, charged the Oregon Republican with sexually harassing and/or physically assaulting them. When it appeared that the Senate was letting Packwood serve without a challenge, it was pressure from angry and determined feminists that forced his colleagues to acknowledge on the floor of the Senate that Packwood was being seated conditionally, pending the outcome of the Senate Ethics Committee investigation.

Sexual harassment is just the tip of the iceberg. Fear of violence on the street and domestic abuse controls too many women's lives. Three to four million women in this country are abused annually by so-called "loved ones," and one out of three women will be raped in her lifetime. We must pass a federal Violence Against Women Act, laws against stalking, and other legislation to stop the epidemic of killings and beatings.

Women voters propelled Bill Clinton, who had embraced many key feminist issues, into the White House. President Clinton then appointed a record number of women to his cabinet, as he attempted to fulfill his promise that he would shape an administration that "looked like America." Clearly, the feminist movement has made significant strides in the campaign to move more women into positions of power. But the treatment of attorney general candidates Zoë Baird and Kimba Wood were painful signs that we still have a long way to go to attain full equality.

Like the Thomas–Hill hearings, the Baird and Wood fiascos struck a chord with women. They reminded us that sexism is alive and well, and that the feminist movement is still very necessary in this country. As is the case with employed women at every economic level, Baird and Wood were caught in a double bind. If Zoë Baird's husband had been appointed attorney general, could you imagine him being questioned about what arrangements were made for the care of his children? Our culture professes a boundless love of babies in theory, if not in practice, but it is still primarily the job of women to find good child care.

Baird's and Wood's cases also put a spotlight on the problems poor and working-class women face in the workplace. Women continue to be stuck in the traditional "women's work," which usually amounts to low-paying, dead-end jobs. And we're paid less, even for performing the very same tasks—women earn only 70 cents for every dollar men are paid. Many women are so desperate for work that they are forced into the underground domestic economy with no job security, few benefits, and the constant fear that this status will be disclosed. For undocumented immigrant women, being found out means deportation. Also, for many poor and older women who are trying to keep their families together and make ends meet, disclosure means the loss of Medicaid coverage and/or their already meager Social Security and welfare payments.

Economic issues aside, the most basic reason feminism remains critically important today is that women know they do not yet enjoy equal rights with men. They also realize that they cannot count on men to hand over those rights out of the goodness of their hearts. The day-to-day realities women face are the impetus behind our movement. It was, therefore, no surprise when a Time/CNN poll released last year found that 78 percent of women support the women's rights movement. Women know that no one will stand up for women's rights the way women will. Feminism is as important, vibrant, and powerful today as ever.

Questions for Discussion

1. What is feminism? Has feminism been a success or failure?
2. Are feminist leaders, such as Gloria Steinem and Patricia Ireland, hypocrites? What are the reasons for your answer?
3. Is feminism antimale? What are the reasons for your answer?
4. What is sexual harassment? Is it a constant threat to women?
5. Does the feminist movement respond to women's needs? What are the reasons for your answer?

Suggested Readings

Davidson, Nicholas. "Feminism and Sexual Harassment." *Society*, 28, no. 4 (May/June 1991), 39–44.

Faludi, Susan. *Backlash: The Undeclared War against American Women.* New York: Crown, 1991.

Friedan, Betty. *The Feminine Mystique.* New York: Norton, 1963.

————. *The Second Stage.* Rev. ed. New York: Summit Books, 1986.

Gibbs, Nancy R. "The War against Feminism." *Time,* 139, no. 10 (March 9, 1992), 50–55.

Leo, John. "The Trouble with Feminism." *U.S. News and World Report,* 112, no. 5 (February 10, 1992), 19.

Nasar, Sylvia. "Women's Progress Stalled? Just Not So." *Washington Post,* October 18, 1992, sec. III, pp. 1, 10.

Phelps, Timothy M., and Helen Winterwitz. *Capitol Games: Clarence Thomas, Anita Hill, and the Story of a Supreme Court Nomination.* New York: Hyperion, 1992.

Reed, Ishmael. "Feminists v. Thomas." *Washington Post,* October 18, 1992, pp. C1, C4.

Roife, Katie. *The Morning After: Sex, Fear and Feminism on Campus.* Boston: Little, Brown, 1993.

Salter, Stephanie. "Sally Quinn, Wake Up and Join Your Sisters." *San Francisco Examiner,* February 2, 1992, p. A13.

Young, Cathy. "Women, Sex, and Rape." *Washington Post,* May 31, 1992, pp. C1, C3.

Civil Liberties and Civil Rights

P olitical systems make rules that are binding upon their members. But political systems differ in the amount of freedom permitted to citizens. In twentieth-century totalitarian dictatorships, the state imposed severe restrictions on individual liberty. Not only was it concerned with what people did, but it sought to mold people's minds to a government-approved way of thinking.

Modern democracies permit a large amount of individual freedom. As a modern democracy, the U.S. government accepts the principle of civil liberties, recognizing that individuals have freedoms the government cannot take away. Among these are freedom of speech, freedom of the press, and freedom of assembly. The Constitution as originally written in 1787 contains some protections for the individual against the encroachment of government, but the most important are set forth in the first ten amendments to the Constitution, known as the Bill of Rights and adopted in 1791. They are also found in federal government laws and court decisions, as well as in state constitutions and laws.

As the arbiter in constitutional disputes between the government and the individual, the Supreme Court is often at the center of the storm when it tries to determine whether government has overstepped the bounds and illegally violated the liberties sanctioned by the Constitution. And so, the Court has decided issues such as whether the government can force a person whose religion forbids worship of graven images to salute the flag (it cannot) and whether the government can ban obscene books, magazines, motion pictures, or television programs (it can).

The Court's decisions on privacy have been particularly controversial. Privacy is the right of an individual to deal with his or her personal life without government interference. The Constitution does not specifically mention a right of privacy. The Court, however, decided that such a right can be inferred from the First, Fourth, Fifth, Ninth, and Fourteenth Amendments to the Constitution. The right of privacy has been a consideration in the Court's decisions allowing for the right of a woman to have an abortion under certain conditions. And it is now central to cases involving fetal rights.

Court decisions on freedom of speech issues have also been very controversial. The Court has often supported the rights of unpopular groups, such as Nazis and communists, to make speeches advocating their political ideas. It has at times also set limits on speech.

Like many modern democracies, the United States contains citizens of different religions, races, and ethnic backgrounds. In addition to promoting civil liberties, the U.S. government is committed to protecting civil rights—those rights that assure minority group equality before the law.

As the speech by Thurgood Marshall in Chapter 1 indicates, the record of civil rights protection for African Americans has been a sorry one. Brought to the New World as slaves, black people were not granted U.S. citizenship until after the Civil War. And even after the adoption of the Thirteenth, Fourteenth, and Fifteenth Amendments, which eliminated slavery and gave legal and political rights to black people, those rights were often denied in practice until the 1960s.

Although the formal barriers to civil rights have largely fallen, many African Americans believe that the nation still does not adequately promote genuine equality. They point to discrimination in employment, housing, and professional advancement as examples of unfinished business.

Part III deals with five issues of civil liberties and civil rights: government controls on pornography, the responsibility of the media in withholding or releasing the name of a rape victim, freedom of the press in wartime, the death penalty, and affirmative action.

Chapter 7

Should Government Impose Stricter Regulations on Pornography?

Americans have been inundated with graphic materials of a sexually explicit nature, including film, videos, and telephone lines. The fact that the American people spend billions of dollars for such items demonstrates the popularity of what critics used to call "smut." But a growing chorus of voices is calling for increased government regulation of sexually explicit material.

Any discussion of the permissibility of sexually explicit material requires a definition of the terms "obscenity" and "pornography." "Obscenity" is a legal term for written or photographic materials of a sexual or violent nature. "Pornography" is a broader term, referring to material designed to be sexually arousing. The terms are often used interchangeably, however. In the United States the courts have determined that obscene materials are not protected under the First Amendment and can be banned by government.

Historically, government agencies have taken steps to keep material regarded as obscene away from the public. But what the government has regarded as obscene has varied over time. A few prominent works of twentieth-century literature—including books by Henry Miller and D. H. Lawrence—could not be sold in the United States for many years after they were published because they were characterized as obscene. Magazines, movies, and hard-core videos have also been suppressed when found to be obscene.

Even when there is agreement about the desirability of curbing obscenity, a continuing problem is determining whether a particular work is obscene. The mere fact that sex and violence are depicted in a particular work is not sufficient to find it obscene from a legal point of view. Some people who are opposed to the sale or display of any works depicting graphic scenes of sex and violence are not interested in legal niceties, however, and just want to censor any works they do not like. But the courts have had to grapple with the problem of applying standards to distinguish obscene work from materials protected by the First Amendment.

The battle over obscenity is a continuing one and has produced some unusual political alliances of conservatives and liberals. Traditionally in the United States, criticism of pornography has come from conservative sources, particularly religious groups. They regard pornography as corrupting traditional values of respect for women and the sanctity of marriage and the family.

The conservative critique was exemplified during the Reagan administration by the establishment of a commission under the jurisdiction of Attorney General Edwin Meese III to investigate the impact of pornography on society. The commission's report concluded that there was a direct relationship between pornography and violence. In 1986, the federal government then set up a special section in the Criminal Division of the Justice Department to aid the prosecution of pornography.

But conservatives have found support for regulating pornography from some feminists, most notably Catharine A. MacKinnon and Andrea Dworkin. While generally regarded as liberals, they find common cause with conservatives on this issue. They condemn pornography because they feel that it causes harm to women, encouraging exploitation and rape. They favor legislation allowing the victims of pornography (such as women who have been raped) to collect civil damages from the people who create or sell pornographic material that may have prompted the rape.

Although most feminists agree that pornography demeans women, many—if not most of them—feel that government involvement in this area is a violation of the First Amendment. In this view, they share the opinion of most liberals that any censorship is dangerous to freedom of speech. Liberals worry that antiobscenity legislation will only stifle ideas.

The debate that follows features a traditional conservative-liberal division on the issue. Ernest van den Haag, a professor of jurisprudence and public policy at Fordham University in New York City, argues from a conservative perspective in defense of legislating against pornography. Speaking before the Heritage Foundation, a conservative think tank, he contends

1. Pornography reduces males and females simply to bearers of impersonal sensations of pleasure and pain; in short, it dehumanizes people. In this way, the empathy that restrains us ultimately from sadism and nonconsensual acts is eliminated.
2. Pornography lacks artistic value.
3. It undermines the social bond on which human association—from family to nation—must depend.
4. The First Amendment does not protect pornography.
5. Distinctions can be made between pornography and literature.
6. Regulating pornography is not the beginning of a police state.

Testifying before a congressional committee considering new initiatives to regulate pornography, Barry W. Lynn, legislative counsel for the American Civil Liberties Union (ACLU), argues against further restrictions. He contends

1. Pornography cannot be objectively defined.
2. Pornography—unlike obscenity—is protected by the First Amendment and should not be abridged.

3. New antipornography legislation would threaten the livelihood not only of distributors who deal only in sexually explicit films but of every owner of a major bookstore chain.
4. Antipornography laws would impose a "chilling effect" on literature or art.
5. Pornography is speech and not an act or a practice.
6. Pornography is not a central cause of sex discrimination.
7. The fact that pornography asserts an often repugnant world view graphically or persuasively does not place it in a special category distinct from literature.
8. The evidence is not conclusive that most pornography is an incitement to violence against women.

Lynn argues that there are ways to fight pornography other than to ban it or regulate it severely. In his view, the ultimate answer to the existence of offensive images must be the production of "affirmative" alternative images.

Should Government Impose Stricter Regulations on Pornography?

ERNEST VAN DEN HAAG

Pornography and the Law

The Meese Commission report on pornography was released last year and is now old hat. Perhaps this is a good time to examine with some detachment the question on which it sought to shed light: Should we continue to outlaw pornography while, in effect, tolerating it? Should we legalize it? Or should we find a method of outlawing it effectively?

For those who wish to legalize pornography the answer is simple. Whether or not pornography is distasteful or morally harmful, it affects only those who buy it. The government is not in charge of their morals. It is part of one's freedom to make choices that are harmful to oneself or disapproved by others. Those offended by pornography can readily refrain. There is no need for the law to protect them; no one compels them to see X-rated movies or buy pornographic magazines. Legitimate questions about advertising, public visibility, and access by children are marginal and could be solved by such measures as plain wrappers and inconspicuous signs.

RIDICULE BY "CIVIL LIBERTARIANS"

Surely the people who want to legalize pornography are right if, as they con-tend, pornography does no harm to those who do not volunteer to buy it. This is the question the Meese Commission addressed. The Commission has been ridiculed by all the usual "civil libertarians." However, if one actually looks at its report, one finds that the Commission did quite reasonable work in trying to answer the question it focused on: Does pornography lead to crime? If it does, obviously it harms persons who did not volunteer for the harm. They are entitled to protection, provided that protection is consistent with constitutional principles.

The Commission decided that pornography, particularly sado-masochistic pornography, stimulates, to say the least, sex crimes. One can argue about this. There is a chicken and egg problem. Does the prospective rapist consume pornography because he independently is a prospective rapist, or is it the pornography which causes, or stimulates, a disposition to rape that did not pre-exist or was minor? Which comes first? However, there seems to be little doubt that a disposition to commit sex crimes may be strengthened or activated by pornography, which appears to legitimize them and to weaken internal re-straints.

CHANGING SEXUAL MORES

The general evidence strongly suggests that crime can be stimulated by com-munications, ideas and sensations aroused by movies or books. Few sayings are as silly as the *dictum* attributed to Jimmy Walker (the late New York mayor) to the effect that "No girl has ever been seduced by a book." Books do not seduce directly any more than whiskey does. But they help. After all, even if one discounts the "sexual revolution," one cannot deny that sexual mores have changed over time, owing not to changes in biology, but to changed ideas and sentiments that infect people and lead them to action. Books such as the Bible or *Das Kapital* influence people's actions because of the ideas they expound. Pornography, which is bereft of ideas, influences people because of the sensa-tions and attitudes it stimulates. It is consumed for the sake of these sensations as drugs are and may influence actions analogously.

But pornography is not the only thing that may lead to sex crime, and certainly it does so only sometimes. Many people consume it without being led to crime. Others become criminals without pornography. Further, alcohol too may lead to crime, or TV violence—indeed myriad things. We cannot outlaw everything, not even every communication, that sometimes leads to crime. Why then outlaw pornography?

EXPLOITS SEX

If the Meese Commission conclusion—let's prohibit pornography because it may lead to crime—does not quite follow from its evidence, the idea of some feminists, that pornography is a male conspiracy against females to exploit them, and foster, or help, violence against them, is even less well founded. Pornography exploits sex, not females. The criminal effects are not intended, let alone conspired for. Women are accidental. Pornographers would be just as willing to present pictures of males as of females if there were a market for them. There isn't, except for male homosexuals, who indeed are catered to by pornographers. Most females—be it for cultural, psychological, or biological reasons—do not seem to want to consume pornography. Actually males, who spend good money for the stuff, are more, not less, exploited than the females who earn it. At any rate, I can't see exploitation (a cloudy concept to begin with, meaning not much more than "I don't like it"), since both buyers and sellers volunteer and both have alternatives. They do what they want to do; they are not compelled to do it. Exploitation without compulsion is hard to figure out.[1]

O.K., forget about the feminists. Why should we punish the sale of pornography? (Nobody advocates prior restraint censorship, which is a pseudo-issue.) The Meese Commission reason, that it may lead to crime, is not sufficient. Are there other reasons? I believe there are. The social damage pornography does is greater, yet more diffuse than indicated by individual crimes. Just as chemical pollution may erode stones, statues, and buildings, so pornography erodes civility and our social institutions.

AVOIDING ART AND HUMANITY

By definition, pornography deindividualizes and dehumanizes sexual acts. By eliminating the contexts it reduces males and females simply to bearers of impersonal sensations of pleasure and pain. This dehumanization eliminates the empathy that restrains us ultimately from sadism and non-consensual acts. The cliche-language and the stereotyped situations of characters not characterized, except sexually, are defining characteristics of pornography. The pornographer avoids distraction from the masturbatory fantasy by avoiding art and humanity. Art may "cancel lust" (as Santayana thought) or sublimate it. The pornographer desublimates it. Those who resort to pornographic fantasies habitually are people who are ungratified by others (for endogenous or external reasons). They seek gratification in using others, in inflicting pain (sometimes in suffering it), at least in their fantasy. In this respect, *The Story of O*, which, itself pornographic, also depicts the rather self-defeating outcome of pornographic fantasy, is paradigmatic.

In a sense, pornographic and finally sadistic literature is anti-human. Were it directed against a specific human group—e.g. Jews or blacks—the same liberal ideologues who now oppose outlawing pornography might advocate prohibiting it. Should we find a little black or Jewish girl tortured to death and her death agony taped by her murderers,[2] and should we find the murderers imbued with sadistic anti-Semitic or anti-black literature, most liberals would advocate that the circulation of such literature be prohibited. Why should humanity as such be less protected than any of the specific groups that compose it? That the sexualized hate articulated is directed against people in general, rather than against only Jews or Negroes, makes it no less dangerous; on the contrary: it makes it as dangerous to more people.

WITHOUT ARTISTIC VALUE

But shouldn't an adult be able to control himself and read or see, without enacting, what he knows to be wrong or, at least, illegal? Perhaps he should. But we are not dealing with a homogeneous group called grown-ups, nor is it possible in the modern American environment to limit anything to adults. Children and adolescents are not supervised enough. Further, the authority of their supervisors has been diminished too much to make effective supervision possible. As for grown-ups, many are far from the self-restrained healthy type envisaged by democratic theory. They may easily be given a last, or first, push by the materials I would like to see prohibited.

Now, if these materials had artistic, indeed any but pornographic value, we would have to weigh the loss against the importance of avoiding their deleterious influence. We may even be ready to sacrifice some probable victims for the sake of this value. But pornographic "literature" is without literary value. It is printed, but it is not literature. Else it cannot be defined as pornography. Hence there is nothing to be lost by restricting it, and much to be gained.

AFFECTS THE QUALITY OF LIFE

Self-restrained and controlled individuals exist and function in an environment which fosters reasonable conduct. But few such individuals will be created, and they will function less well, in an environment where they receive little social support, where sadistic acts are openly held up as models and sadistic fantasies are sold to any purchaser. To be sure, a virtuous man will not commit adultery. But a wise wife will avoid situations where the possibility is alluring and the opportunity available. Why must society lead its members into temptation and then punish them when they do what they were tempted to do? But more than individual cases are at issue.

Pornography affects the quality of our lives. It depreciates emotional ties and individual relationships in favor of fungible ones, in which physical pleasure is, in principle, separated from any emotional or even personal relationships. Yet, without "emotional ties which hold the group together," according to Freud there is "the cessation of all feelings of consideration" and therewith social disintegration and crime. "Emotional ties" are systematically depreciated by pornography.

EROSION OF THE SOCIAL BOND

Thus pornography undermines the social bond on which human association—from family to nation—must depend. It is this social bond which deters most of us, most of the time, from using our neighbors as we please, without regard to their own preferences. We are taught, and most of us learn, to perceive others as ends in themselves and not merely as means to our pleasure. This learning is the basis of society. Yet it is precarious. We need to be socialized continuously. Pornography undermines the internal restraints on which society must depend and which the criminal law with its sanctions can reinforce but not create. This seems quite enough to limit pornography (we will never succeed in doing more). No need (or possibility) to prove a direct and unavoidable relationship to crime. Such a direct causal relationship is likely occasionally, perhaps often. But it is largely beside the point when compared to the erosion of the social bond.

I prefer to live in a society in which public invitations to do without love in individual relationships, to regress to an infantile level of sexuality, stripped of emotion, are not consistently extended. Such invitations are all too likely to be tempting. We all are vulnerable to regression. After all, each of us developed laboriously and with much social effort from anti-social infants into acceptable adults. Invitations to regression should not be socially endorsed. Wherefore the case for prohibition of obscenity seems to be quite strong regardless of whether pornography can be shown to be among the many causes of crime.

PORNOGRAPHY NOT PROTECTED

Interstate commerce in pornography is already illegal under federal statutes, and intrastate pornography is illegal in most states. As interpreted by the Supreme Court the First Amendment does not protect pornography, defined as that which:

1. taken as whole predominantly appeals to the prurient interest (a morbid interest in sex); and
2. lacks serious literary, scientific, artistic, or political value (i.e., does not predominantly offer new ideas or aesthetic experiences); and

3. describes sexual conduct in ways judged to be patently offensive by the standards of the community in which the material is sold.

These legal criteria are rather porous. For instance, the depiction of intercourse with animals may be legal, since it may not appeal to the prurient interest of the average person. The depiction of excretion may be legal, since it may not appeal to the prurient interest of the average person either. The standards of the local community are vague (and costly to ascertain), unless the jury is taken to mean the community. The court could have been more concrete and specific.

CAMOUFLAGE AND PRETENSE

Further, present law requires that the material at issue be considered "as a whole" to determine whether it "predominantly" appeals to the prurient interest. This makes perfect sense for, say, novels, works meant to be taken as a whole, but no sense for periodicals, which, by definition, consist of independent articles or pictures. Why should it not be sufficient if some pictures, or other contributions, to a periodical are obscene, even if the rest consists of non-obscene essays? The non-obscene material usually serves as camouflage or pretense. For a movie, if more than 5 percent of its running time is devoted to images which, taken in isolation, would be regarded as obscene, the movie should be so regarded.

Traditionally pornography has not been thought to be protected by the First Amendment. The idea that the First Amendment licenses pornographers, though widespread, is quite recent. It has no legal basis. Further the First Amendment prohibits only abridging freedom of speech and of the press. Yet current interpretations have led the courts to conclude that the First Amendment protects "expression" (such as nude dancing) as well. Although expression, dancing is certainly not speech, let alone print. Nothing in the First Amendment protects speechless expression, such as music or dance, or for that matter, pictures.

Thus, in accordance with the First Amendment, legislatures cannot abridge the communication of information or of ideas. But pornography as defined by the courts is bereft of either. Legislatures can constitutionally allow pornography or nude dancing, but they need not. The legal question is not, can we prohibit pornography? (The answer is yes.) What is in dispute in each case is only: Is this material obscene according to the legal definition given above?[3]

EXPLICIT VISUAL DEPICTIONS

Of course there will be doubtful cases—but no more so than in other areas of the law. Courts exist to decide doubtful cases and can do so in this area as well as in any other. Standards of obscenity vary over time. Yet at any time there are standards discoverable by the courts. There is no great difficulty in discerning them—as lawyers are aware, though they often pretend otherwise. Yet, although often professing to be unable to distinguish obscene from non-obscene material, lawyers do not expose their genitals in court. They must have some knowledge of prevailing standards.

Depiction of the nude body, even in alluring poses, is no longer regarded as offensive. Nor is explicit prose. Visual depictions that focus on the genitals—rather than to merely include them—are. Detailed and explicit visual depictions of genital actions, including copulation, masturbation, and depiction of genital arousal, are prurient and offensive. So are prurient depictions which make public what traditionally has been private and intimate.

MAKING DISTINCTIONS

The perception of pornographic qualities in any work depends on literary or aesthetic criticism. Therefore, some argue, it is a matter of opinion. In court, serious critics often behave as though they believed criticism to be a matter of opinion. But why be a critic—and teach in universities—if it involves no more than uttering capricious and arbitrary opinions? If criticism cannot tell pornography from literature, what can it tell us? Of course, critics may disagree; so do other witnesses, including psychiatrists and handwriting experts. The decision is up to the courts; the literary witnesses only have the obligation to testify truthfully as to what is, or is not, pornography.

Some of the critics who claim that they cannot make the distinction do not wish to, because they regard pornography as legitimate; others fear that censorship of pornography may be extended to actual literature. Whatever the merits of such views (I don't see any), they do not justify testifying that the distinction cannot be made. A witness is not entitled to deny that he saw what he did see, simply to save the accused from a punishment he dislikes. A critic who is really incapable of distinguishing pornography from literature certainly has no business being one; a critic who is capable of making the distinction has no business testifying that he is not.

200 YEARS OF OUTLAWING OBSCENITY

Oh yes, there is one bugaboo: A "police state," it is feared, may develop from prohibiting the sale of pornography and punishing violators. That argument is not too plausible. To begin with, America did not become a "police state" although obscenity has been punished for the last 200 years. Not a single instance is known, throughout history, of a police state, or a dictatorship, developing by prohibiting obscenity, or even by censoring it, or by censoring anything else. It is the other way around. Once you have a police state, censorship follows. A police state cannot continue without it. But no democracy has ever become a police state by using the criminal law to restrain obscenity. The Weimar Republic in Germany was not replaced by Nazism because it did. It did not. Once Hitler was in power, he used it to abolish all freedom and to institute censorship.

NOTES

1. Depiction of females merely as sexual objects, expressions of hostility or contempt for them, and depictions of sadistic humiliation, are sometimes called "exploitation." If not exploitative, pornography of this sort is certainly antisocial. One may favor prohibition for this reason as much as for the sake of women.

2. This was done by the "Moor murderers" in England.

3. There are the usual ancillary questions: Was it offered for sale? Was it properly seized? But they need not detain us.

☑ N O

Should Government Impose Stricter Regulations on Pornography?

BARRY W. LYNN

Pornography and Liberty

We live in a country where the equality of men and women is neither generally portrayed nor routinely practiced. It is also a nation in which there is persistent violence against women by men who resent their achievements and the challenges they present to a male-dominated society. Against this volatile backdrop it is possible to reach for drastic proposals, including ones which could erode vital constitutional guarantees. One such flawed avenue is the new effort to curb sexually explicit material by creating broad new civil remedies so that individuals offended by it may hinder its use, sale, and distribution.

Many of the witnesses who have appeared during your previous two days of hearings, and several here today, have called for new legislative initiatives to regulate "pornography," which they erroneously assert can be objectively defined. They have made claims which would allegedly permit "pornography," now protected by the Constitution, to be excised from First Amendment protection just as "obscenity" and "child pornography" have been.[1]

Unfortunately, this approach blurs critical distinctions between advocacy and action and between cause and symptom, distinctions which must be retained in order to preserve important First Amendment guarantees. It is clearly contrary to the guarantees of free speech and a free press, because it ultimately rests on the constitutionally-forbidden premise that governments can be parties to the suppression of offensive ideas and images.

The recently adopted Indianapolis ordinance which has been embraced by several witnesses makes actionable "the graphic sexually explicit subordina-tion of women, whether in pictures or in words" if it also includes one or more specific elements, including, for example, the portrayal of women "as sexual objects . . . who enjoy humiliation" or the presentation of women "through postures of servility . . . or display." Such language as "presented as sexual objects" lacks intrinsic or objective meaning. It either requires inquiry into the motive of the producer or allows even the most sensitive viewer's characteriza-tion to be the ultimate determination.

(The ACLU has filed an *amicus* brief in the case challenging the facial constitutionality of the Indianapolis ordinance. This is not a hearing on that ordinance *per se*. However, it is important to note that any approach to regula-tion of sexually explicit material which seeks to cover material not included within the Supreme Court's definition of "obscenity" in *Miller* v. *California,* 413 U.S. 15 (1973) or its description of "child pornography" in *United States* v. *Ferber* 458 U.S. 747 (1982) will face insurmountable constitutional "over-breadth" and "vagueness" problems.)

These phrases can in fact be construed by reasonable people to cover vast amounts of literature, art, and popular culture in today's marketplace. Novels by Norman Mailer, Erica Jong and John Irving, sex education "self-help" books, much "erotic" and even religious art of Eastern and Western cultures, and popular music videos could clearly be included. Likewise, many of the highest grossing films of 1984, including *Indiana Jones, Tightrope,* and *Purple Rain,* all contain sufficient graphic thematic messages about subordination of women to result in legal actions. It would not be simply the proprietor of the "Adam and Eve" bookstore who would have to wonder whether a court would find some of his sales items "pornographic"; it would be every movie exhibitor and every owner of a major bookstore chain.

That problem is the essence of a "chilling effect"—that persons will not write, or photograph, or sell because they do not want to risk that some partic-ularly sensitive or particularly zealous individual will decide that their product is covered by the statutory language. Creating broad individual civil causes of action, particularly ones which allow injunctions against continued distribu-tion, will lead to "self-censorship." This can have as drastic an effect on the free flow of ideas as direct government censorship.

THE ALLEGED EFFECTS OF PORNOGRAPHY

The underpinning of new efforts to control "pornography" is that recently discovered and newly articulated factors take the material outside the scope of the First Amendment. However, the new framing of the argument against pornography, combined with the varieties of empirical research data, still meet no test ever articulated by the Supreme Court which would allow the state directly or its citizens indirectly to suppress this sexually explicit material.

The so-called "findings" section of the Indianapolis ordinance and other proposals notes that "Pornography is a discriminatory *practice* based on sex which denies women equal opportunities in society. Pornography is *central* in creating and maintaining sex as a basis for discrimination. . . . The bigotry and contempt it promotes, with the acts of *aggression it fosters,* harm women's opportunities for equality of rights . . ." (emphasis added). Many previous witnesses have made statements suggesting agreement with this analysis. However, these conclusions are unsupported by the actual evidence available.

Pornography as a "Practice"

Pornography includes words and pictures. It is "speech," not an act or a practice. The parallels between certain racist activity and pornography drawn by some pornography critics are inappropriate. Racial segregation is an "act" and it can be prohibited in spite of First Amendment claims of a "right of association." However, racist speech by the American Nazi Party or the Ku Klux Klan which may, implicitly or explicitly, urge segregation cannot be barred. *Collin* v. *Smith* 578 F.2d 1197 (7th Cir. 1978), *cert. denied* 439 U.S. 916 (1978).

Even the vilest and most graphic sexist or racist speech is not transformed into action because of the intensity with which its critics detest it or the success it demonstrates in getting others to accede to its viewpoint. It is important to guarantee as a "civil right" that no person is denied a job, an education, or entry to a public facility on the basis of race or sex. This is true whether the decision to discriminate is based on listening to well-reasoned academic discourse, reading "hate literature," or watching old movies containing negative stereotypes. However, our "civil rights" laws do not, and may not, insulate individuals from the repugnant speech of others which urges the denial of such opportunities.

Pornography as a Central Cause of Sex Discrimination

Another "finding" is that pornography is "central" to maintenance of women's inequality. The "centrality" of pornography as a source of inequality is not empirically supportable. Unless one works in an adult bookstore, graphic, sexually explicit "pornography" is not a major source of sensory input for many people. However, if all that critics define as "pornography" were to disappear tomorrow, and it had *in fact* been central to subordination, the central position would then be taken up by other images from comic books, cartoon shows, jean advertising, television situation comedies, and dozens of other sources which assault our eyes and ears on a regular basis. Precisely the same arguments that undergird the efforts to eliminate graphic sexual images showing the subordination of women would then be applicable to a variety of remaining images which cast women in a demeaning light.

It may be popular to start the process of eliminating negative views of women by proceeding against graphic sexual images, since allies in such an effort could include those persons who see the issue simply as one of "indecency." However, there is no logical reason to stop there, given the vastly greater number of persons who are exposed to the concept of "subordination" in other, "non-explicit" media. Once we accept the premise upon which this "pornography" regulation is based—the eradication of contemptuous images—there is nowhere to stop the regulatory process.

In fact, once the decision to suppress "negative" portrayals is made, it is only a short trip to mandating "positive" portrayals. As Justice Brennan noted in his dissent in *Paris Adult Theatre I* v. *Slaton* 413 U.S. 49 (1973):

> For if a state may, in an effort to maintain or create a moral tone, prescribe what its citizens cannot read or cannot see, then it would seem to follow that in pursuit of that same objective a state could decree that its citizens must read certain books or must view certain films.

The sexually explicit messages labeled "pornographic" have not been demonstrated to be central to any discriminatory practices. However, even if such evidence was present, it would not dispose of the guarantees of the First Amendment.

Pornography as Behavioral Stimulus, Not Advocacy

There is also the claim that pornography is somehow different than other cultural expressions because it is not "speech." Professor Catharine MacKinnon, the co-author of several proposed anti-pornography ordinances, noted in the *amicus* brief she prepared in the Indianapolis case, that "unlike the 'literature' of other inequalities, pornography works as a behavioral conditioner, reinforcer and stimulus, not as idea or advocacy."

That assertion is simply incorrect. Sexually explicit material may communicate that the activity depicted is pleasurable and appropriate. It is often a rejection of ascetic lifestyles, rational analysis, and prudence. Women's studies professor Ann Barr Snitow notes that it promotes "the joys of passivity, of helpless abandon, of response without responsibility. . . ." According to *Village Voice* writer Ellen Willis the meaning of sexually explicit material is highly individual and complex:

Sex in this culture has been so deeply politicized that it is impossible to make clear-cut distinctions between "authentic" sexual impulses and those conditioned by patriarchy. Between, say, *Ulysses* at one end and *Snuff* at the other, erotica/pornography conveys all sorts of mixed messages that elicit complicated and private responses.[2]

Of course, it also may communicate a more sinister message, that women do, or should, gain pleasure solely from subordination to men. Repulsive as that construct may be, it is a political philosophy which has been dominant in most civilizations since the beginning of human history. It is clearly an "idea" and much pornography serves as a tool for its advocacy.

Similarly, virtually all printed and visual material seeks not only to communicate ideas, but also to act as a "behavioral conditioner, reinforcer, and stimulus." Books and movies frequently: (1) teach people to view an issue in a certain way ("behavioral conditioner"), (2) legitimatize particular ways of thinking ("reinforcer"), or (3) urge people to act in accord with the images presented by the author ("stimulus"). The fact that pornography asserts an often repugnant world-view graphically or persuasively does not place it in a special category from other literature.

The Supreme Court recognized this in *Cohen v. California* 403 U.S. 1526 (1970), where it assessed the impact of Cohen entering the trial court wearing a jacket emblazoned with the words "Fuck the Draft."

> [M]uch linguistic expression serves a dual communicative function: it conveys not only ideas capable of relatively precise, detached explication, but otherwise unexpressible emotions as well. In fact, words are often chosen as much for their emotive as their cognitive force. We cannot sanction the view that the Constitution, while solicitous of the cognitive content of individual speech, has little or no regard for that emotive function which, practically speaking, may often be the more important element of the overall message sought to be communicated. . . .

There is yet another dimension of this false "stimulus-advocacy" dichotomy. A number of commentators have criticized the new effort to regulate pornography as an effort to totally rationalize human sexuality. Historian Alice Echols has lamented the rejection by some feminists of "the notion that fantasy is the repository of our ambivalent and conflictual feelings," which she says leads to "a highly mechanistic and behavioristic analysis that conflates fantasy with reality and pornography with violence."[3] Indeed, it is as dangerous for the state, directly or indirectly, to police fantasies as to police politics.

Pornography as a Cause of Sexual Violence

Finally, much has been claimed about new data purporting to demonstrate a causal connection between certain types of pornography and sexual violence against women. Unfortunately, there is little recognition of distinctions between "causes" and "symptoms" in much of this discussion. This error is compounded by drawing unwarranted implications from the evidence.

For example, at a previous hearing several researchers reported findings that in a sample of "serial murderers," 81 percent noted a "high interest" in pornography and that in another sample of persons arrested for various forms of child exploitation, all had at least some "pornography" (from *Playboy* on down) in their homes. However, the presence of two phenomena, criminal activity and pornography, does not necessarily demonstrate a causal connection between them; it is at least as likely to demonstrate that persons with certain abusive personalities are attracted to both crime and use of pornography.

It is also possible to misdirect the outrage against specific instances of sexual violence. It is undeniable that there are examples of media portrayals of sexual violence whose elements are replicated almost identically by persons during the commission of a criminal act. These occurrences do not permit broad intrusions into First Amendment rights, even if it were demonstrated that *but for* the media portrayals, no crime would have occurred (something which has not been proven in any case). Certainly, the results of psychological experiments on male college students which demonstrate only that some tend to react temporarily more aggressively under laboratory conditions after seeing "aggressive-erotic" films provides no basis for suppressing speech.[4] As Kate Ellis notes in "Pornography and the Feminist Imagination": "In all of these studies a single stimulus and response is being made to stand in for a long conditioning process."

The First Amendment may not be suspended because an image or an idea causes the most susceptible or most malleable person who hears it or sees it to behave in an anti-social manner. This was recognized by the Supreme Court in *Roth* v. *United States* 354 U.S. 476 (1957). An uncomfortable volume of previous testimony before this subcommittee suggests a return to this "most susceptible" standard. It is carried to its greatest extremes in some ordinance language permitting injunctions against the future distribution of a specific book or film if it can be linked to one act of violence.

An even more direct argument is that pornography is a form of "incitement" to violence against women. However, even sexually explicit material which implicitly advocates the subordination of women does not urge that viewers commit criminal activity. In the event that some piece of literature did urge criminal activity its possible suppression would be measured on the basis of well-established constitutional principles.

Supreme Court decisions on speech which allegedly incites listeners to criminal acts make it clear that mere speculative damage is insufficient to suppress speech and that only if there is a close and demonstrable causal nexus between speech and violence may speech be barred. This is the "clear and present" danger standard announced first in *Schenck* v. *United States* 249 U.S. 47 (1919). The Court has subsequently ruled that not even "advocacy" of "revenge" against public officials by Ku Klux Klan members carrying guns, *Bran-*

denburg v. *Ohio* 395 U.S. 444 (1969), or student revolutionaries' threat to "take the fucking street later," *Hess* v. *Indiana* 414 U.S. 105 (1973), could be suppressed. A violent criminal act was not likely to be the direct and imminent result of the speech in these cases. A review of the data on "incitement" to violence against women by pornography demonstrates nothing to meet the *Brandenburg* standard.

WHAT CAN BE DONE?

It is important to use the means of communication available to make it clear that remedies already exist for some of the conduct which has been previously described at your hearings. There has, for example, been testimony in regard to husbands forcing their spouses into sexual activity, described in "pornography," which they did not desire. That constitutes rape in most jurisdictions. The ACLU [American Civil Liberties Union] has been actively supporting elimination of "spouse" immunity in rape cases in those states where it still exists. We would not minimize the problem of getting prosecutors to charge in such cases, but that is no excuse for not empowering the public with the knowledge that such actions can be taken.

Similarly, at previous hearings, Ms. Linda Marchiano testified regarding her physical coercion into the production of the film *Deep Throat.* It appears that the statute of limitations has run, precluding any criminal prosecution. Assuming the facts as she reported, however, she would seem to retain the possibility of civil actions without need for new ordinances or federal intervention.[5]

Privacy-related torts which could already cover Ms. Marchiano's situation include "public disclosure of private facts" (since there was the intimate portrayal of sexual activity), placing one in a "false light in the public eye" (since she could argue that the film gave the false impression that she was enjoying what was actually repugnant coerced activity) or "wrongful appropriation" (her unwanted activity was photographed and appropriated by the perpetrators of a crime for commercial advantage).

Damages or even injunctive relief could certainly be sought in such individual cases, but depending upon the precise facts elicited, First Amendment limitations on such actions could also arise. The ACLU is exploring whether narrow legislation covering such coerced activities would be consistent with such constitutional concerns.

Obviously, this would be costly litigation, with substantial attendant problems of proof. However, any action brought under an Indianapolis-type statute would be similarly expensive, since there could be no statutory presumption of coercion in regard to all women appearing in pornography.

In addition, in a society which has the regard for openness and tolerance found in the United States, the ultimate answer to the existence of offensive images must be the production of "affirmative" alternative images. It means the replacement of images of female subordination with images of equality and authority. The First Amendment was designed to protect the "marketplace of ideas" because of a deeply rooted belief that when ideas and images compete (even if they begin in "unequal" status), the "true" and "accurate" have the best chance to prevail.

No one could seriously suggest that women have an equal "voice" in institutions in the United States. On the other hand, there has already been a historically unprecedented increase in the number of women's voices speaking in every academic field, from law to medicine to theology, and in every artistic endeavor. Those are the sources for the positive views of women which will help shape the future.

In addition to the creation of alternative images, it is certainly constitutionally acceptable to work to create a "negative image" for pornography: to urge that our society would be healthier without it, to critique its moral and aesthetic value, and to urge its disuse by all persons.

CONCLUSION

It is unfortunate when the issues raised by the Indianapolis ordinance are couched as ones of "women's rights" versus "civil liberties." It is clearly possible to protect and enhance both. There is a right to be free from sexual coercion; however, there is no similar right to be free from offensive and insulting images. There may be instances where genuine constitutional claims will clash, where, for example, the constitutional right of privacy runs squarely into the free press guarantees of the First Amendment. The ACLU would be happy to review any statutory language in these delicate areas.

NOTES

1. "Obscenity" has been defined by the Supreme Court as requiring proof of three crucial elements: (1) that it appeals to the "prurient interest" as judged by the average person applying contemporary community standards; (b) that it describes or depicts, in a patently offensive way, specific sexual conduct defined by statute; (c) that, as a whole, it lacks serious literary, artistic, political, or scientific value. The ACLU believes this standard violates the First Amendment. However, "pornography" definitions would restrict even more material since there are no "average person" or "lacking value" tests.

2. "Feminism, Moralism, and Pornography," in *Powers of Desire: The Politics of Sexuality,* ed. Ann Snitow, Christine Stansell, and Sharon Thompson (New York: Monthly Review Press, 1983), p. 463.

3. "The New Feminism of Yin and Yang" in *Powers of Desire,* p. 448.

4. See, for example, Edward Donnerstein and Leonard Berkowitz, "Victim Reactions in Aggressive Erotic Films As a Factor in Violence against Women," *Journal of Personality and Social Psychology,* Vol. 41, No. 4 (1981), pp. 710–724.

5. The ACLU believes that some of these causes of actions, particularly when applied to a broad range of facts, may be inconsistent with the First Amendment.

Questions for Discussion

1. What criteria would you use in determining whether a particular work is art or pornography?
2. Should the regulation of child pornography be considered in any way different from the regulation of other forms of pornography? What are the reasons for your answer?
3. Is the regulation of pornography consistent with the First Amendment? What are the reasons for your answer?
4. What effect would a scientific finding determining conclusively that pornography increases the likelihood of violence against women have on your view of the subject?
5. What effect would new antipornography legislation have on writers, artists, and bookstore owners? What are the reasons for your answer?

Suggested Readings

Baird, Robert M., and Stuart E. Rosenbaum, eds. *Pornography: Private Right or Public Menace?* Buffalo, N.Y.: Prometheus Books, 1991.

Berger, Ronald J., Patricia Searles, and Charles E. Cottle. *Feminism and Pornography*. New York: Praeger, 1991.

Bryden, David. "Between Two Constitutions: Feminism and Pornography." *Constitutional Commentary*, 2, no. 1 (Winter 1985), 147–180.

Committee on Federal Legislation and the Committee on Communications and Media Law. "Pornography Victims Compensation Act." *Record of the Association of the Bar of the City of New York*, 47, no. 3 (April 1992), 326–334.

Delgado, Richard, and Jean Stefanic. "Pornography and Harm to Women: 'No Empirical Evidence?'" *Ohio State Law Journal*, 53, no. 4 (1992), 1037–1055.

Elson, John. "Passions over Pornography." *Time*, 139, no. 13 (March 30, 1992), 52–53.

Hentoff, Nat. "*MacKinnon* v. *Free Speech*." *Progressive*, 56, no. 9 (September 1992), 14–15.

Irving, John. "Pornography and the New Puritans." *New York Times Book Review*, March 29, 1992, pp. 1, 24–25, 27. *See also* "Pornography and the New Puritans: Letters from Andrea Dworkin and Others." *New York Times Book Review*, May 3, 1992, pp. 15–16.

Kaminer, Wendy. "Feminists against the First Amendment." *Atlantic*, 270, no. 5 (November 1992), 110–112, 114–116, 118.

MacKinnon, Catharine A. "Pornography as Defamation and Discrimination." *Boston University Law Review*, 71, no. 4 (July 1991), 793–815.

———. "Pornography, Civil Rights, and Speech." *Harvard Civil Rights–Civil Liberties Law Review*, 20, no. 1 (Winter 1985), 1–70.

Oliver, Charles, "Sexual Fantasies." *Reason*, 24, no. 2 (June 1992), 46–47.

Ross, Mary Ellen. "Censorship or Education? Feminist Views on Pornography." *Christian Century*, 107, no. 8 (March 7, 1990), 244–246.

Russell, Diana E. H., ed. *Making Violence Sexy: Feminist Views on Pornography.* New York: Teachers College, Columbia University, 1993.

Segal, Lynne, and Mary McIntosh, eds. *Sex Exposed: Sexuality and the Pornography Debate.* New Brunswick, N.J.: Rutgers Univ. Press, 1993.

Stoller, Robert J. *Porn: Myths for the Twentieth Century.* New Haven: Yale Univ. Press, 1991.

Teller. "Movies Don't Cause Crime." *New York Times,* January 17, 1992, p. A29.

Tisdale, Sallie. "Talk Dirty to Me: A Woman's Taste for Pornography." *Harper's,* 284, no. 1701 (February 1992), 37–39, 42–46.

U.S. Cong., Senate. *Effect of Pornography on Women and Children.* Hearings before the Committee on the Judiciary, 98th Cong., 2d Sess., 1985.

———. *Legislative Proposals for Compensation of Victims of Sexual Crimes.* Hearing before the Committee on the Judiciary, 102d Cong., 1st Sess., 1991.

Wickerson, Isabel. "Foes of Pornography and Bigotry Join Forces." *New York Times,* March 12, 1993, p. B16.

Wilson, Elizabeth. "Against Feminist Fundamentalism." *New Statesman and Society,* 2, no. 55 (June 23, 1989), 30–33.

Chapter 8

Should the Media Name the Accuser When the Crime Being Charged Is Rape?

On March 31, 1991, a woman told police in Palm Beach, Florida, that she had been raped at the compound of the Kennedy family where Senator Edward Kennedy and his nephew were staying. The woman charged that the rapist was William Kennedy Smith. Although most rapes are not even mentioned in media accounts since most are unreported, this story not only appeared in the media but became sensational because the accused rapist was a member of the Kennedy family.

Although the press mentioned Smith by name and discussed his background and life, it did not at first mention the name of the accuser. The news organizations were following a longtime practice of not mentioning names of rape victims. The practice reflects the belief that rape is a crime unlike others because it is personal and traumatic and carries a stigma against the victim.

But after two tabloids published the name of the accuser, *NBC Nightly News* did the same. The woman, Patricia Bowman, did not want her name disclosed publicly, but soon the *New York Times* and several other news organizations followed suit. Most of the media did not reveal her name, however.

The naming of the accuser by such major media organizations produced a storm of controversy both within the journalism profession and among the general public as well. People who sympathized with the alleged victim on the subject say that the injured party has a right to privacy. But the media contend that the public has a right to information and the First Amendment protects news organizations in printing the facts, however heinous they may be.

From a legal perspective, the Constitution itself does not mention the word privacy. But the Supreme Court has recognized the right of privacy since the 1920s in such matters as marriage, reproduction, and child rearing. It also recognizes a right of privacy in education and abortion. Speaking for the Court in *Griswold* v. *Connecticut*, Justice William O. Douglas said that the enumerated rights in the Bill of Rights have penumbras, or shadows, that protect individuals' privacy interests.[1]

But the courts have accorded First Amendment protection of freedom of the press to news organizations in reporting truthful information, including naming an alleged victim of a rape. A few states have enacted laws prohibiting the news media from disclosing the names of alleged rape victims, but their legal status is still to be determined by the federal courts. In 1989, however, the Supreme Court overturned a Florida court decision that awarded damages to a rape victim who had sued under a Florida statute prohibiting the identification of rape victims by news organizations.[2]

Most news organizations have not worried about the legal constraints dealing with the naming of accusers in rape cases. Instead, they have generally withheld the name because of professional and ethical considerations. But as we have seen in the Palm Beach story, some news organizations have reversed their long-standing policy in dealing with the subject.

It may be that the behavior of the media in the Smith case was unique because of the popular interest in the Kennedy family. More reporters covered the trial of William Kennedy Smith than reported from the scene of the Persian Gulf War. The trial was televised, although the accuser's face was blurred from the screen. Smith was acquitted. In December 1991, after the trial was over, Patricia Bowman came forward and agreed to be identified both in picture and in voice and be interviewed on the ABC News program *Prime Time Live*. At that point, other news organizations identified her by name.

The issue of a news organization's responsibility to report the news versus the right of privacy is hotly contested, as is clear from the debate in this chapter. The articles below are drawn from a symposium, "The Privacy Rights of Rape Victims in the Media and the Law," given at Fordham Law School in New York City on January 28, 1993. Michael Gartner, the former president of NBC News, defends the decision he made to reveal the name of the woman who claimed that she had been raped by William Kennedy Smith. He contends

1. Journalists are in the business of disseminating news, not suppressing it.
2. News organizations, not lawyers or legislators, should make the decision about naming rape victims. Journalists do not give newsmakers in any other category of news the option of being named or not being named.
3. Not naming rape victims does a disservice to the public by reinforcing the idea that there is something shameful about being a rape victim.
4. Naming the rape victim is fair since the name of a suspect in a rape case is published. Suspects are not always guilty, however.

Linda Fairstein, chief of the Sex Crimes Prosecution Unit, New York County District Attorney's Office, argues for a rape victim's right to privacy. She contends

1. Rape as a crime is treated differently from other crimes.
2. Rape is the only crime that is generally viewed as victim-precipitated, and rape victims have always been stigmatized.
3. It is not true that the media are not in the business of keeping

secrets, since news organizations abided by a gentleman's agreement not to name rape victims for a long time.

4. Revealing names in the media does not add credibility to a story.
5. Naming the accused does not justify naming the accuser.
6. At this point, naming the victim does not help destigmatize the victim.

NOTES

1. 381 U.S. 479; 14 L. Ed. 510; S. Ct. 1678 (1965).
2. *Florida Star* v. *B.J.F.* 491 U.S. 524 (1989).

☑Y E S

Should the Media Name the Accuser When the Crime Being Charged Is Rape?

MICHAEL GARTNER

Shaking the Foundations of Free Speech

Why did NBC News name the victim in the William Kennedy Smith rape case? How was that decision made? I am President of NBC News and was instrumental in making that decision. What follows is a discussion of the reasons supporting the decision and the procedural steps NBC News took in making it.

For years, journalists and feminists have debated whether the names of rape victims (or alleged rape victims) should be made public. Among both journalists and feminists, there is no agreement. At NBC, we debated the journalistic arguments.

The function of journalists is not to change the world, or to change the public's views. People who want to change the world should become teachers or politicians, not newsmen and newswomen. Journalists have only one duty—to present the news as clearly, as fairly, as thoroughly, and as accurately as possible. That is why, after great debate, I chose to air the name of the alleged rape victim in the Palm Beach case. In my opinion, a number of reasons supported this decision: First, we are in the business of disseminating news, not suppressing it. Names and facts are news. They add credibility to stories and give viewers or readers information they need to understand issues. Accordingly, my inclination is always toward telling the public all the germane facts that we possess.

Second, it is my view that producers, editors, and news directors should make editorial decisions, rather than lawyers or legislatures. For this reason, I oppose preventing news organizations from disclosing the names of rape victims who prefer to remain anonymous. Importantly, we do not give newsmakers in any other category of news the option of being named or not being named.

Third, by not naming rape victims, we are participating in a conspiracy of silence which does a disservice to the public by reinforcing the idea that there is something shameful about being raped. Rape is a despicable crime of violence, and rapists are deplorable people. Rape victims, on the other hand, are blameless. One role of the press is to inform the public, and one way of informing the public is to destroy incorrect impressions and stereotypes.

Fourth, and finally, is the issue of fairness. There was no debate in our newsroom about whether to name the suspect in the Palm Beach rape case even though at the time we ran the story the defendant, William Kennedy Smith, had not yet been charged with the commission of a crime. We dragged his name and his reputation into the public domain, however, without regard to what might happen to him should he be acquitted, or indeed, should he not even be charged. Unquestionably, rapists are contemptible people. Suspects, however, are not necessarily rapists.

Those are the points made in our internal debates at NBC News. I first raised this issue when the "Central Park jogger" was raped.[1] We reported that story on *Nightly News,* and afterward I told my colleagues that if this story were to gain a continuing national interest, we should debate the question of naming the victim. As it turned out, the story did not receive continuing national interest, and we never needed to address the issue of naming the victim for that story.

In early April of 1991, I first started to consider naming the victim in the Palm Beach rape case. A week later, I discussed this issue with some colleagues from outside NBC News. On Monday, April 16, 1991, I raised the issue with three colleagues within NBC News. The next day, these discussions continued. They were passionate and spirited. By the end of that day, the debate encompassed approximately thirty people, men and women of all views. There was no unanimity of opinion. If a vote had been taken, however, the result probably would have been to not print the victim's name. Nevertheless, I decided, for the reasons listed above, to name her. The fact that her identity was known to many in her community was another factor—but not a controlling one—in my decision.

A number of people at NBC News—including people who were involved in the preparation, production and presentation of the piece—disagreed with my decision. No one, however, asked to be removed from the story, and everyone did a thorough job. The story was fair and accurate; it was not sensational or promoted in an effort to boost our ratings. It was presented merely as one of many interesting stories on our *Nightly News* broadcast that evening.

At 5 p.m., we advised our affiliates that we were naming the rape victim. Our Florida affiliates, especially, needed to be told in advance. In the time since we aired this story, six of our 209 affiliates have complained to us about the decision; at least one, WBZ in Boston, actually bleeped out the woman's name and covered her picture. Several affiliates said that although our decision ran counter to their own policies, they respected our judgment and aired the story. Several other affiliates called to say they agreed with our decision. Most affiliates said nothing.

I am particularly proud of the process we went through in reaching our conclusion. In fact, the process may have been more important than the conclusion itself. We vigorously and freely debated an important issue of journalism; all sides were discussed. The story was shaped and reshaped as a result of that debate. And when we ultimately decided to air the victim's name, everyone involved in that decision at least understood the reasons for our doing so.

Our decision engendered a national debate. Although much of the debate has been focused on the wrong issues, some of it has been focused on the right issue: the crime of rape. The debate has raised the public's awareness of the vileness of the crime, the innocence of the victims, and the baseness of rapists. That has been a beneficial side effect.

Rape is rarely a national story. If another rape receives national attention, however, we will have the same debate again. The position at NBC News is this: We will consider the naming of rape victims or alleged rape victims on a case-by-case basis.

I think the duty of a free press is to allow people to make their own decisions. Censorship is one crime that may be as repulsive as the crime of rape. I would hate to see any laws passed, or any government pressures, that would interfere with the decisions news organizations make to name anyone for any issue.

NBC named the rape victim in the Palm Beach case in an effort to be thorough as reporters and fair as journalists. It was a controversial decision that was made with some anguish. But I believed then, and I believe now, that it was the right decision.

NOTE

1. See Craig Wolff, "Youths Rape and Beat Central Park Jogger," *New York Times,* April 21, 1989, p. B1.

Should the Media Name the Accuser When the Crime Being Charged Is Rape?

LINDA FAIRSTEIN

The Privacy Rights of Rape Victims

Sir Matthew Hale, who was Lord Chief Justice of the King's Bench in England, once wrote an opinion in a rape case which has been paraphrased in court-rooms and in living rooms almost ever since. According to Justice Hale, rape is an accusation that is so easy for a woman to make and so difficult for a man to defend against that it must be examined with more caution than any other crime.

Unfortunately, Justice Hale wrote that opinion in 1671. And yet, the extra caution that Justice Hale required to support the testimony of a rape victim became in the laws of this country something that was known as the corroboration requirement. The corroboration requirement remained a part of our laws for three centuries and was eliminated only recently from our legal system.

I cannot help but frame this issue in a somewhat personal perspective. I graduated from law school in 1972 and joined the Manhattan District Attorney's office that year. At that time, there were no sex crimes prosecutors or sex crimes prosecution units anywhere in the country. In fact, in 1971, although more than 2000 rapes were reported to the New York City police, only eighteen men were convicted of crimes of sexual assault in that year.

The reason for such a small number of convictions was due to the corroboration requirement. This requirement was still in effect when I joined the Manhattan District Attorney's office. The corroboration requirement mandated that the rape victim prove three elements of her case by independent evidence. First, the victims had to provide independent evidence identifying their attacker. Victims often experienced difficulty proving this element because unlike many crimes, like muggings and bank robberies, that occur in broad daylight and are witnessed by a number of people, sexual assaults, on the other hand, rarely occur in such surroundings. Second, there had to be independent evidence that the defendant used force during the attack. A weapon recovered at the crime scene or an injury to the victim could suffice. This evidence was used to prove that the victim had been assaulted. And third, there had to be evidence of the sexual nature of the attack, usually in the form of seminal fluid. This left open the problem that if the sexual act had not been completed, there was no way to prove that the crime was of a sexual nature.

The existence of the corroboration requirement made it virtually impossible for the state to prosecute rapists. Whether past legislation governing crimes of sexual violence was drafted in reaction to the prevailing public attitudes existing at the time about the crime, or whether these public attitudes were formed and reinforced by the laws and the legal mandates, it is clear that rape and other sexual assaults were treated differently from any other category of crime within the criminal justice system.

Correspondingly, victims of sexual assault also have been treated differently for centuries. When I started in 1972 at the Manhattan District Attorney's office, a woman who was robbed at gunpoint by an assailant caught three weeks later without a weapon and identified in a lineup was considered legally competent to testify to the armed robbery because of the corroborating circumstances. Yet, if the same man at the same time had raped her and there was no corroboration of those elements, she could not testify about the sexual assault.

Rape has been the only category of crime requiring corroboration. It was not eliminated as a requirement in New York State until 1974. Consider, however, that one could convict someone of murder on circumstantial evidence alone.

Also consider that victims of sexual assault have always been treated differently. It is the only crime that is generally viewed as victim-precipitated, occurring because the victim in some way allowed the crime to occur. Rape victims have always been stigmatized for their behavior, and for their participation or victimization in this type of crime.

I believe that we as a society have made progress in our response to rape victims. Our progress, however, has been extraordinarily slow and has occurred in only some segments of society. Moreover, this progress has occurred only in regard to certain kinds of victims of sexual assault cases. Professor Benedict accurately outlines in her book eight factors that frequently cause the public and the press to blame rape victims. It is still quite commonplace for the community to look with suspicion on victims who are known to their assailants, commonly referred to as "date rape" cases, or to victims who are attacked in particular occasions at particular times of day and night, or to victims who do not offer resistance to their offenders.

Until we can respond to more survivors with more dignity, I believe one small measure of respect we can and must offer to rape victims is their privacy. Those who choose to report the crime should not be named by the media. As Mr. Gartner stated, it seems clear that every broadcaster and every publication has the absolute right to publish the victim's name. Therefore, in my opinion, it is a matter of decency to ask that those names be withheld.

I agree with Geneva Overholser, the editor of the *Des Moines Register*, who encourages women who have been raped to identify themselves and put their faces to these crimes that have been hidden away for so long. Each victim, however, must come to terms with her own experience in her own way. It should be the right of each victim to decide if and when she will become identifiable to the public beyond the courtroom, if she even chooses to go that far. For some women, it is an important step in their recovery to be publicly identified as a rape victim. For others, however, it will never be acceptable to take this step.

Before hearing Mr. Gartner's remarks today, I was aware of four media justifications for printing the names of rape victims. Professor Benedict refers to these in greater detail in her book. One justification, derived from remarks made by Mr. Gartner around the time of the victim naming in the Palm Beach rape, is that the media is not in the business of keeping secrets. Obviously, this idea was a relatively recent change of policy for the media who, for a long time, abided by a gentleman's agreement not to name rape victims.

A second justification is that names lend victims credibility. I find this argument implausible. I do not understand how a story would obtain more credibility when people who do not know the victim, and who live outside the community where the victim lives, hear or read the victim's name. There are occasionally humorous moments in this business. We have a courthouse reporter who has been with one of our local tabloids for forty years and who just celebrated his fortieth anniversary. At every press conference after a press release in our office, this reporter raises his hand and says, "please describe the victim," a question that has been facetiously translated as "what color was the victim's hair"? The resulting newspaper accounts of these crimes frequently refer to the raven-haired woman who was attacked, or to the blonde who was coming out of her office building late at night. Interestingly, there is no other category of crime in which the physical description of the victim plays any part in the case. Therefore, I do not understand how naming the victim in rape cases gives the story more credibility.

A third justification, advanced by Alan Dershowitz, is that naming the accused but not the accuser unfairly prejudices the accused. Although I agree with this argument in principle, I do not think that naming the accuser rectifies this inequity. Mr. Gartner said that there was never a debate at NBC News about naming the accused in the Palm Beach rape. I feel, however, that it was outrageous for the media to name the accused before he had even been formally charged with the commission of a crime. Accordingly, I do not think that naming the victim is an appropriate answer to this problem.

The fourth justification is that naming the victim is a way of destigmatizing the victim. I think that it would be wonderful to live in such an accepting society. But I also think that until we reach that point, it is each individual victim's right to decide when, and by whom, she should be identified.

Questions for Discussion

1. Would not publishing a rape victim's name be an act of press self-censorship? What are the reasons for your answer?
2. What effect would a law or practice that requires the media not to publish a rape victim's name have on the willingness of rape victims to report the crime to the police? Explain.
3. What effect would reporting the names of rape victims have on destigmatizing the crime of rape? Explain.

4. In terms of the public's right to know, what is the difference between reporting a mugging incident and reporting a rape incident? Does the public have the right to know the names of victims?
5. What criteria should be used by journalists in deciding whether to withhold information in publishing any stories, whether about rape or other subjects?

Suggested Readings

Benedict, Helen. *Virgin or Vamp: How the Press Covers Sex Crimes.* New York: Oxford Univ. Press, 1992.

Butterfield, Fox, with Mary B. W. Tabor. "Woman in Florida Rape Inquiry Fought Adversity and Sought Acceptance." *New York Times,* April 17, 1991, p. A17.

Carmody, Deidre. "News Media's Use of Accuser's Name Is Debated." *New York Times,* April 18, 1991, p. A22.

Cohen, Roger. "Should the Media Name the Accuser When the Crime Being Charged Is Rape?" *New York Times,* April 21, 1991, sec. IV, p. 4.

DeCrow, Karen. "Stop Treating Victims as Pariahs; Print Names." *USA Today,* April 4, 1990, p. A8.

Denno, Deborah W. "Perspectives on Disclosing Rape Victims' Names." *Fordham Law Review,* 41, no. 5 (April 1993), 1113–1131.

Glaberson, William. "*Times* Article Naming Rape Accuser Ignites Debate on Journalistic Values." *New York Times,* June 25, 1989, p. A18.

Goodman, Ellen. "Pursuing Justice, Protecting Privacy." *Boston Globe,* April 18, 1991, p. 13.

Goodman, Walter. "When Broadcast Matter Is Considered Offensive." *New York Times,* December 21, 1991, p. 47.

Jones, Alex S. "Editors Debate Naming Rape Victims." *New York Times,* April 13, 1991, p. 6.

Kwitny, Jonathan. "Public Interest, Public Naming." *New York Times,* May 8, 1991, p. A23.

Quindlen, Anna. "Public and Private: A Mistake." *New York Times,* April 21, 1991, sec. IV, p. 17.

Chapter 9

Are Government Regulations on Freedom of the Press during Wartime Justified?

For democracy to succeed, people and their elected representatives must have access to truthful information. In this way, they can debate issues and influence opinion in a rational manner.

In domestic matters involving economic and social policy, advocates of democracy generally encourage the full disclosure of information necessary for public discussion. In matters of foreign policy and national security, however, many of the same advocates object to revealing all relevant information on issues. Some matters, such as the deployment of troops in wartime, require secrecy lest an enemy obtain advantages that can result in great harm to U.S. lives.

War, the threat of war, and the needs of national security have been cited as justification for government restrictions on freedom of the press. And yet even in these situations, precisely because the stakes are so high there is also good reason for the American people to be properly informed. The decision to use force, the way that force is implemented, and the effectiveness of military action are all of vital interest for public debate.

Government regulation in national security reporting is a risky business, particularly in a political system that accepts the principle of freedom of the press. The risk is that, although the United States government can impose secrecy for legitimate security reasons, it can do so for less justifiable reasons as well—including protection against revealing illegal actions or mismanagement.

For their part, reporters want to cover the news. That is their job, and many of them have shown great courage in reporting from combat areas. Some of them have been injured or killed, too, while doing their jobs.

Because of the difference in goals, the relationship between the press and the military is often uneasy. The case of the Vietnam War provides an example. U.S. reporters, roaming pretty much at will throughout South Vietnam, sometimes portrayed the U.S. military in a negative manner. As the war continued, some American military and political leaders argued that the stories about abuses by the U.S. military helped undermine support by the American people for U.S. involvement in the war, to the disadvantage of the United States and to the comfort of the communist enemy. For their part, however, reporters defended their actions, arguing that they were doing their job—covering the war—so that the American people could have correct information about what was really going on in Vietnam.

During the Reagan and Bush administrations, the Pentagon imposed restrictions on war coverage of U.S. military actions. Reporters were barred from military operations in Grenada in 1983. And during the U.S. intervention in Panama in 1989, a press pool system was established in which a few reporters were selected to accompany military units and furnish information to their fellow reporters. The system did not work, because it was not activated in time.

During the Persian Gulf War, the military imposed pool and escort systems on reporters. This time, the pool system was activated. The escort system required that journalists be accompanied by U.S. military personnel, who could determine where the journalists could go. Reporters disliked the press arrangements and felt that the government was manipulating them so that only stories favorable to the United States would reach the American people.

Conflict between the military and the reporters raged during the war and continued after hostilities had ended. The character of the controversy is shown in the selections below.

Major Melissa Wells-Petry, a member of the Office of the Staff Judge Advocate in the U.S. Army, defends the military restrictions on reporters during the Persian Gulf War. Writing in *Military Review*, a U.S. Army publication, she contends

1. The American people were able to get information about the war in spite of the restrictions on reporters. Public opinion polls show that the American people approved of the press coverage of the war.
2. Reporters are not as knowledgeable as military officials in reporting military developments.
3. The press cannot know better than the military the effect of any given piece of information on military operations. Unrestricted freedom to report may result in loss of American lives.
4. When reporters are free to go where they want during wartime, they may be captured. U.S. military personnel would then have to be deployed to find and rescue them, actions that would place U.S. soldiers at risk.
5. Press restrictions in earlier U.S. wars were much greater than during the Persian Gulf War.
6. The press is a business whose commercial interest in selling papers should not be allowed to jeopardize the military's interest in controlling the conduct of military operations.

In a statement prepared for the Senate Committee of Government Operations, Paul McMasters makes the case for greater press freedom to report wars. McMasters spoke on behalf of the Society of Professional Journalists. He argues:

1. The restrictions on the press are too stringent and should be eased.
2. The pools do not work effectively, resulting in poor coverage of the war.
3. Security reviews of press reports cause delays and impede accurate reporting.
4. The First Amendment to the Constitution gives the people and the press the right of free speech. Pentagon restrictions of war coverage infringe on that right.
5. The notion that the new rules are made necessary by press abuses during the Vietnam War is a myth.
6. The Pentagon rules for covering the war show a distrust of the American people. If the American people lose trust in their political and military leaders because they lack confidence in the information they are receiving, they will not support a war effort. In addition, there should be more press pools and more freedom to gather news by those who cannot get into the pools.

 Y E S

Are Government Regulations on Freedom of the Press during Wartime Justified?

MELISSA WELLS-PETRY

Reporters as the Guardians of Freedom

The commander's major task is to fight a war, not a lawsuit.[1]

In the borough of Manhattan in the city of New York, far from the vast roar and dust of the battlefields in Iraq, the military faced a minor skirmish on its home flank. A group of journalists filed a lawsuit protesting the press pool and escort system imposed on reporters in the Persian Gulf theater. The suit demanded that the judge order the U.S. military to stop restricting the press in the Gulf theater in any way. The suit further demanded that the judge order the military to provide the press free access to every area U.S. forces were deployed or engaged in combat action.[2]

Much has been written about the dynamics of the media-military relationship during the Gulf War. Indeed, Assistant Secretary of Defense for Public Affairs Pete Williams has commented that "the subject of press pools and escorts is nearly the most frequently written about item around, with the possible exception of Princess Di and Fergie."[3] Much of the debate is couched in constitutional terms. In this debate, the media frequently champions the free press guaranteed by the Constitution—in the media's view, a press that is completely free, at all times, under all circumstances—as the decisive guardian of freedom itself.

The media has many motivations for railing against restrictions. Some motivations spring from constitutional concerns for a free press, some from commercial interests. But regardless of motive, four primary assumptions underlie the media's arguments that, if our constitutional way of life is to survive, the press must have unfettered access to military operations and unfettered ability to report those operations.

The assumptions underlying the media's arguments are

- The absence of reporters equals the absence of truth.
- Reporters are uniquely qualified to obtain and relay military operational information.
- Reporters are better positioned or better qualified than the military to resolve competing interests in information and to judge what should be reported.
- The safety of reporters is not a legitimate factor in restricting the media and, in any event, reporters' safety is not the military's problem.

ASSUMPTION 1. THE ABSENCE OF REPORTERS EQUALS THE ABSENCE OF TRUTH

One of the earliest casualties in America's desert war was the truth, wounded by an information directorate bent on controlling the words and images that flow from the battlefields.

—U.S. News & World Report

The absence of reporters—that is, the absence of reporters freely ranging over the whole battlefield, instantaneously transmitting interviews and video, filing copy at will and without any official review—is often proclaimed as certain death for the truth. This is a bold assumption indeed, and there is little evidence to support it. While military regulation of the press has sometimes resulted in information distortion, it can hardly be said that the truth is regularly, or forever suppressed by restrictions on press coverage of military operations.[4] Moreover, as a practical matter, even when the widest latitude is granted, there is no guarantee that information will be accurate or full.[5]

During the Gulf War, the military imposed a pool and escort system on reporters. At the height of military operations, approximately 1,400 journalists were in the Gulf region and 1,351 pool print stories were written. While the war was actually underway, 131 reporters were moving with ground units. There was, on average, one television crew with every division, although the Army was moving too quickly for television crews to set up portable satellite links—in one instance, a unit marched for 47 out of 50 hours. Additional reporters were on ships, with medical units and at Air Force bases.[6]

Was the truth doomed by the pool and escort system in the Gulf? Hardly. To put the operation in historical context, 27 reporters went ashore with the first wave at Normandy on D-day. Their reports were subject to strict military censorship and, unlike the system in the Gulf, there was no mechanism for appeal.[7]

To put the operation in practical context, surveys show that nearly 80 percent of adults polled thought press coverage of the Gulf War was "good" or "excellent." An impressive 78 percent of those polled were "satisfied that the military is not hiding bad news, and 57 percent said the Pentagon should exert *more* control over reporting of the war [and] 88 percent supported some censorship of the press under the circumstances."[8] As *Time* magazine reported, "one fact was nearly obscured [in the debate on military press restrictions]: the gulf war was covered exhaustively."[9]

Finally, to those who argue that the public was satisfied with what it heard *because* the absence of free-roaming reporters kept the public from knowing the truth, congressional oversight, such as that provided by the Governmental Affairs Committee, ensured a check on the system.[10] This congressional check, as will be seen, is unique. This check cannot be provided by reporters, even when reporters are given the widest access to battlefields or soldiers. In short, it is baseless to assume that the absence of reporters equals the absence of truth. Moreover, it is equally baseless to assume that the *presence* of reporters *ensures* the truth.

ASSUMPTION 2. REPORTERS ARE UNIQUELY QUALIFIED TO OBTAIN AND RELAY MILITARY OPERATIONAL INFORMATION

Are you going to keep your air supremacy jets up there, you know, flying around?

—At a U.S. Central Command briefing

There are little . . . they almost look like [flapping hands up and down] . . . hay wagons that will pick up bales on the front of a tank, will also, will also take out mines, won't it?

—A CNN anchor

I ain't got no education and I can understand what them people at the Pentagon are talking about. Them reporters are just ignorant.

—A caller to C-Span

Reporters generally are not soldiers, and no one expects them to know as much about the profession of arms as those who wear the uniform. While the media claims that it must be free of any restriction by the military, this claim makes sense only if the media can bring something unique or insightful to the process of obtaining and relaying military information. Otherwise, the operational risks involved in opening the battlefield to the press are taken without any hope of a corresponding informational gain to the public.

Journalists obviously bring a great deal of professionalism to their craft. Still, it is not clear that the net information benefit from allowing free-roaming reporters and unreviewed reports in a combat environment would be very great. Reporters, in practical terms and regardless of how wide their access to battlefields or soldiers, are able to report only what they can see, hear and understand. This is no more of the "big picture" of a military operation than is perceived by the private who stoked the guns, the sergeant who drove the tank or the lieutenant who called in the tactical fire support.

Reporters on the battlefield, nevertheless, may skillfully bring us the human side of war—the individual interest story, the pathos, the personal drama. These stories may charm or dismay us, and certainly they may sell papers. As a check on military operational "truth," however, such stories have little value. Indeed, as one World War II correspondent who was with the troops in North Africa stated:

> From first to last, we never "saw" a battle in the desert. We were simply conscious of a great deal of dust, noise and confusion. The only way we could gather a coherent picture was by driving hard from one headquarters to another and by picking up the reports from the most forward units. . . . Then, when the worst was over, we went forward ourselves to . . . hear the individual experiences of the soldiers.[11]

If reporters—like individual soldiers—rarely are able to discern the whole dynamic of a battle for themselves, unrestricted access does little to further constitutional concerns for truth. On the other hand, unrestricted access poses real risks to military security, political quandaries in the event reporters are captured or killed and practical problems in providing logistic support to the press. Negotiating these risks and problems is simply unwarranted if there is no substantial informational—that is, *constitutional*—benefit to be gained by opening the battlefield to all-comers.

This conclusion takes nothing away from the validity of the adage that "there are no bad questions." There are no bad questions. But that fact does not demonstrate that it is helpful, much less constitutionally required, for reporters in a combat environment to ask questions wherever, whenever and of whomever they please.

ASSUMPTION 3. REPORTERS ARE BETTER POSITIONED OR BETTER QUALIFIED THAN THE MILITARY TO RESOLVE COMPETING INTERESTS IN INFORMATION AND TO JUDGE WHAT SHOULD BE REPORTED

Journalists are not duty bound to coddle people with the information they want to hear, but to provide them with the information they should hear [in the judgment of the reporter].

—Time

There is [in the press pool and escort system] a terrible sense of loss: What would the reporter have gotten on his own, free to make his own decisions, ask his own questions, judge for himself what might constitute a violation of valid military security concerns?

—U.S. News & World Report

It is not too candid to say that few soldiers are willing to vest the authority to judge "what might constitute a violation of valid military security concerns" in just anyone. Because it is their lives on the line, obviously soldiers will urge the greatest caution and the application of at least some military expertise in deciding what information should be published at a particular point in time. Moreover, the destiny of the individual soldier is inextricably tied to the destiny of the nation. Thus, the nation cannot hope to achieve its objectives if it cannot protect its soldiers to the maximum possible extent.

The fallacy of the assumption that reporters are in a better position than the military to decide what people "should" hear seems self-evident—the press *cannot* know better than the military the effect of any given piece of information on military operations. Yet, this assumption, to one extent or another, underlies every attack on military press restrictions. This assumption does not comport with either the Constitution or common sense.

Under the Constitution, the military is accountable to the American people primarily through Congress. The press performs an important, indeed critical, function in providing news coverage of wars, but its function is not necessarily to provide a mechanism for military *accountability*. Not only is the press peculiarly ill-suited to judge "what might constitute a violation of valid military security concerns," such judgments are clearly outside its charters. Thus, this assumption, like those already discussed, provides no comfort to those who argue for unfettered access to and unrestricted reporting of military operations.

ASSUMPTION 4. THE SAFETY OF REPORTERS IS NOT A LEGITIMATE FACTOR IN RESTRICTING THE MEDIA, AND REPORTERS' SAFETY IS NOT THE MILITARY'S PROBLEM

Saying that [the military's] prime concern is for the physical safety of the war correspondents. . . . Your war correspondent now carries on his back, in military parlance: Editor, Model 1991—ME, field-transportable.

—*U.S. News & World Report*

Several bureau chiefs told me last fall that in planning for the war coverage, the security of reporters was their concern and not mine. But I don't think that's realistic, because I couldn't ignore that even if I wanted to. It is not morally possible. We were on the phone to CBS News nearly every day that Bob Simon was missing . . . [a]nd when a group of U.S. journalists was captured in Iraq . . . four news industry executives wrote to the President saying that no U.S. forces should withdraw from Iraq until the issue of the journalists was resolved.

—DOD spokesman Pete Williams

Reporters charge that physical security concerns are a pretext on the part of the military to control information. By contrast, Williams states that the media must drop the pretense that the military is not, or should not be, concerned for the physical security of reporters.[12] The latter position is the one borne out by common sense and decency, as well as the law. Not only would a failure of concern for reporters' physical security be morally indefensible and completely unrealistic, the simple fact is the law requires the U.S. government to be concerned about its citizens who are in enemy hands.

Thus, the capture or mistreatment of U.S. citizens, journalists or otherwise, is bound to have both political and military ramifications, particularly in a combat environment. This is why the State Department often imposes travel restrictions to unstable areas on all U.S. citizens. Moreover, if the safety of war correspondents is not the military's legitimate concern, then whose concern is it? What resources does the news industry have to protect or regain the safety of its reporters? Even if industry had suitable resources, how could they be employed in a combat environment without impacting on military operations?

As seen in the events described by Williams previously, when security is lost or jeopardized in a combat theater, the news industry must turn to the government, in general, and the military, in particular, for help. Since physical security is, then, the military's problem, the military rightly must be able to impose restrictions that minimize the danger to reporters and the danger that the conflict will be exacerbated by the capture or mistreatment of civilian journalists. Reporters may blithely dismiss military security concerns while inside a courtroom in Manhattan. But in a real-world situation, it is the military, and ultimately the nation, that must pay the bill. Thus, the assumption that reporters' safety is not the military's problem is simply false.

In sum, the assumptions that underlie the media's arguments that they must have unfettered access to the battlefield, as well as the unfettered ability to report military operations, are invalid. They certainly do not support the type and scope of risk taking on the part of the military that results from opening the battlefield to all-comers or in allowing reporters to roam freely and to file without any, or with only cursory, official review. Moreover, these invalid assumptions are implicit in legal challenges to military restrictions on the press, such as the lawsuit filed in New York. Therefore, the legal complaints against the military by the media often are not well-grounded, even in practical terms.

Day after day during the war there were letters sent to me at the Pentagon saying something like this: "Will you please ask reporters to give their names when they ask questions and then we can write to their employers and tell them to buzz off."

—DOD spokesman Pete Williams

Letters to the Los Angeles Times have been overwhelmingly critical of the press. "They hate us," [the page editor said]. . . . "They wish we would go away."

—Time

There is probably greater public anger with the press [during the war with Iraq] than at any time since the end of the war in Vietnam.

—A First Amendment lawyer

While Americans were sending 55,000 letters to CNN, 60 percent were negative reactions to the perception that the network's "special privileges in Baghdad" made it "too cozy with the enemy," reporters and their lawyers were pushing for ever-greater access to the war.[13] The New York lawsuit embodies three themes frequently heard in all complaints about military restrictions of the press. These themes are that the type of restrictions imposed in the Gulf War are unprecedented in the history of war correspondence, that the restrictions denied the public an "honest look at war in its full context" and that, because of the restrictions, "the American public has been and will be deprived of full and accurate information on important public policy issues."[14] The next sections will discuss these legal complaints in practical terms.

The new restrictions [in the Persian Gulf] impose a policy of censorship for the first time in the era of modern warfare.

—Plaintiffs' brief

But something else . . . is at stake [in the Persian Gulf]: more than likely, the most restrictive war-time policy on release of information the U.S. government has ever imposed on the media.

—At the National Press Club

[T]hose reporters who long for the good old days of Vietnam should visit the archives . . . [t]hey would find no historical precedent for the expensive and detailed Desert Storm *coverage.*

—*Washington Post*

History often instructs the law and policy because it is a record of practical solutions that have worked over time. Laws allowing for censorship of military information existed as early as the Revolutionary War. There were few press reports on the War of 1812, and the Mexican War was reported primarily by soldiers, some of whom had been journalists before taking up arms. The Civil War was covered by larger numbers of professional reporters, but there were more restrictions on the press, including occasional exclusion of reporters from both Union and Confederate camps.

In the 1898 Spanish-American War, reporters were restricted by appointed censors or military officers and were sometimes banished from the battlefield. In the initial stages of the American Expeditionary Force's entry into World War I, the military imposed an accreditation system, stiff censorship and restrictions on battlefield access. In World War II, the Office of Censorship was created and heavy review was imposed. Nevertheless, the press, though relatively few in number, had fairly easy transit around the battlefields of World War II. Even so, several important operations, such as the Battle of Midway and the atomic bombing of Hiroshima, were closed to coverage.

In the Korean War, reporters themselves asked for full, mandatory censorship as an alternative to expulsion from the theater for poorly received stories. In Vietnam, reporters had greater access to the fighting, but were still dependent upon the military to get them there. Reporters were excluded from the military operation in Grenada.[15] During Operation Just Cause in Panama, a press pool system was imposed, although it was not activated in time to work effectively.[16]

In short, it is an exaggeration to claim that the restrictions imposed on the press in Operation Desert Storm are either unprecedented or unheard of in scope. Indeed, as technology enlarges the ability and speed of reporters to transmit information around the world, it may be that new types of restrictions will become necessary to meet operations security requirements. But clearly the establishment of press pools and escorts in the Persian Gulf does not exceed the historical resolution of the competing interests of the military and the press in combat information.

[President] Bush and his men imprisoned the journalists in military briefing rooms and on guided tours with Pentagon babysitters. The public was denied an honest look at war in its full context.

—Newsday

If [Peter] Arnett were awarded "the Iraq Medal of Honor by Saddam Hussein," suggested one letter writer in the New Orleans Times-Picayune, "I for one feel he would deserve it."

—Time

"An honest look at the war in its full context" may be everyone's ideal. But it is not clear that the absence of press pools or escorts would result either in reporters relaying an "honest"—that is, an objective, informed and complete—look at the war, or in the illumination of the war's "full context." No one presumes deception on the part of a reporter. But no one takes a reporter's account without some skepticism that it is colored by the reporter's individual views and experience and by a variety of professional and personal interests.

Clearly, even if reporters had unfettered access to the battlefield and unfettered opportunity to report, that does not guarantee that press reports will be— or would be *perceived* as—more "honest," or more objective, informed or complete, than those filed under the pool and escort system. Indeed, there may be a perception that the reports of independent, unchecked and fiercely competitive reporters are a less reliable source of information about the war.

The full context of a war simply is not made more understandable by unfettered access to the battlefield. In fact, on the battlefield perhaps more so than anywhere else, a correspondent can report essentially what is in front of him, and that is all. Even the cumulative effect of many battlefield correspondents reporting what is in front of them does not necessarily suggest or illuminate the full context of the war. Thus, even if there exists a problem with honest reporting of wars in their full context, the media is pushing for a solution that will not fix that problem. Indeed, to do away with the pool and escort system or other forms of restrictions on the press, might subject the military to a variety of operational risks, while at the same time providing no real advantage to reporters and no enhancement of the information benefit to the public.

Because of the restrictions imposed on the press by the military, "the American public has been and will be deprived of full and accurate information on important public policy issues."

—Plaintiffs' brief

There is an idea somehow that we're trying to sort of pretend like people don't get killed in a war and that we do that by not allowing coverage at Dover [of coffins in transit to places designated by next of kin], which, of course, is ludicrous.

—DOD spokesman Pete Williams

The argument that press restrictions in the Persian Gulf theater deprived the public of "full and accurate information on important public policy issues" is nothing more than a summary statement of the four assumptions previously discussed. It relies on the ideas that without reporters, there can be no truth, that reporters are able to provide a check on military operational truth, that they know better than the military what is full and accurate information in light of operations security requirements and they can roam the battlefield without imposing additional physical security obligations on the military.

As already demonstrated, even if reporters are given unfettered access to the battlefield and the unfettered ability to report, nothing suggests that this would result in "full and accurate information on important public policy issues." Information that is relevant to public policy issues is not of the type that is elicited by interviewing individual tank crews while the smoke swirls around them. Relevant public policy information is, by definition, disseminated in other forums such as high-level briefings, congressional hearings and statements by department and administration officials.

Again, this conclusion does not detract from the critical function of the press in reporting such information or in providing a forum for public comment on and scrutiny of such information. Yet, the point remains that unfettered access and reporting from the battlefield does nothing to advance the constitutional cause of the press, while at the same time it exposes the military to certain and unwarranted risks to successful military operations.

Military restrictions on the press are, as they have been over history, tailored to operational requirements and the nature of the warfighting at hand. A simple cost-benefit analysis proves that such restrictions strike an appropriate balance between the interest of the press in gathering information and the interest of the military, and the nation, in winning our wars. As the Court of Military Appeals has stated, "no [soldier] has a right, constitutional, statutory, or otherwise, to publish any information which will imperil his unit or its cause."[17] No lesser standard can be applied to reporters.

A final point to consider in evaluating the media's criticisms of military press restrictions in combat theaters is the plain fact that reporting is a *business,* and information has *commercial value.* No matter how much elegant constitutional language is employed, the fact remains that one major source of irritation with military press restrictions, as the lawsuit in New York makes clear, is the media perception that such restrictions "threaten to interfere with [reporters'] ability to pursue a profession."[18] Indeed, one reporter felt that the press restrictions made reporters "essentially unpaid employees of the Department of Defense."[19]

Viewed as a business enterprise and a commercial interest, unfettered access to and reporting of military operations is even less justified. The military's single, fixed, inviolable mission is to win our wars.[20] To do so, the military, so far as possible, must have maximum security for its force and operations and complete control of the battlefield, both at the forward line of its own troops and behind its own lines. Plainly put, the desire to pursue a profession or a commercial interest in selling papers simply is not a sufficient basis for ignoring, or slighting, the military's vital interests in controlling the conduct of military operations.

Press restrictions are necessary to strike a balance on the battlefield. Press restrictions balance the professional interests of reporters, the informational benefit to the public of unfettered access to and reporting from the battlefield, operational considerations that may determine whether soldiers live or die and whether the nation succeeds or fails in the task it has given its Army. It is soldiers, not reporters, who take an oath to defend with their lives the U.S. Constitution. When soldiers are about that dangerous task, common sense, as well as the law counsels the appropriateness of restricting the press.

NOTES

The views expressed in this article are those of the author and do not purport to reflect the position of the Department of the Army, the Department of Defense or any other government office or agency.

1. From *United States versus Voorhees*. 16 Court of Military Review 83 (Court of Military Appeals, 1954), 107.

2. "News Groups Sue Over Limits on Persian Gulf Coverage." Reuters, 10 January 1991. Plaintiffs in the suit are *The Nation, Harper's, Mother Jones, In These Times, The Progressive* and the *L.A. Weekly.*

3. National Press Club Luncheon Speaker Pete Williams, Assistant Secretary of Defense for Public Affairs, Federal Information Systems Corporation, 14 March 1991.

4. Cassell, "Restrictions on Press Coverage of Military Operations: The Right of Access, Grenada, and 'Off-the-Record Wars,'" *Georgetown Law Journal,* 73 (1985), 931.

5. Ibid.

6. All information and statistics are from National Press Club speech, *supra* note 3.

7. Ibid.

8. "Just Whose Side Are They On?," *Time* (February 25, 1991):53 (emphasis added).

9. "The Press; It Was a Public Relations Rout Too," *Time* (March 11, 1991):56.

10. "Pentagon Aims to 'Discourage' Restrictions on Media," *Washington Post* (February 21, 1991), p.A28.

11. Cassell, 965.

12. National Press Club speech.

13. "Just Whose Side Are They On?"

14. See for example, National Press Club speech; "Losers: Iraq and the First Amendment," *Newsday* (March 8, 1991): 55; and from Plaintiffs' brief, quoted in "News Groups Sue."

15. All historical data is based on the excellent and detailed survey of press coverage of military operations in Cassell.

16. National Press Club speech.

17. *United States versus Voorhees,* 106.

18. Plaintiffs' brief, quoted in "News Groups Sue."

19. "Pentagon Aims to 'Discourage' Restrictions," p.A28.

20. From Gen. Douglas MacArthur's address on "Duty—Honor—Country," U.S. Military Academy, 1962.

Are Government Regulations on Freedom of the Press during Wartime Justified?

PAUL McMASTERS

Government, Censorship, and Freedom of the Press

By being here today, we journalists risk looking petty or unpatriotic or both, so I'd like to start with a general statement of the position [of the Society of Professional Journalists]. We are not here to speak against the war or the U.S. military personnel serving in the Gulf. We are not here to seek special privileges for members of the press. We are not here asking to be able to report military secrets that would endanger our troops or allied operations.

We are here to make the best possible case for a more complete and diverse report to the public about the war.

Everyone agrees there must be some information withheld from general dissemination during wartime, so military censorship is not the issue. The issue is the unprecedented restrictions on the press by the Pentagon in this war. Specifically, we would like to see the Pentagon relax its requirements for security reviews of reporters' dispatches from the war zone. Further, we would like to see more press pools and more freedom to gather news for those who cannot get into the pools.

The pools are a mess. There are not enough of them to accommodate the reporters there, or to cover all units; entire divisions have no news going back to their troops' home towns. The pools are too restrictive; when a reporter does get a rare opportunity to interview a soldier, there is a military minder looking over his shoulder. Often, the pools are taken to areas away from where the news is occurring. And the pool system tends to produce a sameness to the coverage, since a small number of reporters file stories from a small number of sources.

We were gratified to learn this weekend that the military has added 40 journalists to the pools. But the fine print was that Gen. Norman Schwarzkopf, commander of the Central Command, also ordered a closer scrutiny of reporters' stories during the review process.

The security reviews present a number of problems for correspondents. They can cause undue delays, sometimes days, in getting copy back to the home front. They can involve petty editing, such as changing the word "giddy" to "proud." They can diminish the depth of reporting and create self-censorship by reporters trying to get as much as possible through before deadline.

The Society has compiled an illustrative list of the problems associated with the pool system and the security reviews. That list is included with my written testimony.

The pool system and security reviews are procedural problems. People of

145

reason and good will should be able to work them out. There is an underlying problem, however, that must be addressed before all else. That is the pervasive atmosphere of mistrust of the press in the military. It has little to do with military security and much to do with political insecurity. That is why the military has imposed these restrictive guidelines. These guidelines narrow the news coverage and make it more superficial. They deny independent verification. They keep pertinent information from the public and elected leaders.

All this sanitizes the images of war reaching policy-makers and the public back home. This Nintendo war atmosphere is a cruel hoax on the families and friends of those who have to serve and suffer. I'm speaking of such things as the Pentagon canceling ceremonies at Dover Air Force Base for soldiers who have fallen in battle. Of shutting off the flow of information about defense contractors providing equipment and supplies for battlefield operations. Of instilling in troops such fear and distrust of reporters that they have held journalists at gunpoint, thumped a photographer with the butt of a rifle, and detained and interrogated journalists for hours.

Journalists in the Gulf just want to do their jobs. That is not nearly so threatening as the military and others would have you believe. For the most part, doing our job is a pretty simple matter. It's certainly not a sinister matter. We want to tell the soldier's story. We want to capture the grit and sacrifice of combat. We want to offer to the American people an independent source of information that verifies and validates. We want to give the American people reason to trust what their leaders are telling them.

This year, we celebrate the 200th birthday of the Bill of Rights. One of the most enduring of those rights, the right of free speech, is guaranteed by the First Amendment. It is a right of the American people, not just the press. That right is an empty promise, however, if there is not a concomitant right to know. That must be a signal feature of a democratic society. But the public has been denied crucial information in all recent military actions.

In Grenada, the American people were held hostage to Fidel Castro's Cuban Radio for hours after the U.S. invasion began because the military kept the American press out.

In Panama, the press pool that had been organized to avoid the problems of Grenada was an abject failure. The press pool arrived late and then was kept at an air base outside Panama City—away from the fighting. At one point, Air Force officials assured everyone that two bombs dropped at Nato Rio by two Stealth fighters—the first use ever of these planes in action—were right on target. A few weeks later, reporter Michael Gordon went to see for himself; one of the bombs was on target but the other had landed 300 yards away. Before writing his story for the New York Times, Gordon checked with Defense Secretary Dick Cheney and other Pentagon officials. That's how Cheney learned that the Stealth mission hadn't been as successful as he and the public had been told.

Now for that canard about the media losing the war in Vietnam. The military's own historian and a host of studies and commissions have refuted that myth. Yet it persists. The truth is that the military and the government misled the

American public about such matters as the Gulf of Tonkin, the extent of U.S. advisers' involvement in the fighting, the corruption of the Diem government, and the inability and unwillingness of South Vietnam troops to prosecute the war. Later, the Pentagon Papers revealed how the military had misled the public and Congress about the bombing in Cambodia. If our military had been more forthcoming about such matters, the outcome of that war could have been much different. But the people and their leaders were denied information essential to shaping public policy.

In 1917, Hiram Johnson, a cantankerous U.S. senator from the state of California, said, "The first casualty when war comes is truth." Sen. Johnson hasn't been wrong yet. It's not too naive to suggest, however, that we have an opportunity to prove him wrong this time around.

An informed citizenry is democracy's best defense, according to Thomas Jefferson. I would add that an informed citizenry is our military's best support, too. The tradition of civilian control of the military demands that the American people not be kept in the dark. There are dire consequences when the public is not fully informed.

Last Wednesday when our television screens displayed those grisly photos of Iraqi civilians killed in an allied bombing raid, we sampled the real danger of the military's tight-fisted control of information from the war zone. Those images of charred and battered women and children made us recoil in surprise. The years of peace since Vietnam had lulled us into forgetting the terrible face of war, and in the first month of fighting, our military has kept us from confronting that reality. It took photos of the enemy's dead to jolt us awake to that ugly reality. The irony should not be lost on the Pentagon.

During a January 23 briefing at the Pentagon, Gen. Colin Powell, chairman of the Joint Chiefs of Staff, was fielding the questions. At one point in the session, he fixed his journalistic interrogators with a friendly but firm gaze and said, "Trust me." Most of us watching on TV chuckled, but we took the general at his word, too. Here was a tested warrior, an honest man, a worthy leader. And in the awful hours of war, we need leaders we can trust. But our leaders must trust the people, too. And both must trust the truth—even if it is sometimes inconvenient or bitter.

That is why military leaders must loosen their stranglehold on the flow of information from the Persian Gulf and the Pentagon. Unless they do, public support for the war effort will wane over time. The military will have suffered a self-inflicted wound. That, more than trusting the public with the truth, will hurt our ability to successfully prosecute this war.

ANNEX TO TESTIMONY BY PAUL McMASTERS

Here is an illustrative list of incidents involving press pools and security reviews under Pentagon press guidelines in the Persian Gulf war zone. This list was compiled by the Freedom of Information Committee of the Society of professional Journalists.

Press Pools

Correspondents covering the allied side of the Gulf War are complaining of severe censorship restrictions. Almost 700 pool reports have been issued, all of which have been cleared through a censor. And journalists continue to have problems.

1. An unescorted *Time* magazine photographer who tried to take a picture of a tank was seized by U.S. military police, blindfolded and held at a desert camp for the night.
2. A Reuters photographer who stopped by a U.S. Marine position near the Kuwait border and asked permission to take pictures was held at gunpoint for nine hours.
3. Television crews from Britain's Independent Television News and BBC were detained trying to report on an oil slick threatening Saudi shores.
4. A carload of French photographers near the front was stopped by a burst of warning fire from a Marine detachment.
5. Times of London correspondent Christopher Walker said a wire service photographer working outside the pool was held for six hours by armed U.S. Marines who threatened to shoot him if he left his car.

—REUTERS, RODNEY FINDER, FEB. 12, 1991

More than two dozen reporters and photographers have been detained by the U.S. or the Saudi military for trying to cover the war on their own. Others have managed, without being detected, to go out on their own. Among those having been detained are Eric Schmitt, John Kifner and Chris Hedges, all of the *New York Times*. Others who have been detained include: Guy Gugliotta of the *Washington Post,* John King and Fred Bayles of the Associated Press, Joseph Albright of Cox Newspapers, a six-member team from the BBC and several French freelance photographers.

—NEW YORK TIMES, FEB. 12, 1991

An Associated Press writer and photographer were held six hours by a unit of the 1st Cavalry Division. They were given dinner, shown B-52 air strikes and provided with other glimpses of camp life that generated a story.

Wesley Boxce, a *Time* photographer, was held for 30 hours by members of the Alabama National Guard. At times during his captivity, Boxce was blindfolded and interrogated.

New York Times reporter Chris Hedges was detained for six hours and his credentials were temporarily lifted after he tried to ask officials at a military hospital for permission to conduct an interview. He was told he could lose his credentials, have his visa revoked and asked to leave. His credentials were returned the next day. Hedges said he was also taken into custody by the Alabama National Guard when he was interviewing Saudi shopkeepers in a civilian area about the local economy.

Associated Press reporter Mort Rosenblum was detained by authorities for three hours in what an editor calls "a strong arm fashion" for reporting without an escort. A BBC television crew had its credentials removed for three days.

—ASSOCIATED PRESS, FEB. 12, 1991
—WASHINGTON POST, FEB. 11, 1991

A French TV crew reported that it received a warning shot from friendly troops. Another reporter said that he was stopped by an armed man, not in uniform and driving an old car, who demanded the reporter's passport.

—GANNETT NEWS SERVICE, FEB. 11, 1991

Agence France-Presse [AFP] threatened legal action against the U.S. Pentagon for denying AFP the right to participate in Department of Defense pools and for denying it total access to photo pools in Saudi Arabia. AFP has sought access to these pools and has been denied. No reason has ever been provided. There are no standards or criteria for pool participation.

—PRESS RELEASE FROM AGENCE FRANCE-PRESSE, JAN. 31, 1991

The U.S. military has required that anyone going out on a combat pool to cover the war must be in good physical condition and meet the minimum physical standards as set by the Army or the Navy. The military said the test was designed to ensure that reporters, photographers and camera crews could keep up with troops and not slow them down or needlessly risk their lives. Most people said they had no problems with the test as long as it wasn't being used to unfairly screen out reporters. Policy later rescinded.

—ASSOCIATED PRESS, JAN. 2, 1991
—EDITOR AND PUBLISHER, JAN. 12, 1991

Security Reviews

Several tests of controversial military security reviews of war news reports have been decided by Pentagon spokesman Pete Williams and other military officials. Among decisions made were:

1. Williams gave permission to release a dramatic photograph of Iraqi prisoners of war and a news story about U.S. troops in southeast Saudi Arabia.
2. Williams also allowed a story by *Boston Globe* reporter Colin Nickerson to be released. The story described the collaboration of units from two different military services—a reference left unchallenged by the public affairs officer accompanying him. Military officials in the Persian Gulf thought the story revealed too much to the Iraqis. Because a reference had already appeared in an earlier pool report, Williams decided to leave the story unchanged.

Both decisions were made in several hours. Parts of at least two other stories—one describing electronic jamming capabilities of the 390th Electrical Combat Squadron in southeast Saudi Arabia, the other the number of aircraft involved in a mission by the 48th Tactical Fighter Wing in southwest Saudi Arabia—were altered Saturday after intense debate.

—USA TODAY, JAN. 20, 1991

Several major news organizations protested Pentagon ground rules for covering war in the Persian Gulf that restrict descriptions of combat and require military review of combat dispatches. The organizations said that the rules would give the military too much control over reporting. "Specifically, we object in the strongest possible terms to the so-called 'security review' provisions that set up cumbersome barriers to timely and responsible reporting and raise the specter of government censorship of a free press," said four network news presidents—Roone Arledge of ABC, Eric Ober of CBS, Michael Gartner of NBC and Tom Johnson of CNN—in a letter.

The Associated Press also objected to the security review. But Defense Secretary Dick Cheney said the rules were necessary to protect troops and provide security for missions.

—ASSOCIATED PRESS, JAN. 10, 1991

Several news organizations said that they would appeal to the Pentagon to drop rules requiring journalists in combat-coverage pools to submit their work to a military review. Pentagon spokesman Pete Williams said that the military had no intention of censoring the dispatches and had no authority to delete any material. Several provisions have been dropped from the original Pentagon rules. Among those dropped was a requirement that all troop interviews be on the record. Also dropped were rules banning impromptu interviews with senior American military officials entering and leaving installations and prohibiting coverage of religious services in Saudi Arabia.

—ASSOCIATED PRESS, JAN. 8, 1991
—NEW YORK TIMES, JAN. 6, 1991

Questions for Discussion

1. What professional qualities do reporters bring to the coverage of war?
2. Should the U.S. press report unfavorable stories about U.S. military operations (e.g., atrocities, poor leadership, and operational failures)? What are the reasons for your answer?
3. What are "legitimate" restrictions on press coverage during wartime?
4. What effect does adverse coverage of U.S. military operations have on the outcome of war?
5. Under what conditions would Pentagon control of the media in war coverage be successful? Why?

Suggested Readings

Andrews, Peter. "The Media and the Military." *American Heritage,* 42, no. 4 (July/August 1991), 78–85.

Blanchard, Margaret A. "Free Expression and Wartime: Lessons from the Past, Hopes for the Future." *Journalism Quarterly,* 69, no. 1 (Spring 1992), 5–17.

Getler, Michael. "Do Americans Really Want to Censor War Coverage This Way?" *Washington Post,* March 17, 1991, pp. D1, D4.

Katz, Steven L., ed. "Symposium on the Military and the Media during the Persian Gulf War." *Government Information Quarterly,* 9, no. 4 (1992), 375–496.

Klein, Michael W. "The Censor's Red Flair, the Bombs Bursting in Air: The Constitutionality of the Desert Storm Media Restrictions." *Hastings Constitutional Law Quarterly,* 19, no. 4 (Summer 1992), 1037–1076.

MacArthur, John R. *Second Front: Censorship and Propaganda in the Gulf War.* New York: Hill and Wang, 1992.

Sidle, Winant. "The Gulf War Reheats Military-Media Controversy." *Military Affairs,* 71, no. 9 (September 1991), 52–63.

Thompson, Loren B. "The Press and the Pentagon: Old Battles, New Skirmishes." *American Enterprise,* 3, no. 1 (January/February 1992), 14–16, 18.

U.S. Cong., Senate. *Pentagon Rules on Media Access to the Persian Gulf War.* Hearing before the Committee on Governmental Affairs, 102d Cong., 1st Sess., 1991.

Williams, Pete. "Let's Face It, This Was the Best War Coverage We've Ever Had." *Washington Post,* March 17, 1991, pp. D1, D4.

Chapter 10

Should the Death Penalty Be Abolished?

The Eighth Amendment to the Constitution forbids "cruel and unusual punishments" but does not specify what makes a punishment cruel or unusual. When the Bill of Rights was adopted, the death penalty, or "capital punishment" as it is called, was not considered cruel or unusual. But particularly since the nineteenth century, there has been continuing controversy about the morality of capital punishment, not only in the United States but throughout the world. The global trend has been away from capital punishment. Today the United States is the only Western industrial country that allows the death penalty.

The death penalty has been brought before the Supreme Court on a number occasions. In 1972, the Supreme Court decided in *Furman* v. *Georgia* to bar the death penalty as it was imposed under statutes at the time, objecting to the randomness of procedures.[1] As a result of the decision, most state legislatures enacted new laws complying with the decision in *Furman* so that capital punishment could still be used as a punishment for major violent crimes.

The Supreme Court again considered capital punishment in 1976 in *Gregg* v. *Georgia*. In that case and in four related cases it accepted the constitutionality of the death penalty under certain conditions.[2]

The death penalty is under continuous legal challenge. One related issue the Supreme Court considered involved racism. In 1987, the Court rejected a challenge that capital punishment was more likely to be inflicted on black defendants than whites and therefore violated the Equal Protection Clause of the Fourteenth Amendment.[3] The death penalty is also under continuous consideration in the legislative branch. Bills to abolish the death penalty have been introduced but not enacted into law. Some members of Congress, representing the opposite view, have sought to apply the death penalty to acts of treason and drug trafficking instead of only to the most extreme cases of murder.

Amnesty International, the Nobel Peace Prize–winning human rights organization, argues against the death penalty. In written testimony submitted to the House Judiciary Committee in 1991, it attacked the Bush administration's efforts to expand use of the death penalty for certain heinous crimes. Amnesty International makes the following key points:

1. There is a global trend toward abolition of the death penalty, which is rooted in respect for universal human rights norms.
2. Legal scholars conclude that definitions of capital murder are

subjective and unreliable and that no known legal formula can eliminate arbitrary and discriminatory application of the death penalty.

3. The death penalty provides no special deterrent to violent crime and enshrines no viable principle of retributive justice.
4. There is no humane manner to execute a person, and medical societies throughout the world have urged their members not to participate directly or indirectly in executions.
5. Executing people who are mentally impaired violates international humanitarian standards.
6. There is no relationship between the death penalty and rates of violent crime.
7. There are alternatives to the death penalty, most notably life imprisonment, that can protect society against criminals.
8. Vengeance is not a tolerable basis for public policy or penal law.
9. There is always the possibility that an innocent person can unjustly be subjected to capital punishment.
10. Racial disparities subject African American defendants to a greater likelihood of being sentenced to death than white people.
11. Some prisoners are killed because they do not get competent legal representation.

James C. Anders, an attorney in South Carolina, argues for the death penalty. Speaking before the Senate Judiciary Committee, he contends

1. Capital punishment is a deterrent to violent crime.
2. Capital punishment satisfies society's compelling desire to see justice done.
3. The death penalty is a sentence sanctioned by law and implemented only after exhaustive criminal proceedings through the courts. In no way can it be equated with murder.
4. To say that some people are put to death while others who commit similar offenses are not is no argument against the death penalty, since the same argument could be used against subjecting any criminal to penalties.
5. The criminal justice system in the United States is so sophisticated that it is unlikely that an innocent person will be executed.
6. Because prisoners escape or are paroled or furloughed, sentences other than the death penalty offer no real assurance that these criminals will not commit violent crimes again.

NOTES

1. *Furman* v. *Georgia,* 498 U.S. 238 (1972).
2. *Gregg* v. *Georgia,* 428 U.S. 153 (1976).
3. *McCleskey* v. *Kemp,* Supreme Court docket no. 84-6811 (April 22, 1987).

☑ Y E S

Should the Death Penalty Be Abolished?

AMNESTY INTERNATIONAL

The Case against the Death Penalty

Protecting citizens from violent crime is an urgent issue for U.S. legislators. To provide the illusion of protections not only betrays citizens' trust in their government but also wastes public resources. It can also undermine the very values, namely the sanctity of human life and respect for the security of the person, which make violent crime utterly unacceptable in American society.

The death penalty provisions of the Comprehensive Violent Crime Control Act of 1991, a bill proposed by the Bush Administration on March 11, are illusory protections. They constitute an assault on the U.S. justice system and on U.S. credibility as a leading proponent of human rights world-wide.

The Administration repeatedly has defended its bill with references to a "war on crime." Affinity between war and killing is undeniable. Violent crime in the United States, however, is a domestic social problem. On a practical level, killing prisoners held in government custody will do nothing to solve that problem. On an ethical level, killing is not an acceptable program for addressing societal stability.

The Administration's bill expands the number of federal crimes punishable by death and includes both unintentional homicides and offenses which do not involve loss of life. Several procedural provisions, which will be discussed below, restrict safeguards against injustices. Together, these provisions would pull the U.S. justice system in an regressive direction. They would diminish human rights protections.

There is a global trend toward abolition of the death penalty which is rooted in respect for universal human rights norms. Governments throughout the world are recognizing that the death penalty does not deter heinous crimes. They increasingly perceive that their societies should not bear the cost of this brutal punishment.

Western Europe achieved wide-scale abolition during the 1980s. The last execution in Turkey took place in 1984, and the United States remains the only NATO [North Atlantic Treaty Organization] member which executes its citizens. Ireland abolished the death penalty in 1990.

Dramatic moves toward democracy by several countries during recent years have included abolition of the death penalty. In 1987, following the "people power revolution" ending the repressive dictatorship of Ferdinand Marcos, the Philippine people approved a new Constitution which abolished the death penalty. Subsequently, the sentences of 528 condemned prisoners were commuted to life in prison by the cabinet of Corazon Aquino. In Haiti, the termination of the Duvalier family dictatorship was followed by adoption of a new Constitution abolishing capital punishment.

The transition to democracy in several Eastern European countries has led to abolition of the death penalty. The Czechoslovakian Parliament amended the country's Penal Code in July 1990 to abolish the death penalty. The Constitutional Court of Hungary declared the death penalty unconstitutional in October 1990, describing the punishment as cruel, arbitrary, and a violation of human rights. An official of the Polish Ministry of Justice stated in December 1990 that the new draft Penal Code for Poland contains no death penalty provisions.

Changes in Southern Africa have also included changes with respect to the use of the death penalty. In Namibia, following the end of the illegal occupation by South Africa, the Namibian Constituent Assembly approved unanimously a constitution which includes a provision outlawing use of the death penalty. The constitution states: "The right to life shall be respected and protected. No law may prescribe death as a competent sentence. No court or tribunal shall have the power to impose a sentence of death upon any person. No executions shall take place in Namibia." The liberalizing trend in South Africa has been reflected in its attitude toward the death penalty. President F. W. de Klerk announced in February 1990 that "all executions have been suspended and no executions will take place until Parliament has taken a final decision on the new proposals [for changes in penal provisions]."

Worldwide moves to eliminate the death penalty accelerated in other countries as well throughout 1990. In addition to the countries mentioned above, capital punishment was abolished for all crimes in Andorra, Mozambique, and Sao Tome and Príncipe. In addition, Nepal barred the death penalty as punishment for ordinary peacetime criminal offenses.

The most striking feature of this acceleration is that when countries shed the yoke of repression, they also rid themselves of one of the tools of repression—the death penalty. Why is this lesson lost on the United States?

Use of the death penalty is exceptional in democratic societies. The United States is perhaps the most striking example of such an exception. Researchers and statistical analysts have repeatedly failed to find social benefits in capital punishment. Legal scholars have concluded that definitions of capital murder are subjective and unreliable, while no known legal formula can eliminate arbitrary and discriminatory application of the death penalty.

Nevertheless, the Bush Administration proposes extension of the death penalty in the United States. The killing of Kurds in Iraq and the mass executions of petty criminals in China, roundly condemned by the U.S. Government have links to current U.S. death penalty proposals. In its "war on crime" proposals, the Administration joins the governments it criticizes by choosing the death penalty as its response to a perceived threat of social instability.

Advocates of the penalty, no matter which particular justifications they present publicly, maintain that killing prisoners serves a "greater good" for society. Government authorities differ, of course, in their interpretations of "greater good." What moral authority can the U.S. Government claim in criticizing other governments for killing prisoners if our government also kills for a "greater good"? Not coincidentally, the greater-good line of reasoning is used by governments in attempts to justify all human rights abuses, ranging from unjust imprisonment to summary legal proceedings to torture and the death penalty.

The beneficiaries of the "greater good," in fact, are the relatively few government officials who wish to appear actively concerned about threats to society while failing to address difficult issues. The death penalty provides no special deterrent to violent crime and enshrines no viable principle of retributive justice. Instead of protecting society, it teaches citizens of all ages that physical violence is an accepted means of dealing with personal and social problems.

Despite use of medical technology in the United States to make executions seem more "humane," killing remains a uniquely cruel punishment. Current practices here place death penalty supporters at odds with both domestic and international medical organizations.

The House of Delegates of the American Medical Association adopted a resolution in 1980 stating that "a physician, as a member of a profession dedicated to preserving life when there is hope of doing so, should not be a participant in a legally authorized execution." The same year the American Psychiatric Association declared that it "strongly opposes any participation by psychiatrists in capital punishment, that is, in activities leading directly or indirectly to the death of a condemned person as a legitimate medical procedure."

According to the Committee on Ethics of the American Nurses Association, it is a "breach of the nursing code of ethical conduct to participate either directly or indirectly in a legally authorized execution."

The Assembly of the World Medical Association has also taken a strong stand on the issue of health professionals assisting in executions. The Assembly resolved in 1981 that "it is unethical for physicians to participate in capital punishment." At least 19 national medical associations worldwide have formally stated their opposition to actions by medical personnel which facilitate executions.

In addition, international humanitarian standards generally maintain that people who are not of sound mind should not be held criminally responsible for their acts. A related principle holds that these people should not be executed because they are incapable of understanding the nature of their punishment.

Yet a 1989 U.S. Supreme Court ruling permits states in this country to execute prisoners who are mentally impaired or retarded. The Administration's crime bill contains no provisions for excluding the mentally impaired from execution. Estimates on the number of mentally impaired people now held on death rows in the United States range from 10 percent to over 30 percent. Several prisoners who were clearly mentally impaired have been executed here in recent years.

While admitting the cruelty and occasional injustices inherent in the premeditated killing of prisoners, a majority of U.S. authorities who support the death penalty claim that the punishment is a necessary deterrent to violent crime. The deterrent argument has wide common-sense appeal. People who act according to common sense, however, are not the violent criminals subjected to death penalty statutes. People who kill in the heat of passion or under the influence of drugs or alcohol do not act with the benefit of common sense. Because ideologically motivated killers choose to put themselves in life-threatening situations before they commit terrorist acts, the prospects of execution at a future date will hardly serve as a deterrent. Hired killers, acting upon the assumption that arrest and prosecution are unlikely, are also improbable candidates for deterrence.

Study after study in countries with varying cultural traditions and social norms fail to show any significant relation between the death penalty and rates of violent crime. In France and Canada, homicide rates have actually fallen after executions ceased.

Over 20 countries now have death penalty laws for drug trafficking. Despite hundreds of executions for drug offenses in recent years, no clear evidence links a decline in drug trafficking with either the threat or use of the death penalty. No reported changes in drug trafficking accompanied over 1,000 executions for drug offenses in Iran during 1989. A United Nations Expert Group on Countermeasures to Drug Smuggling concluded in 1985 that the death penalty provided no special deterrence to drug trafficking. In fact, the Group found that provisions for a death penalty sometimes hindered prosecution and conviction of drug smugglers.

A detailed report of the United Nations Committee on Crime Prevention and Control noted in 1988 that research "has failed to provide scientific proof that executions have a greater deterrent effect than life imprisonment. Such proof is unlikely to be forthcoming. The evidence as a whole still gives no positive support to the deterrent hypothesis."

Incapacitation of violent offenders has also lost credibility as a reason for execution. As the world's abolitionist governments have shown, society can be protected from dangerous people without recourse to killing. While governments have a duty to protect citizens from criminals, the only effective means of meeting this obligation are practices consistent with society's own values. Physical elimination is barbaric in today's world. The killing of prisoners is incompatible with respect for life.

Just retribution is perhaps the pro–death-penalty argument with the greatest emotional appeal. Some people strongly believe that other people deserve to die. But however satisfying visions of revenge may be, vengeance is not a tolerable basis for public policy or penal law. The history of societies' efforts to establish the rule of law shows progressive restriction of personal or societal vengeance as a basis for punishment.

As compensation for a victim's suffering, vengeance has no social utility. It neither restores life to victims of murder nor reduces the loss suffered by victims' families. Instead of helping to heal lives wrenched by violent crime, it freezes people in patterns of hatred and revenge.

Revenge is rooted in fear, social instability, and a culture of violence. It is an attempt to vent anger rather than to seek effective solutions to complex dilemmas. Revenge is an act of desperation and has no place in the legal system of the United States or any other country.

Since World War II, the United Nations and regional intergovernmental organizations have recognized the death penalty as a human rights issue. International standards promote restriction of offenses punishable by death, stronger safeguards for people facing the death penalty, and most recently, abolition of capital punishment.

The Universal Declaration of Human Rights, proclaimed without dissent by the United Nations General Assembly in 1948, declares that "everyone has the right to life" (Article 3) and that "no one shall be subjected to torture or to cruel, inhuman or degrading treatment or punishment" (Article 5). Killing, the ultimate physical assault on a person, violates both of these rights. Whether legally sanctioned or committed outside the law, killing is a cruel punishment which denies the value of human life.

The General Assembly affirmed in 1971 that "in order to fully guarantee the right to life, provided for in Article 3 of the Universal Declaration of Human Rights, the main objective to be pursued is that of progressively restricting the number of offenses for which the death penalty may be imposed, with a view to the desirability of abolishing this punishment in all countries."

The two international human rights Covenants provide contours of the rights set forth in the Universal Declaration. The International Covenant on Civil and Political Rights, an agreement which entered into force in 1976 but has not yet been ratified by the U.S. Government, prohibits reintroduction of the death penalty by countries which have abolished it and restricts the punishment to only "the most serious crimes" (Article 6).

The Human Rights Committee, an international implementing body established under the Covenant, has recognized the right to life as "the supreme right from which no derogation is permitted." In a general comment issued in 1982, the Committee stated that "all measures of abolition [of the death penalty] should be considered as progress in the enjoyment of the right to life."

A resolution adopted by the United Nations Economic and Social Council and endorsed by the UN General Assembly in 1984 underscored the importance of fair trials in capital cases. The Council reinforced these standards in 1989, including emphasis on provisions of adequate legal representation in capital cases.

In July 1991, the Second Optional Protocol to the International Covenant on Civil and Political Rights will enter into force. All states party to the Protocol are bound to prohibit the execution of prisoners. This Protocol, the first international treaty envisaging abolition of the death penalty, represents significant progress in preventing human rights abuses.

On regional levels, the death penalty also has been condemned. The American Convention on Human Rights states that the death penalty "shall not be extended to crimes to which it does not presently apply" and that "the death penalty shall not be re-established in states that have abolished it" (Article 4). The Inter-American Commission on Human Rights called on all member nations in 1984 to abolish the death penalty. In 1990 the Optional Protocol to the American Convention on Human Rights was opened for signature. This Protocol requires that the death penalty be abolished for all but extraordinary crimes committed during wartime.

The Sixth Protocol to the European Convention on Human Rights, which entered into force in 1985, declares that "the death penalty shall be abolished. No one shall be condemned to such penalty or executed." In January 1986, the European Parliament unequivocally stated that "the death penalty is a cruel and inhuman form of punishment and a violation of the right to life, even where strict legal procedures are applied."

The U.S. Supreme Court ruled in 1972 that death sentencing in this country was arbitrary and capricious and, therefore, unconstitutional. Several justices found that the death penalty had fallen disproportionately on economically poor people and on members of ethnic minorities. Guidelines set by the Supreme Court later in the 1970s have failed to ensure fair, consistent application of the death penalty. Substantial evidence shows that death sentencing in the United States, as elsewhere in the world where it is practiced, continues to be discriminatory, arbitrary, and unfair.

The death penalty is a uniquely irrevocable punishment. Unlike other punishments, executions cannot be revoked. An executed prisoner can never receive compensation for judicial errors.

Last year Texas authorities released Randall Adams, and Florida authorities released James Richardson. Both men had been sentenced to death and had remained in prison for years before convincing evidence of their innocence emerged. A study released in 1987 by Hugo Bedau of Tufts University and Michael Radelet of the University of Florida reached what they called the "conservative" conclusion that 350 innocent people had been sentenced to death within the past century in the United States. Twenty-three of these people were executed.

With some 2,400 people on death rows in the United States today, the largest death row population in the world, the likelihood that some prisoners have been unjustly convicted remains high.

The case of Charles Brooks, executed by Texas authorities in 1982, is an example of disparate sentencing imposed on co-defendants. Despite evidence of the defendants' equal guilt, Charles Brooks received the death penalty while his co-defendant received a sentence of life imprisonment.

Several studies show significant racial disparities in death sentencing. Black people convicted of murdering white people are more frequently sentenced to death than any other category of offender in the United States. White defendants charged with killing a black person rarely receive the death penalty. In some jurisdictions, blacks who kill whites are as much as 11 times more likely to face execution than whites who kill blacks.

In the case of Warren McCleskey, a black man convicted of killing a white police officer, the Supreme Court ruled in 1987 that statistical evidence of discrimination based on the race of a defendant or victim is insufficient to show denial of equal protection. Title X of the Administration's new crime bill, the so-called Equal Justice Act, reaffirms such disregard of international norms for fairness.

Publicly available statistical analyses of racially biased sentencing no longer would be considered as permissible evidence. Under this statute, neither state nor federal courts could invalidate death sentences on such evidence of racial discrimination. In an odd twist of logic, the Administration has argued that proof of racially discriminatory sentencing patterns somehow reflects attempts to reinforce discriminatory quota systems.

The Administration's bill severely restricts a defendant's ability to challenge his or her death sentence, despite a finding by the General Accounting Office in 1990 of "racial disparities in the charging, sentencing, and imposition of the death penalty."

The Supreme Court's June 1991 ruling in *Payne* v. *Tennessee* permitting "victim impact" evidence in capital cases also raises grave questions about equal protection in this country. "All are equal before the law," proclaims the Universal Declaration of Human Rights and subsequent international treaties. The U.S. Constitution enshrines this principle of equal protection. Yet aspects of particular victims' lives and the types of pain suffered by particular victims' relatives have been judged as valid considerations in sentencing procedures. This judgment encourages judicial decisions based on distinctions in the value of individual human lives. Comparison of victims' intrinsic worth is an abhorrent remnant of past times which should never be permitted in a modern justice system.

Economic status may be an even more significant factor in death sentencing within particular jurisdictions than race is. A large majority of prisoners sentenced to death in the United States are from the poorest sectors of society. According to a former warden of San Quentin Prison in California, capital punishment appears to be "a privilege of the poor." Compelling evidence of inadequate legal representation has long been grounds for overturning the death sentences of defendants who lacked resources to pay lawyers' fees.

Congress gave the Federal courts jurisdiction in 1867 to challenge states' confinement of prisoners. Since that time, between one-third and one-half of all death sentences have been overturned in habeas corpus proceedings. In its 1990 *Butler* v. *McKeller* decision, the Supreme Court applied its ruling in *Teaque* v. *Lane* to death penalty cases. In *Butler,* the Supreme Court judged that "reasonable, good faith" decisions made by state courts cannot be overturned, even if such decisions prove contrary to subsequent court rulings. Federal habeas corpus appeals, therefore, are no longer available to state prisoners seeking to either establish a "new rule" of law or benefit from "new rules" post-dating the appeal of their convictions and imposition of death sentences. A prisoner may be executed even if the sentence proves unconstitutional under Federal court rulings.

The Supreme Court's *McCleskey* v. *Zant* decision in April of this year provides further restrictions on the scope of federal review of state death penalty cases. The effect of this ruling is to impose a new standard for attorneys, requiring extreme degrees of proof rather than a "good faith" test for introduction of issues not raised in the first petition procedure. These increasingly stringent standards will allow most prisoners sentenced to death to file only one federal habeas petition. Error of new evidence will no longer be sufficient to open the process to further review.

State defendants who are granted evidentiary hearings during federal habeas proceedings, however, do not even have the right to counsel under the new bill. Counsel would be guaranteed to defendants only in state post-conviction proceedings, although states that impose the death penalty traditionally have been reluctant to provide adequate resources for defendants lacking the means to pay lawyers and investigators. In addition, the bill provides no standards of competency for lawyers in capital cases.

The Administration's bill further eviscerates the right to habeas corpus by proposing a statute of limitations for filing habeas petitions. After a state post-conviction appeal, the bill would give defendants facing the death penalty only six months to file for federal review of their cases. In February, Justice Scalia announced that extensions would no longer be automatic for appeals by death row prisoners who are unable to retain counsel. Justice Scalia has administrative responsibilities for the U.S. Circuit Court of Appeals in Texas, Louisiana, and Mississippi. Each of these states has a large death row population. Lack of adequate counsel, according to Justice Scalia, is no longer considered "good cause" for extending appeal deadlines.

Another worrisome trend reinforced by the Administration's crime package is removal of safeguards against introduction of unfairly obtained or prejudicial evidence during capital trials. Evidence obtained without proper warrant would be admissible, provided that federal officers acted "in good faith." Firearms and "related evidence" would be admissible whether or not "good faith" could be proved. International standards of fair trial preclude use of evidence illegally obtained. U.S. exclusionary rules support these standards. The Administration's proposal severely undermines a critical tenet of human rights protection.

Coerced confessions, adamantly condemned by jurists worldwide, have also been exempted under some circumstances from exclusion during trial proceedings. According to the 1991 *Arizona* v. *Fulminante* Supreme Court decision, a coerced confession will not invalidate a conviction or sentence of death if an appellate court rules that its introduction into evidence was "harmless error."

The Court upheld Oreste Fulminante's conviction for murder, which was based on evidence provided by an FBI informant paid to coerce information from him.

A Supreme Court ruling this year permits police to hold citizens in custody for 48 hours before judicial authorities rules on just cause for indictment. Amnesty International's 30 years of international experience unequivocally shows that torture and other coercive techniques usually occur in the initial period of custody. Two days and nights certainly can be sufficient time to extract a "confession" from some detainees.

In conjunction with the *Fulminante* decision, the 48-hour habeas corpus decision bodes ill for the cause of justice in this country, especially in death penalty cases. U.S. authorities have rightly criticized use of coerced confessions in other countries. These condemnations will carry less authority if our justice system permits a similar practice.

The Administration's current crime control package weakens or eliminates critical safeguards against unjust or disparate death sentencing. Added to several recent court decisions which remove guarantees of due process, provisions of the crime bill would propel the U.S. justice system away from international human rights norms.

The history of executions in the United States demonstrates that some prisoners are killed because their lawyers lack skills necessary to defend them adequately. Some die because of unredressed injustices in legal proceedings, because of capricious decisions made at varying stages of prosecution, or because of discriminatory practices within particular jurisdictions. Some defendants convicted of heinous crimes receive sentences of imprisonment, while defendants convicted of less abhorrent crimes are executed.

More than 80 countries in the world have abolished the death penalty in law or in practice. They have recognized that the death penalty is uncivilized in principle and unfair in practice. None of these countries report social or political ill-effects resulting from abolition. Instead, they find that society benefits from law enforcement built upon values other than those it condemns. A government does not condemn deadly violence by killing.

Abolition is a victory of reason over emotion and justice over revenge. The Administration's 1991 crime bill would move this country further from abolition. The death penalty provisions and eviscerations of judicial safeguards contained in the bill will encourage disregard for the value of human life and tolerance of rights violations. If enacted, the new federal death penalty laws will unleash a brutalizing force on society. We deserve better. We deserve real protection from violent crime, real assistance for victims, and a real commitment by the U.S. Government to uphold basic human rights at all times and in all places.

Should the Death Penalty Be Abolished?

JAMES C. ANDERS
The Case for the Death Penalty

There are in this world a number of extremely wicked people, disposed to get what they want by force or fraud, with complete indifference to the interests of others, and in ways which are totally inconsistent with the existence of civilized society.

—James Fitzjames Stephen

What is society to do with these people? I believe that in certain cases, the death penalty can be shown to be the only rational and realistic punishment for an unspeakable crime. But before embarking on a discussion on the merits of the death penalty, a fundamental philosophical question must be answered. What is the purpose of punishment? Harmonious coexistence among people in any society is dependent upon the advancement of mutually agreed upon goals for the good of the whole society. Obviously, the most basic right a citizen has is the right to be secure in his person, the right to be safe from physical or economic harm from another. Laws to protect citizens and advance the harmony of society are founded upon these principles. To enforce these laws, created in the best interest of society as a whole, there has to be a deterrent for a breach of the law. Therefore, deterrence is the first aim of a system of punishment.

Deterrence is only one side of the punishment coin, however. An equally fundamental reason to punish lies in society's compelling desire to see justice done. Punishment expresses the emotions of the society wronged, the anger and outrage felt, and it solidifies and reinforces the goals, values and norms of acceptable behavior in the society. Punishment is justified purely on the ground that wrongdoing merits punishment, and that it is morally fitting that one who does wrong suffers, and suffers in proportion to his wrongdoing.

Consider the facts of a 1977 case from my jurisdiction. Codefendants Shaw, Roach and Mahaffey spent the morning of October 29th drinking and shooting up drugs. That afternoon the three decided to, in Mahaffey's words, "see if we could find a girl to rape." They drove to a nearby baseball field where they spotted a car parked with two teenagers inside. They robbed and killed the young man on the spot. The girl was carried to a dirt road a short distance away where she was repeatedly raped and sodomized over a period of hours. When they finished with her, they forced her to place her head in a circle they had drawn in the dirt, and they executed her. Later that evening, Shaw returned by himself and sexually mutilated the girl's body.

The deterrent effect of the death penalty is the favorite criticism of the opponents of capital punishment. The social scientists' studies have been mixed at best and there is no authoritative consensus on whether or not the death penalty deters anyone from committing a crime. Threats of punishment cannot and are not meant to deter everybody all of the time. They are meant to deter most people most of the time.

"The threatened punishment must be carried out—otherwise the threats are reduced to bluffs and become incredible and therefore ineffective."
—Ernest van den Haag

Therefore, the death penalty can only be a deterrent if it is meted out with a reasonable degree of consistency. The deterrent effect lies in the knowledge of the citizenry that it will more likely than not be carried out if the named crime is committed.

Even if one is not fully convinced of the deterrent effect of the death penalty, he or she would surely choose the certainty of the convicted criminal's death by execution over the possibility of the deaths of new victims. These new deaths could either be deterred by the execution, or prevented by the executed criminal's obvious incapacity. Simply put, one should opt to execute a man convicted of having caused the death of others than to put the lives of innocents at risk if there is a chance their deaths could be prevented by the deterrent effect.

Death penalty opponents argue that if life is sacred (as, presumably, we all believe) then the murderer's life, too, is sacred and for the State to punish him by execution is barbaric and causes the State to bend to the murderer's level. The only similarity between the unjustified taking of an innocent life and the carrying out of a convicted murderer's execution is the end result—death. The death penalty is a legal sentence, enacted by the legislatures of various states which presumably reflect their constituents' desires. It is a penalty that can finally be carried out only after a trial where the defendant is afforded all of his constitutional rights, and the lengthy appellate process has been exhausted. It is a penalty that has been sanctioned by the United States Supreme Court, a majority of whose members have said, regardless of their personal feelings, that the death penalty is a constitutionally valid punishment. How then can its invocation be compared to the senseless, irrational murder of an innocent victim who is afforded no rights, and is tried and convicted by his murderer for the crime of being in the wrong place at the wrong time? Legal execution and murder are no more comparable than driving a car and knowingly driving a stolen car. Although the physical act of driving either is the same, the two acts are separated by the crime involved in the latter, and that makes all the difference.

Death penalty opponents are also troubled by the studies that purport to show that the death penalty is applied capriciously, that it discriminates racially and economically. They cite these studies as justification for eliminating the penalty. Notice that they are not claiming that some innocent person may be executed, but, rather, that not all the guilty are executed. Assuming that premise for the sake of argument, is that a rational reason to abolish the death penalty? Is the fact that some guilty persons escape punishment sufficient to let all guilty persons escape it? If it is then, in practice, penalties never could be applied if we insisted that they cannot be inflicted on any guilty persons unless we are able to make sure that they are equally applied to all other guilty persons. There is no more merit in persuading the courts to let all capital defendants go because some escaped penalties than it is to say let all burglars go because some have escaped detection and imprisonment. If discrimination exists in the application of the death penalty, then the remedy is statutory reform to minimize or abolish the discrimination, not the abolition of the penalty itself.

The capricious/discriminatory complaint seems by and large to be an abolitionist sham. The abolitionists would oppose the death penalty if it could be meted out without any discretion, if it were mandatory under certain conditions. They would oppose it in an homogeneous country without racial discrimination. It is the death penalty itself, not its possible maldistribution that the abolitionists oppose. Opponents rarely raise the objection that an innocent person might be sent to the electric chair. With the sophistication of the criminal justice system today, the likelihood of convicting, let alone executing, an innocent man is all but nil. But there is another more subtle reason abolitionists no longer advance the "innocent man proposition" as a justification for their opposition to the penalty and that is because this argument too would be a sham. Death penalty opponents would rid the world of the death penalty for everyone, including the admittedly guilty.

To defend the death penalty should not lead to one's being labeled "cold," "blood-thirsty" or "barbaric." A person who commits capital murder simply cannot and should not expect to be given a pat on the back and told to "go and sin no more." If the death penalty can deter one murder of an innocent life or if it can make a statement to the community about what will and will not be tolerated, then it is justified.

Opponents of the death penalty advocate the life sentence in prison as a viable alternative to execution. My experiences lead me to believe that life imprisonment is not a satisfactory means of dealing with the most horrid of criminals. Early release programs, furloughs, and escapes combine to place a shockingly high number of convicted murderers back on the streets in record time. Hardly a day goes by when one cannot pick up a newspaper and read a gruesome account of the crimes committed by a now liberated "lifer." But that is not the worst of it. Consider the plight of the victims' families, forced to relive the nightmare again and again each time a parole hearing is scheduled. Year after year they endure the uncertainty and agony while waiting on the decision of the parole board. Will this be the year the man who turned their lives upside down will be released to live out his life, perhaps to put another family through the same nightmare?

The life without parole sentence is no solution either. First the possibility of escape cannot be completely eliminated, even in the most secure of institutions. For example, convicted triple murderer and death row inmate Fred Kornahrens escaped with a ploy so simple it caught prison officials completely by surprise. During a body search prior to being transported to court, Kornahrens concealed a key between his index and middle fingers. When handcuffed, he simply uncuffed himself and made good his escape. Given enough time, I am certain Fred Kornahrens could escape again. Second, the life without parole sentence places a tremendous burden on prison administrators. Faced with controlling inmates who have already received the worst punishment society can mete out, they can only throw their hands up in frustration. Lastly, the true lifer is not only capable of continuing to murder, but may actually be more likely to do so. Every prison in the country has its own stories of the lifer who killed another inmate over a cigarette or a piece of chicken. In my home state this scenario was taken one step farther when disenchanted crime victim Tony Cimo hired convicted mass murderer Donald "Pee Wee" Gaskins to kill another convicted murderer Rudolph Tyner, the slayer of Cimo's parents. Pee Wee Gaskins in a perfect example of why life imprisonment is never going to be an acceptable alternative to the death penalty and why the death penalty for murder by a federal prisoner serving a life term is a viable proposal.

I recently prosecuted a capital case involving the murder of a state highway patrolman. Trooper George Radford was brutally beaten and executed with his own weapon over a $218 ticket. All Trooper Radford did was show his murderer the same consideration and courtesy he exhibited to all every day on duty. Rather than handcuffing the defendant, Warren Manning, whom he had ticketed for driving under suspension, Trooper Radford allowed him to remain unhandcuffed for the twenty minute ride to the police station so that he would be more comfortable. Manning surprised Trooper Radford halfway there and callously murdered him. Law enforcement personnel deserve the additional protection and security the death penalty affords them. The scores of highway patrolmen who travelled to Camden, South Carolina for the sentencing of Warren Manning show exactly how important the death penalty issue is to them.

Based on the foregoing analysis, the death penalty takes on special significance in deterrence and punishment of federal law violations. Serious problems exist in American society on a large scale basis or threaten to grow to such a basis. As discussed above, the benefits of deterrence and social justice on crimes such as murder, murder for hire and attempts to assassinate the President are obvious under the death penalty.

Drug-related murders are on the rise and the death penalty could be particularly effective in combating this murder-for-profit trend. Law enforcement officers who are often required to work undercover in the drug community would be protected to a degree under the deterrence effect of the death penalty. In order to support President Bush's plan to combat the drug problem nationally and internationally, it seems obvious that drug kingpins should know that they are subject to the death penalty. What group of individuals create more chaos and death than these?

Other heinous crimes which pose a threat of great magnitude are those of terrorism. Crimes such as explosions, air piracy, mailing bombs and taking hostages, all where death results, very simply and obviously demand the strongest punishment and deterrent the law can impose. The effects of terrorism are so potentially great and devastating that the death penalty is the only conceivable punishment. The death penalty is not merely an alternative but a necessity for dealing with these large scale national problems.

One leading proponent of the death penalty, E. van den Haag, wrote "never to execute a wrongdoer, regardless of how depraved his acts, is to proclaim that no act can be so irredeemably vicious as to deserve death." In the question of deterrence this principle is exacerbated by a special group of sane murderers who, knowing that they will not be executed, will not hesitate to kill again. If opponents of the death penalty admit that there is a reasonable probability that such wrongdoers will murder again and/or attempt to murder again, and still insist they would never approve of capital punishment, I would conclude that they are indifferent to the lives of the human beings doomed to be the victims of the unexecuted criminals. "Charity for all human beings must not deprive us of our common sense," [said] Hugo Adam Bedau. To those who could not impose the death penalty under any circumstances, van den Haag attributed what he called "a failure of nerve," a feeling that they themselves are incapable of rationally and justly making a life and death decision and that, therefore, everyone else is equally unqualified to decide life or death.

Such a view grossly and tragically underestimates our system of justice. I have always been impressed with the intelligence, compassion and common sense jurors display. Jurors really are the "conscience of the community." That is more than just a phrase lawyers bandy about in closing arguments. I have seen how seriously jurors take their oath to decide the issues, based on the law, regardless of their personal prejudices, and biases. The juries and the courts can evade decisions on life and death only by giving up paramount duties: those of serving justice, securing the lives of citizens and vindicating the norms that society holds inviolable. Justice requires that the punishment be proportional to the gravity of the crime. The death penalty comes closest to meeting this supreme standard while still falling short because those criminals sentenced to execution still had the luxury of choosing their fate when their victims did not.

Questions for Discussion

1. How could you determine whether the death penalty is an instrument of racial oppression?

2. What role should family members of a murdered victim play in influencing a sentence involving the death penalty?
3. If the death penalty is acceptable, in what kinds of cases should it be applied? Why?
4. What effect would public executions have on violent crimes?
5. What role does arbitrariness of capital punishment sentences play in your evaluation of this issue?

Suggested Readings

Baldus, David C., George Woodworth, and Charles A. Pulaski. *Equal Justice and the Death Penalty: A Legal and Empirical Analysis.* Boston: Northeastern Univ. Press, 1990.

Berns, Walter. *For Capital Punishment: Crime and the Morality of the Death Penalty.* Lanham, Md.: University Press of America, 1991.

Black, Charles L., Jr. *Capital Punishment: The Inevitability of Caprice and Mistake.* 2d ed. New York: Norton, 1981.

Goldberg, Steven. "So What If the Death Penalty Deters?" *National Review,* 41, no. 12 (June 30, 1989), 42, 44.

Paternoster, Raymond. *Capital Punishment in America.* New York: Lexington Books, 1991.

Radelet, Michael L., Hugo Adam Bedau, and Constance E. Putnam. *In Spite of Innocence: Erroneous Convictions in Capital Cases.* Boston: Northeastern Univ. Press, 1992.

Trombley, Stephen. *The Execution Protocol: Inside America's Capital Punishment Industry.* New York: Crown, 1992.

U.S. Cong., House of Representatives. *Death Sentence Issues.* Hearings before the Subcommittee on Civil and Constitutional Rights of the Committee on the Judiciary, 102d Cong., 1st Sess., 1991.

———, House of Representatives. *Death Penalty Legislation and the Racial Justice Act.* Hearings before the Subcommittee on Civil and Constitutional Rights of the Committee on the Judiciary, 101st Cong., 2d Sess., 1990.

———, House of Representatives. *Federal Death Penalty Legislation.* Hearings before the Subcommittee on Crime of the Committee on the Judiciary, 101st Cong., 2d Sess., 1990.

———, Senate. *Death Penalty.* Hearings before the Committee on the Judiciary, 101st Cong., 1st Sess., 1989.

U.S. General Accounting Office. *Death Penalty Sentencing: Research Indicates Pattern of Racial Disparities.* Report to Senate and House Committees of the Judiciary, 1990.

White, Welsh S. *The Death Penalty in the Nineties: An Examination of the Modern System of Capital Punishment.* Ann Arbor: Univ. of Michigan Press, 1991.

Chapter 11

Is Affirmative Action a Desirable Policy to Remedy Discrimination?

In the decades following World War II, the civil rights movement in the United States achieved notable successes. The Supreme Court ruled that racially discriminatory practices were unconstitutional, and laws were adopted at the national, state, and local level ending practices of segregation and other forms of discrimination.

The civil rights movement focused initially on political gains—voting rights, school integration, and access to public accommodations. Although resistance was strong, the movement achieved legal guarantees of equal treatment. Achieving equal economic opportunity proved to be a more intractable problem. As many African Americans pointed out, it is all well and good to have the legal right to go to any fine restaurant or hotel, as civil rights laws required, but the legal right does not make much practical difference to the people who cannot afford to pay.

Clearly, civil rights legislation did not secure economic equality. Many companies hired only a few African Americans, and often the jobs held by blacks were low level. Few black people rose to top positions in business. Many departments in colleges and universities had few black teachers or administrators. And even professional sports—baseball, basketball, and football—which welcomed blacks to their teams as athletes, hired few blacks as coaches or executives.

Many people in the civil rights movement saw this economic and social disparity between blacks and whites as just another form of discrimination. They called upon government to guarantee equal employment opportunities.

Government responded in two ways: by enforcing antidiscrimination laws, and by adopting affirmative action programs, which required employers to take special measures to recruit, hire, train, and upgrade members of groups that have suffered harm from past discrimination. Both policies were not limited to African Americans but were applied to other racial minorities and to women.

Support for the enforcement of antidiscrimination laws was broad. Government agencies sought to ensure that employers made job information available to all groups, did not use tests that were unrelated to performance of jobs as an unfair screening device against minority groups, and placed no discriminatory barriers to advancement within an organization.

Affirmative action was—and remains—controversial. It is based on the idea that special measures are needed to benefit groups of people who suffered from a long history of discrimination. In this view, affirmative action is needed to make previously excluded groups of people more competitive in economic and professional life.

When a government agency or court determines that a private or public organization is engaged in discriminatory hiring practices, it may require the organization to end those practices. But detecting discrimination in hiring practices is difficult. At times, the government relies on a statistical analysis based on the composition of either the work force in an organization or the number of applicants to particular jobs there. Government agencies sometimes require employment "guidelines" or "targets," which the organizations are expected to follow to comply with civil rights regulations. But critics of affirmative action complain that these guidelines are actually "quotas" in which specific percentages are allotted to targeted groups.

Quotas are illegal in the United States. According to a landmark case, *Regents of the University of California* v. *Bakke,* the Supreme Court decided that an affirmative action program using quotas for medical school admissions violates the Civil Rights Act of 1964. The Court, however, declared that admissions committees can consider race as one of a complex of factors involved in admissions decisions.[1] Critics of affirmative action say that guidelines inevitably become quotas, while supporters of the policy say that they do not.

The legal basis of affirmative action in the federal government is Title VII of the Civil Rights Act of 1964 and Executive Order 11246. Subsequent affirmative action measures extended the role of the federal government in encouraging active efforts to recruit specific targeted minority groups. The U.S. Equal Employment Opportunity Commission (EEOC) enforces the law through hearing individual complaints and providing remedies for people who have suffered from discriminatory employment practices.

The Office of Federal Contract Compliance Programs (OFCCP) in the Department of Labor implements Executive Order 11246. Its primary mission is to ensure that federal contractors take affirmative action to promote equal employment opportunity.

Affirmative action has been bitterly contested by people who believe the policy discriminates against them. They argue that they have not been hired or advanced because their employer has been forced to give preference to minorities or women. They say affirmative action is unfair, counterproductive, and unjust. Defenders argue that the policy is fair, just, and necessary to end discrimination. Some of the flavor of the controversy is seen in the debate below.

Nadine Strossen, a law professor at New York Law School and president of the American Civil Liberties Union, supports affirmative action in an article appearing in *Cornell Law Review.* The article is the text of a speech she delivered before the Federalist Society Fifth Annual Lawyers Convention: Individual Responsibility and the Law.

Strossen contends

1. Alternatives to affirmative action, such as self-help, are not sufficient to remedy the evils of racial discrimination.
2. Contrary to assertions by critics of affirmative action, there is no evidence to indicate that there are psychological injuries to both the beneficiaries and nonbeneficiaries of this policy. Beneficiaries are not stigmatized.
3. Because racism continues to be pervasive in U.S. society, social justice requires the continuation of affirmative action programs.
4. Critics of affirmative action complain about preferential treatment for minority or other groups that have suffered from discrimination but do not complain about the preferential treatment the economically and politically privileged receive in U.S. society.
5. Awareness of future opportunity that affirmative action makes possible should be expected to bolster one's resolve and ability to help oneself in meaningful ways.

Writer Jay R. Girotto criticizes affirmative action in an essay especially written for this anthology. He contends

1. Affirmative action heightens racial tensions.
2. Affirmative action programs perpetuate doubt about the professional competence of African Americans in the workplace.
3. The rewards of affirmative action are reaped by middle class rather than poor members of the African American community.
4. Affirmative action programs decrease incentives for African Americans to develop responsibility for their own advancement.
5. Most Americans disapprove of affirmative action.

NOTE

1. 438 U.S. 265; 57 L. Ed. 2d 750; 98 S. Ct. 2733 (1978).

Is Affirmative Action a Desirable Policy to Remedy Discrimination?

NADINE STROSSEN

Blaming the Victim: A Critique of Attacks on Affirmative Action

Randy Kennedy helped focus the discussion when he said that on the level of principles we all agree, but we disagree about the means for pursuing those principles. Without being disparaging, I would say that we all agree on the level of platitude. First, we are all in favor of individual liberty. Second, we abhor racism and poverty as disproportionately impeding certain segments of our society from enjoying the benefits of liberty. We disagree, though, on what remedies will effectively foster our shared goals of promoting liberty on an equal basis.

Dr. Keyes stressed the fact that we have rights as individuals rather than as members of groups. That is certainly true. An equally true fact, though, is that, throughout our history, people have been denied liberty disproportionately, and to this day are being denied liberty disproportionately, based on their membership in particular groups. In the same vein, I completely agree with Dr. Keyes that people should be treated not as numbers but as individuals. However, it is irresponsible for us to ignore the shockingly disproportionate extent to which the liberty of people who belong to certain groups is violated.

Bearing in mind the useful general focus that Randy provided, I would like to narrow the focus even further. I would like to concentrate on one particular critique that Dr. Keyes made, and that I have heard in similar gatherings, about one particular means for addressing the ongoing crisis in this society's maldistribution of liberty on the basis of race. I am referring to affirmative action.

In his opening remarks, Brad Reynolds talked about the "good old days" when people were not embarrassed to talk about affirmative action. Well, I stand here before you and say I still am not embarrassed to be an advocate of affirmative action. Brad also referred to a civil rights orthodoxy. Perhaps he and many of you see affirmative action as an outmoded part of this orthodoxy that should now be rejected. I agree that we should not simplistically look upon one particular remedy as a panacea. This is particularly true when the remedies encompassed by the term "affirmative action" include a wide panoply of measures, some of which may be more appropriate than others. Still, I do not think it is appropriate, in a knee-jerk fashion, to reject the entire concept of affirmative action.

Just as Brad Reynolds cautions against what he views as outmoded orthodoxies, so too, I think we also must guard against questionable new orthodoxies. A term that seems fashionable in these circles describes another remedy that should not be viewed as a panacea: the notion of "self-help." As I listened to

Dr. Keyes invoke that seemingly magic buzzword, I was reminded of a state-ment that Dr. Martin Luther King Jr. made many years ago. He said it is a cruel hoax to tell a man he should lift himself up by his bootstraps when he has no boots. So, just as affirmative action may not be a panacea, let us not overesti-mate the efficacy of alternative measures such as self-help.

The specific critique of affirmative action on which I would like to focus is the idea of victimization. I see it as a sort of blame-the-victim phenomenon. The argument is that the intended beneficiaries of affirmative action programs are really stigmatized by these programs. Dr. Keyes made the argument that they are diminished, they are disempowered, they are made to feel their inferi-ority. I echo Randy Kennedy's request for evidence to demonstrate this sup-posed phenomenon. It is asserted as though it were a self-understood truth, and yet I am unaware of any empirical studies that prove this is, in fact, a psycho-logical impact of affirmative action programs.

Like Randy, I too looked into the empirical evidence. During my search, I came across an interesting article in *Law & Policy* by a psychologist named Rupert Barnes Nacoste, who analyzed the studies that had been done on the psychological impacts of affirmative action. He was responding to what he perceived as widely stated but never empirically demonstrated conclusions that beneficiaries of affirmative action programs experience self-doubt, that non-beneficiaries experience resentment, and consequently, that these pro-grams cause an increase in interracial tensions. The evidence did not support conclusions that these adverse psychological effects are the inevitable conse-quences of affirmative action programs. Rather, the evidence strongly suggests that psychological responses are contingent on the accuracy or inaccuracy of the information and the understanding that a person has about affirmative action. This does not strike me as surprising.

Dr. Nacoste concluded that people's psychological reactions to affirmative action depend in particular on two variables. The first factor is the nature of the specific program involved. One of the problems with the current public discus-sion of this subject is that it often does not address the many reasonable, well-conceived, and fairly implemented programs in effect all over the county. Instead, the term "affirmative action" is often used in a sweeping, condemna-tory way, and discussions will often focus on particular ill-advised or bizarre examples that masquerade under that term.

In this respect, the phrase "affirmative action" reminds me of another current buzzword about which Professor Kennedy and I have previously debated—"political correctness." That term has taken on a pejorative meaning because too often it is associated with a few extreme and exaggerated applications of policies that, at bottom, reflect some positive impulse toward important, laud-able goals of diversity and equality. The same thing has happened with respect to affirmative action. The surveys to which Dr. Nacoste referred showed that most people, if they associated affirmative action with quotas, opposed it. Unfortunately, recent political discussion has tended to equate affirmative ac-tion with quotas. In fact, in the recent political discourse about affirmative action, it is not only the people who are allegedly benefited by these programs who are said to be stigmatized but, even worse, the whole notion itself has become stigmatized in a way that obscures meaningful analysis and debate.

According to Dr. Nacoste, the other variable factor that affects the perception of affirmative action, and whether or not it has negative psychological consequences for the intended beneficiaries and the rest of society, is how well people understand and accept the underlying rationale. In particular, he found that beneficiaries did not feel stigmatized and non-beneficiaries felt more positive when they understood that the target group was in fact needy and that it was receiving just compensation for actual past harm.

Dr. Nacoste also found that statements by top political leaders had a profound influence on how people perceived these programs. So, not surprisingly, certain political leaders who have relentlessly associated "the Q word," "quota," with affirmative action have played a major, unconstructive role in obscuring the debate about the underlying merits of affirmative action. If people truly understood the actual facts about the disproportionate denial of liberty on the basis of race throughout our history to this day, neither the intended beneficiaries, nor the rest of society, could rationally attach a stigma or a resentment to those programs.

This morning I re-read the brief that the American Civil Liberties Union [ACLU] filed in the *Bakke* case [*Regents of the Univ. of Cal. v. Bakke,* 438 U.S. 265 (No. 76-811) (1978)], and I was struck by how timely many of those statements, written in 1976, are today. I find that very sad. The ACLU supported the affirmative action program that the University of California at Davis had adopted in that case, on the rationale that the program promotes the individual equality necessary to the enjoyment of individual liberty. I would like to read part of the introduction to that brief:

> [T]he major civil liberties issue still facing the United States is the elimination, root and branch, of all vestiges of racism. No other asserted claim of right surpasses the wholly justified demand of the nation's discrete and insular minorities for access to the American mainstream from which they have so long been excluded.

I read the foregoing passage because I know some people in Federalist Society circles see a disparity or tension between the values of liberty and those of equality. I believe, though, that both sets of constitutional values are inextricably intertwined for the reason explained in the quoted passage.

Consistent with the foregoing statement in the ACLU's *Bakke* brief, Justice Blackmun's powerful dissenting opinion in that case said that, given the then current state of deprivation of rights and liberties on the basis of race in our society, affirmative action measures were justified in terms of fundamental social justice. Hoping that racial injustice would mark only a passing phase in our social history, Justice Blackmun expressed the view that affirmative action measures should be only temporary. He voiced the hope that these measures would help us to attain a state of equality of opportunity that is not mal-distributed on the basis of race.

Justice Blackmun speculated in *Bakke*, back in 1976, that a decade might be the limited period during which affirmative action remedies would be necessary for meaningful progress toward racial equality. We have long since passed that ten-year mark. The current year, 1991, is 15 years after *Bakke* was decided and, unfortunately, we have not substantially progressed toward racial equality. Justice Blackmun would probably acknowledge this fact, and the ACLU certainly does.

Along with other ACLU leaders, I believe that the most pervasive, overarching civil liberties problem in this country continues to be racial discrimination. Among all the victims of civil liberties violations that the ACLU represents, regarding a wide range of issues, people of color are disproportionately included. Therefore, if affirmative action is a remedy that is only going to be necessary on a temporary basis, we are still in that temporary phase.

In sum, there is a compelling social justice rationale for race-based affirmative action programs. Why should they be seen as more stigmatizing than other group-based programs? Indeed, we have many group-based preferences that are not intended to be compensatory and that do not have the compelling social justice rationale that affirmative action has. When I read the ACLU's brief in the *Bakke* case this morning, I was reminded of two such preferences.

Allen Bakke, the white medical student who sued the University of California at Davis because he was denied the particular preference that accrued to members of racial minorities, was also denied two other group-based preferences that were meted out by the medical school, neither of which he challenged. One was a preference for applicants who intended to practice medicine in northern California following their graduation. The other was a preference for applicants whose spouses were enrolled in the medical school. It is telling that Allen Bakke did not challenge those non-racial preferences. Too often, race-based affirmative action is singled out as the only type of group-based preference in our society that should be seen as connoting the beneficiary's inferiority, thus making the beneficiary into a victim who bears a stigma.

There is a racist cast to this disparity in societal attitudes toward different kinds of group-based preferences. Preferences designed to help traditionally oppressed racial minorities are said to be stigmatizing, but nobody questions whether the many other group-based preferences prevalent in our society are stigmatizing. Let me read you a passage which forcefully makes this point. It is from a book by Philip Green, written in 1981:

> Do all those corporate directors, bankers, etc., who got their jobs, first, because they were somebody's son, second, because they were male, third, because they were Protestant, and fourth, because they were white feel demeaned thereby? It would be interesting to ask them—and to ask the same question of the doctors who managed to get into good medical schools because there were quotas keeping out Jews, the skilled trades-

men who were admitted to the union because two members of their family recommended them and so on. Implicit in this critique of affirmative action, clearly, is a notion that whereas it's never painful to be rewarded because you are in the majority or the established elite, it's always painful to be rewarded because you're in the minority or a marginal group.

Indeed, should those of us who are unintended but actual beneficiaries of years of racial discrimination or gender discrimination in this society feel stigmatized? Should we feel victimized because we have, in fact, reaped the benefits of past discrimination?

Another argument that has been raised against affirmative action, which is akin to the notion of stigmatization and victimization, is the idea that it breeds passivity and leads to a lack of will. Dr. Keyes made this point. Again, I am not aware of any psychological studies that support this assertion. Indeed, some of the evidence Professor Kennedy described seems to call that conclusion into question.

It also seems a matter of common sense that a group of people who know they are to be systematically denied certain opportunities would become discouraged, and such discouragement would breed a lack of will, a lack of motivation, a lack of incentive. Systematic discrimination should be expected to breed passivity. A corresponding inference is that the awareness of future opportunity should be expected to bolster one's resolve and ability to help oneself in meaningful ways.

In conclusion, if affirmative action is fairly understood as a matter of basic social justice, two other, important realizations should follow: first, that there are no special, undeserving, victimized, stigmatized beneficiaries, but that all of society is a beneficiary; and second that any stigma should attach to those who unfairly criticize such a basic tool for pursuing social justice rather than to those who benefit from the removal of traditional barriers to their full and meaningful participation in this society.

Is Affirmative Action a Desirable Policy to Remedy Discrimination?

JAY R. GIROTTO
The Mythology of Affirmative Action

Most Americans agree that African Americans have been cruelly and unfairly treated in the United States. The historic legacy of slavery, lack of political empowerment, and denial of economic opportunity produced obstacles that have been difficult for African Americans to overcome. Most Americans welcomed the attempts to promote genuine civil rights by ending the barriers of segregation, providing equal voting rights, and creating equal opportunities. However, some Americans argue that the legacy of racial discrimination is an obstacle too large to overcome with only equal opportunities. They believe the nation should do something about providing equal results along with equal opportunities. The most common policy for achieving equal results is affirmative action.

Affirmative action is a plan to offset past discrimination by giving preferential treatment to a group that experienced the discrimination. The proponents of affirmative action believe that equality and fairness can be achieved by making special efforts to recruit, hire, and promote specified groups that were barred by discrimination in the past.

However lofty its goals, affirmative action is based on myths rather than facts. This essay examines those myths to show that affirmative action is not effective in promoting equality and fairness. Specifically, the myths of affirmative action are

1. Affirmative action reduces racial tension by promoting a racially heterogeneous neighborhood, workplace, and educational environment.
2. The preferential advancement of some African Americans improves the popular respect for all African Americans.
3. The rewards of affirmative action are reaped by the poor members of the African American community.
4. Affirmative action programs promote individual responsibility by placing African Americans in jobs and schools.
5. Most Americans approve of affirmative action.

MYTH 1. AFFIRMATIVE ACTION REDUCES RACIAL TENSION BY PROMOTING A RACIALLY HETEROGENEOUS NEIGHBORHOOD, WORKPLACE, AND EDUCATIONAL ENVIRONMENT

Affirmative action does not reduce racial tensions. In fact, affirmative action serves to heighten them. Evidence of affirmative action inflaming racial tension

177

is demonstrated in a study by sociologist Stephen Johnson in 1980. Johnson conducted thirty-two formal interviews of college students and found that Caucasian American male students who lost puzzle exercises to fake competitors were more hostile toward the opponents when told that the opponents were African Americans who were given a bonus score to compensate for historic disadvantages. The Caucasian American male students expressed less hostility toward African American victors when told they lost because of their opponents' ability.[1]

This study illustrates the ineffectiveness of affirmative action in reducing racial tension. The idea of adding a bonus score to African American test scores is used in hiring practices today and is known as "race-norming."[2]

Most state employment services use the General Aptitude Test Battery (GATB) to evaluate candidates for jobs. The GATB measures reading, math, vocabulary, and perceptual skills. Private companies, too, use this test when they ask state employment agencies for a list of the highest-qualified applicants for an open job. Affirmative action policy requires that GATB test scores be segregated by race; that is, an individual's score is compared with a nationwide pool of applicants of the same race. The consequence is that an African American and a Caucasian American with the same raw score on the GATB will have vastly different final scores. The African American, for example, will be listed as scoring seventy-five (signifying he was in the seventy-fifth percentile of the African American applicants), while the Caucasian American has a score of forty.

The employer receiving the list of GATB scores, however, is not informed of candidates' race. Nor does the list include the raw scores. Therefore, it appears that the African American candidate has scored twice as high as the Caucasian American applicant.[3]

The process of "race-norming" for the GATB is identical to the use of a bonus score in the Johnson study. It is reasonable to conclude that the Caucasian American applicants are hostile toward the African American applicants when they realize African Americans are given a bonus score to compensate for historic disadvantage. The mechanism of "race-norming" of the GATB serves to heighten racial tension. Since the GATB is a very popular hiring procedure, its effect on racial tension is probably widespread.

MYTH 2. THE PREFERENTIAL ADVANCEMENT OF SOME AFRICAN AMERICANS IMPROVES THE POPULAR RESPECT FOR ALL AFRICAN AMERICANS

Preferential advancement places African Americans in highly visible or politically powerful positions; some are television newscasters, others are federal commissioners. Affirmative action proponents believe that the general public reacts favorably to the appearance of African Americans in influential and high-status positions as a sign that talented African Americans are "making it" in the system.

The idea that affirmative action improves the reputation of African Americans is a myth. Affirmative action programs actually perpetuate doubt about the professional competence of African Americans in the workplace because Caucasian American workers are often left to wonder, Was he or she just another affirmative action hire?

The doubt and frustration of both Caucasian Americans and African Americans are exemplified by developments within the Chicago police force and the Detroit Symphony. Since 1973, the Chicago police force has followed an aggressive court-ordered hiring plan to increase the number of minorities in its ranks. The plan expanded minority and African American representation on the 12,004-member police force from 16 to 24 percent.[4]

Does the plan improve the reputation of African Americans? According to Roy V. Smith, an African American eighteen-year veteran of the Chicago police force, the affirmative action policy means frustration and doubt. Smith believes that the policy hinders his opportunities in the workplace. He feels that if he is promoted to sergeant, the achievement will be perceived as an affirmative action appointment and doubt will be cast on his abilities as a police officer. In fact, Smith is so adamant about the trappings of affirmative action that last fall he joined a reverse-discrimination suit against the city of Chicago bought by 313 police officers. Smith and the other police officers who filed the lawsuit believe that racial discrimination is now being practiced against Caucasian American police officers.[5]

In 1989, the Detroit Symphony, one of the leading orchestras in the United States, hired Richard Robinson, an African American bass player, without the formality of an audition. The decision to hire Robinson came as pressure was brought to bear by several Michigan state legislators to hire more African Americans in the symphony.

The initial reaction to Robinson's employment was positive. The chief executive officer of the American Symphony Orchestra League said, "The Detroit Symphony Orchestra is to be applauded." But the individual with the most serious reservations was Robinson. He appeared unsure of himself. He later commented, "I would have rather auditioned like everybody else. Somehow this [my appointment] devalues the audition and worth of every other player."[6]

The complaints continued to come from African Americans within the orchestral community. The African American assistant conductor of the Chicago Symphony, Michael Morgan, said, "Now, even when a black player is hired on the merits of his playing, he will always have the stigma that it was to appease some state legislator."[7] African American conductor James DePriest turned down the role as music director in Detroit. "It's impossible for me to go to Detroit because of the atmosphere," he said.[8] There was a perception that African Americans hired by the Detroit Symphony were "affirmative action hires."

The affirmative action policies of the Chicago police force and Detroit Symphony are counterproductive. The policies reinforce the common stereotype of African Americans held by many individuals in American society—that African Americans are not good enough to make it on their own ability.

MYTH 3. THE REWARDS OF AFFIRMATIVE ACTION ARE REAPED BY THE POOR MEMBERS OF THE AFRICAN AMERICAN COMMUNITY

Affirmative action proponents believe that affirmative action programs are designed to help the African Americans in poverty. In principle, the policy should reduce the number of African Americans in poverty by giving them a better chance in education and employment.

The principal beneficiaries of affirmative action, however, are not the poor but are, rather, the middle class. The following facts are examples of the ineffectiveness of affirmative action in dealing with problems of poverty. First, there are more African American males of college age in prison or on parole than in college. Second, fewer African Americans are in college today than ten years ago.[9] These developments have occurred with the machinery of affirmative action in place.

To the extent that middle-class African Americans benefit from affirmative action, the gap between poor and middle-class African Americans has *widened*. As Yale Law School professor Stephen Carter observes, "What has happened in black America in the era of affirmative action is this: middle-class black people are better off and lower-class black people are worse off. The most disadvantaged people are not in a position to benefit from preferential admission."[10]

Affirmative action succeeds in placing more African Americans in better positions and better schools but does not achieve the goal of greater social equity. Americans are being deflected from the real economic problems facing African Americans by the lure of quick-fix affirmative action programs. The focus needs to shift from affirmative action policies to policies that lift individuals out of poverty.

If affirmative action is not effective, then what is a good public policy? The most useful public policy is the two-phased approach advocated by Shelby Steele. First, an educational and economic development program is needed that would help all disadvantaged people, whether they are African American or Caucasian American. Second, racial discrimination needs to be eliminated through close monitoring and severe sanctions.[11] Affirmative action achieves neither of these goals and is not a successful public policy.

MYTH 4. AFFIRMATIVE ACTION PROGRAMS PROMOTE INDIVIDUAL RESPONSIBILITY BY PLACING AFRICAN AMERICANS IN JOBS AND SCHOOLS

Individual responsibility is the foundation of character building. Responsible people know that the quality of their lives is something they will have to define within the confines of their abilities. The quality of an individual's life reflects the quality of his or her efforts.[12]

Advocates of affirmative action assert that, with this policy, African Americans will develop a greater sense of personal responsibility than they had when racial discrimination was practiced in the United States. At first glance this assertion appears to be true. When African Americans faced severe discrimination, they invested less effort in developing skills and felt they were not responsible for their own advancement because of the obstacles they faced. Affirmative action similarly stifles the emergence of personal responsibility.

If, for example, an affirmative action policy is adopted that requires an employer to promote African American and Caucasian American workers at the same rate, the employer may believe the African American workers are less skillful because they require an affirmative action policy. Therefore, to comply with the affirmative action policy, the employer makes positions easier to attain for African American workers. African American workers, realizing they do not have to be as skilled as Caucasian American workers to achieve the same success, will have less incentive to enhance their productivity. If African Americans decide their advancement does not depend on their performance, they may choose to invest less in improving their abilities and skills than will Caucasian Americans.[13] Both discrimination and affirmative action, by relieving them of the responsibility for their own advancement, decrease the incentive of African Americans.

The solution to the problems of discrimination and affirmative action is shared responsibility. Caucasian Americans must be responsible for a free and fair society in which people are regarded because of ability rather than race, while African Americans must be responsible for taking charge of their own lives.

MYTH 5. MOST AMERICANS APPROVE OF AFFIRMATIVE ACTION

During the 1970s, the emergence of affirmative action legislation created a number of backlash effects. The most significant example of backlash was the transformation of traditional Democrats into Reagan voters during the 1980 presidential election. A study performed by Stanley Greenberg, a Democratic party pollster, indicates that a contributing factor in the defection of the Reagan Democrats was a distaste for African Americans spawned by affirmative action programs.

Greenberg performed this study in late 1985 for the Democratic party. Greenberg writes:

> The special status of African Americans (affirmative action) is perceived by almost all of these individuals (Reagan Democrats) as a serious obstacle to their personal advancement. Indeed, discrimination against Caucasian Americans has become a well-assimilated and ready explanation for their status, vulnerability and failures.[14]

The bitterness of these former Democratic party voters shows the central tragedy of affirmative action: these policies generally do more harm than good by inspiring backlash hatred toward the individuals who benefit from the policy.

The overwhelming distaste for affirmative action is reflected in a Gallup poll. While most Americans approved of the early civil rights movement, they oppose preferential treatment. The Gallup poll asked one question in several different ways. One was: "Some people say that to make up for past discrimination, women and minorities should be given preferential treatment in getting jobs and places in college. Others say that ability, as determined by test scores, should be the main consideration. Which point of view comes close to how you feel on the subject?" Every survey produced the same overwhelming result: 81–84 percent favored "ability," while 10–11 percent sided with "preferential treatment." Along racial lines the results were similar, with 56 percent of African Americans favoring "ability" and only 14 percent supporting "preferential treatment."[15]

When the question was presented somewhat differently, the result was the same: "Should we make every effort to improve the position of blacks and other minorities if it means giving them preferential treatment?" This question contains no mention of test scores, but still 71–72 percent opposed "preferential treatment," while 24 percent supported it. Again, the result generally held across racial lines, with 66 percent of African Americans opposing preference and only 32 percent favoring it.[16] The results of these two public opinion polls show a resounding rejection by the American people of the basic affirmative action principle of preferential treatment.

The issue of affirmative action and racial justice is exceedingly divisive. The solution to the problems of racial injustice is found by assuring equal rights for all and discrimination against none. This is the principle that civil rights leader Martin Luther King Jr. asserted most eloquently when he said, "I have a dream that my four little children will one day live in a nation where they will not be judged by the color of their skin but by the content of their character."[17] This color-blind ideal means, and racial justice demands, that people address one another in economic and social activities without reference to skin color. By its very nature, affirmative action moves us steadily away from King's worthy goal. Affirmative action violates the concept of discrimination against none and is inconsistent with the hope of achieving racial justice. The United States cannot believe in a discrimination-free society while public policy sets a precedent of racial discrimination.

NOTES

1. Fredrich R. Lynch, "Surviving Affirmative Action (More or Less)," *Commentary*, August 1990, pp. 44–47.

2. Peter A. Brown, "Normin' Stormin,'" *New Republic*, April 29, 1991, p. 12.

3. Ibid., p. 13.

4. Sylvester Monroe, "Does Affirmative Action Help or Hurt?" *Time*, May 27, 1991, p. 22.

5. Ibid.

6. Quoted in James Blanton, "A Limit to Affirmative Action?" *Commentary,* June 1989, pp. 28–32.

7. Quoted in *New York Times,* final ed., March 5, 1989, sec. A, p. 1, col. 1.

8. Ibid.

9. Ibid.

10. Stephen L. Carter, *Reflections of an Affirmative Action Baby* (New York: Basic Books, 1991), p. 121.

11. Shelby Steele, *Content of Our Character* (New York: St. Martin's Press, 1990), p. 124.

12. Ibid., p. 33.

13. Glenn C. Loury, "Incentive Effects of Affirmative Action," *Annals of the American Academy of Political and Social Science,* September 1992, p. 21.

14. Quoted in Thomas Byrne Edsall, "Race," *Atlantic Monthly,* May 1991, p. 56.

15. *Gallup Poll Monthly,* December 1989, p. 18.

16. Ibid.

17. Quoted in William Safire, *Lend Me Your Ears* (New York: W. W. Norton, 1992), p. 499.

Questions for Discussion

1. What criteria should be used in deciding which groups should be included in a category warranting affirmative action?
2. Do guidelines inevitably lead to quotas? What are the reasons for your answer?
3. What criteria should be used by a university admissions committee of a prestigious college or university in selecting students for admission? What is the relevance of your answer to the issue of affirmative action?
4. What effect does affirmative action have on the beneficiaries of affirmative action programs?
5. How would you recognize when affirmative action programs should be ended?

Suggested Readings

"Affirmative Action Revisited." *Annals of the American Academy of Political and Social Science,* 523 (September 1992), 1–120.

Cahn, Steven M., ed. *Affirmative Action and the University: A Philosophical Inquiry.* Philadelphia: Temple Univ. Press, 1993.

Carter, Stephen L. *Reflections of an Affirmative Action Baby.* New York: Basic Books, 1991.

Clayton, Susan D., and Faye J. Crosby. *Justice, Gender, and Affirmative Action.* Ann Arbor: Univ. of Michigan Press, 1992.

Cooper, Mary H. "Racial Quotas." *CQ Researcher,* 1, no. 2 (May 17, 1991), 277–300.

Ezorsky, Gertrude. *Racism and Justice: The Case for Affirmative Action.* Ithaca, N.Y.: Cornell Univ. Press, 1991.

Groarke, Leo. "Affirmative Action as a Form of Restitution." *Journal of Business Ethics*, 9, no. 3 (March 1990), 207–213.

Kinsley, Michael. "Class, Not Race." *Washington Post*, August 1, 1991, p. A15.

Lipset, Seymour Martin. "Affirmative Action and the American Creed." *Wilson Quarterly*, 16, no. 1 (Winter 1992), 52–62.

Lloyd, Mark. "Affirmative Action: Solution or Problem?" *Christian Science Monitor*, January 18, 1991, p. 19.

Lynch, Frederick R. "Race Unconsciousness and the White Male." *Society*, 29, no. 2 (January/February 1992), 30–35.

Nieli, Russell, ed. *Racial Preference and Racial Justice: The New Affirmative Action Controversy.* Washington, D.C.: Ethics and Public Policy Center, 1991.

Robinson, Robert K., Billie Morgan Allen, and Yohannan T. Abraham. "Affirmative Action Plans in the 1990s: A Double-Edged Sword?" *Public Personnel Management*, 21, no. 2 (Summer 1992), 261–272.

Scanlan, James P. "The Curious Case of Affirmative Action for Women." *Society*, 29, no. 2 (January/February 1992), 36–41.

Starr, Tama. "So Sue Me." *Washington Post*, April 11, 1993, pp. C1, C5.

Thernstrom, Abigail. "Affirmative Action: Solution or Problem?" *Christian Science Monitor*, January 18, 1991, p. 19.

Policy Making Institutions

A s indicated in Part I, the Framers of the Constitution established a system of separation of powers and checks and balances constituted in three branches of government—legislative, executive, and judicial. The Framers feared that the concentration of powers in the hands of one branch would be a danger to liberty.

The Constitution, as has so often been said, is a living document, and it has changed over time through formal constitutional amendment, statutes, political practices, and customs. In part because of the ambiguities in some provisions of the Constitution and in part because of historical developments, power has shifted in different eras from one branch to another.

Constitutional amendments have modified the major branches of government. For example, the Seventeenth Amendment, adopted in 1913, changed the method of choosing U.S. senators from election by the state legislatures, as provided in Article I of the Constitution, to direct popular election in each state. Statutes have also changed the Constitution. Congress passed numerous laws in the nineteenth and twentieth centuries establishing new departments and government agencies. When the Constitution was adopted, the role of government in society was minimal, but through statutes passed, particularly in this century, Congress has given executive agencies—the bureaucracy—vast powers in both domestic and foreign policy.

The formal constitutional actors in the U.S. political system have had their own impact on constitutional development. The Constitution says nothing about the power of judicial review, but the Supreme Court, under John Marshall, asserted that power in *Marbury* v. *Madison* in 1803. Today the power of judicial review is an accepted principle of the U.S. political system. The Constitution, moreover, says nothing about the organization of Congress into committees, but congressional committees today play important roles in the enactment of legislation.

Custom, too, influences the Constitution. George Washington left office at the end of his second term, and a two-term tradition was widely accepted over time until Franklin D. Roosevelt was elected to a third term in 1940 and a fourth term in 1944. Adopted in 1951, however, the Twenty-Second Amendment limited presidential terms to two, thus giving formal constitutional sanction to what had been a custom until Roosevelt's third term.

The power of the principal institutions of government depends, then, on a variety of factors. The Constitution and laws provide the basic structure and define the formal powers of the major actors in the political system. The relationship of policy makers over time, however, depends on the personalities of the policy makers, the ties between the president and influential members of Congress, the character of judicial decisions, the astuteness of top bureaucrats, and historical developments.

Part IV deals with some of the important issues about the power, role, and behavior of policy makers in the national government today. The debates consider the power of the president, the limitation of terms for members of Congress, the relationship between bureaucracy and democracy, the philosophy of the Supreme Court, and the character of questions that should be asked a Supreme Court nominee.

Chapter 12

Is the President Too Powerful in Foreign Policy?

In May 1987 a special committee of members of both the Senate and the House of Representatives opened hearings to investigate the actions of President Ronald Reagan, other members of the executive branch, and private citizens in secretly selling arms to Iran and in using the profits illegally to aid the Contras, a group of anticommunist fighters at war against the Sandinista government in Nicaragua. With massive media coverage, the committee investigated in detail the activities of the principal actors in what has come to be called the Iran-Contra affair.

Congressional investigations such as these into the conduct of foreign policy derive from specific authority granted in the Constitution as well as historical developments involving war and peace. The Constitution gives roles in foreign policy to *both* the president and the Congress. Article I of the Constitution grants Congress the powers to declare war; raise and support armies; provide and maintain a navy; make rules for the government and regulation of the land and naval forces; provide for calling forth the militia to execute the laws of the Union; and provide for organizing, arming, and disciplining the militia. Other provisions add to Congress's constitutional role. Such provisions include the Necessary and Proper Clause of Article I, Section 8, allowing Congress broad scope to carry out the powers specifically enumerated in the Constitution and its general constitutional powers of taxation and appropriation.

The Senate is given specific foreign policy powers. The ratification of a treaty requires approval by two-thirds of the senators present and voting. The Senate also has the power to confirm most presidential appointments.

The president's constitutional powers are set forth in Article II. That article gives the president executive power and designates the holder of that office as commander in chief of the armed forces. In addition, the president is given power to make appointments and to make treaties, "with the Advice and Consent of the Senate." The president's oath of office includes a statement that the president agrees to "preserve, protect, and defend the Constitution."

Inherent in the Constitution itself are conflicts between the legislative and executive branches of government. Some of the principal issues that have developed over time have involved the president's right to send military forces into combat situations without the consent of Congress, the use of executive agreements instead of treaties, and the reliance on covert operations by the president and members of the agencies involved in the conduct of foreign policy.

One of the most important reasons for the growth of executive power anywhere is the existence, or the imminent prospect, of war among nations or war within a nation. Executive power tends to increase during wartime, sometimes because the legislature grants the president emergency powers and sometimes because the executive takes action without asking for the approval of Congress.

At the outbreak of the Civil War, President Abraham Lincoln took steps that, according to the Constitution, were illegal. These included spending money that had not been appropriated by Congress and blockading southern ports. Lincoln expanded the powers of the president as commander in chief beyond the intent of the Framers of the Constitution. In 1940, President Franklin Roosevelt transferred fifty ships to Great Britain in return for the leasing of some British bases in the Atlantic—without congressional authorization to take such actions. He also ordered U.S. ships to "shoot on sight" any foreign submarine in waters that he regarded were essential for the nation's defense. In giving such an order, he was making war between the United States and Germany more likely.

Since the end of World War II, the United States has become a principal actor in world politics—a status in the international community that will be discussed at greater length in Part V. Here it is only essential to state that as a major world power, the United States has had to concern itself with global security issues in a manner unprecedented in its history.

The permanent emphasis of foreign and national security considerations has plagued executive-legislative relations since 1945. President Harry Truman sent U.S. troops to Korea without a formal declaration of war. President Dwight Eisenhower approved actions by the Central Intelligence Agency (CIA) to help bring down one government in Guatemala and put the shah in power in Iran. John Kennedy authorized the CIA to assist a military operation planned by Cuban exiles against a communist regime in Cuba—an operation that turned out to be a foreign policy disaster for the young president. He also increased the number of military advisers to Vietnam from several hundred to about seventeen thousand.

The actions of Presidents Lyndon Johnson and Richard Nixon in the war in Indochina sparked an increasing involvement by Congress in the conduct of foreign policy. Johnson raised the number of U.S. troops to five hundred thousand. Nixon engaged in a "secret" air war in Cambodia in 1969 and sent U.S. troops into that country in 1970.

The 1970s were marked by massive congressional involvement in the conduct of foreign policy. In 1971 Congress adopted legislation forbidding the expenditures of funds to carry on the war in Cambodia. Overriding a veto by President Nixon, it passed a War Powers Act (1973) sharply limiting the president's ability to send troops. Under the act the president has the power on his own authority to send U.S. armed forces into an area for a period of sixty days but then must get the approval of Congress or terminate the use of armed forces. The president is also required to consult with Congress, if possible, before military intervention is ordered.

Every president since Nixon has taken the position that the War Powers Act is unconstitutional because a statute cannot take away powers that are traditionally the preserve of presidents in the conduct of foreign policy. But every president has complied with its provisions. If and when a time comes in which a president refuses to comply with the law, the Supreme Court will decide on the constitutionality of the act.

Throughout the 1970s Congress continued to impose restrictions on executive actions in the conduct of foreign policy. To restrict some arms transfers, Congress used the legislative veto, which under certain conditions allowed either one or both chambers to cancel a proposed executive action. (The legislative veto, which had originated under Herbert Hoover in 1932 and had been applied to both domestic and foreign policy matters, was struck down as unconstitutional by the Supreme Court in 1983.)

Congress took steps to limit the actions of the president in areas other than arms transfers. In 1973 and 1974 it linked improved trade status of the Soviet Union in its dealings with the United States to a liberalization of Soviet emigration practices. The Senate failed to approve the Strategic Arms Limitation Treaty, known as SALT II, in 1979 and 1980, so President Jimmy Carter withdrew the treaty from the Senate's consideration. In an attempt to undermine President Reagan's policy in Nicaragua, Congress adopted the Boland Amendments restricting aid to the Contras in a variety of ways from 1983 to 1985. In 1986, however, Congress authorized a resumption of aid to the Contras, but stipulated that it could not be used to purchase weapons or other military equipment. In 1987, Congress approved assistance to the Contras with few restrictions, and, consequently, the U.S. government was permitted to supply the Contras with weapons and other military equipment. But the Boland Amendments had been directly responsible for the most important crisis of the Reagan administration's second term—the Iran-Contra affair—an intensive investigation of the executive branch by both Congress and the media.

Neither the administration of President George Bush nor that of Bill Clinton featured the kinds of executive-legislative clashes on foreign policy that characterized the Reagan presidency. President Bush sought the approval of Congress under the War Powers Act for the commitment of U.S. forces in the Persian Gulf. President Clinton had the support of Congress in continuing and ending U.S. peacekeeping efforts in Somalia. Nevertheless, the history of the president in foreign policy suggests that clashes about power are likely to resume when there are strong differences over the desirability of using U.S. forces abroad.

Is the president too powerful in foreign policy? Political scientist Daniel P. Franklin argues the affirmative. He contends

1. Presidential power in the conduct of foreign policy is often in conflict with democratic processes of popular consent, popular control, and freedom of speech and of the press.
2. Because presidents often operate beyond the control of the other

branches of government, there is a tendency in the Executive Office for presidents and their advisers to conduct foreign policy through illegal means.

Political scientist Ryan J. Barilleaux argues the negative. He advances seven propositions designed to clarify the nature of presidential power in foreign affairs:

1. The United States needs a strong president for foreign affairs.
2. Presidential power, while substantial, is constrained by the Constitution, law, and public opinion.
3. Abuses of presidential power in foreign affairs are doomed to fail.
4. There is very little that a president can do in foreign affairs without congressional acquiescence or approval.
5. Attempts to inhibit presidential power through mechanical "solutions" are self-defeating.
6. The current level of presidential power in foreign affairs, however imperfect, is about the best that can reasonably be expected.
7. Realistic reforms that would not upset the basic structure of the U.S. government could help improve the situation.

Is the President Too Powerful in Foreign Policy?

DANIEL P. FRANKLIN

The President Is Too Powerful in Foreign Affairs

In the nuclear age, presiding over the government of a superpower state, the president is in a position to determine not only the fate of our nation but, in some sense, the fate of the world. That sort of responsibility is much too important to be left to the haphazard, incoherent process of foreign policy decision making in the presidency that has become common since the end of World War II. Specifically, the presidency in its conduct of foreign affairs suffers from the absence of adequate democratic control. Democratic control is essential in the making of foreign policy not only because it is "right" in the philosophical sense, but because it is more likely to succeed.

The assertion that the president has too much power in foreign policy making involves two separate but related arguments. First, in the liberal democratic sense, the president is too powerful. The president exercises too much responsibility in foreign affairs without having to account to Congress or directly to the public and the press. Accordingly, presidents are too powerful because their actions violate the separation of powers doctrine.[1]

Second, because presidents often operate beyond the control of the other branches of government, there is a tendency in the Executive Office for presidents and their advisers to conduct foreign policy through illegal means. The Iran-Contra affair, in which the "Reagan White House" (President Ronald Reagan has always denied his direct involvement) delivered arms to Iran and funds to rebels fighting to topple a left-wing government in Nicaragua in direct contravention of the law, is simply one in a succession of scandals in the modern presidency that involve violations of the law in the pursuit of national security goals.[2]

To be fair, this lack of democratic control in foreign policy making is not merely the consequence of the unrestrained ambitions of unscrupulous presidents. Rather, three general factors account for this lack of control. First, the nature of modern warfare, airpower, and nuclear weapons dictate that the president be able to act quickly and without restraint in real emergencies. Second, because of its parochial orientation, Congress does not always display a great deal of initiative or oversight in the conduct of foreign affairs. This is particularly the case in the review of covert intelligence operations and the use of force. After all, there is little electoral benefit to be gained for the member of Congress who is actively involved in all but a few foreign policy issues (two exceptions to this rule are in the consideration of foreign trade legislation and foreign aid appropriations). Finally, a tradition has developed, based on precedent, that legitimizes an expanded role for the modern presidency in foreign affairs. The courts, for their part, have either declined to intervene in preventing the expansion of presidential power in foreign policy or actively supported presidential claims in this regard. Thus the loss of democratic control has been a gradual process in which the ambitions of individual presidents have played only a partial role.

THE PROBLEM OF DEMOCRATIC CONTROL

Most analysts agree that a democracy is a system of government characterized by the "rule of the people." Beyond this simple definition, however, there is tremendous disagreement about the other requisites of a democratic government. In fact, there is a broad variation in the structures of democratic regimes, but certain unifying characteristics seem to be common to all democracies. These basic conditions are popular consent, popular control, and freedom of speech and of the press. It is essential that all of these conditions be present, at the same time, for a democracy to maintain its viability. In its conduct of foreign policy, however, the presidency does not always satisfy these conditions necessary for democratic control.

Popular Consent

Popular consent in a democracy is maintained through uncoerced participation. To the extent that the president is popularly, freely elected, the presidency is subject to popular consent. In the realm of foreign policy, however, where much of the decision making in the postwar era is carried out by the president's staff who are subject to neither the will of Congress nor the restraints of the professional bureaucracy, popular consent is limited. Activist, experienced presidents (Dwight Eisenhower, for example) are able to control rather than be controlled by their own foreign policy staffs. However, since there is no prior experience quite like the presidency, individuals chosen to serve as president are likely to have limited experience (and, perhaps, limited interest) in the conduct of foreign affairs as commander in chief. Consequently, in the administration of a president who is relatively inexperienced (as was John Kennedy at the time of the Bay of Pigs invasion, Jimmy Carter during the Iran hostage crisis, and Ronald Reagan during the Iran–Contra affair), foreign policy decision making authority, by default, falls on the shoulders of the president's unelected staff. This situation is not only a violation of the notion of popular consent; it is a dangerous way to make policy.

As noted presidential scholar Thomas Cronin argues, "Perhaps the most disturbing aspect of the expansion of the presidential establishment is that it has become a powerful inner sanctum of government, isolated from traditional, constitutional checks and balances."[3] For presidents, there are very real problems associated with depending too heavily on their own staffs for foreign policy expertise. Specifically, a president may become isolated in the White House from the rest of the policy-making community.[4] For example, even though President Lyndon Johnson was an active manager of his own Vietnam policy, he was also isolated from dissenting views because staffers were either deferential to the president, in agreement with the president, or excluded because of their dissenting views.[5] This kind of decision-making arrangement calls into question the wisdom of making foreign policy in the White House without including, whenever possible, presidential consultation with officials and individuals from outside the Executive Office.

Popular Control

"Popular control" means that there must be some relationship in a democracy between what the public wants and what the government does. For the most part, popular control is maintained through periodic elections. Politicians will try to anticipate the desires of voters in their quest for reelection. In that sense, the president is subject to popular control. This control, however, has eroded. For one thing, pursuant to the Twenty-Second Amendment, which limits presidential terms, the president cannot run for a third term and thus is a "lame duck" after reelection.

There is, in addition, a more subtle violation of the principle of popular control associated with presidential foreign policy making. The public is generally poorly informed and uninvolved in foreign affairs. There are, of course, exceptions to this rule. Certain ethnic and interest groups do have an intense interest; Jews, for instance, are often very concerned about U.S. policy toward Israel, as are American automobile manufacturers and labor unions about the U.S. relationship with Japan. In the main, however, elected officials have very little popular guidance in these matters. In fact, the flow of influence tends to be in the other direction; public officials, and particularly the president, have a tremendous impact on public opinion in regard to foreign affairs. This influence gives the president a great deal of leeway in foreign policy making. However, just because the public may have no *opinion* on foreign affairs does not mean that the public has no *stake* in foreign affairs. Thus, in the conduct of foreign policy decision making it is incumbent upon public officials to seek out the public interest rather than strike out on their own. Freedom of action is not an unrestricted license for a public official in a democracy. Since there is really no such thing as a "unified" public interest but only an amalgam of many points of view, representation of the public interest entails the inclusion of actors from outside the presidency in the decision-making process (including members of Congress). Yet, this type of extensive consultation rarely occurs. Foreign policy decision making in the Executive Office can be, and often is, carried out largely by fiat, even including those decisions that do not involve any time constraints. This pattern is an overall derogation of popular control over foreign policy decision making.

Freedom of Speech and the Press

Finally, freedom of speech and of the press is an essential component of any democratic system. After all, public participation from a position of ignorance cannot really be considered democratic participation at all. However, behind the twin veils of "executive privilege"[6] and "national security," the president has managed to arrogate the flow of information regarding national security affairs. It is not that the press cannot print or the Congress cannot investigate foreign policy activities of the presidency; the problem is that in dealing with the obstacle of government secrecy, Congress and the press may not know which questions to ask or what information to request. As the House Foreign Affairs Committee once noted,

> Congress has repeatedly experienced difficulty in getting sufficient, accurate, and timely information. This was demonstrated in the Dominican Republic intervention in 1965, the *Mayaguez* incident in 1975, and the Iranian hostage rescue attempt in 1980, to name only a few examples. Having little information beyond that available in the media, Members of Congress enter discussions with executive branch officials on an unequal footing.[7]

President George Bush, in the manner of this tradition, did not consult with congressional leaders in advance of his decision to invade Panama in 1989, dispatch U.S. forces to the Persian Gulf in 1990, and send troops to Somalia as part of a United Nations relief effort in 1992.

Ostensibly, this barrier of secrecy is intended to protect the nation's security—to keep our enemies from sharing our most sensitive intelligence. While it is true that certain information must be protected, the classification of information for security purposes may have gone well beyond the limits of what is acceptable and necessary in a viable democracy. As one frustrated (anonymous) member of Congress stated, "The actions of the United States are not secret to other nations, only to Congress and the American people."[8] As this comment implies, much of what passes for classified information is labeled secret not because it should not be or is not known by our adversaries, but because that information is embarrassing to the administration and is not and should not be known (from the administration's perspective) by the people and the Congress of the United States.

White House officials will argue that this secrecy is necessary because Congress is incapable of protecting sensitive information. However, in the aftermath of a series of revelations concerning misconduct by the Central Intelligence Agency (CIA) in the 1970s, Congress set up an intelligence review structure that is designed specifically to prevent leaks. Intelligence committee staffs are screened and given security clearances, committee meeting rooms are "bug proofed," and access to sensitive information reported to the committees is restricted. Besides, members of Congress have plenty of options other than leaking information to the press when they object to a particular intelligence operation. Members can use their leverage with the president, who has, after all, an entire program to pass on the Hill. In any event, it is probably the case that most leaks originate in the permanent bureaucracy or in the Executive Office itself. Nevertheless, despite these congressional precautions and despite the legal requirement that the president "fully inform the intelligence committees in a timely fashion of intelligence operations in foreign countries,"[9] President Bush reiterated the Reagan administration view that "the 'timely fashion' language [of the law] should be read to leave the President with virtually unfettered discretion to choose the right moment for making the required notification."[10]

In the absence of at least a congressional review, the executive's penchant for secrecy violates the third minimum standard for democratic control. How can the voters, or their representatives, pass judgment on presidential actions they know nothing about?

CONSEQUENCES OF THE LOSS OF CONTROL

Since the earliest days of the Republic, the role and implications of a relatively unfettered executive branch have been debated. In 1795 Alexander Hamilton and James Madison engaged in a spirited public exchange over the foreign policy powers of the president. President George Washington had proclaimed

U.S. neutrality in a conflict between Britain and France. Hamilton defended the president's action arguing, in part, that the executive powers of the president pursuant to Article II of the Constitution were "subject only to the exceptions and qualifications which are expressed in the instrument." Consequently, Hamilton argued, short of a declaration of war or some other action specifically authorized by Congress pursuant to its constitutional authorities, the president set the U.S. agenda in foreign affairs. For his part, Madison responded by warning that to allow the president to set the policy agenda without consulting Congress would impose on Congress an "obligation" that would constitute a violation of the legislative function. In other words, by acting without the participation of Congress, the president would by his actions present Congress a *fait accompli*.[11] For example, President Bush's penchant for unilateral intervention abroad in effect presented Congress with a bill for the cost of the deployment plus the obligation to provide support for the consequences of intervention—the rebuilding of Panama, Kuwait, and Somalia.

While Hamilton's broad interpretation of the president's foreign policy authority has come to dominate, we would be well advised to heed Madison's warning. This disregard of the necessity of democratic control has very real consequences for the viability of policy execution. The strength of a democracy is in the public sense of involvement created by popular participation. A true democratic government is not only representative of the public, it *is* the public. Therefore, when a democratic regime makes a ruling or imposes a restriction, that policy is representative of the "general will" and is, for the public, a self-imposed restraint or obligation. In the absence of meaningful participation, the public feels no compulsion (nor is it morally bound) to live up to its legal obligations.[12]

For one thing, if the public and its representatives do not get a sense that they are being consulted in matters of foreign affairs, support for administration policies will be "shallow." Pollsters have identified the so-called rally-around-the-flag effect, or the tendency of the public to support the bold foreign policy moves of a president in the short term but not in the long term.[13] Political commentators interpret this effect to mean that the public does not have the "stomach" (anymore) for foreign involvement.[14] But what if this obvious distaste for interventionism is more a function of the feeling the public gets in a nondemocratic state that it has no investment (except for tax dollars, of course) in decisions made: no public involvement, no public support? If this is the case, this lack of public commitment robs us, as a democracy, of one of our primary sources of power—popular mobilization. The leader of a democratic state can count on popular support of a kind that can tap a nation's strength in no other comparable way. With public support we fought the Second World War, helped rebuild Western Europe, defended South Korea, and sustained a war effort in Vietnam for more than a decade. These examples are evidence of a tremendous public tolerance for the sacrifice associated with interventionism. The people of the United States had, and have, "what it takes" to support a superpower foreign policy.

At the same time, the administration that operates beyond democratic control will often behave with a certain arrogance. This "arrogance of power" is the tendency of unrestrained leaders "to equate power with virtue and major responsibilities with a universal mission."[15] In other words, the presidency that is beyond democratic control not only has the latitude to go beyond constitutional constraints; it has a mistaken sense of virtue in doing so. Corruption is a consequence of a lack of democratic control. It is not that all presidents are corrupt, but that an institution that is beyond control will at some point be corrupted.[16] In that event, citizens are viewed contemptuously by their leaders as "subjects" rather than as equals and participants. The administration that trades in arms in direct contravention to the law, as did the Reagan administration, is an administration that holds the public and its representatives in contempt. Only a president who agrees to and, indeed, is obliged to consult with the public's representatives from outside the Executive Office will overcome the arrogance of power.

IMPLEMENTATION

To say that we need to impose a democratic structure on foreign policy decision making is not to say that we should run our foreign policy by plebiscite. The vast majority of voters are neither interested nor qualified enough to be involved with governmental decision making on a day-to-day basis. Rather, through our representatives, we can have a participatory foreign policy without having a plebiscitary one. In a representative democracy, voters designate elected officials who, as part of their job responsibility, develop an expertise in public affairs. Thus, while it is impractical to involve the general public in routine or emergency foreign policy making, there are plenty of foreign policy specialists on Capitol Hill who represent a component of the public interest and who can be tapped by the Executive Office. For example, as of 1993 Claiborne Pell (chair of the Senate Foreign Relations Committee) and Lee Hamilton (chair of the House Foreign Affairs Committee) had served in Congress and specialized in foreign affairs for a combined total of sixty-two years! There is no reason to believe that there is a monopoly of foreign policy expertise at the White House. Furthermore, not only does the president sacrifice policy expertise when members of Congress are excluded; the president also loses the political expertise and the opinions of actors who are not presidential sycophants. Members of Congress, even from the president's own party (had they been consulted), would have flagged President Reagan's decision to approve an arms-for-hostage trade with Iran.

No one is going to argue that the president should be required to consult Congress (or other outsiders) in every situation. Sometimes there are circumstantial barriers (the principals may be out of town) or time constraints. After all, the president may have as little as ten or fifteen minutes to respond to a "bolt-out-of-the-blue" nuclear attack. No one expects the president confronted with this situation to convene and consult with Congress or even to call congressional leaders. However, these situations are so rare or unlikely as to be virtually nonexistent. The "time constraint" argument is more often used as an excuse to avoid congressional involvement or consultation *while* the decision is being made. Congress is thoroughly capable of acting quickly when the need arises. Congressional leaders can be summoned to the White House at a moment's notice. And, if in the course of being consulted, congressional leaders disagree with the president's proposals, perhaps the commander in chief would be well advised to listen seriously to and consider their objections.

Neither reform nor any amount of democratic involvement in foreign policy decision making is going to guarantee success. Mistakes will be made, the difference being that the responsibility for mistakes in a democracy is shared. In 1983, when President Reagan (under duress) negotiated an agreement with Congress to authorize the deployment of peacekeeping troops in Lebanon, the president took one of the most fateful steps of his administration. The subsequent deaths of 241 Marines in their Beirut barracks led not only to a shared sense of national grief but a shared sense of responsibility among decision makers in Washington. In contemplating an expanded role for the U.S. military in Somalia, Bosnia, and future crises, President Bill Clinton would be well advised to seek, in advance, the counsel of congressional leaders. Not only would he gain the benefit of their advice; he would likely benefit from their long-term support.

Presidential consultation is not only right; it is responsible. If a democratic government is to be a responsible government, no political leader should have the right to control, nor bear the sole responsibility of controlling, the fate of the nation. Such exclusive conduct of policy making is not only wrong in the philosophical sense; it is unlikely to succeed.

NOTES

1. The separation of powers doctrine was the Framers' way of preventing tyranny. By ensuring the separateness of the different branches of government, the Framers hoped that no one interest or individual could come to dominate the entire decision-making process. The Framers recognized that the delay and conflict associated with the separation of powers were a necessary price to pay in preventing corruption. In particular, see John Jay, Alexander Hamilton, and James Madison, *The Federalist Papers,* ed. Clinton Rossiter (New York: New American Library, 1961), nos. 10, 48.

2. Other obvious examples include the secret bombing of Cambodia and White House–authorized covert activities of the Central Intelligence Agency (CIA) both inside and outside the United States, including CIA participation in the break-in at Daniel Ellsberg's psychiatrist's office during the Nixon administration. Ellsberg was a Department of Defense official who leaked the contents of a secret report about the Vietnam War to the *Washington Post* and the *New York Times.*

3. Thomas Cronin, "The Swelling of the Presidency," in *Classic Readings in American Politics,* ed. Pietro S. Nivola and David H. Rosenbloom (New York: St. Martin's Press, 1986), p. 415.

4. For a discussion of the detrimental consequences of presidential isolation, see Irving L. Janis, *Groupthink: Psychological Studies of Policy Decisions and Fiascoes,* 2d ed. (Boston: Houghton Mifflin, 1982).

5. For an excellent account of Vietnam War policy making in the Johnson White House, see James G. Thompson, "How Could Vietnam Happen? An Autopsy," *Atlantic Monthly,* 221, no. 4 (April 1968), 47–53.

6. Executive privilege is the principle, upheld by the courts, that permits presidents and their staffs to withhold certain information regarding national security matters (and other administrative responsibilities) from Congress. The limits of executive privilege are not well defined (criminal investigations are exempt), and presidents tend to be broad in their definition of what sort of information can be withheld. See Chief Justice Warren Burger's decision in *United States* v. *Nixon,* 418 U.S. 683 (1974).

7. U.S. Congress, House of Representatives, Foreign Affairs Committee, *Strengthening Executive–Legislative Consultation on Foreign Policy,* Congress and Foreign Policy Series, no. 8 (October 1983), p. 65.

8. Quoted in *Congressional Quarterly Weekly Report,* 34, no. 46 (November 13, 1976), p. 3170, and in Charles W. Kegley and Eugene R. Wittkopf, *American Foreign Policy: Pattern and Process,* 2d ed. (New York: St. Martin's Press, 1982), p. 412.

9. National Security Act, as amended, Section 501 (b).

10. President George Bush to Senator David L. Boren, chair of the Senate Select Committee on Intelligence, October 30, 1989. A copy of this letter was made available to the author. As of this writing, the Clinton administration has yet to take a position on this issue.

11. See the "Pacificus-Helvidius [Hamilton-Madison] Debates on the Nature of the Foreign Relations Power 1793," reprinted from the *Gazette of the United States,* June 29, 1793, in Jean E. Smith, *The Constitution and American Foreign Policy* (St. Paul: West Publishing Co., 1989), pp. 49–58.

12. For a classic discussion of this justification for democracy, see Jean-Jacques Rousseau, *The Social Contract,* trans. Richard W. Crosby (Brunswick, Ohio: King's Court Press, 1978). (The book was originally published in 1762.) Rousseau ultimately came to the conclusion that a direct democracy was the only appropriate structure for a democratic state. The French Revolution and its aftermath eventually discredited Rousseau's view of democratic structure but did not necessarily discredit his overall moral and practical justifications for democracy in some form.

13. Jong R. Lee, "Rallying around the Flag: Foreign Policy Events and Presidential Popularity," *Presidential Studies Quarterly,* 7, no. 4 (Fall 1977), 252–256.

14. Charles Krauthammer, "Divided Superpower: The Real Cause of the North Affairs," *New Republic,* 195, no. 25 (December 22, 1986), 14–17.

15. The statement from which this definition is adapted is J. William Fulbright, *The Arrogance of Power* (New York: Random House, 1966), p. 9. Fulbright is former chair of the Senate Foreign Relations Committee.

16. This is precisely the point Madison was trying to make in *Federalist,* no. 47, when he argued, "The accumulation of all powers, legislative, executive, and judiciary, in the same hands, whether of one, a few, or many, and whether hereditary, self-appointed, or elective, may justly be pronounced the very definition of tyranny." *Federalist Papers,* p. 301.

 ☑ *NO*

Is the President Too Powerful in Foreign Policy?

RYAN J. BARILLEAUX

Understanding the Realities of Presidential Power

The presidency has long been plagued by the question of whether it endows a single official with too much power. Before the office was created, many of the nation's political leaders feared the rule of a king and wanted to ensure that the chief executive of the United States could never become one. Their descendants criticized presidential power in the succeeding generations of U.S. history, from "King" Andrew Jackson to the "imperial" presidencies of Lyndon Johnson and Richard Nixon. Today, in an age of nuclear weapons and guerrilla war, there is even more concern about the possible excesses of executive power.

Is the president too powerful? The question is not merely a rhetorical one, because it reflects a long-standing U.S. fear of tyrants. Americans want a government that is strong, but not one so strong as to threaten liberties and the lives of citizens.

With regard to the presidency, the question essentially comes down to the issue of the president's powers in foreign affairs. Scholars have noted a distinction between presidential power in foreign affairs and domestic matters, with the former considerably outweighing the latter in its impact on the U.S. political system. As Aaron Wildavsky puts it: "The United States has one President, but it has two presidencies. . . . Presidents have had much greater success in controlling the nation's defense and foreign policies than in dominating its domestic policies."[1] In domestic policy presidential power is understood to be "the power to persuade," because the president must convince Congress, the public, interest groups, and others to accept his policies. His actual ability to command is limited.

In foreign policy, however, the situation is different. The president has much greater ability to shape policy on his own: he is commander in chief of the armed forces, controller of all diplomacy, keeper of nuclear weapons, and leader of the world's only superpower. He decides when and on what terms the United States will negotiate with foreign nations. He controls the military might of the nation, even to the use of force in emergency situations. He can recognize foreign governments or refuse to do so. He alone speaks for the nation in world affairs and often speaks on behalf of all democracies. The president's prerogative power in foreign affairs—that is, power to choose on his own—is extensive.

But is it too great? Many critics believe so. They argue that the president is far too powerful for his or the nation's good, because he can launch an invasion or start World War III on his own. Consequently, the nation finds itself caught in an endless series of military encounters—wars in Indochina in the 1960s and early 1970s, the invasion of Grenada in 1983, the toppling of Manuel Noriega's dictatorship in Panama in 1989, the dispatch of American forces to Somalia in 1992 and to Macedonia in 1993. The nation, moreover, finds that its leaders have engaged in embarrassing political intrigues, such as what has come to be known as the Iran–Contra affair—the events in 1985 and 1986 involving the sale of U.S. armaments to Iran in exchange for the release of U.S. citizens held captive in Lebanon and the illegal U.S. government funding of Nicaraguan rebel forces, known as Contras, who were resisting the Marxist Sandinista government in Nicaragua. All of these events, critics contend, add up to a presidency out of control.

These charges about excessive presidential power are wrong. Of course, there are legitimate grounds for criticism of presidential foreign policy conduct. There have been excesses committed by presidents, and room for reasonable reforms certainly exists. But it is too much to say that the president is too powerful in foreign affairs. What happens is that critics see certain problems and generalize them into flaws in the basic nature of the presidency. They fail to understand the realities of presidential power.

A better understanding of presidential power is exactly what we need. To provide it, this article advances seven propositions designed to clarify the nature of presidential power in foreign affairs.

1. THE UNITED STATES NEEDS A STRONG PRESIDENT FOR FOREIGN AFFAIRS

Alexander Hamilton noted government's need for a strong executive, particularly for the conduct of foreign policy. In his famous phrasing, Hamilton declared that "energy in the executive is a leading character in the definition of good government." He pointed to the virtues of "unity, secrecy, and dispatch" that executives embody, all of which are necessary in the international arena.[2] The speed with which international events move, in a world of nearly two hundred nations and a growing list of nuclear powers, demands decisiveness and action such as is beyond the reach of a legislative body. Without a strong president, the United States would soon be forced to isolate itself from the world or sit by while events overwhelmed us.

To that extent, the president's foreign policy power cannot be measured against some ideal of an unaggressive and "tame" executive. Rather, any charge of too much presidential power can be made only if his powers far exceed the rather great strength that the president needs to act at all in the world arena.

2. PRESIDENTIAL POWER, WHILE SUBSTANTIAL, IS CONSTRAINED BY THE CONSTITUTION, LAW, AND PUBLIC OPINION

Even as great as it must be, the president's foreign policy power is not unlimited. Chief executives are always mindful of the limits on their powers. Indeed, President Lyndon Johnson once complained that he had only one real power (i.e., to launch a nuclear attack), and it was one that he could not use.

How is the president limited? First, the Constitution sets a number of conditions under which he can conduct foreign affairs. Presidential appointments, whether to the position of secretary of defense or ambassadorships, require Senate confirmation. Thus the Senate is able to impose limits, albeit broad ones, on the kinds of individuals it will accept for office. For example, the Senate denied President George Bush his first choice for the job of secretary of defense, John Tower, because many senators had doubts about Tower's personal character and fitness for the post. All treaties require Senate approval, and all money spent by the president, whether on weapons or foreign aid, must be appropriated by Congress. Congress also regulates the size of the armed forces and the number and kinds of weapons in the U.S. arsenal. President Bill Clinton's plan to drop the ban on gays in the U.S. military met considerable opposition on Capitol Hill, and in the end the commander in chief was forced to compromise with his critics. In short, the president must play by the rules, and the rules already include extensive congressional participation in the foreign policy process.

Second, Congress has created a number of laws that further restrict the president. The Case Act (named for Senator Clifford Case of New Jersey) (1972), for example, requires the president to inform Congress of all agreements other than treaties that he makes with foreign nations.[3] Congress can and does limit the purposes for which money may be spent, such as prohibiting a president to use federal funds to conduct a war in Southeast Asia.[4] The president must notify Congress of any use of U.S. forces in hostile situations and receive congressional approval for maintaining them in conflict for more than sixty days.[5] The president has extensive power of initiative in international affairs but limited power of fulfillment.

Third, a further constraint on the president is public opinion. Even when the president has unilateral power and/or the approval of Congress, public disapproval may cause him to reconsider his actions. Sensing a strong public antipathy to Vietnam-type conflicts, chief executives since the mid-1970s have been reluctant to engage the nation in any military actions that cannot be resolved quickly and with few American lives lost. While President Bush was able to win broad support for his decisive war against Iraq in 1991, that policy had clear limits and an obvious goal. In contrast, public opinion certainly did not pressure President Clinton to intervene in the complex war in Bosnia in 1993. White House caution was reinforced by public reluctance to become mired in a "Vietnam in the Balkans."

What this all means is that in reality presidential power in foreign affairs is more limited than it appears to be. It is not the unrestrained power that critics often suggest but is an extension of the "power to persuade" that is recognized in domestic matters. The difference between foreign and domestic policy is that Congress and the American people are willing to grant the president more latitude abroad than they do at home.

3. ABUSES OF PRESIDENTIAL POWER IN FOREIGN AFFAIRS ARE DOOMED TO FAIL

Critics of presidential power usually focus their attention on various real or alleged abuses of power by chief executives: Vietnam, the Iran-Contra affair, and so forth. Their argument is that abuses prove the disproportionate power of the president and warrant greater restraints on the chief executive. In other words, what these critics are saying is that it is better to have a president who is too weak than to risk abuses of power.

The problem with this argument is that it is both unrealistic and incorrect. It is unrealistic because there is no way to design political institutions that cannot be abused, and efforts to do so will probably only make things worse. Restraining presidential power to the degree necessary to prevent any abuse will yield an executive incapable of the kind of "unity, secrecy, and dispatch" that the nation needs. The nation must live with the risk of abuse and be vigilant against it.

Moreover, the argument is incorrect. Abuses of presidential foreign policy power are ultimately doomed to fail. Because the government of the United States is one of separate institutions sharing power, Congress can investigate abuses such as the Iran-Contra affair. Because the government historically has been unable to keep most things secret, problems such as Iran-Contra do not survive for long. The only "abuses" of presidential power that continue for any time are those, like the Vietnam War, in which Congress allows the president to act unilaterally.

There is no way to make the government foolproof against abuses and still maintain effective government. Perhaps that means that the United States will swing back and forth between too much presidential autonomy in foreign affairs and too little, but the alternative is a consistently weak executive.

4. THERE IS VERY LITTLE THAT A PRESIDENT CAN DO IN FOREIGN AFFAIRS WITHOUT CONGRESSIONAL ACQUIESCENCE OR APPROVAL

This point is even more important than the last for understanding the realities of presidential power. In truth, the president's power in foreign affairs is that of initiation and persuasion: the president initiates actions, negotiations, diplomacy, policy changes, and commitments; then he attempts to persuade Congress to go along with him. Extended presidential war making, as in Vietnam and Korea, depends on congressional acquiescence. So do treaties, national commitments, defense expenditures, foreign aid, and all other significant foreign policy decisions.

This point does not mean that the president is weak but that many of the so-called abuses of presidential power in foreign affairs occurred with the full knowledge of Congress. For example, for six years the United States observed the nuclear arms limitation provisions it had concluded with the Soviet Union in a proposed Strategic Arms Limitation Treaty (SALT II) of 1979. It took action despite the absence of Senate approval of the agreement and in apparent violation of U.S. law, because Congress was tacitly willing to let the president do so.[6] Moreover, although the president can commit U.S. forces to hostile situations for a short time, as in bombing Libya or invading Grenada, he must inform Congress of what he is doing and obtain its approval of any extended actions. Thus presidents are careful about the kinds of situations in which they place themselves, for they will need Congress's support and the public's as well.

So, while the president has the upper hand in foreign policy making, he does not have absolute power. If Congress acquiesces in presidential actions or commitments, then the problem does not lie in the executive alone.

5. ATTEMPTS TO INHIBIT PRESIDENTIAL POWER THROUGH MECHANICAL "SOLUTIONS" ARE SELF-DEFEATING

Despite the fact that many presidential "abuses" of power occur with the acquiescence or even approval of Congress, the legislature occasionally objects to such actions and tries to prevent future problems by creating mechanical "solutions." The best example of this approach is the War Powers Act (1973), which creates a set of deadlines and requirements for the president to follow. The purpose of the resolution is to prevent a long-term, Vietnam-type commitment of U.S. forces without Congress's approval. But the War Powers Act has not solved the problem as intended. It has made presidents more careful about the use of force, but it has not produced a situation of legislative control over executive assertiveness in the use of force.[7]

The point here is that Congress, if it wants to restrain presidential power in foreign affairs, cannot do so by developing these mechanical "solutions." When it relies on such devices, it becomes complacent about controlling executive power or it impairs the president's ability to act effectively. If Congress wants to maintain an active role in foreign policy, it can do so only by aggressively pursuing its traditional rights, powers, and responsibilities in that area.

6. THE CURRENT LEVEL OF PRESIDENTIAL POWER IN FOREIGN AFFAIRS, HOWEVER IMPERFECT, IS ABOUT THE BEST THAT CAN REASONABLY BE EXPECTED

The United States could do much worse than having the current system for controlling foreign policy. It could have a system of weak executive power, which might prevent presidential abuses but cost the nation its ability to cope with a dangerous world. It could have a more powerful president, checked only by his conscience and the persuasiveness of advisers, but that situation would surely mean tyranny.

What the nation does have is a system with a strong, but restrained, executive who exercises his power within a system of checks and balances in which he is held accountable for his actions. The United States Constitution establishes a government of three branches, each checking and balancing the wielding of power by the other two. The president has great power, but it is not absolute power. This situation is not perfect, but it is a workable and reasonable one. It allows the president to exercise the leadership and decisiveness needed by the United States, but obligates him to pay attention to Congress and the public. It does not create perfect equilibrium, with presidential power waxing and waning over time as circumstances and congressional and public attitudes change, but in politics equilibrium often means paralysis. Attempts to alter the system significantly, as in removing the president's power to conclude executive agreements or employ U.S. forces abroad without congressional authorization, would not be worth whatever benefits they might bring.

7. REALISTIC REFORMS THAT WOULD NOT UPSET THE BASIC STRUCTURE OF THE U.S. GOVERNMENT COULD HELP IMPROVE THE SITUATION

For all that a clear view of presidential power reminds us of the excessiveness of critics, it is also true that the current situation is not perfect. There are realistic reforms that could make things better without damaging needed presidential powers. For example, the Case Act could be amended to require the president to report to Congress on all significant agreements he concludes with other nations, even informal ones. Without hampering the president, this action would give Congress better information about U.S. foreign policy. Similarly, Congress could enhance its ability to play an active and responsible role in foreign affairs by coordinating its oversight of executive actions and decisions in that area: it could create a joint intelligence committee, or even a joint national security committee, to simplify and thus improve executive-legislative consultation on foreign policy. At present, foreign affairs and intelligence matters in Congress are divided between the House and the Senate and within each chamber among committees on Foreign Affairs, Armed Services, and Intelligence. The result is a confusion that inhibits Congress's ability to oversee and respond to executive actions and decisions in foreign affairs. The president could also make a concerted effort to increase his consultation with congressional leaders, even if he did so only with members of his own party. In these ways, the chief executive could head off many potential problems.

CONCLUSION

In the final analysis, the president will consult with Congress and restrain his power only to the extent he feels it necessary to do so. Therefore, critics of presidential power ought to look to Congress as well as to the executive. The legislature's interest in and involvement with foreign policy are determined largely on Capitol Hill and not in the White House. The president does not have too much power in foreign affairs, but neither does Congress have too little. What counts is what is done with power. Perhaps Congress needs to do more.

NOTES

1. Aaron Wildavsky, "The Two Presidencies," in *The Presidency,* ed. Aaron Wildavsky (Boston: Little, Brown, 1969), p. 230.
2. John Jay, Alexander Hamilton, and James Madison, *The Federalist Papers,* ed. Clinton Rossiter (New York: New American Library, 1961), no. 70, p. 423.
3. PL 92-403; 86 Stat. 619, August 22, 1972; 1 U.S.C. 112.
4. See Thomas M. Franck and Edward Weisband, *Foreign Policy by Congress* (New York: Oxford Univ. Press, 1979), pp. 13–57.
5. PL 93-148; 87 Stat. 555; 50 U.S.C. 1542, 1543.
6. Ryan J. Barilleaux, "Executive Non-Agreements and the Presidential-Congressional Struggle in Foreign Affairs," *World Affairs,* 148 (Spring 1986), 217.
7. Daniel Paul Franklin, "War Powers in the Modern Context," *Congress and the Presidency,* 14 (Spring 1987), 77–92.

Questions for Discussion

1. What are the constitutional powers of Congress in foreign policy?
2. How should the United States go about requiring and implementing "meaningful" consultation between the president and Congress, particularly in emergency situations?
3. What effect would the adoption by the United States of a parliamentary-type government have on legislative power in foreign policy?
4. How does the war against international terrorism affect the debate over presidential powers?
5. How would the Framers of the Constitution have viewed presidential power in foreign policy since the administration of Franklin Roosevelt?
6. Does George Bush's handling of the Persian Gulf crisis of 1990–1991 demonstrate presidential strength or weakness? What are the reasons for your answer?

Suggested Readings

Burgin, Eileen. "Congress and Foreign Policy: The Misperceptions." In *Congress Reconsidered,* edited by Lawrence C. Dodd and Bruce I. Oppenheimer, pp. 333–363. 5th ed. Washington, D.C.: Congressional Quarterly Press.
Crabb, Cecil V., and Pat M. Holt. *Invitation to Struggle: Congress, the President, and Foreign Policy.* 4th ed. Washington, D.C.: Congressional Quarterly Press, 1992.

Fisher, Louis. *The Politics of Shared Power: Congress and the Executive.* 3d ed. Washington, D.C.: Congressional Quarterly Press, 1993.

Franklin, Daniel P. *Extraordinary Measures: The Exercise of Prerogative Powers in the United States.* Pittsburgh: Univ. of Pittsburgh Press, 1991.

Glennon, Michael J. *Constitutional Diplomacy.* Princeton, N.J.: Princeton Univ. Press, 1990.

Gonzalez, Henry B. "The Relinquishment of Co-Equality by Congress." *Harvard Journal on Legislation,* 29, no. 2 (Summer 1992), 331–356.

Henkin, Louis, Michael J. Glennon, and William D. Rogers, eds. *Foreign Affairs and the U.S. Constitution.* Ardsley-on-Hudson, N.Y.: Transnational Publishers, 1990.

Koh, Harold H. *The National Security Constitution: Sharing Power after the Iran-Contra Affair.* New Haven: Yale Univ. Press, 1990.

Lindsay, James M. "Congress and Foreign Policy: Why the Hill Matters." *Political Science Quarterly,* 107, no. 4 (Winter 1992–1993), 607–628.

U.S. Cong., Senate. *The Constitutional Roles of Congress and the President in Declaring and Waging War.* Hearing before the Committee on the Judiciary, 102d Cong., 1st Sess., 1991.

Chapter 13

Should the Number of Congressional Terms Be Limited?

The Constitution specifies the duration of the terms of office for members of Congress: two years for representatives and six years for senators. Although the Framers considered limiting the number of terms a member of Congress may serve, they abandoned the idea. They did not limit the number of presidential terms either.

George Washington established a precedent for the presidency when he voluntarily stepped down at the end of his second term. Franklin D. Roosevelt upset the tradition of a two-term presidency when he won reelection to third and fourth terms. Roosevelt's experience may never be duplicated because in 1951 the Twenty-Second Amendment, limiting the number of presidential terms to two, was adopted. Though spearheaded by Republicans, it may have adversely affected two Republican presidents, Dwight D. Eisenhower and Ronald Reagan, who would have been strong contenders for third terms had they chosen to run again.

From time to time, proposals for limiting congressional terms have been put forward. The idea has won the support of Presidents Abraham Lincoln, Harry S. Truman, Dwight D. Eisenhower, and John F. Kennedy. In 1990 new proposals were made, most notably by a group composed largely of Republicans—Americans to Limit Congressional Terms.

It is not difficult to understand why Republican support for limiting congressional terms is strong. The Democratic party has been in continuous control of the House of Representatives since 1955 and has been the majority party in the Senate for most of those years. Democrats have benefited most from incumbency, since incumbents tend to get reelected. Since 1974, more than 90 percent of the incumbents who have run have been reelected.

The movement for term limits also developed a momentum because of popular dissatisfaction with legislators. Particularly in the late 1980s and early 1990s, the prestige of Congress was hurt by stories about "perks" of legislators, such as no-interest loans for members of the House of Representatives at the House Bank and special parking spaces at National Airport reserved for senators and representatives. Scandals involving sexual harassment and the taking of bribes and questionable contributions from private and corporate sources contributed to the further tarnishing of Congress's image. In the minds of many people, Congress was becoming a privileged class with benefits and behavior patterns that were unreasonable and costly to the American people. To many, it seemed that one reason Congress had lost touch with ordinary people was because so many members were in Congress too long.

The dissatisfaction with Congress had grown to such a point that in 1992 term limitation measures were placed on the ballots in fourteen states. All of them were passed. Some members of Congress and legal scholars question whether a state ballot is sufficient to limit terms for federal legislators. They say that only a constitutional amendment can achieve this objective. And some legislators who come from states that have adopted term limits are challenging the constitutionality of the term limits. Advocates of term limits are working on adopting a constitutional amendment so that even if the Supreme Court invalidates the action in the states, the amendment would be binding.

In articles appearing in the monthly magazine *World and I*, Paul Calamita, articles editor of the *Journal of Law and Politics*, and Thomas K. Plofchan Jr., research associate at the Center for National Security Law at the University of Virginia School of Law, argue for term limits. Timothy S. Prinz, assistant professor in the Department of Government and Public Affairs of the University of Virginia, argues against them.

Calamita and Plofchan contend

1. Term limits are already an established institution, affecting city mayors, state governors, state legislators, and the president of the United States.
2. Term limits have broad support of the American people.
3. Congressional incumbents have so many advantages that they are virtually invincible. Thus, talented individuals are discouraged from running for congressional office.
4. The concept of citizen-legislators will be resurrected and replace the failed idea of professional politicians.
5. Lame-duck legislators (that is, officials who are in their last term in a particular elected office) will remain responsive and responsible political figures.
6. Women and minority groups will be likely to have a greater representation than they currently do because incumbency would no longer provide so many advantages in the electoral process.
7. Political alliances within the legislature, which can create long-term infighting, will be eliminated.
8. Legislators will not have to spend so much time in winning reelection. Instead, they can focus their attention on issues.
9. Term limits will destroy seniority, which rewards legislators with influence based on the number of years they are on a committee. Instead, legislators will be rewarded on the basis of competence.
10. Term limits will put into office men and women who are every bit as knowledgeable as the legislators they are replacing.
11. Term limits will not result in an entrenched congressional staff powerhouse since new members of Congress will sign on staff members who are directly known to them.

12. Voters will not be compelled to reelect a legislator who may be incompetent for fear that the defeat of the legislator will result in lower legislative influence for them.

Timothy S. Prinz argues against term limits. He contends

1. Most members of Congress do not come from safe seats. They are reelected because they serve the needs of their constituents.
2. Although public opinion polls show that most people are highly critical of Congress as an institution, they usually approve of the representatives of their particular constituencies.
3. Legislative matters are so complex and important that they require legislators with professional competence. Citizen-legislators, on the other hand, would need the highest professional political skills if they are to serve effectively.
4. It is hard to make the case that incumbents dominate the House of Representatives since there is considerable turnover with each election.
5. Like it or not, most of the political offices in the country have become professionalized. Term-limit advocates refuse to accept this reality.
6. Term limits will mean that talented people will not seek legislative office since their political career prospects will be limited.
7. Term limits will make congressional staff, the executive branch, and interest groups more important than they are since new legislators will be dependent upon their expertise.
8. Term limits will increase the power of the special interests. Legislators will be looking for jobs once they become lame ducks, and the special interests offer more future employment possibilities than nearly any other sector of society.
9. Incumbents not facing reelection prospects will face even fewer challenges for reelection than is currently the case.
10. Term limits are not the panacea for the problems that ail U.S. society. The solution to the problems must come from voters who are willing to pay the price for the programs they favor.

☑ Y E S

Should the Number of Congressional Terms Be Limited?

PAUL CALAMITA AND THOMAS K. PLOFCHAN JR.
Term Limitation: Its Time Has Come

The 1990s have been an especially troubled time for the U.S. Congress. The 1990 budget fiasco, self-awarded pay raises, the Keating Five scandal, the savings and loan debacle, paralysis in confronting the Persian Gulf crisis, the recent disclosures regarding "rubbergate" and not paying for food service, parking ticket fixing, the growing realization that Congress exempts itself from many laws, and the Thomas confirmation fiasco have resulted in the highest public *disapproval* rating for Congress ever (72 percent). Predictably, cries for reform have been heard across the nation.

One cry recalls an idea that has been around since the Articles of Confederation: Limit congressional tenure. Why not? We already limit the tenure of many city mayors, 29 state governors, a growing number of state legislators, and even the president of the United States.

Support for term limitation evidences a growing sentiment among the electorate that long-awaited remedial measures short of such a step, such as reforms of the redistricting process and campaign finances, will not suffice. Indeed, American voters support the idea of limiting congressional tenure by a 72 percent to 24 percent margin.

Despite claims of partisan politics, the campaign for term limitation has garnered support from all of the major sectors of our society: Republicans and Democrats, men and women, blacks and whites, liberals and conservatives. Prominent members of the term limitation parade, to name a few, include President George Bush, Vice-President Dan Quayle, Senators Dennis DeConcini (D-Az.) and Paul Wellstone (D-Minn.), 1992 presidential candidate and former governor of California, Edmund G. Brown, Jr., Ohio Governor George Voinovich (R), Colorado State Senator Terry Considine (R), Texas Governor Ann W. Richards (D), John R. Silber (D-Massachusetts gubernatorial candidate in 1990), retired Senator Gordon Humphrey (R-N.H.), California Attorney General John K. VandeKamp, columnist George Will, and Ralph Nader. Also, national groups like Americans to Limit Congressional Terms (with affiliated organizations in 33 states and over 100,000 members), the National Taxpayers Union, and Citizens for Congressional Reform are championing the cause in addition to numerous groups organized at the state level.

In 1990, voters in California, Oklahoma, and Colorado passed initiatives that limit the tenure of their state legislators. Bolstered by these successes, proponents of term limits have initiated petitions to limit the terms of state legislators and even state congressional delegates in 20 states—including a measure in Washington State that would force Speaker of the House Tom Foley out in 1994. In 25 other states where binding voter initiatives are not used, proponents of term limits have commenced campaigns designed to pressure state legislators to impose term limits themselves.

More importantly, in 1992, 80 to 100 seats in the House of Representatives are expected to open up due to incumbents retiring from office or redistricting that will result from the 1990 census figures. This presents a window of opportunity for voters to elect representatives who support limited congressional tenure. As a result, the possibility of federal action, including the proposal of a Constitutional amendment, to limit congressional terms increases dramatically.

THE NEED FOR CHANGE

It is not enough to identify the breadth of the limitation movement. The reasons for its genesis must be examined.

Today, it appears that members of Congress, once they are elected, serve virtually at their own pleasure. Large staffs, many offices, travel allowances, franking privileges, media access, and massive campaign war chests courtesy of PACs [political action committees] and special interest groups serve to make congressional incumbents very comfortable and virtually invincible. These factors demonstrate the need for congressional reform. Yet it has become obvious to many that such reform will not occur until new people occupy the seats of power. This is only likely to happen with term limitation, as the above-mentioned abuses clearly indicate that Congress is incapable of policing or reforming itself.

Financially, the growth of PACs has made the idea of a fair election of a citizen-politician at best a historical artifact. Recently, Common Cause reported that of the 405 House members up for reelection in 1990, 79 had no major party challenger, 158 had challengers who raised less than $25,000 each, and another 132 faced opponents that managed to raise less than half of each incumbent's war chest. Thus, 361 (91 percent) of the House incumbents up for reelection did not face a serious challenger (at least financially, if not politically speaking).

House incumbents entered the 1990 election year with $177.5 million in campaign funds, while their opponents began with a paltry $14.8 million. As for the Senate, in the 1988 election, the average electoral victor spent $4 million, with some senators spending as much as $25 million.

Given the financial hurdle that challengers face, it comes as no surprise that only one out of the 405 congressmen up for reelection in 1990 lost in a primary election, with the one loser having been convicted of having sex with a teenager prior to the primary. Moreover, 96.2 percent of House incumbents seeking reelection ultimately prevailed, as did 97 percent of incumbent senators—a reelection rate higher than in the pre-perestroika Soviet politburo.

Opponents of term limits argue that limiting tenure will discourage America's finest from running for state legislatures and Congress, as such a short stay in public office provides no incentive to leave their present occupations. To the contrary, for the first time in decades, talented individuals from all walks of life would run for Congress since they would have a decent chance of getting elected.

The concept of citizen-legislators will be resurrected. People will know from the beginning that this is not a career. Political service will be like serving on a local public interest board.

Furthermore, it is predicted that the resultant increase in competitive elections will foster a new enlightenment among the voters as they seek to gain candidates' perspectives on issues rather than merely accepting the opinions of incumbents, as they currently do. In addition, congressmen returning to their communities after the limit of their terms will bring their knowledge and expertise with them.

Perhaps the biggest criticism of term limitations is that limiting tenure will result in an unprecedented number of lame-duck legislators who will be less responsive to their constituents and who will be more concerned, during their final terms, with feathering their postlegislative nests than with legislating. Three arguments rebut this cry of alarm.

First, many term limitation advocates contend that the lame-duck myth is exactly that. America's experience within the executive branch since 1951, when the Twenty-Second Amendment limited the president to serving two terms, belies such concern. No president since that time can be considered to have suffered a lame-duck final term. Notably, President Reagan sustained vetoes and actually moved forward with many of his domestic and foreign policies during his final term. Furthermore, the 29 states that limit gubernatorial tenure have not raised claims of being held hostage by such restrictions.

Second, term limits will mean that congressional seats will become filled by individuals who are successful within their niche in the private sector. Such people would be loathe to tarnish their reputations by feathering their nests during their final terms when they already have such bright futures in the private sector from whence they came.

Finally, even if the feared corruption during a congressman's final term becomes a problem, the limited stay at the public trough should provide relief to the voters. Further, revolving door policies and limits on outside income should be sufficient to restore fidelity.

Other collateral societal benefits would occur if legislative tenure is limited. First, women and minority groups would have a better opportunity to elect candidates of their choice, thereby more closely bringing proportionality of representation. (Women and minorities currently hold a mere 53 out of the 535 congressional seats.)

Second, Congress' current political alliances would be eliminated. Moreover, the relentless turnover created by tenure limitation would prevent the antagonism and decades-long infighting that presently are fostered under the current electoral system.

Third, congressmen would no longer be compelled to devote large percentages of their time and our resources (especially staffing and the franking privilege) toward ensuring reelection. Instead, they would be able to focus more on the matters at hand.

SENIORITY AND EXPERIENCE

Today, many congressmen attain leadership positions within Congress based upon seniority, rather than on merit. As Senator Byrd (D-W.Va.) continues to demonstrate, committee and subcommittee chairmen are often powerful enough to single-handedly garner significant amounts of federal pork for their district or state.

Limiting congressional tenure should help change the seniority system to a system in which leadership is based upon ability and effectiveness. Congressmen would still spend their first few years in office learning how the system works before competing for leadership positions. However, congressmen would no longer have to wait years, or even decades, before getting leadership positions.

Further, all members of Congress would stand on nearly equal footing and be able to speak their convictions without fear of retaliation by entrenched senior congressmen. As good-government advocate Ralph Nader recently observed, long-term incumbents are currently so powerful that junior incumbents are more afraid of them than they are of the people back home.

A related counterargument to term limitation is that congressional experience is so valuable and necessary for proper legislation that we should not arbitrarily force congressmen out of office lest we become the victims of inexperience or fall at the mercy of senior congressional staff members. But, each district or state certainly can call upon numerous qualified individuals to replace legislative giants such as Sam Nunn, Bob Dole, and Tom Foley who would be lost to term limitation. Also, while congressional experience is generally considered to be valuable, it is not a prerequisite for effective public service. After all, being a Congressman cannot be more difficult than being a mayor, state legislator, governor, or president of the United States. Yet all of those positions are subject to limited tenure.

It is ridiculous to assert that newly elected congressmen will blindly retain all staffers of the previous officeholder. Such coveted positions will certainly go to the new congressman's campaign leaders and trusted confidantes.

Finally, it is unlikely that newly elected members of the House or Senate will arrive in Washington without having gained experience in public office on the local or statewide level. Further, senators who are precluded by term limits from running again for the Senate may run for a seat in the House and vice versa.

Many American voters agree that limited terms pose no threat to effective leadership. A recent national survey asked voters whether they believed it more important to "keep experienced people in the House and Senate" or to "elect new people with fresh ideas." Seventy percent chose to elect new people with fresh ideas, with as many Democrats as Republicans in favor.

THE VOTERS' DILEMMA

It has been said of the congressional seniority system that to ensure the most powerful representation, voters must devote themselves to their congressional representatives as if they were married. Under the present system, an increase in seniority usually ensures that a congressman will receive more important and influential duties, resulting in more powerful representation for the home district or state than if a new congressman were elected. Thus, it is not uncommon to find members of Congress whose tenures span decades as, once elected, a divorce is too costly for a district or state in terms of the loss of powerful representation.

The system, in which seniority rather than merit determines political clout in Congress creates the perverse incentive to reelect incumbents who have become less competent in order to maintain their place on the seniority ladder. This dilemma explains the phenomenon that while the congressional disapproval rate during 1990 was at a then all-time high (69 percent), voters still reelected incumbent representatives and senators at a rate of 96 percent and 97 percent respectively.

Term limitations would solve this voters' dilemma. Critics of term limitation assert that term-limitation laws enacted by some states would create an incentive for the remaining states not to adopt such laws in the hope that they can more easily secure positions of leadership for their delegates to Congress based upon their seniority. However, in the practical realm, this would not be a problem. As members of Congress become subject to limited tenure, most likely they will take measures to eliminate the benefits of seniority.

CONCLUSION

It is apparent that significant problems exist within our present congressional structure. Many of these problems are a direct result of our system, which tolerates tenure at will by our incumbent congressmen. Limiting congressional tenure will increase the number of congressional vacancies, thereby improving the opportunities for our ablest citizens to step forward and serve in Congress.

Moreover, tenure limits for Congress will provide incentives to many of our citizens to put their private pursuits on hold in order to answer the call to public service. Ability and merit, rather than seniority, will become the most important determinants of not only who is elected, but who will attain leadership positions within the Congress.

Finally, congressmen who have served their time in office will return to their appreciative constituents to disseminate the valuable knowledge that they have acquired in Washington, thereby creating a more enlightened electorate ready to formulate America's future political agenda.

Should the Number of Congressional Terms Be Limited?

TIMOTHY S. PRINZ

Term Limitation: A Perilous Panacea

As Congress has been rocked by scandal and perceptions of incompetence, critics and reformers describe members of Congress as a privileged class, out of touch with the people in their districts, unresponsive to district concerns, and even corrupt. Frustration with Congress, and with Washington in general, is by all accounts widespread among the American public.

This dissatisfaction has fueled the hopes of those who would place limits on congressional terms. Even an observer as sanguine about American politics as George Will has decided that the career legislators currently in place in Washington have served altogether too long and have lost touch with their constituents. With recent polls indicating that 74 percent of Americans favor some form of term limits, it is time to think seriously about the implications of any proposal to limit congressional terms.

The case against limiting congressional terms presented here advances several interlocking arguments revolving around the nature of the contemporary political career. For one, members of Congress are not nearly as insulated or invulnerable as the term-limitations movement would have us believe. Despite record-high reelection rates for incumbents, substantial turnover still occurs with each election. In addition, a straightforward analysis of the incentives and constraints surrounding the contemporary political career highlights several difficulties associated with proposals to limit congressional terms.

Finally, the disadvantages brought on by any successful proposal to limit the terms of members of Congress have serious implications for the American system of government. Our commonplace understandings of representation, the separation of powers, and good governance will be dramatically altered if term limits are adopted.

Much of the current movement for term limitations is rooted in a pervasive sense that incumbents have lost touch with voters and that Congress is enmeshed in governmental gridlock, unable to muster the political will necessary to address society's most pressing problems. Term limitations will do little to address either of these concerns.

IN DEFENSE OF PROFESSIONAL POLITICIANS

One of the most common arguments advanced in favor of term limitations described members of Congress as professional politicians. Implicit in this criticism is the idea that somehow professional politicians are less able to reflect the desires of their constituents (due perhaps to the lure of big money from PACs [political action committees] and interest groups, or maybe they are blinded by the power and glamor of serving in Washington), and that what the country really needs is to replace these professional incumbent politicians with a new class of citizen legislators.

There are several problems with this argument. For one, as most close observers of American politics recognize, the vast majority of incumbent members of Congress do not come from safe seats. Rather, they work very hard to retain their seats in Washington. They do so in a variety of ways: by serving the needs of their constituents before the bureaucracy in Washington, by pursuing district interests in legislation before the Congress, and most generally by assiduously working to ensure that the voters in their district have little reason to reject them at the polls the next time around. Most members of Congress pursue a seemingly endless array of responsibilities—committee meetings, votes on the floor, working on legislation, meetings with other legislators, and the executive branch, fund-raising and constituency service—with one eye always on the district and how it will respond to his or her actions.

Most of us would be hard-pressed to find instances where a member of Congress deliberately ignored the wishes of the vast majority of his or her constituency. Simply because members of Congress win by overwhelming margins does not mean that they are then free to ignore their constituents; on the contrary, the fact that they are so good at representing the interests of their constituents may explain why they do so well at election time. It is not far-fetched to claim that most members of Congress remain in office because they do a good job of serving as their district's representative. Incumbents have been accurately described as "running scared," and they win 90 to 95 percent of the time not because they are unbeatable but because they work very hard at winning reelection.

If voters disapproved of the performance of their elected representative, presumably they would elect someone else. The fact that incumbents return to Washington with such regularity says something about voters as well as about incumbents. Public opinion polls largely confirm this approval of incumbents. By and large, most polls find highly favorable ratings for a particular district's member of Congress, but unfavorable ratings for the Congress and its legislative product. This separation (or schizophrenia) between views of the representatives and views of the Congress will hardly be cured by a reform like term limitations and provides little justification for such a radical change in the current system of representation.

Criticizing members of Congress as professional politicians misses the point. Like it or not, serving in Congress is now a full-time job. Never mind that career legislators must constantly work to preserve their seat if they want to retain their career. That is only half the issue.

A seat in the cockpit of government carries with it weighty responsibilities, and to believe that instilling "new blood" in the institution is somehow going to relieve members of Congress of these hard choices and difficult problems is misguided at best. Given the demands of the job, both electoral and otherwise, the reformers' notion of a citizen-legislator going to Washington and dealing with the complexities of contemporary governance is largely a chimera.

TURNOVER IN CONGRESS

More to the point, despite the fact that incumbents work hard to remain in office, turnover in Congress has not fallen off noticeably. Turnover in the House of Representatives—the number of new representatives in the legislature due to incumbent defeat or replacement via retirement—has brought an average of 53 new members to the House in each election in the 1980s and has averaged 61 new members since 1970. Similar figures apply to the Senate, which has averaged about 10 new members each election. Further, average tenure in the Senate is still less than two full terms, and mean tenure in the House is now a little under 6 terms, the same period suggested by advocates of term limitations.

Of course, it means little to claim that the House averages 50 new members each election cycle if the same 50 members are being replaced, but that has not been the case in the last two decades. A simple comparison of the 98th Congress (elected in 1982) with the current Congress reveals that more than one-third of the seats (163 of 435) have changed hands at least once.

Interestingly, the states where the movement to limit congressional terms has the greatest momentum have seen a good deal of turnover in a relatively short period of time—with the exception of Patricia Schroeder's seat, every other seat in the Colorado delegation has changed hands once since 1982. The state of Washington's experience is a little more typical, where just under half of the delegation (3 of 7) has been replaced since 1982. If we go back as far as the Watergate class of 1974 and include the effects of redistricting, 338 incumbents (78 percent) elected in the 1974 Democratic landslide have since been replaced in Congress.

Thus, it is hard to make the case that incumbents are dominating the institution. Clearly, incumbents win with great regularity, but incumbent reelection rates can mask the large amounts of real turnover in the House that occur with each election.

In short, present rates of turnover seem to indicate that the political life cycle of the House of Representatives is currently about 10 to 15 years. In other words, a new generation of representatives replaces the previous sitting incumbents at about the same rate as would be imposed by current proposals to limit congressional terms. Given the numbers, it is hard to make the case that new blood is not entering the House or the Senate.

TERM LIMITS AND POLITICAL CAREERS

A final defense of incumbents, and the most significant critique of proposals to limit service in Congress, is rooted in the current character of the system of electoral competition in the United States. At bottom, proposals to limit congressional terms appear to seriously miscomprehend the current system of incentives and constraints facing most candidates for public office.

Like it or not, most of the political offices in this country have become professionalized. From city councils to the United States Senate, these positions are pursued by individuals who view them as full-time jobs. Politics and the getting and keeping of public office are a career, not something people do on the side while being a lawyer, business professional, teacher, or whatever.

This notion of a political career has important implications for the way individuals seek and hold public office. For one, the notion of a political career engenders competition and creates a loose structure of career opportunities—a sort of hierarchy or ladder of advancement. As one moves up the ladder, positions tend to be more attractive (they have greater power and prestige attached to the office). In addition, there are generally fewer of these more attractive positions available and greater competition for them.

The structure of political opportunities guides the behavior of career politicians in important ways. Perhaps the most important factor is competition—the pyramidal structure has multiple points of entry, but movement up the ladder becomes more difficult and more uncertain as competition increases. The system also creates an overlapping set of constituencies, so that the progression from office to office to office is often a logical one.

For example, congressional districts often contain a number of state legislative districts, making the move from state legislator to member of Congress a relatively easy one. The similarity of tasks involved in the two jobs helps as well. In this sense, the system provides ready advantages to certain candidates—those with prior experience in public office.

Given this overview, one might conclude that a large number of competitors for the local seat in Congress might be readily available. State legislators, city councillors, and other local officials provide a ready pool of candidates. These officials are also the best candidates: They have the experience of running for office and they share a portion of the district's constituency. For these reasons, they should be able to mount a strong challenge to sitting incumbents. Upon closer inspection, however, it becomes readily apparent why incumbents so often face only token opposition.

The problem is that politics is a career: To the extent that a position currently held by a politician is an advantage in seeking to move up the ladder and challenge for the seat in Congress, that position also becomes a risk in the decision to move up the ladder. Any decision to challenge an incumbent member of Congress entails risking the seat presently held, thereby threatening an end to a political career. And for politicians who have made political office a career, this is no small consideration. Given such circumstances, it is in their interest to wait for an appropriate time to challenge the incumbent. And the most likely times are when there is a widespread perception that the incumbent might be particularly vulnerable or when the incumbent retires and leaves the seat open.

The problem here, of course, is that incumbents are for the most part able to create the impression of invulnerability, which means that, for the present, significant turnover occurs only when members retire. There is a good deal of evidence that the present system of opportunities for political office functions in this manner. The best candidates wait until a seat is open to run, leaving incumbents to face only token opposition. Other campaign resources, particularly money, follow the same sort of logic: PACs and other contributors give overwhelmingly to incumbents because it makes sense to back the best candidate.

Term limitations will do little to obviate this system of political opportunities, and they stand to do considerable damage. Limitations on congressional terms will upset the system of incentives for office currently in place for those now in public office, most likely by reducing the incentive to run for Congress. The best and the brightest pool of candidates—those in positions immediately below—will have little incentive to run if they are forced to give up the seat in 12 years and have no future prospects for their career.

In its current incarnation, the electoral system provides a recognizable system of incentives and constraints in the pursuit of office, and every politician recognizes them and takes risks accordingly. Term limitations remove some of the most powerful incentives while retaining the restraints, a situation that most strategic politicians are going to avoid.

THE DISADVANTAGES OF TERM LIMITATIONS

In addition to altering the political career structure in important ways, term limits pose a number of significant disadvantages. Many of these disadvantages are by now well known and have been thoroughly discussed by a number of observers. Nonetheless, a brief recounting of some of the more prominent problems created by term limits would be useful in assessing the case against term limitations.

The most common complaint against term limits is the loss of power Congress would suffer as a result. Reform movements of any stripe typically assume that if power can be taken away from the object of reform, it will devolve to ordinary citizens. Experience has shown, however, that this assumption is naive: when one party of interest in Washington loses power, a different one generally gains.

With term limitations in effect, congressional staff would become much more important, since members will have less time to develop the technical expertise necessary to pass judgment on the intricacies of public policy. By the same argument, the executive branch and interest groups will become more powerful as well, since members of Congress will be more dependent on them for the information and analysis crucial to the policy process.

With staff and the permanent bureaucracy as the principal source of expertise in the federal government, unelected representatives would exert considerable influence over the most important decisions in Washington. And the only way for amateur members of Congress to reduce the role of the executive is to rely on other sources such as interest groups. These groups would undoubtedly be happy to supply the information and expertise legislators need.

Ironically, then, a reform designed to enhance the representative character of the electoral system will in fact reduce it by making our representatives more dependent on outside sources of information and expertise. In the more benign case, the executive branch will grow in power and authority vis-a-vis the Congress. The more troubling scenario involves congressional staff or special interests wielding significant influence over congressional decisions. But reliance on outside groups for knowledge and expertise is not the only danger to representation.

Perhaps the most dangerous consequence of term limitation is the effect it would have on the incentives of representatives described above. But the logic does not stop there. Members of Congress currently have the option of planning a career in Congress. Despite the risks and the hard work involved, most either plan to stay in Congress or to use their seat to pursue a higher office—a seat in the Senate or a governor's chair. Those few who do leave electoral politics with useful years remaining can usually accept a job in the executive branch or can command lucrative positions as lobbyists on the Hill.

What happens when terms are limited? Members of Congress are forced to start thinking right away about their future—about what they will do ten or twelve years hence. The situation forces them to start planning their next move—either to a higher seat (the problem is that these are scarce and very competitive), to an appointive position (these, too, are scarce and hard to pursue), or to a lucrative position in the private sector (clearly the easiest of the three). With a limit on the amount of service in Congress, representatives will be looking ahead to their next position. This result will almost certainly enhance the power of special interests to influence representatives, inasmuch as they are the most likely source of future positions. As Patrick Henry noted on a similar subject during the constitutional debates, "Virtue will slumber. The wicked will be constantly watching: consequently you will be undone."

To go one step further, with term limitations in place, who will challenge a representative during his or her six terms in office? Most citizens do not have the luxury of putting their own careers on hold for ten years or so while serving their district's interest in Washington. Local politicians will have little incentive to challenge an incumbent for a congressional seat, inasmuch as it is in their interest to bide their time and wait for the current representative to serve out the term.

It is likely, then, that sitting members of Congress will face even less opposition than under the current system. Again, the irony is that a proposal designed to enhance the representative relationship will in fact undermine it. The likely outcome of term limitations is that the people's control over their representatives will be lessened, not strengthened.

In the atmosphere of overwhelming dissatisfaction with incumbents and official Washington in general, term limitations have become only the most recent panacea for a public anxious for quick fixes to national problems. While there is much that lies behind the current discontent, term limits are not the answer. There is much that ails the contemporary body politic in America, but much of the responsibility lies with voters, not with elected officials.

For whatever reasons, voters have fallen into the habit of sending contradictory messages. Citizens criticize the Congress but still overwhelmingly approve of their own representatives. Voters refuse to raise taxes and even favor tax cuts, while at the same time protesting any cuts in their pet programs. Voters also appear to like the idea of one party holding the White House and the other party running Congress.

That voters do not approve of the results of this situation—governmental gridlock—is a sign of the need to reform voter attitudes, not governmental institutions. The ideal systemic solution is to give voters more choice, not limit those choices through a clumsy vehicle like term limitations.

Questions for Discussion

1. Are term limits for members of Congress democratic? Why or why not?
2. Why do incumbents have an advantage in getting reelected?
3. What effect would public financing of congressional campaigns have on incumbent reelection prospects?
4. What effect would term limits have on the character, integrity, and professional competence of candidates for congressional office?
5. What effect would term limits have on the power of special interests?
6. What effect would term limits have on voting turnout?

Suggested Readings

Benjamin, Gerald, and Michael J. Malbin, eds. *Limiting Legislative Terms.* Washington, D.C.: Congressional Quarterly Press, 1992.

Borger, Gloria. "Can Term Limits Do the Job?" *Newsweek,* 111, no. 11 (November 11, 1991), 34–36.

Broder, David S. "Pox Populi." *Washington Post,* April 25, 1993, pp. C1, C4.

Calamita, F. Paul. "Solving the Voters' Dilemma: The Case for Legislative Term-Limitation." *Journal of Law and Politics,* 8, no. 3 (Spring 1992), 559–607.

Committee on Federal Legislation. "Term Limitations for United States Representatives and Senators." *Record of the Association of the Bar of the City of New York,* 46, no. 7 (November 1991), 755–783.

Crane, Edward H. "Six and Twelve: The Case for Serious Term Limits." *National Civic Review,* 80, no. 3 (Summer 1991), 248–255.

Evans, Rowland, and Robert Novak. "The Best Way to Clean Up Congress." *Reader's Digest,* 138, no. 827 (March 1991), 112–116.

Frenzel, Bill. "Term Limits and the Immortal Congress: How to Make Congressional Elections Competitive Again." *Brookings Review,* 10, no. 2 (Spring 1992), 18–22.

Kesler, Charles R. "Bad Housekeeping: The Case against Congressional Term Limitations." *Policy Review,* no. 53 (Summer 1990), 20–25.

Kristol, William. "Term Limitations: Breaking Up the Iron Triangle." *Harvard Journal of Law and Public Policy,* 16, no. 1 (Winter 1993), 95–100.

Ledbetter, Carl, Jr. "Limiting Legislative Terms Is a Bad Idea." *National Civic Review,* 80, no. 3 (Summer 1991), 243–247.

Mann, Thomas E. "The Wrong Medicine: Term Limits Won't Cure What Ails Congressional Elections." *Brookings Review,* 10, no. 2 (Spring 1992), 23–25.

Payne, James L. "Limiting Government by Limiting Congressional Terms." *Public Interest,* no. 103 (Spring 1991), 106–117.

Petracca, Mark P. "The Poison of Professional Politics." *USA Today* (Magazine), 120, no. 2560 (January 1992), 10–13.

Polsby, Nelson. "Some Arguments against Congressional Term Limitations." *Harvard Journal of Law and Public Policy,* 16, no. 1 (Winter 1993), 101–107.

Reynolds, Alan. "Time for Term Limits." *National Review,* 44, no. 7 (April 13, 1992), 43–44.

Wills, Garry. "Undemocratic Vistas." *New York Review of Books,* 39, no. 19 (November 19, 1992), 28–34.

Chapter 14

Is a Big Government Bureaucracy Inherently Incompatible with Democracy?

When the Constitution was adopted in the late eighteenth century, only a few hundred people were employed by government at the national level. Today, however, there are more than 3 million civilian federal government employees. Millions of other public employees serve in the armed forces and the agencies of state and local governments. About one out of every six employed people in the United States works for government at the national, state, or local level.

Government has grown remarkably in this century because of its increased activities in foreign affairs, the domestic economy, and welfare. In the late eighteenth century the United States was a small power on the periphery of the world's major powers of Europe. For more than four decades after World War II, it became one of the two strongest military powers, challenged principally by the other superpower, the Soviet Union.

Even after the disintegration of the Soviet Union, the United States was the world's only superpower. The United States still requires the services of large numbers of people in the armed forces. Government, moreover, is engaged in dispensing foreign aid, gathering intelligence information, assisting individuals and groups abroad, and helping to promote international trade.

In addition to the growth of foreign policy activities, domestic factors are responsible for government expansion. Business asks for government assistance to build highways, improve railroads, construct dams, widen waterways, and administer tariffs. It also requests government support for research in energy, transportation, and military technology. The demands of labor also increase government involvement in the economy. Labor asks for government inspection involving safety at work sites, government supervision of minimum wage laws, and government employment of those who cannot find jobs in the private sector. Labor seeks government protection of unions against the power of business.

Finally, the welfare state contributes to government growth. Individuals and groups demand government help to provide health care, Social Security, housing, and education. All these goals require programs that are administered by government, and that administration is the bureaucracy.

Big government receives its share of criticism. In the election of 1976, for example, Jimmy Carter ran under a campaign promise to reduce the size of the federal government. Ronald Reagan became even more identified than Carter with such a reduction. Both Carter and Reagan failed to achieve their stated purposes. The best that Reagan could do was to reduce the rate of growth of the federal government.

George Bush talked much about cutting government spending, but his administration was no more successful than its predecessors in doing so. In fact, the Bush administration presided over the growth of an even larger bureaucracy than his predecessors.

Critics of bureaucracy argue that government is now so big and unwieldy that it is undermining democracy. In an article in *Policy Review*, a Heritage Foundation publication, attorney Brink Lindsey echoes this view. He contends

1. There is too much government for the American people or their elected representatives even to comprehend, much less control.
2. As the force of public opinion is weakened by big government, policy making is disproportionately influenced by parochial interests that are often not in accord with the common welfare.
3. Even elected representatives cannot keep informed about public matters because of the immense size and scope of government programs.
4. Because of system overload, power slips from elected representatives to congressional staff members and pressure-group lobbyists.
5. The enormity of government has meant a shift in power from the legislative to the executive branch, and to the bureaucracy in particular.
6. Big government demands that legislators spend much of their time helping constituents deal with the big government that the legislators have created.

Political scientist Kenneth F. Warren takes issue with this point of view. In a forum "Public Administration and the Constitution" appearing in *Public Administration Review*, he argues:

1. Big government is a reality that we have to deal with whether we like it or not.
2. The federal courts have never seriously questioned the legitimacy of the administrative state since 1938. In fact, the Supreme Court has upheld the granting of broad delegations of power to agency administrators.
3. Congress has accepted the legitimacy of the administrative state through delegation of power to government agencies.
4. Although it is true that Americans oppose big government in principle, polls show that they want government programs to continue.

Is a Big Government Bureaucracy Inherently Incompatible with Democracy?

BRINK LINDSEY

System Overload: The Size of Our Government Is Unsafe for Democracy

American democracy has seen better days. Across the political spectrum there is a growing sense that our system has fallen into corruption—not just hum-drum venality (although there is plenty of that), but rather a sweeping and pervasive institutional degradation.

The recently concluded budget fiasco [1991] is symptomatic. The episode played like a comedy of errors: the "summit" deal blindsided by public outrage and trashed by the congressional rank-and-file; the government wavering in and out of mandated shut-down; and in the end, the final package passed in the dead of night, its details unknown to those who voted on it. The overall picture is of a government both out of touch and out of control.

Numerous ills underlying democracy's malaise have been identified. The malignant influence of political action committees, the unfair advantages that incumbents enjoy over challengers, the vacuousness of campaigns dominated by media consultants, and the paralysis of divided government have all received substantial attention.

Beyond the more visible troubles with American self-government, though, there is a deeper and more basic problem. Simply put, the size and complexity of contemporary government have made it impossible for democracy to function properly. No matter what "good government" reforms are instituted, there remains a deep-seated and ineradicable conflict between the realities of big government and the aspirations of self-government.

LIMITED ATTENTION SPAN

Democracy means the rule of the people—government by consent of the governed. In a representative democracy such as our own, popular control may be exercised in two basic ways. First, the people may guide policy directly through public opinion, which when focused and firm on a particular issue is always influential and usually irresistible. Second, the public rules vicariously through its elected representatives; it is presumed that such officials, coming from the people and accountable to them, will act in the public's interest even on those matters where public opinion is silent or nebulous.

Both of these aspects of democratic control are now visibly slipping under the bloated bulk of the federal government's innumerable activities and responsibilities. The problem is system overload: there is too much government for the public and its representatives even to comprehend, much less control.

The effectiveness of democratic control faces one inescapable limitation— the number of issues that can be squeezed into the public agenda at any one time. For ordinary citizens in normal times, political issues will inevitably assume a low priority. The demands of job and family, the diversions of recreation, and the press of strictly local concerns impose rather harsh limits on the range of national issues that can engage the public's interest and consideration. Accordingly, the larger the scope of government's responsibilities, and the more complex its programs and policies, the greater is the likelihood that vast areas of government will operate wholly outside public scrutiny or even cognizance.

This threat to democracy is not new; it was clear to our Founders that an overextended government is incompatible with popular control. As Publius observed in the *Federalist Papers:*

> It will be of little avail to the people that the laws are made by men of their own choice if the laws be so voluminous that they cannot be read, or so incoherent that they cannot be understood; if they be repealed or revised before they are promulgated, or undergo such incessant changes that no man, who knows what the law is today, can guess what it will be tomorrow.

THE FEDERAL ICEBERG

This is exactly the situation in America today. Notwithstanding the considerable accomplishments of the Reagan Revolution, big government remains an unshakable basic premise of American political life. Federal funding and regulation have become inextricably connected with every aspect of social existence, and the scope of federal responsibility for social problems is virtually without limit.

Consider, for example, this random sampling of the forgotten and the never-heard-of: the Export-Import Bank, which provides subsidized loans and loan guarantees for U.S. exporters; the Federal Energy Regulatory Commission, which, among other things, sets rates for natural gas pipelines; the Delaney Amendment, which prohibits addition of a substance to food if any dose of that substance has ever been found to produce cancer in lab animals; the Job Training Partnership Act, which funds training of "disadvantaged" and "dislocated" workers; and the Pension Benefit Guaranty Corporation, which insures pension plans in case employers default on their obligations. These programs and policies, and hundreds of others like them, exist in the large and growing blind spot of American democracy, their fate determined not by the broad electorate, but by "experts" and "insiders."

Under these conditions, it is flatly impossible for the larger public to keep track of anything but a fraction of the nation's ongoing business. Everything else is out of sight and out of mind—the great body of the iceberg, submerged and invisible.

Even when there is general public interest in some issue, there may still be a lack of real democratic influence on the formulation and maintenance of policy. For instance, Americans in recent years have grown increasingly concerned about protecting and preserving the environment. A number of legislative initiatives have been aided by this perceived shift in national mood, among them the recently enacted Clean Air Act amendments bill. The actual content of the Clean Air bill, though, has received scant attention in our public debate and is almost certainly a complete mystery to most Americans. Will its cost to the economy, estimated to run $30 billion, be justified by the resulting gains in air quality? Or are the new controls unduly onerous and unlikely to produce significant benefits? These questions have not been put to the American people.

PLEBISCITARY DEMOCRACY

The promise of government by consent of the governed is fulfilled only where there is *informed* consent by the public for actions taken on its behalf. With the present hypertrophy of regulations and spending programs and accompanying bureaucracy, informed consent has become impossible. And as the force of public opinion loses its relevance, policymaking is disproportionately influenced by parochial interests whose alignment with the common welfare is haphazard at best. Publius identified the problem over 200 years ago:

> Another effect of public instability is the unreasonable advantage it gives to the sagacious, the enterprising, and the moneyed few over the industrious and uninformed mass of the people. Every new regulation . . . presents a new harvest to those who watch the change, and can trace its consequences; a harvest, reared not by themselves, but by the toils and cares of the great body of their fellow-citizens. This is a state of things in which it may be said with some truth that laws are made for the *few*, not for the *many*.

Public control over government will increase only if there is significantly less government to control. The people's representatives remain accountable in the sense that they must regularly run for reelection. On a day-to-day basis, however, they are unconstrained by public opinion on the great preponderance of the issues with which they deal. This is a condition known as plebiscitary democracy: an all-powerful centralized state combined with democratic trappings. Alexis de Tocqueville, in his magisterial analysis of American democracy, derided this attenuated and debased form of self-government:

> Their imagination conceives a government which is unitary, protective, and all-powerful, but elected by the people. Centralization is combined

with the sovereignty of the people. That gives them a chance to relax. They console themselves for being under schoolmasters by thinking that they have chosen them themselves.

It was evident to Tocqueville that representative democracy thrives only within the framework of limited government:

It is really difficult to imagine how people who have entirely given up managing their own affairs could make a wise choice of those who are to do that for them. One should never expect a liberal, energetic, and wise government to originate in the votes of a people of servants.

LEGISLATORS IN A FOG

Under present circumstances even plebiscitary democracy is overwhelmed by the size of government. The culprit is the physical inability of our elected officials to keep up with the unruly sprawl of federal programs and responsibilities.

Congress, the nation's preeminent democratic body, is widely regarded as an institution in crisis. Most certainly Congress suffers from many ills, but one fundamental problem is that 535 human beings cannot possibly master the details of all the matters that come before them. This has nothing to do with lack of conscientiousness; it has to do with the limited number of hours in the day. Measures pass into law whose relevance, meaning, and even existence are known only to a few legislators at best. Accordingly, the linkage between policymaking and popular control is becoming more and more tenuous.

Contemporary legislation is both sweeping and comprehensive in the scope of its concerns, and narrow and particularistic in the level of detail at which these concerns are addressed. The legislative process may begin with some general, even simple idea, but inevitably it descends into a maze of complexities: definitions of terms, attempts to settle ambiguities and anticipate loopholes, exceptions made for special circumstances, assignment of administrative responsibilities, establishment of proper procedures, and so forth. At the same time, the legislation is shaped—or rather distorted—by a steady bombardment of interest-group lobbying designed to secure favorable treatment for this or that narrow constituency. The end result, the bill ultimately enacted, is an ungainly agglomeration of provisions, some of general concern, others technical and obscure, still others tailored to suit the special circumstances of some narrow interest.

The rank-and-file lawmaker, faced with a piece of pending legislation, does not have the expertise to evaluate its technical intricacies, nor is he privy to the back-room deals that larded the bill with special-interest provisions. He may be well versed on some narrow issue dear to an important constituent or contributor; otherwise, he is unlikely to know anything but the general outlines of the major issues involved. He may not even know that much.

With legislators often in a fog about what they're voting on, Congress's status as a deliberative assembly is severely compromised. For a major bill, the time allotted for floor debate would be consumed many times over just reviewing, section by section, what the legislation is proposing, not to mention arguing its merits. In 1988 alone, the legislation enacted by Congress—not just considered, but actually passed and signed—came to a total of 4,839 pages. And those are pages not of ordinary English, but of twisting, circuitous, cross-referenced legalese. Furthermore, bills are often passed in the frantic final push at the end of a congressional session, the necessary votes accumulated through a slew of last-minute compromises. Inevitably, things will slip through without any discussion at all—straight from the back rooms to the statute books without any public airing.

TWENTY-FOUR-POUND MONSTER

The spectacle of last fall's [1991] budget agreement provides a telling illustration of how Congress now operates. In an attempt to avoid the quagmire of the congressional appropriations committees, the administration and House and Senate leaders bypassed normal legislative procedures in favor of a budget "summit." The strategy failed miserably: after months of posturing, maneuvering, and just plain stalling, the summiteers waited until the last day of the fiscal year to agree on a "deficit reduction" plan, which was then summarily scuttled as soon as it reached the full Congress. In the tragicomic weeks that followed, the government hovered on the edge of insolvency while legislators worked feverishly to put together a new package.

Finally, after all-night marathon sessions and only a few days before elections, Congress managed to pass a budget agreement. Copies of the 10-inch thick, twenty-four-pound monster were few and hard to find; people were voting on language they had never even seen. The core of the deal—141 pages of new "spending restraint" mechanisms—had been finalized in negotiations with the administration only hours before being put to a vote. The deliberative function of Congress was little more than a sham.

UNELECTED REPRESENTATIVES

This overload situation places the power in the hands of people other than elected representatives—in particular, congressional staff members and pressure-group lobbyists. The growth in congressional staff reflects the general expansion of the federal government: the total number of staff jumped from 11,500 in 1973 to 32,000 in 1990. Among other things, staff members have front-line responsibility for drafting and revising legislative proposals; they also prepare the committee reports that give the official explanation of what legislation means. They are the masters of the details their elected bosses don't have time for; they are the true policy experts. They are also unelected and unaccountable.

At times it appears that legislators are simply puppets being manipulated by their staffs. Staff members brief their senator or congressman on what is going on in committee hearings, and provide his talking points and the questions he will ask; they prepare him for meetings with other members, constituents, contributors, and lobbyists; they write his speeches and his op-ed articles; they whisper deferentially in his ear when he says the wrong thing; they negotiate with other staffers on his behalf; and on particularly rushed occasions, they even tell him how to vote.

FARMING OUT TO LOBBYISTS

Even the staff cannot keep up with the demands of contemporary government. Consequently, much of the work of legislating is farmed out to private-sector lawyers and lobbyists. Working closely with the staff, these private contractors draft legislative provisions, prepare talking points and position papers on specific issues, draft committee report language, and even write what the congressman or senator will say during floor debate. In short, they do exactly what legislators and their staffs do—except that they do it on behalf of paying clients, and they are paid to advance those clients' interests without any regard to the larger public good.

The control that staff members and lobbyists exert over committee reports and what is said in floor debates is particularly insidious. These items, known as "legislative history," are the records that courts turn to as evidence of "congressional intent." They provide detailed explanations of a statute's provisions, and even give concrete examples of what the law actually entails in specific circumstances. Judicial interpretations of statutory provisions frequently turn on what is contained in the legislative history. Even when the meaning of a statute is not litigated, lawyers consult legislative history to advise clients on how the law should be observed.

This canned legislative history is seldom read by congressmen and senators, and it is never debated or voted on; nonetheless, it can become the effective law of the land. From the lobbyist's perspective, inserting favorable language in the legislative history is frequently the perfect vehicle for advancing a client's interests; getting a provision in the actual bill is much more difficult, and the attempt to do so could attract unwanted attention to the client's situation.

SEVENTEEN FEET OF REGULATIONS

This *sub rosa* transfer of power, though, is minor compared to what has happened publicly and openly—namely, the massive shift of policymaking responsibility from the legislative to the executive branch that has taken place over the past few decades. From the Agriculture Department to the Veterans Administration, cabinet departments and administrative agencies have been delegated broad authority to fill in the blanks of legislation with their own regulations. These regulations are substantively indistinguishable from statutory law; their content on the whole may be more detailed and specific than legislation, but there are certainly statutory provisions that are as narrow and technical as any regulation. It is on the procedural level that the two are chiefly distinguishable: legislation is voted on by the people's chosen representatives, and regulations are not.

While it is impossible to measure the degree to which legislative power now rests with the federal agencies, one indicator is the size of the Code of Federal Regulations, the official compendium of all formally promulgated regulations. Its nearly 200 volumes form a stack seventeen feet high—over 100,000 pages in all.

As elected officials lose control over policymaking and all its mind-boggling complexities, the focus of the Congress is shifting away from legislation and toward more tangible and comprehensible pursuits. The new center of congressional attention is "constituent services"—interceding with the federal bureaucracy on behalf of voters and contributors. This can be as innocuous as helping the proverbial little old lady get her Social Security check, and as sinister as running interference for Charles Keating. In any event, this kind of casework has become the bread and butter of congressional offices. For example, the Pentagon is flooded with over 100,000 written inquiries from Capitol Hill a year—not to mention 2,500 phone calls every business day. And in a recent poll of House administrative assistants (representatives' chiefs of staff), 56 percent identified constituent services as the single most important factor behind their boss's political success, as opposed to only 11 percent who considered their congressman's legislative record to be most important.

The basic character of Congress is changing from a body of lawmakers to a group of ombudsmen. Representative government is quite simply disintegrating, as general policymaking gives way to the much more comprehensible and manageable task of doing favors for specific constituents.

A FEW WELL-DEFINED TASKS

For democracy to be redeemed from its present corruption, a massive rollback in government is needed. The present political culture, unconstrained by any limiting principles and addicted to federal "solutions" to every conceivable problem, must be abandoned. What is needed instead is government that is limited to a few well-defined tasks, tasks whose connections to the general welfare are matters of broad-based consensus. Within this delimited public sphere, effective popular control can again become a reality. With so much less to oversee, the electorate's attention would be sharper and more focused, and lawmakers would have the chance to weigh and consider before they vote.

Reduced to manageable proportions, its responsibilities clearly drawn, government could actually be made governable again.

Short of such basic change, though, American democracy will continue to deteriorate. Elimination of PACs [political action committees], reduction of the franking privilege, term limitations—all are welcome, but these and other proposed reforms are at best half-measures. A real solution must address the root of the matter: the irresolvable conflict between democracy and Leviathan.

Is a Big Government Bureaucracy Inherently Incompatible with Democracy?

KENNETH F. WARREN

We Have Debated Ad Nauseam the Legitimacy of the Administrative State—But Why?

THE ADMINISTRATIVE STATE IS LEGITIMATE BECAUSE THE LAW SAYS IT IS

I have had a difficult time listening to arguments which have focused on the legitimacy of the administrative state itself (not some of its specific features, actions, or programs) because the deeply entrenched traditional role the administrative state has been playing in our political system is a major reality we cannot ignore. Whether the big governmental bureaucracy or the administrative state is legitimate under most scholarly definitions and applications is really beside the point. In *The Bureaucratic Experience* Ralph Hummel (1987) discusses many functional aspects of the administrative state today that many critics regard as "illegitimate," but he realistically acknowledges that "the agonies of the bureaucratic age" constitute reality, and we can best deal with big bureaucracy if we acknowledge its existence, try to understand it, and then do what we can to cope with it.

I interviewed the distinguished Professor Walter Gelhorn on various administrative law topics for the first edition of my administrative law textbook (Warren, 1982). I will never forget his reaction when I asked him whether he believed our administrative state was legitimate since the "law-making" powers delegated to our public administrators were probably unconstitutional because only Congress under Article I, Section I, had the exclusive power to make laws. Dismissing politely my naive tone in blatant body language, he noted that very technically speaking the administrative state is obviously illegitimate if we interpret the Constitution literally because a strict interpretation of the Constitution clearly did not permit such broad delegation. Practically speaking, he maintained, it did not make any difference because lawyers must work in court with the administrative state as it legally or actually exists. In a sobering remark, he exclaimed that you political scientists may want to spend your time debating the legitimacy of the administrative state, but we lawyers have to deal with its actual legal status (Gellhorn, 1990).

Is Gellhorn's insight wrong? I think not. The bottom line is that we may debate the legitimacy of the administrative state forever, but the administrative state with all of its functional parts is what the courts from day to day say it is. That means that the administrative state's complete legal or legitimate status changes from court decision to court decision, although its basic acceptance as legitimate or constitutional has been upheld for over half a century. The irony, in light of the recent debate during the Reagan-Bush years on the administrative state's legitimacy, is that although the courts have oftentimes overruled a particular action by the administrative state as illegal or illegitimate, the federal courts have never seriously questioned the legitimacy of the administrative state since 1936 when the Supreme Court itself in *United States* v. *Curtiss-Wright Export Co.* (299 U.S. 304) legitimated the administrative state by upholding a significant delegation of law-making powers by Congress to the administrative branch. The federal courts, led by the Supreme Court, have never reversed this position, although a few state courts have questioned the wisdom of legally legitimating the administrative state by refusing to uphold "unreasonably broad" delegations of authority to administrative agencies in the absence of any clear legislative intent that authorized it.[1]

In fact, after a long series of Supreme Court decisions, which upheld increasingly broader delegations of power to agency administrators since the 1936 *Curtiss-Wright* ruling, Justice Thurgood Marshall apparently wanted to put an end to the debate concerning the legitimacy of the administrative state by declaring the nondelegation doctrine dead in *National Cable Ass'n* v. *United States,* 415 U.S. 336 (1974). Justice Marshall asserted that non-delegation "was briefly in vogue in the 1930s, has been virtually abandoned by the Court for all practical purposes," and today "is surely moribund as the substantive due process approach of the same era" (at 352–53). A year later, the spirit of Marshall's position was reiterated in *Algonquin SNG, Inc.* v. *Federal Energy Administration,* 518 F.2d 1051, 1063 (1975), when the court held: "Here the delegated power is broad, and Congress has had repeated opportunities to limit it or withdraw it altogether. It has not done so, and I think this court should not do so."[2]

It should be stressed that both liberal and conservative courts have upheld the power of the administrative state by deferring time and time again to agency discretion and expertise. Only rarely do the courts challenge and overrule the use of administrative power, even when deregulation was in high gear during the late 1970s and 1980s. In the 1980s, Bernard Schwartz noted: "Of course, the scope of review is normally dominated by the doctrine of deference to the agency. This has not yet been altered by the changed atmosphere that is starting to prevail in the regulatory area" (Schwartz, 1980). Martin Shapiro also maintained that the courts have expressed an increasing willingness to defer to agency discretionary authority and expertise. Ironically, this came at a time when the Republican party, especially its large and influential conservative wing, was vehemently attacking the legitimacy of the administrative state (Shapiro, 1983).

Over 50 years ago, the Supreme Court gave a big boost to the administrative state's legitimacy in our governmental system by holding: "Where, as here, a determination has been left to an administrative body, this delegation will be respected and the administrative conclusion left untouched" (*Gray* v. *Powell*, 314 U.S. 402, 412; 1941). In 1992, the Supreme Court upheld this same perspective in *Arkansas* v. *Oklahoma*, 112 S. Ct. 1046, when it again routinely deferred to agency authority. The Court made a strong argument in support of the administrative state's independent power, stressing that courts should honor agency rulings unless "the agency has . . . *entirely* failed to consider an important aspect of the problem" (quoting from *Motor Vehicle Mfrs. Ass'n.* v. *State Farm Mutual Auto Ins.*, 463 U.S. 29, 43; 1983) (my emphasis). The Court concluded: "It is not our role . . . to decide which policy choice is the better one, for it is clear that Congress had entrusted such decisions to the Environmental Protection Agency" (at 1061) (i.e., the administrative state).

THE ADMINISTRATIVE STATE'S LEGITIMACY HAS BEEN DEMOCRATICALLY SANCTIONED

Congress has sanctioned the legitimacy of the administrative through delegation. Our public administrators, including our presidents, have accepted and even expanded such delegated powers, while the courts have been very willing to declare constitutional the awesome powers exercised by our administrative state. So it seems that our governmental leaders through their actions have legitimated the administrative state, but has the public? Francis Rourke suggests that the real test for legitimacy in a democratic country is whether the people perceive as legitimate governmental institutions or actions. So he poses the question: "Is the power that bureaucracies wield legitimate power, in the sense that is it accepted by those subject to it as being rightfully exercised?" (Rourke, 1987). The answer is resounding, "Yes!" Several scholars in recent years have written that the administrative state has a legitimacy crisis[3] and that this can be seen in the negative attitudes Americans have experienced toward big government and its civil servants. Although it is true that public opinion polls consistently show that Americans oppose big governmental bureaucracy in principle, poll data nevertheless disclose that Americans want the very things that have required the administrative state to emerge and flourish. That is, Americans consistently favor supporting an almost endless list of governmental programs, which require big bureaucracy, and generally support maintaining or increasing current funding levels for these programs.

For example, in 1989 the Gallup Poll asked whether a list of governmental programs should be "increased," "kept the same," or "decreased." Ninety-three percent said "same" to "increased" for combating the drug problem; 90 percent answered "same" to "increased" for AIDS research; 95 percent said "same" or "increased" for programs for the elderly; 93 percent responded "same" or "increased" for Social Security; 88 percent answered "same" or "increased" for environmental protection; 87 percent said "same" or "increased" for scientific research; and 60 percent answered "same" or "increased" for defense[4] (Gallup, 1990). In other words, this public opinion poll, as well as others, makes clear that the American people, despite their dislike for the administrative state in the abstract, overwhelmingly legitimize its role in American society through their firm approval of the numerous governmental programs that only the administrative state can implement. Thus, in the future, we should focus on improving the operations of the administrative state and stop dwelling on questions concerning its legitimacy.

NOTES

1. For example, *Bio-Medical Laboratories, Inc. v. Trainor,* 1977. 370 N.E. 2d 223; and *State v. Broom,* 1983. 439 So. 2d 357.

2. Although this was said by Judge Robb in dissent, the Supreme Court upheld the wisdom of Robb's opinion in reversing the appeals court's majority (426 U.S. 548; 1976).

3. See, for example Rosen (1986), Farazmand (1989) and Freedman (1978).

4. Over the years, American public opinion has favored continued or increased support for practically every program mentioned.

References

Farazmand, Ali, 1989. "Crisis in the Administrative State." *Administration and Society,* vol. 21 (August).

Freedman, James O., 1978. *Crisis and Legitimacy.* Cambridge, Eng.: Cambridge University Press.

Gallup, George Jr., 1990. *The Gallup Poll: Public Opinion 1989.* Wilmington, VA: Scholarly Resource, Inc., pp. 103–104.

Gellhorn, Walter, 1990. Personal interview.

Hummel, Ralph P., 1987. *The Bureaucratic Experience,* 3d ed. New York: St. Martin's Press, pp. viii, 1–21, 247–269.

Rosen, Bernard, 1986. "Crisis in the U.S. Civil Service." *Public Administration Review,* vol. 46 (May-June).

Rourke, Francis E., 1987. "Bureaucracy in the American Constitutional Order." *Political Science Quarterly,* vol. 102 (Summer), p. 228.

Schwartz, Bernard, 1980. "Administrative Law Cases During 1979." *Administrative Law Review,* vol. 32 (Summer), p. 435.

Shapiro, Martin, 1983. "Administrative Discretion: The Next Stage." *Yale Law Journal,* vol. 92 (July), pp. 1490–95.

Warren, Kenneth F., 1982. *Administrative Law in the American Political System.* St. Paul, MN: West Publishing Co.

Questions for Discussion

1. What effect would the dismantling of big government have on U.S. society?
2. What evidence can be used to determine whether the American people support big government?
3. How can waste in government be reduced?
4. What powers does the Congress have to control the bureaucracy?
5. What powers does the bureaucracy have to thwart the will of Congress?

Suggested Readings

Goodsell, Charles T. *The Case for Bureaucracy: A Public Administration Polemic*, 3d ed. Chatham, N.J.: Chatham House, 1994.

Goldstein, Mark L. *America's Hollow Government: How Washington Has Failed the People*. Homewood, Ill.: Business One Irwin, 1992.

Gormley, William T., Jr. *Taming the Bureaucracy: Muscles, Prayers and Other Strategies*. Princeton, N.J.: Princeton Univ. Press, 1989.

Ingraham, Patricia W., Donald F. Kettl, and Charles H. Levine. *Agenda for Excellence: Public Service in America*. Chatham, N.J.: Chatham House, 1992.

Ledeen, Michael. "Busting the Bureaucracy." *American Spectator*, 25, no. 10 (October 1992), 41–42.

Meier, Kenneth J. *Politics and the Bureaucracy: Policymaking in the Fourth Branch of Government*, 3d ed. Pacific Grove, Calif.: Brooks/Cole, 1993.

Osborne, David, and Ted Gaebler. *Reinventing Government: How the Entrepreneurial Spirit Is Transforming the Public Sector*. Reading, Mass.: Addison-Wesley, 1992.

Parkinson, C. Northcote. *Parkinson's Law, and Other Studies in Administration*. Boston: Houghton Mifflin, 1957.

Rosen, Bernard. *Holding Government Bureaucracies Accountable*. 2d ed. New York: Praeger, 1989.

Walters, Jonathan. "The Shrink-Proof Bureaucracy." *Governing*, 5, no. 6 (March 1992), 32–38.

Wilson, James Q. *Bureaucracy: What Government Agencies Do and Why They Do It*. New York: Basic Books, 1989.

Chapter 15

Should the Supreme Court Abide by a
Strict Constructionist Philosophy?

Of the three branches of the federal government—president, Congress, and the Supreme Court—the last is the least democratic. Although representative democracy requires periodic elections, the members of the Supreme Court are appointed, never run for office in popular elections, and once on the Court, usually remain there for life or until they retire. Presidents, senators, and representatives may envy the justices' luxury of not having to run for public office.

The Supreme Court's power of judicial review is—at least on the surface—another undemocratic feature of this arm of government. Judicial review is the power of the Supreme Court to examine state and federal laws and the acts of state and federal public officials to determine whether they are in conflict with the Constitution. If these laws and acts are in conflict, then the Court may declare them invalid. The fact that a majority of nine unelected members of the Court may declare null and void the laws enacted by the representatives of the majority of the people who vote seems to be a limitation on the principle of majority rule. The argument is often made, however, that the specific content of court decisions has strengthened rather than weakened democracy.

Judicial review is not the practice in all representative democracies. The British system of government, for example, permits the courts to interpret the laws but not to declare an act of Parliament void. Judicial review is not specifically mentioned in the Constitution of the United States. Debate surrounds the question of whether the Framers intended the Supreme Court to have this power over the laws of the federal government. There is general agreement, however, that the Framers understood that judicial review is applicable to acts of state legislatures in conflict with the Constitution. The Supreme Court first declared an act of Congress unconstitutional in *Marbury* v. *Madison* (1803). In this case the court found the Judiciary Act of 1789 to be in conflict with Article III of the Constitution. Today the Supreme Court's authority to declare a statute unconstitutional is unchallenged.

Over the past century the Supreme Court has exercised its power of judicial review in a variety of cases. Those who have benefited from the Court's decisions have hailed the wisdom of the Court. The "losers" have called for a variety of responses, including limiting the jurisdiction of the Court, amending the Constitution, enlarging the size of the Court, or impeaching the chief justice.

Court decisions have not supported one group of people exclusively. In the early part of the twentieth century, for example, Court decisions were more favorable to big business, states' rights advocates, and segregation-ists. Since the days of the Warren Court (for former Chief Justice Earl Warren) in the mid-1950s, however, Court decisions have been more fa-vorable to groups demanding extension of civil rights and civil liberties. The changing character of Supreme Court decisions is a reflection of such factors as the composition of the Court, legal precedents, and the political environment. One other factor that has received much attention, how-ever, is the philosophical outlook of the judges.

Two principal philosophical outlooks have guided judicial decision making, and they are always in conflict. As we saw in Chapter 1, William Bradford Reynolds held the intentions of the Framers of the Constitution in the highest regard, while Thurgood Marshall argued that the wisdom of the Constitution lies in its adaptability to changing social needs. Strict constructionists, like Reynolds, believe that the Supreme Court should be bound by the intent of the Framers and the language in the document itself. Loose constructionists argue that strict constructionism is miscon-ceived, impossible, or even fraudulent. At various times in U.S. history, conservatives have supported strict constructionism, but liberals, too, at times, have taken a similar philosophical approach.

The debate below elicits the main arguments of the contending schools. Federal appeals court judge J. Clifford Wallace makes a case for interpre-tivism—the principle that judges, in resolving constitutional questions, should rely on the express provisions of the Constitution or upon those norms that are clearly implicit in its text. He contends

1. The Constitution itself envisions and requires interpretivist re-view.
2. Interpretivist review promotes the stability and predictability essential to the rule of law.
3. Judges are not particularly well suited to make judgments of broad social policy.
4. The argument put forward by noninterpretivists that certain constitutional provisions invite justices to use value judgments outside the Constitution is invalid.
5. Although the Framers' intent cannot be ascertained on every issue, interpretivism will exclude from consideration entire ranges of improper judicial responses.
6. The Fourteenth Amendment did not produce so fundamental a revision in the nature of U.S. government that the intentions of the Framers are scarcely relevant any longer.
7. The Constitution can still be changed by the only legitimate means for which it provides: formal amendment.
8. When noninterpretivists justify their actions on the basis of "doing justice," they act improperly because they are incapable of deciding what is just.

9. An activist judiciary undermines the very principles of democracy.
10. An interpretivist view shows respect for precedent.

Law professor Jeffrey M. Shaman takes the negative position on the issue. He contends:

1. History shows that whenever the Supreme Court makes a decision that someone does not like, the justices are accused of holding to their own personal views and not to the words of the Constitution or the intent of the Framers.
2. From its early history, the Supreme Court has had to go outside the written Constitution and the intent of the Framers in making some decisions.
3. The Court often must create meaning for the Constitution because the document is rife with general and abstract language.
4. There is no reason to pay greater attention to the intent of the Framers than to that of the people who ratified the Constitution or to the succeeding generations who retain it.
5. The intent of the Framers is difficult to discern.
6. The conditions that shaped the Framers' attitudes have changed in two centuries of constitutional experience.
7. The Constitution provides only the bare bones; its meaning must be augmented by the justices.
8. The Court is subject to popular constraints that keep its power limited.

 YES

Should the Supreme Court Abide by a Strict Constructionist Philosophy?

J. CLIFFORD WALLACE
The Case for Judicial Restraint

This year we celebrate the 200th anniversary of our Constitution. This remarkable document has structured our government and secured our liberty as we have developed from 13 fledgling colonies into a mature and strong democracy. Without doubt, the Constitution is one of the grandest political achievements of the modern world.

In spite of this marvelous record, we will celebrate our nation's charter in the midst of a hotly contested debate on the continuing role that it should have in our society. Two schools of constitutional jurisprudence are engaged in a long-running battle. Some contend that the outcome of this conflict may well determine whether the Constitution remains our vital organic document or whether it instead becomes a curious historical relic. The competing positions in this constitutional battle are often summarized by a variety of labels: judicial restraint versus judicial activism, strict construction versus loose construction, positivism versus natural law, conservative versus liberal, interpretivism versus noninterpretivism.

In large measure, these labels alone are of little assistance in analyzing a complex problem. Ultimately, what is at stake is what Constitution will govern this country. Will it be the written document drafted by the Framers, ratified by the people, and passed down, with amendments, to us? Or will it be an illusive parchment upon which modern-day judges may freely engrave their own political and sociological preferences?

In this article, I intend to outline and defend a constitutional jurisprudence of judicial restraint.[1] My primary thesis is that a key principle of judicial restraint—namely, interpretivism—is required by our constitutional plan. I will also explore how practitioners of judicial restraint should resolve the tension that can arise in our current state of constitutional law between interpretivism and a second important principle, respect for judicial precedent.

INTERPRETIVISM VERSUS NONINTERPRETIVISM

What is the difference between "interpretivism" and "noninterpretivism"? This question is important because I believe interpretivism to be the cornerstone of a constitutional jurisprudence of judicial restraint. By "interpretivism," I mean the principle that judges, in resolving constitutional questions, should rely on the express provisions of the Constitution or upon those norms that are clearly implicit in its text.[2] Under an interpretivist approach, the original intention of the Framers is the controlling guide for constitutional interpretation. This does not mean, of course, that judges may apply a constitutional provision only to situations specifically contemplated by the Framers. Rather, it simply requires that when considering whether to invalidate the work of the political branches, the judges do so from a starting point fairly discoverable in the Constitution.[3] By contrast, under noninterpretive review, judges may freely rest their decisions on value judgments that admittedly are not supported by, and may even contravene, the text of the Constitution and the intent of the Framers.[4]

INTERPRETIVIST REVIEW

I believe that the Constitution itself envisions and requires interpretivist review. To explore this thesis, we should first examine the Constitution as a political and historical document.

As people read the Constitution, many are struck by how procedural and technical its provisions are. Perhaps on first reading it may be something of a disappointment. In contrast to the fiery eloquence of the Declaration of Independence, the Constitution may seem dry or even dull. This difference in style, of course, reflects the very different functions of the two documents. The Declaration of Independence is an indictment of the reign of King George III. In a flamboyant tone, it is brilliantly crafted to persuade the world of the justice of our fight for independence. The Constitution, by contrast, establishes the basic set of rules for the nation. Its genius lies deeper, in its skillful design of a government structure that would best ensure liberty and democracy.

The primary mechanism by which the Constitution aims to protect liberty and democracy is the dispersion of government power. Recognizing that concentrated power poses the threat of tyranny, the Framers divided authority between the states and the federal government. In addition, they created three separate and co-equal branches of the federal government in a system of checks and balances.

The Framers were also aware, of course, that liberty and democracy can come into conflict. The Constitution, therefore, strikes a careful balance between democratic rule and minority rights. Its republican, representative features are designed to channel and refine cruder majoritarian impulses. In addition, the Constitution's specific individual protections, particularly in the Bill of Rights, guarantee against certain majority intrusions. Beyond these guarantees, the Constitution places its trust in the democratic process—the voice of the people expressed through their freely elected representatives.

Raoul Berger argues persuasively in *Government by Judiciary* that the Constitution "was written against a background of interpretive presuppositions that assured the Framers their design would be effectuated."[5] The importance of that statement may escape us today, when it is easy to take for granted that the Constitution is a written document. But for the Framers, the fact that the Constitution was in writing was not merely incidental. They recognized that a written constitution provides the most stable basis for the rule of law, upon which liberty and justice ultimately depend.

As Thomas Jefferson observed, "Our peculiar security is in the possession of a written constitution. Let us not make it a blank paper by construction."[6] Chief Justice John Marshall, in *Marbury* v. *Madison*, the very case establishing the power of judicial review, emphasized the constraints imposed by the written text and the judicial duty to respect these constraints in all cases raising constitutional questions.[7]

Moreover, the Framers recognized the importance of interpreting the Constitution according to their original intent. In Madison's words, if "the sense in which the Constitution was accepted and ratified by the Nation . . . be not the guide in expounding it, there can be no security for a consistent and stable government, [nor] for a fruitful exercise of its powers."[8] Similarly, Jefferson as President acknowledged his duty to administer the Constitution "according to the safe and honest meaning contemplated by the plain understanding of the people at the time of its adoption—a meaning to be found in the explanations of those who advocated . . . it."[9] It seems clear, therefore, that the leading Framers were interpretivists and believed that constitutional questions should be reviewed by that approach.

Next, I would like to consider whether interpretivism is necessary to effectuate the constitutional plan. The essential starting point is that the Constitution established a separation of powers to protect our freedom. Because freedom is fundamental, so too is the separation of powers. But separation of powers becomes a meaningless slogan if judges may confer constitutional status on whichever rights they happen to deem important, regardless of textual basis. In effect, under noninterpretive review, the judiciary functions as a superlegislature beyond the check of the other two branches. Noninterpretivist review also disregards the Constitution's careful allocation of most decisions to the democratic process, allowing the legislature to make decisions deemed best for society. Ultimately, noninterpretivist review reduces our written Constitution to insignificance and threatens to impose a tyranny of the judiciary.

PRUDENTIAL CONSIDERATIONS

Important prudential considerations also weigh heavily in favor of interpretivist review. The rule of law is fundamental in our society. To be effective, it cannot be tossed to and fro by each new sociological wind. Because it is rooted in written text, interpretivist review promotes the stability and predictability essential to the rule of the law. By contrast, noninterpretivist review presents an infinitely variable array of possibilities. The Constitution would vary with each judge's conception of what is important. To demonstrate the wide variety of tests that could be applied, let us briefly look at the writings of legal academics who advocate noninterpretivism.

Assume each is a judge deciding the same constitutional issue. One professor seeks to "cement a union between the distributional patterns of the modern welfare state and the federal constitution." Another "would guarantee a whole range of nontextually based rights against government to ensure 'the dignity of full membership in society.'" A third argues that the courts should give a "concrete meaning and application" to those values that "give our society an identity and inner coherence [and] its distinctive public morality." Yet another professor sees the court as having a "prophetic" role in developing moral standards in a "dialectical relationship" with Congress, from which he sees emerging a "more mature" political morality. One professor even urges that the court apply the contractarian moral theory of Professor Rawls' *A Theory of Justice* to constitutional questions.[10] One can easily see the fatal vagueness and subjectivity of this approach: each judge would apply his or her own separate and diverse personal values in interpreting the same constitutional question. Without anchor, we drift at sea.

Another prudential argument against noninterpretivism is that judges are not particularly well-suited to make judgments of broad social policy. We judges decide cases on the basis of a limited record that largely represents the efforts of the parties to the litigation. Legislators, with their committees, hearings, and more direct role in the political process, are much better equipped institutionally to decide what is best for society.

NONINTERPRETIVIST ARGUMENTS

But are there arguments in favor of noninterpretivism? Let us consider several assertions commonly put forth by proponents. One argument asserts that certain constitutional provisions invite judges to import into the constitutional decision process value judgments derived from outside the Constitution. Most commonly, advocates of this view rely on the due process clause of the Fifth and Fourteenth Amendments. It is true that courts have interpreted the due process clause to authorize broad review of the substantive merits of legislation. But is that what the draftsmen had in mind? Some constitutional scholars make a strong argument that the clause, consistent with its plain language, was intended to have a limited procedural meaning.[11]

A second argument asserts that the meaning of the constitutional text and the intention of the Framers cannot be ascertained with sufficient precision to guide constitutional decisionmaking. I readily acknowledge that interpretivism will not always provide easy answers to difficult constitutional questions. The judicial role will always involve the exercise of discretion. The strength of interpretivism is that it channels and constrains this discretion in a manner consistent with the Constitution. While it does not necessarily ensure a correct result, it does exclude from consideration entire ranges of improper judicial responses.

Third, some have suggested that the Fourteenth Amendment effected such a fundamental revision in the nature of our government that the intentions of the original Framers are scarcely relevant any longer. It is, of course, true that federal judges have seized upon the Fourteenth Amendment as a vehicle to restructure federal/state relations. The argument, however, is not one-sided. Berger, for example, persuasively demonstrates that the framers of the Fourteenth Amendment sought much more limited objectives.[12] In addition, one reasonable interpretation of the history of the amendment demonstrates that its framers, rather than intending an expanded role for the federal courts, meant for Congress (under section 5 of the amendment) to play the primary role in enforcing its provisions.[13] Thus, it can be argued that to the extent that the Fourteenth Amendment represented an innovation in the constitutional role of the judiciary, it was by limiting the courts' traditional role in enforcing constitutional rights and by providing added responsibility for the Congress.

Advocates of noninterpretivism also contend that we should have a "living Constitution" rather than be bound by "the dead hand of the Framers." These slogans prove nothing. An interpretivist approach would not constrict government processes; on the contrary, it would ensure that issues are freely subject to the workings of the democratic process. Moreover, to the extent that the Constitution might profit from revision, the amendment process of Article V provides the only constitutional means. Judicial amendment under a noninterpretivist approach is simply an unconstitutional usurpation.

Almost certainly, the greatest support for a noninterpretive approach derives from its perceived capacity to achieve just results. Why quibble over the Constitution, after all, if judges who disregard it nevertheless "do justice"? Such a view is dangerously shortsighted and naive. In the first place, one has no cause to believe that the results of noninterpretivism will generally be "right." Individual judges have widely varying conceptions of what values are important. Noninterpretivists spawned the "conservative" substantive economic due process of the 1930s as well as the "liberal" decisions of the Warren Court. There is no principle result in noninterpretivism.

But even if the judge would always be right, the process would be wrong. A benevolent judicial tyranny is nonetheless a tyranny. Our Constitution rests on the faith that democracy is intrinsically valuable. From an instrumental perspective, democracy might at times produce results that are not as desirable as platonic guardians might produce. But the democratic process—our participation in a system of self-government—has transcendental value. Moreover, one must consider the very real danger that an activist judiciary stunts the development of a responsible democracy by removing from it the duty to make difficult decisions. If we are to remain faithful to the values of democracy and liberty, we must insist that courts respect the Constitution's allocation of social decisionmaking to the political branches.

RESPECT FOR PRECEDENT

I emphasized earlier the importance of stability to the rule of law. I return to that theme now to consider a second principle of judicial restraint: respect for precedent. Respect for precedent is a principle widely accepted, even if not always faithfully followed. It requires simply that a judge follow prior case law in deciding legal questions. Respect for precedent promotes predictability and uniformity. It constrains a judge's discretion and satisfies the reasonable expectations of the parties. Through its application, citizens can have a better understanding of what the law is and act accordingly.

Unfortunately, in the present state of constitutional law, the two principles of judicial restraint that I have outlined can come into conflict. While much of constitutional law is consistent with the principle of interpretivism, a significant portion is not. This raises the question how a practitioner of judicial restraint should act in circumstances where respecting precedent would require acceptance of law developed under a noninterpretivist approach.

The answer is easy for a judge in my position, and, indeed, for any judge below the United States Supreme Court. As a judge on the Ninth Circuit Court of Appeals, I am bound to follow Supreme Court and Ninth Circuit precedent even when I believe it to be wrong. There is a distinction, however, between following precedent and extending it. Where existing precedent does not fairly govern a legal question, the principle of interpretivism should guide a judge.

For Supreme Court justices, the issue is more complex. The Supreme Court obviously is not infallible. Throughout its history, the Court has at times rejected its own precedents. Because the Supreme Court has the ultimate judicial say on what the Constitution means, its justices have a special responsibility to ensure that they are properly expounding constitutional law as well as fostering stability and predictability.

Must Supreme Court advocates of judicial restraint passively accept the errors of activist predecessors? There is little rational basis for doing so. Periodic activist inroads could emasculate fundamental doctrines and undermine the separation of powers. Nevertheless, the values of predictability and uniformity that respect for precedent promotes demand caution in overturning precedent. In my view, a justice should consider overturning a prior decision only when the decision is clearly wrong, has significant effects, and would otherwise be difficult to remedy.

Significantly, constitutional decisions based on a noninterpretivist approach may satisfy these three criteria. When judges confer constitutional status on their own value judgments without support in the language of the Constitution and the original intention of the Framers, they commit clear error. Because constitutional errors frequently affect the institutional structure of government and the allocation of decisions to the democratic process, they are likely to have important effects. And because constitutional decisions, unlike statutory decisions, cannot be set aside through normal political channels, they will generally meet the third requirement. In sum, then, despite the prudential interests furthered by respect for precedent, advocates of judicial restraint may be justified in seeking to overturn noninterpretivist precedent.

CONCLUSION

It is obvious that courts employing interpretivist review cannot solve many of the social and political problems facing America, indeed, even some very important problems. The interpretivist would respond that the Constitution did not place the responsibility for solving those problems with the courts. The courts were not meant to govern the core of our political and social life—Article I gave that duty, for national issues, to the Congress. It is through our democratically elected representatives that we legitimately develop this fabric of our life. Interpretivism encourages that process. It is, therefore, closer to the constitutional plan of governance than is noninterpretivist review.

After 200 years, the Constitution is not "broke"—we need not fix it—just apply it.

NOTES

This article is adapted from an address given at Hillsdale College, Hillsdale, Michigan, on March 5, 1986.

1. I have elsewhere presented various aspects of this jurisprudence. See, e.g., Wallace, "A Two Hundred Year Old Constitution in Modern Society." 61 *Texas Law Review,* 1575 (1983); Wallace, "The Jurisprudence of Judicial Restraint: A Return to the Moorings." *George Washington Law Review* 1 (1981).

2. Wallace, "A Two Hundred Year Old Constitution," *supra* n. 1; Ely, *Democracy and Distrust* 1 (Cambridge, MA: Harvard University Press, 1980).

3. Ely, *supra* n. 2, at 2.

4. See *id.* at 43–72.

5. Berger, *Government by Judiciary* 366 (Cambridge, MA: Harvard University Press, 1977).

6. *Id.* at 364, *quoting* Letter to Wilson Cary Nicholas (Sept. 7, 1803).

7. *Marbury v. Madison,* 5 U.S. (1 Cranch) 137, 176–180 (1803).

8. Berger, *supra* n. 5, at 364, quoting *The Writings of James Madison* 191 (G. Hunt ed. 1900–1910).

9. Id. at 366–367, citing 4 Elliot, *Debates in the Several State Conventions on the Adoption of the Federal Constitution* 446 (1836).

10. Monaghan, "Our Perfect Constitution," 56 *New York University Law Review,* 353, 358–360 (1981) (summarizing theories of noninterpretivists).

11. See, e.g., Berger, *supra* n. 5, at 193–220.

12. See *id.*

13. See *id.* at 220–229.

Should the Supreme Court Abide by a Strict Constructionist Philosophy?

JEFFREY M. SHAMAN

The Supreme Court's Proper and Historic Function

Considerable criticism, frequently quite sharp, has recently been directed at the Supreme Court for the way it has gone about its historic function of interpreting the Constitution. In particular, Edwin Meese, the current Attorney General of the United States [1987], has accused the Court of exceeding its lawful authority by failing to adhere strictly to the words of the Constitution and the intentions of the Framers who drafted those words.[1]

The Attorney General's attack upon the Court echoes a similar one made by Richard Nixon, who, campaigning for the Presidency in 1968, denounced Supreme Court Justices who, he claimed, twisted and bent the Constitution according to their personal predilections. If elected President, Nixon promised to appoint to the Court strict constructionists whose decisions would conform to the text of the Constitution and the intent of the Framers. (Ironically, it is some of the Nixon appointees to the Court that Meese now accuses of twisting and bending the Constitution.)

I hasten to add that it is not only politicians who sing the praises of strict constructionism; there are judges and lawyers, as well as some scholars, who join the song. Among legal scholars, though, the response to strict constructionism has been overwhelmingly negative. There are legal scholars, for instance, who describe strict constructionism as a "misconceived quest,"[2] an "impossibility,"[3] and even a "fraud."[4]

Those who criticize the Court point to rulings during the tenure of Chief Justice Burger, most notably the decision in *Roe* v. *Wade*[5] legalizing abortion, as examples of illegitimate revision or amendment of the Constitution based upon the personal beliefs of the justices. Some years ago, similar charges were leveled at the Warren Court for its ruling requiring reapportionment along the lines of one person-one vote,[6] its decision striking down school prayer,[7] and other rulings, even including the one in *Brown* v. *Board of Education* outlawing school segregation.[8]

It should not be supposed, however, that strict constructionism is always on the side of conservative political values. In the 1930s it was the liberals who claimed that the Supreme Court was not strictly construing the Constitution when the justices repeatedly held that minimum wage, maximum hour, and other protective legislation violated the Fourteenth Amendment.[9] As the liberals then saw it, the conservative justices on the Court were illegitimately incorporating their personal values into the Fourteenth Amendment, which had been meant to abolish racial discrimination, not to protect the prerogatives of employers.

HISTORY LESSONS

The lesson of this bit of history seems to be that, whether liberal or conservative or somewhere in between, whoever has an ox that is being gored at the time has a tendency to yell "foul." Whenever the Supreme court renders a decision that someone doesn't like, apparently it is not enough to disagree with the decision; there also has to be an accusation that the Court's decision was illegitimate, being based upon the justice's personal views and not the words of the Constitution or the intent of the Framers.

We can go back much further in history than the 1930s to find the Supreme court being accused of illegitimacy. In 1810, for instance, Thomas Jefferson condemned Chief Justice John Marshall for "twistifying" The Constitution according to his "personal biases."[10]

History also reveals something else extremely significant about the Court, which is that from its earliest days, the Court has found it necessary in interpreting the Constitution to look beyond the language of the document and the intent of the Framers. In the words of Stanford Law Professor Thomas Grey, it is "a matter of unarguable historical fact" that over the years the Court has developed a large body of constitutional law that derives neither from the text of the document nor the intent of the Framers.[11]

Moreover, this has been so from the Court's very beginning. Consider, for example, a case entitled *Hylton* v. *United States*,[12] which was decided in 1796 during the term of the Court's first Chief Justice, John Jay. The *Hylton* case involved a tax ranging from $1.00 to $10.00 that had been levied by Congress on carriages. Mr. Hylton, who was in the carriage trade and owned 125 carriages, understandably was unhappy about the tax, and went to court to challenge it. He claimed that the tax violated section 2 of Article I of the Constitution, which provides that direct taxes shall be apportioned among the several states according to their populations. Hylton argued that this tax was a direct one, and therefore unconstitutional because it had not been apportioned among the states by population. This, of course, was years before the enactment of the Sixteenth Amendment in 1913, authorizing a federal income tax. Prior to that, Article I prohibited a federal income tax, but what about a tax on the use or ownership of carriages—was that the sort of "direct" tax that was only permissible under Article I if apportioned among the states by population?

The Supreme Court, with several justices filing separate opinions in the case (which was customary at that time), upheld the tax as constitutional on the ground that it was not direct, and therefore not required to be apportioned. What is most significant about the *Hylton* case is how the Court went about making its decision. As described by Professor David Currie of the University of Chicago Law School, the Court in *Hylton* "paid little heed to the Constitution's words," and "policy considerations dominated all three opinions" filed by the Justices.[13] In fact, each of the opinions asserted that apportioning a carriage tax among the states would be unfair, because a person in a state with fewer carriages would have to pay a higher tax. While this may or may not be unfair, the justices pointed to nothing in the Constitution itself or the intent of the Framers to support their personal views of fairness. Moreover, one of the justices, Justice Patterson, went so far in his opinion as to assert that the constitutional requirement of apportioning direct taxes was "radically wrong," and therefore should not be extended to this case. In other words, he based his decision, at least in part, upon his antipathy to a constitutional provision.

While Justice Patterson went too far in that respect, he and his colleagues on the court could hardly have made a decision in the case by looking to the text of the Constitution or the intent of the Framers. The language of the document simply does not provide an answer to the constitutional issue raised by the situation in *Hylton*. The text of the document merely refers to "direct" taxes and provides no definition of what is meant by a direct tax. Furthermore, as Professor Currie points out, the records of the debates at the Constitutional Convention show that "the Framers had no clear idea of what they meant by direct taxes."[14] Thus, to fulfill their responsibility to decide the case and interpret the law, the justices found it necessary to create meaning for the Constitution.

CREATING MEANING

Indeed, it is often necessary for the Supreme court to create meaning for the Constitution. This is so because the Constitution, being a document designed (in the words of John Marshall) to "endure for ages,"[15] is rife with general and abstract language. Those two great sources of liberty in the Constitution, the due process and equal protection clauses, are obviously examples of abstract constitutional language that must be invested with meaning. The Fourth Amendment uses extremely general language in prohibiting "unreasonable" searches and seizures, and the Eighth Amendment is similarly general in disallowing "cruel and unusual" punishment.

Even many of the more specific provisions of the Constitution need to be supplied with meaning that simply cannot be found within the four corners of the document. The First Amendment, for instance, states that Congress shall not abridge freedom of speech—but does that mean that the government may not regulate obscene, slanderous, or deceptive speech? The First Amendment also says that Congress shall not abridge the free exercise of religion—does that mean that the government may not prohibit polygamy or child labor when dictated by religious belief? These questions—which, by the way, all arose in actual cases—and, in fact, the vast majority of constitutional questions presented to the Supreme Court, cannot be resolved by mere linguistic analysis of the Constitution. In reality there is no choice but to look beyond the text of the document to provide meaning for the Constitution.

There are those, such as Attorney General Meese, who would hope to find meaning for the Constitution from its authors, the beloved and hallowed Framers of the sacred text. By reputation, these fellows are considered saints and geniuses; in actuality, they were politicians motivated significantly by self-interest.

THEORETICAL DRAWBACKS

But even if the Framers do deserve the awe that they inspire, reliance on their intentions to find meaning for the Constitution still has serious theoretical drawbacks. In the first place, why should we be concerned only with the intentions of the 55 individuals who drafted the Constitution and not the intentions of the people throughout the nation who ratified it, not to mention the intentions of the succeeding generations who retain the Constitution? After all, even when finally framed, the Constitution remained a legal nullity until ratified by the people, and would be a legal nullity again if revoked by the people. The Framers wrote the Constitution, but it is the people who enacted and retain the Constitution; so if anything, it is the people's intent about the document that would seem to be the relevant inquiry.

Moreover, there are considerable difficulties in discerning what in fact the Framers intended. The journal of the Constitutional Convention, which is the primary record of the Framer's intent, is neither complete nor entirely accurate. The notes for the journal were carelessly kept, and have been shown to contain several mistakes.[16]

Even when the record cannot be faulted, it is not always possible to ascertain the Framers' intent. As might be expected, the Framers did not express an intention about every constitutional issue that would arise after the document was drafted and adopted. No group of people, regardless of its members' ability, enjoys that sort of prescience. When the Framers did address particular problems, often only a few of them spoke out. What frequently is taken to be the intent of the Framers as a group turns out to be the intent of merely a few or even only one of the Framers.

There are also constitutional issues about which the Framers expressed conflicting intentions. A collective body of 55 individuals, the Framers embraced a widely diverse and frequently inconsistent set of views. The two principal architects of the Constitution, James Madison and Alexander Hamilton, for instance, had extremely divergent political views. Madison also on occasion differed with George Washington over the meaning of the Constitution. When Washington, who had presided over the Constitutional Convention, became President, he claimed that the underlying intent of the Constitution gave him the sole authority as President to proclaim neutrality and to withhold treaty papers from Congress. Madison, who had been a leader at the Constitutional Convention, disagreed vehemently. And so, the man who would come to be known as the father of this nation and the man who would come to be known as the father of the Constitution had opposing views of what the Framers intended.[17]

These examples demonstrate that it simply makes no sense to suppose that a multi-member group of human beings such as the Framers shared a unitary intent about the kind of controversial political issues addressed in our Constitution. We can see, then, that, at best, the so-called Framers' intent is inadequately documented, ambiguous, and inconclusive; at worst, it is nonexistent, an illusion.

Even if these insurmountable obstacles could be surmounted, there are other serious problems with trying to follow the path laid down by the Framers. The Framers formed their intentions in the context of a past reality and in accordance with past attitudes, both of which have changed considerably since the days when the Constitution was drafted. To transfer those intentions, fashioned as they were under past conditions and views, to contemporary situations may produce sorry consequences that even the Framers would have abhorred had they been able to foresee them. Blindly following intentions formulated in response to past conditions and attitudes is not likely to be an effective means of dealing with the needs of contemporary society.

LOCKED TO THE PAST

Some scholars take this line of reasoning one step further by maintaining that the Framers' intent is inextricably locked to the past and has no meaning at all for the present.[18] In other words, because the Framers formed their intentions with reference to a reality and attitudes that no longer exist, their intentions cannot be transplanted to the present day. What the Framers intended for their times is not what they may have intended for ours. Life constantly changes, and the reality and ideas that surrounded the Framers are long since gone.

The futility of looking to the Framers' intent to resolve modern constitutional issues can be illustrated by several cases that have arisen under the Fourth and Fifth Amendments. The Fourth Amendment prohibits unreasonable searches and seizures, and further requires that no search warrants be issued unless there is probable cause that a crime has been committed. Are bugging and other electronic surveillance devices "unreasonable searches"? May they be used by the police without a warrant based on probable cause? What about the current practice of some law enforcement agencies of using airplanes to fly over a suspect's property to take pictures with a telescopic camera—is that an "unreasonable search"? The Fifth Amendment states that no person shall be compelled to be a witness against himself. What about forcing a suspect to take a breathalyzer test, or a blood test, or to have his or her stomach pumped—do those procedures amount to self-incrimination that violates the Fifth Amendment?

Whatever you may think should be the answers to these questions, you cannot find the answers by looking to the Framers' intent. The Framers had no intent at all about electronic surveillance, airplanes, telescopic cameras, breathalyzer tests, blood tests, or stomach pumping, for the simple reason that none of those things existed until well after the days of the Framers. Not even Benjamin Franklin, for all his inventiveness, was able to foresee that in the 20th century constables would zip around in flying machines taking snapshots of criminal suspects through a telescopic lens.

Many of the difficulties in attempting to resolve constitutional issues by turning to the Framers are illustrated by the school prayer cases.[19] The religious beliefs of the Framers ranged from theism to atheism, and among even the more devout Framers there was a wide diversity of opinion concerning the proper relationship between church and state. Moreover, as often happens when human beings ponder complex issues, the views of individual Framers about church and state did not remain the same over time. As a member of Congress, James Madison, for example, once voted to approve a chaplain for the House of Representatives, but later decided that the appointment of the chaplain had been unconstitutional.[20] Insofar as school prayer specifically was concerned, the Framers expressed virtually no opinion on the matter, for the simple reason that at the time public schools were extremely rare. Thus, the Framers had no intention, either pro or con, about prayer in public schools.

Given the theoretical deficiencies of trying to decide constitutional questions by looking to the Framers' intent, it should come as no surprise that this approach has been a failure when attempted by the Supreme Court. Scholars who have closely studied the Court's use of this approach commonly agree that it has not been a satisfactory method of constitutional decisionmaking, because the Court ends up manipulating, revising, or even creating history under the guise of following the Framers' intent.[21] The fact of the matter is that neither the Framers' intent nor the words of the document are capable of providing much constitutional meaning.

BARE BONES

What we are left with, then, are the bare bones of a Constitution, the meaning of which must be augmented by the justices of the Supreme Court. And that is exactly what the justices have been doing since the Court was first established. The overwhelming evidence of history shows that the meaning of the Constitution has undergone constant change and evolution at the hands of the Supreme Court. Through the continual interpretation and reinterpretation of the text of the document, the Court perpetually creates new meaning for the document. Although it is formally correct that we, unlike the citizens of Great Britain, have a written Constitution, its words have been defined and redefined to the extent that for the most part we, like the citizens of Great Britain, have an unwritten Constitution, the meaning of which originates with the Supreme Court.

Strict constructionists argue that it is undemocratic for Supreme Court Justices—unelected officials who are unaccountable to the populace—to create meaning for the Constitution. Of course, using the Framers' intent to interpret the Constitution also is undemocratic; following the will of the 55 persons who supposedly framed the Constitution or the smaller group of them who actually participated in the framing is hardly an exercise in democracy.

When strict constructionists cry that the Court is undemocratic, they are ignoring that our government is not (and was not intended by the Framers) to be a pure democracy. Rather, it is a limited or constitutional democracy. What this means is that there are constitutional limits to what the majority may do. The majority may not, for example, engage in racial discrimination, even if it votes to do so in overwhelming numbers. The majority may not abridge freedom of speech or the free exercise of religion or other constitutional rights guaranteed to every individual.

Article III of the Constitution states that there shall be a Supreme Court, and in combination with Article II, decrees the Court's independence from the electorate. By its very terms, the Constitution establishes a counter-majoritarian branch of government, the Supreme Court, in juxtaposition to the more democratic executive and legislative branches. This scheme reflects one of the guiding principles that underlies the Constitution—the principle of separate powers that check and balance one another. The Supreme Court's constitutionally mandated independence functions as a check and balance upon the more majoritarian branches of federal and state governments. It thereby provides a means of maintaining constitutional boundaries on majoritarian rule.

The role of the Supreme Court is to enforce constitutional requirements upon the majoritarian branches of government, which otherwise would be completely unbridled. As dictated by the Constitution, majority control should be the predominant feature of our government, but subject to constitutional limits.

Moreover, the Supreme Court is not quite as undemocratic as the strict constructionists sometimes like to portray it to be. While it is true that the justices who sit on the Court are appointed rather than elected and that they may be removed from office only for improper behavior, it is also true that they are appointed by a popularly elected president, and their appointment must be confirmed by a popularly elected Senate. Turnover of the Court's personnel, which sometimes occurs frequently, enhances popular control of the Court. Additionally, the Court's constitutional rulings may be overruled by the people through constitutional amendment, which, though a difficult procedure, has been accomplished on four occasions.[22] Thus, while the court is not directly answerable to the public, it is not entirely immune from popular control.

THE ULTIMATE AUTHORITY

The people also have the ultimate authority to abolish the Supreme Court. That they have not done so during our two centuries of experience indicates popular acceptance of the Court's role. Admittedly, there are particular decisions rendered by the Court that have aroused considerable public outcry, but given the many controversial issues that the Court must decide, this is inevitable. More telling about the public attitude toward the Court is that the people have taken no action to curtail the Court's authority to interpret the Constitution. Indeed, the public has shown little, if any, inclination toward abolishing the Court or even restricting its powers. Despite Franklin Delano Roosevelt's overwhelming popularity, his "court-packing plan" was a dismal failure;[23] the proposal to establish a "Court of the Union" composed of state court justices which would have the power to overrule the Supreme Court evoked such widespread public disapproval that it was quickly abandoned;[24] the campaigns to impeach Justices Earl Warren and William O. Douglas never got off the ground;[25] and although various members of Congress often propose bills threatening to restrict the Court's jurisdiction, the full Congress always rebuffs those threats.[26] These experiences suggest that even in the face of controversial constitutional decisions, there has been abiding public consent to the role of the Supreme Court in our scheme of government.

The Court's role, when all is said and done, is to create meaning for a Constitution that otherwise would be a hollow document. It is perfectly appropriate for anyone to disagree with Supreme Court decisions, and to criticize the Court on that basis. But it is not appropriate to attack the Court's decisions as illegitimate on the ground that they do not follow the Framers' intent. Pretending to use the Framers' intent to impugn the legitimacy of the Supreme Court is a spurious enterprise. The Court's legitimate function is, and always has been, to provide meaning for the Constitution.

NOTES

1. Address by Attorney General Edwin Meese, III, before the American Bar Association, Washington, D.C. (July 9, 1985); "Q and A with the Attorney General," *American Bar Association Journal,* 81, no. 44 (July 1985).

2. Brest, "The Misconceived Quest for the Original Understanding," *Boston University Law Review,* 60, no. 204 (1980).

3. Ely, "Constitutional Interpretation: Its Allure and Impossibility," *Indiana Law Journal,* 53, no. 399 (1978).

4. Nowak, "Realism, Nihilism, and the Supreme Court: Do the Emperors Have Nothing But Robes?" 22 *Washburn Law Journal* 246, 257 (1983).

5. 410 U.S. 113 (1973).

6. *Reynolds* v. *Sims,* 377 U.S. 533 (1964).

7. *Engle* v. *Vitale,* 370 U.S. 421 (1962); *Abington School Dist.* v. *Schempp,* 374 U.S. 203 (1963).

8. 347 U.S. 483 (1954).

9. See, e.g., Boudin, *Government by Judiciary* 433–43 (New York: W. Goodwin, 1932); Haines, *The American Doctrine of Judicial Supremacy* (Berkeley, Cal.: University of California Press, 1932).

10. Ford (ed.) 9 *Writings of Thomas Jefferson* 275–76 (1902).

11. Grey, "Origins of the Unwritten Constitution: Fundamental Law in American Revolutionary Thought," 30 *Stanford Law Review* 843, 844 (1978).

12. 3 U.S. (3 Dall.) 171 (1796).

13. Currie, *The Constitution in the Supreme Court,* 1789–1888 34 (Chicago: University of Chicago Press, 1985).

14. *Id.* at 36.

15. *McCulloch* v. *Maryland,* 17 U.S. (4 Wheat.) 316, 414 (1819).

16. See, Rohde & Spaeth, *Supreme Court Decision Making* 41 (1976); 1 *The Records of the Federal Convention of 1787* xii–xiv (Farrand ed. San Francisco: W. H. Freeman, 1937).

17. Burns, *The Vineyard of Liberty* 101–104 (New York: Knopf, 1982).

18. Wofford, "The Blinding Light: The Uses of History in Constitutional Interpretation," 21 *University of Chicago Law Review* 502 (1964).

19. *Supra* n. 7.

20. Strokes & Pfeffer, *Church and State in the United States* 181–82 (Colorado Springs: Shepard's 1975).

21. See, e.g., tenBroek, "Uses by the United States Supreme Court of Extrinsic Aids in Constitutional Construction," 27 *California Law Review* 399, 404 (1939); Kelly, "Clio and the Court: An Illicit Love Affair," 1965 *Supreme Court Review* 119, 122–25; Alfange, "On Judicial Policymaking and Constitutional Change: Another Look at the 'Original Intent' Theory of Constitutional Interpretation," 5 *Hastings Constitutional Law Quarterly* 603, 617 (1978).

22. The Eleventh Amendment overruled the holding of *Chisholm* v. *Georgia,* 2 U.S. (2 Dall.) 419 (1793); the Fourteenth Amendment nullified, in part, the decision in *Dred Scott* v. *Sandford,* 60 U.S. (19 How.) 393 (1857); the Sixteenth Amendment nullified the holding of *Pollack* v. *Farmers' Loan and Trust, Co.,* 157 U.S. 429 (1895); the Twenty-sixth Amendment neutralized *Oregon* v. *Mitchell,* 400 U.S. 112 (1970).

23. "Not all the influence of a master politician in the prime of his popularity was quite enough to carry a program that would impair judicial review," McCloskey, *The American Supreme Court* 177 (Chicago: University of Chicago Press, 1960). The plan was rejected vehemently by the Senate Judiciary Committee. See *Senate Comm. on the Judiciary, Reorganization of the Fed. Judiciary Adverse Report,* S. Rep. No. 711, 75th Cong., 1st Sess. 23 (1937).

24. Pfeffer, *This Honorable Court* 424–25 (Boston: Beacon Press, 1965).

25. Those who campaigned for Chief Justice Warren's impeachment were unable to have impeachment proceedings initiated against him. While impeachment proceedings were instituted against Justice Douglas, they never got beyond the subcommittee stage and were eventually forsaken. See *Special Subcomm. on H. Res., 920 of the House Comm. on the Judiciary,* 91 Cong., 2d Sess., Final Report, Associate Justice William O. Douglas (Comm. Print 1970).

26. "In the fifteen years between 1953 and 1968, over sixty bills were introduced in Congress to eliminate the jurisdiction of the federal courts over a variety of specific subjects; none of these became law." Bator, Mishkin, Shapiro & Wechsler, *Hart & Wechsler's the Federal Courts and the Federal System* 360 (Mineola, NY: Foundation Press, 2d ed. 1973).

Questions for Discussion

1. What kinds of contemporary issues would the Framers have never contemplated?
2. What consequences about strict interpretivism can be drawn from your answer to Question 1?
3. How would you evaluate the qualifications of a person nominated to the Supreme Court who accepts the strict constructionist viewpoint?
4. Can the nonconstructionist view be reconciled with the U.S. system of democratic rule? What are the reasons for your answer?
5. Does the Constitution as written require the judiciary to follow the principle of judicial restraint? What are the reasons for your answer?

Suggested Readings

Barnum, David G. *The Supreme Court and American Democracy.* New York: St. Martin's Press, 1993.

Bork, Robert H. *The Tempting of America: The Political Seduction of the Law.* New York: Free Press, 1990.

Farber, Daniel A. "The Originalism Debate: A Guide for the Perplexed." *Ohio State Law Journal,* 49, no. 4 (1989), 1085–1106.

Freeman, Samuel. "Original Meaning, Democratic Interpretation and the Constitution." *Philosophy and Public Affairs,* 21, no. 1 (Winter 1992), 3–42.

Graglia, Lino A. "Judicial Activism: Even on the Right, It's Wrong." *Public Interest,* no. 95 (Spring 1989), 57–74.

Lively, Donald E. "The Imperial Judiciary: Occupational Hazards of a Constitutional Society." *Villanova Law Review,* 34, no. 1 (February 1989), 1–23.

Louthan, William C. *The United States Supreme Court: Lawmaking in the Third Branch of Government.* Englewood Cliffs, N.J.: Prentice Hall, 1991.

O'Brien, David M. *Storm Center: The Supreme Court in American Politics.* 2d ed. New York: W. W. Norton, 1990.

Pacelle, Richard L. *The Transformation of the Supreme Court's Agenda from the New Deal to the Reagan Administration.* Boulder, Colo.: Westview Press, 1991.

Perry, Michael J. "The Argument for Judicial Review—And for the Originalist Approach to Judicial Review" [Ben J. Altheimer Lecture]. *University of Arkansas at Little Rock Law Journal,* 14, no. 4 (Summer 1992), 613–670.

Snowiss, Sylvia. *Judicial Review and the Law of the Constitution.* New Haven: Yale Univ. Press, 1990.

Wolfe, Christopher. *Judicial Activism: Bulwark of Freedom or Precarious Security?* Pacific Grove, Calif.: Brooks/Cole, 1991.

Chapter 16

Should the Senate Ask Nominees to the Supreme Court Questions about Politics and Ideology?

Article II, Section 2 of the Constitution provides that the president nominate candidates for Supreme Court justices. It also provides that for the nominees to be appointed to the Court, they must be confirmed by the Senate. The Constitution says nothing, however, about the professional and intellectual backgrounds of the nominees; nor does it say anything about the criteria that should be used by the president in nominating candidates or by the Senate in evaluating them for confirmation.

From George Washington's day to the present, presidents have nominated candidates to the Court from a variety of backgrounds, including lower court judges, cabinet members, senators, and governors. In making their choices, presidents have based their considerations on judicial background, legal philosophy, intellectual talent, personal honesty and integrity, party unity, political and ideological compatibility, and other factors.

The Senate has often confirmed the nominees. At times, however, it has rejected them. Senators, too, have used criteria similar to those of the president in voting on confirmation.

The results of the confirmation process have not always been happy for presidents. As early as 1795, the Senate rejected John Rutledge as George Washington's nominee to be chief justice of the Supreme Court. Rutledge, who had been one of the authors of the Constitution, seemed qualified. He had even served as a Supreme Court justice. But he had opposed the Jay Treaty, which would have improved relations between the United States and Great Britain. And the Federalists, who dominated the Senate, favored the treaty. The Senate, consequently, did not confirm Rutledge.

From George Washington to Bill Clinton, presidents have had to be careful in nominating candidates to the Supreme Court for fear that their nominations would not win confirmation. At times, presidents have been willing to engage in major battles with the Senate for their candidates. At other times, however, presidents have made cautious nominations that resulted in quick and favorable confirmation.

For most of the twentieth century, the Senate has confirmed presidential nominees to the court. From 1900 to 1968 only one nominee—John J. Parker in 1930—was rejected by the Senate. But since then, presidents have had a harder time getting their nominees confirmed. Lyndon Johnson could not get Abe Fortas confirmed as chief justice in 1968. Richard Nixon faced defeat with his nominees of Clement Haynsworth and G. Harrold Carswell. Ronald Reagan's candidate Robert Bork went down to defeat, too. One of Reagan's nominees, Judge Douglas H. Ginsburg, was forced to withdraw from consideration after revelations about his personal life brought criticisms from conservative sources.

The Senate confirmation process has become increasingly acrimonious, too. Because the Supreme Court deals with some of the most controversial political issues of our times, such as abortion, affirmative action, criminal justice, and separation of church and state, groups concerned about the outcome of policy have good reason to be vitally involved with decisions dealing with appointments to the Supreme Court. Conservatives favor conservative justices, and liberals support liberal justices— although no one can be certain about how justices will decide cases once they are appointed to the Court. Since the stakes are so high, the fight over court nominations has on occasion become fierce.

Public attention to Supreme Court nomination has been reflected in procedural changes as well as media involvement in the subject. Until the nomination of Harlan Fiske Stone in 1925, Supreme Court nominees did not even personally appear before the Senate Judiciary Committee, the unit responsible for initiating the confirmation process in the Senate. Today, all Supreme Court nominees must personally appear before the committee. The hearings, which are now televised, have given the process an even greater popular notoriety than existed earlier.

Some of the stormiest controversies involving nominees occurred in the Reagan and Bush administrations. Although William Rehnquist, who was an associate justice of the Supreme Court, was confirmed as chief justice, he faced tough hearings. He won confirmation with fewer favorable Senate votes than any successful nominee for the post in the twentieth century. The Robert Bork hearings were stormy, and the Senate voted against him. And the nomination of Clarence Thomas to succeed Thurgood Marshall as associate justice produced extraordinary hearings centered on accusations of sexual harassment by a former associate, Anita Hill. Thomas won confirmation but at great cost to his reputation.

Much dissatisfaction—both within the Senate and among the general public—has been expressed about the confirmation process. One key issue is whether the nominees to the Court should be judged on the basis of their competence (such as judicial temperament, professional background, and personal character) alone or whether ideology and political viewpoints should be considered as well.

The debate on this issue is drawn from articles appearing in *Judicature: The Journal of the American Judicature Society*. The articles were written before Anita Hill accused Clarence Thomas of harassment. Albert P. Melone, a political science professor at Southern Illinois University at Carbondale, argues that the Senate should consider a nominee's political and ideological outlook in the confirmation process. He contends

1. The Framers of the Constitution did not intend the Senate to be a rubber stamp for presidential appointments.

2. The Senate has used political and ideological criteria to evaluate Supreme Court nominees throughout U.S. history.
3. Nominees can give answers about their political and ideological views without bringing into question their impartiality in dealing with cases that will come before them if they are confirmed.

William Bradford Reynolds, who served as assistant attorney general in the Civil Rights Division of the Justice Department during the Reagan administration, opposes the use of political and ideological considerations in the Senate confirmation process. He contends

1. The Framers of the Constitution did not intend that a political litmus test be applied to nominees to the court.
2. So long as nominees have the professional and character qualifications for the Court, they should be confirmed.
3. If political and ideological considerations are the criteria for confirmation, then the Supreme Court will cease to be independent of the other two branches of the federal government.

☑ YES

Should the Senate Ask Nominees to the Supreme Court Questions about Politics and Ideology?

ALBERT P. MELONE

The Senate's Confirmation Role in Supreme Court Nominations and the Politics of Ideology versus Impartiality

Controversy surrounds the appropriate role of the United States Senate in exercising its constitutional responsibility of advice and consent. Conservative thinkers and propagandists, right-wing politicians, and others question whether the Senate should rightly concern itself with anything more than the professional qualifications of judicial nominees. The Senate's rejection of Judge Robert Bork's nomination to the Supreme Court is touted as a particular egregious example of the Senate exceeding its constitutional responsibility. Senator Orrin Hatch of Utah termed the Bork hearing an ". . . ideological inquisition." Iowa's Senator Charles Grassley charged that Bork's critics ". . . prefer judges who will act as some kind of super legislature who will give them victories in the courts when they lose in the legislature." Senator Gordon Humphrey of New Hampshire said that the charges against Bork are "pure political poppycock, 99.9 percent pure, so pure it floats."

Nominees are not passive targets of ideological interrogation. They often refuse to answer questions designed to illicit answers about their judicial attitudes. They do so by appealing to the often misunderstood but powerful norm of judicial impartiality. They state that if they reveal their attitudes today about a case that may come before them tomorrow as sitting jurists they will be unable to participate fairly in decision making. Disqualification and recusation is the only honorable course in such a situation, so goes the refrain. Silence, it is believed, is a better course than failing to decide at all.

It is my view that senators may reasonably inquire into and base their final decision to confirm or reject presidential choices on factors other than the nominees' personal and professional qualifications. Senators may legitimately ask nominees about their political and judicial ideology as it may manifest itself in judicial decision making. I base this conclusion upon an analysis of three related factors.

First, the constitutional framers did not intend the Senate to be a rubber stamp for presidential appointments. The advice and consent clause of the Constitution justifies an independent scrutiny of nominees by members of the Senate.

Second, the historical record reveals that from the beginning of the Republic the Senate has rejected nominees for reasons other than personal and professional qualifications. In one fashion or another, political considerations, including evaluations of the ideological soundness of nominees, influence Senate advice and consent decisions.

Finally, I will clarify the claim that nominees should not give answers to questions that may bring into question their impartiality. Nominees may conduct themselves before the Senate hearing panels with honor and probity while at the same time providing vital political information. Properly understood, statutory and ethical norms do not prohibit nominees from revealing their views on the great issues of the day.

THE MEANING OF ADVICE AND CONSENT

The plain words of the Constitution suggest that the framers contemplated a sharing of responsibility between the executive and legislative branches. Yet, a striking feature of this sharing arrangement is the placement of the appointment and confirmation functions in article II—the executive article, not article I—the legislative article. Section 2 of article II provides that the president shall have the power to nominate by and with the consent of the Senate. Clearly, the president may select the persons he or she wants to nominate. The Senate may advise the chief executive on the initial selection, but it may not select particular nominees. Through its consent function, the Senate has the power to accept or reject presidential choices. Therefore, it is erroneous to conclude, as Richard Nixon once did, that the president may name whomever he pleases without senatorial checks. Indeed, a literal interpretation of the Constitution does not indicate any boundaries for senatorial consent. The Constitution's plain words do not prescribe or dictate justification for confirming or rejecting nominees.

Moreover, because the Constitution is a document limiting the use of power that derives its authority from the consent of the governed, and since the advice and consent provision of article II does not impose any limit to its discretion, it is fair to conclude that the Senate may use its constitutional authority as it sees fit. It may do so for whatever reason, be it professional qualifications, personal integrity, or political and ideological considerations.

Investigating beyond literal interpretation to the framers' probable intent reinforces the shared responsibility view. However, historical evidence introduces ambiguity otherwise not present with the more simplistic literalism approach.

The records of the Philadelphia Convention reveal that the shared responsibility feature of the nomination process was the result of compromise, as is the explanation for many other constitutional provisions. Choices presented by the competing Virginia and New Jersey plans framed many of the debates held in Philadelphia. The original Virginia Plan, the basic proposal supported by the large states, sought to locate the appointment of judges in the two legislative chambers. On at least two occasions, however, James Madison expressed the fear that members of the more numerous branch would be ill-suited to evaluate prospective judges. He thought they might select judicial candidates for the poor reason that they were particularly talented legislators or because the aspirants had assisted ignorant legislative members in their own businesses or those of their constituents. On the other hand, the Senate, being an unelected body and therefore a more select group of persons, would be better qualified to evaluate the abilities of candidates with a higher regard for qualifications. William Paterson, the author of the small state plan called the New Jersey Plan, and James Wilson argued for appointment by the executive alone.

Alexander Hamilton informally suggested what finally emerged as the convention's final recommendation, and the one ultimately ratified by the states. In their initial voting, convention delegates rejected both the plan granting advice and consent to the Senate and a proposal to place the appointing authority in the president alone. Instead, what survived until the final days of the convention was a provision granting the appointing power to the Senate alone. Then, finally, in the last days of the convention, there emerged from the Committee of Eleven the present system: nomination by the president, and advice and consent of the Senate.

As is often the case when attempting to identify the framers' original intention, the precise reasons for the compromise are unknown. However, James E. Gauch, the author of a recent and carefully conducted study, reasonably concludes that the framers were concerned with three related issues: the ability to evaluate potential nominee qualifications; the matter of corruption and intrigue in the nomination process; and finally the matter of small versus large state interests. The import of Gauch's finding is that the framers' concerns went beyond good character and professional qualifications of future judicial officeholders. In one form or another, politics entered their thinking.

Analyzing the ratification debates adds somewhat to our total understanding of the framers' intent. But reading too much into a few paragraphs may result in overstating the case. Alexander Hamilton's *The Federalist* 66 and 76 are the authoritative source for evidence of the framers' intent as expressed during the ratification debate.

Without question, Hamilton reinforces a plain meaning interpretation of the advice and consent provision. To that end, the Senate's role is properly confined to the confirmation or rejection of presidential nominees. *The Federalist* 66 reads:

> There will, of course, be no exertion of choice on the part of the Senate. They may defeat one choice of the Executive and oblige him to make another; but they cannot themselves choose—they can only ratify or reject the choice of the President.

The Senate, then, is a major player in the selection drama. However, the chief executive plays a leading role because he or she is in the position of submitting the names of only those persons thought desirable. For what reason then require senatorial consent? Hamilton's answer is instructive. He writes:

> I answer, that the necessity of their concurrence would have a powerful, though, in general a silent operation. It would be an excellent check upon the spirit of favoritism in the President, and would tend greatly to prevent the appointment of unfit characters from state prejudice, from family connection, from personal attachment, or from a view to popularity.

Thus, at the very least, the Senate must act as a check against a president who might appoint persons of unfit character. Further, the Senate is in a position to embarrass a chief executive for such attempts. The Senate's institutional leverage will deter presidents from such conduct. Hamilton makes this point by writing:

> . . . It will readily be comprehended, that a man who had himself the sole disposition of offices, would be governed much more by his private inclinations and interests, than when he was bound to submit the propriety of his choice to the discussion and determination of a different and independent body. . . .

WRONG REASONS

Hamilton contributes two major points to our understanding. First, he reinforces the literal understanding of the advice and consent clause; namely, the appointment power is a shared responsibility between the president and the Senate. Second, upper house concurrence is a requisite because the chief executive might otherwise appoint persons for the wrong reasons. Hamilton indicates four wrong reasons for appointment. These are: the appointment of unfit characters "from state prejudice," "from family connection," "from personal attachment," or "from a view to popularity." Do these four justifications for senatorial denial of presidential choices pertain to ideological tests for office? The probable answer is yes.

First and paramount, Hamilton's words commit senators to inquire beyond personal and professional qualifications. It requires the Senate to ascertain whether nominees are associated with the president in any of the four ways. If they are, it does not necessarily mean that the nominees are unqualified to serve. It means that the relationship between the president and the nominees bears scrutiny.

Second, each of the four points has ideological elements. In the context of the eighteenth century, "state prejudice" meant more than good will toward one's neighbors. It also signified common points of view or shared consciousness about the political order. Carolinians two centuries ago, as they do even today, had a different perspective on political events than, for example, New Yorkers. Indeed, these differences, that are easily describable as ideological, were a source of political disagreement current at the Philadelphia Convention. Appointing persons "from family connection" and "from personal attachment" likewise has ideological dimensions. Conventional wisdom and modern social science inform us that the family is a strong socializing agent, inculcating attitudes and beliefs including those concerning politics. Further, persons often choose friends who share basic values and attitudes. Finally, appointing persons "from a view to popularity" reasonably entails situations wherein presidents appoint persons meeting with popular approval. Persons with ideological views consistent with those of either elite decision-making bodies, such as the Senate or wider publics, are likely to be popular. The president may then be applauded for his outstanding choices, thereby increasing the value of his political currency.

Third, by his words Hamilton does not exclude any of the four unacceptable reasons as factors in a president's or senator's nomination or a confirmation calculation. He objects to persons named to the judiciary who have "*no other merit than . . . coming from the same State . . . or being in some way or other personally allied to him, or of possessing the necessary insignificance and pliancy to render them the obsequious instruments of his pleasure.*" It is perfectly acceptable, therefore, for a president to nominate an individual of personal and professional qualifications who also comes from a preferable state or region, has family connections, is well-liked by the president, and enjoys widespread popularity.

It is conceivable and probable that each of the four reasons for Senate concern contain non-ideological components. However, understood within the context of the time Hamilton's words leave little doubt that ideology as a belief system, and as reflected in one's character, renders legitimate Senate inquiries into matters other than narrowly conceived personal and professional qualifications.

James E. Gauch suggests that Hamilton's reference to the Senate having a responsibility to explore the "propriety" of executive choices commits senators to look beyond the professional and personal qualifications of the nominees. However, it is unclear to me that Hamilton uses the word "propriety" to mean anything more than a summary term for the four unacceptable reasons for solely nominating persons to the bench: cronyism, family connections, favoring one state over others, or responding to the popular will regardless of qualifications. If this is true, then the word "propriety" is a redundancy and little more than a convenient use of language.

The search for original intention is an interesting exercise. Although others have come to conclusions different from the one found here, the weight of the evidence tends to justify Senate inquiries into nominees' ideology. However, the search for original intention in this case does not render other interpretations incorrect. There is no evidence that the framers' explicitly debated in the eighteenth century what is today a central concern. Unless an issue is explicitly discussed and a record of that debate is available, what the framers really intended remains a matter of intellectual speculation and curiosity.

I suspect there was no full debate and discussion of the appropriate reasons for rejecting nominees, including an explicit analysis of the proper place for ideological inquiries, because it did not occur to the framers that future judges and justices would be asked to perform anything more than traditional judicial tasks. Surely, the framers did not anticipate the considerable institutional authority courts now enjoy. There is considerable doubt the framers envisaged courts with the power to strike down acts of Congress: statutes and administrative acts unrelated to the jurisdiction of the Supreme Court. They could not have imagined an institution as central to the American political system as the contemporary Supreme Court has become.

However, given the framers clear preference for checks on power, and the institutional importance played by the judiciary today, it seems reasonable that they would consider, as do many contemporary senators, the ideology of unelected and unaccountable lawmakers as appropriate objects of inquiry by a popularly elected body. Senators must respond to the constitutional facts of life as they find them. The living constitution requires the responsible evaluation of potential judicial lawmakers whose eighteenth century counterparts enjoyed a different kind of status.

NOMINEE BASHING: THE HISTORICAL RECORD

An examination of past Senate practices reveals the considerable extent to which judicial nominees are evaluated on political and ideological grounds. Otherwise well-qualified persons are rejected for a variety of political reasons. Further, contrary to the supposition of some commentators, nominations preceding the 1987 Robert Bork debacle were marked by questions and speculations concerning the ideological fitness of presidential nominees. Judge Bork's case is dramatic because the nominee himself was more than willing to enter into intellectual discourse, thereby revealing his controversial policy inclinations. The existing literature contains several different classification schemes defining the various reasons judicial nominees are rejected by the Senate.

Depending upon the purpose, the adoption of one scheme over another can be important. What is pertinent to note, however, is that all the schemes point out that past nominees were evaluated on political grounds unrelated to professional qualifications.

During the first decade after the adoption of the 1789 Constitution, the Senate rejected a person for reasons unrelated to professional competence. An extremely well-qualified justice of the South Carolina Supreme Court was rejected because he angered powerful Federalist politicians with his vigorous denunciation of the controversial Jay Treaty. Most Federalists viewed support for the treaty as a true indicator of party loyalty, while Republicans thought the treaty an unnecessary concession to British might. The vote to reject John Rutledge was 14 to 10; it was a party vote with 13 Federalists voting against, and only three voting for confirmation. The remaining votes to confirm came from Anti-Federalists. The Rutledge episode is an early example of how politicians mask their real political reasons for opposing candidates by attacking nominees' personal and professional qualifications. Historians point out that Rutledge was attacked falsely as mentally unsound, and therefore unfit for Supreme Court service. The Federalist press employed this malicious tactic rather than stating the true reason for Federalist opposition. They realized that the Jay Treaty was so unpopular that to publicly attack Rutledge for his opposition to it would cause a political backfire.

There are many other examples of nominee bashing for reasons unrelated to professional competence. The Senate defeat of President James Madison's nomination of Alexander Wolcott was due in large part to the nominee's opposition to the enforcement of embargo and intercourse acts when he was U.S. Collector of Customs in Connecticut. Federalist senators and the press opposed him for this reason, although, in fairness, there were authentic questions raised about Wolcott's judicial qualifications. An otherwise well-qualified Grant appointee, Ebenezer R. Hoar, suffered rejection because as attorney general he championed the merit system in government. He also drew fire from radical Republicans because of his earlier opposition to the impeachment of President Andrew Johnson.

Harlan Stone's 1925 appointment is the first time a nominee appeared before the Senate Judiciary Committee to explain himself. Senators questioned his qualifications because of his prosecution as attorney general of a senator for participation in an oil and land fraud deal. There was vigorous Senate floor debate when his nomination came before the entire body; the nomination was recommitted for further consideration to the Senate Judiciary Committee. Unfortunately, transcripts of that appearance are unavailable, but a biographer describes it as an impressive performance that served to vindicate Stone's nomination.

Nominees have been rejected by the Senate for local political reasons having little if anything to do with their professional ability. Senators concerning themselves with their political power bases have invoked senatorial courtesy to block confirmation of presidential nominees. The Senate's rejection of President Polk's 1845 nomination of George Woodward resulted in large part because of home state opposition. A year earlier, in 1844, senatorial courtesy was invoked and was a lesser factor in the defeat of President Tyler's nomination of Reuben H. Walworth. President Cleveland had two nominations defeated when in each case the Senate would not confirm a nominee who was opposed by the senior senator in the president's party from the nominee's state. There are many more instances of its invocation for lower federal court judges, but the point is indisputable.

THE TWENTIETH CENTURY

The matter of evaluating nominees primarily on ideological grounds is better documented for the present century than for the previous one. There are at least two interrelated explanations. First, in the twentieth century the Senate has become more responsive to popular control. In a recent paper, Charles R. Epp points out that by 1913 the Seventeenth Amendment had shifted the Senate's electoral base from the state legislatures that had theretofore named senators to the popular electorate. This institutional shift in accountability may have made senators more sensitive to interest group and grassroots awareness of judicial policy making. Second, it may be that judicial ideology played a more limited and ordinarily a less obvious role during the first century of the Republic than it does today. During the first 100 years of the Republic, only 17 acts of Congress were declared unconstitutional, but in the next 90 years the Court struck down 87 more, an increase of over 400 percent.

In the nineteenth century there were fewer controversial Supreme Court opinions. Then the full scope of the Court's real and potential ability to affect public policy was not fully understood. However, late in that century and the first third of this century the Court's role in policy making became a matter of considerable debate. It became clear that Supreme Court justices exercise their discretion in dramatic ways including striking down popular congressional acts and state laws. The Court had become a bastion of conservative ideology. By the mid-1960s, it became equally clear that the Court had again become a policymaker; this time, however, it was a vehicle for liberal causes, and once again, many of its decisions were unpopular. In short, because the stakes are high, the judicial philosophy and ideology of potential jurists have become a subject of close scrutiny.

President Wilson's appointment of Louis Brandeis is an early twentieth century example of how ideology has had a probable impact on the selection process. Wilson attempted to name the brilliant Brandeis as attorney general but met considerable opposition from the elitist Boston bar. When that appointment failed, Wilson pledged to name Brandeis to the next important vacancy. That position turned out to be the Supreme Court. The Brandeis appointment was put off for months as the Senate took volumes of testimony. Much of the opposition was due to the liberal crusader's so-called radical views and his sociological jurisprudence. There is also evidence of an unhealthy dose of antisemitism. But many, including William Howard Taft, were opposed to Brandeis for other reasons, including his views in support of the working classes and his alleged animosity toward big business.

Ideology was a factor in 1930 with the nominations of two otherwise well-qualified persons. Charles Evans Hughes was attacked because, among other reasons, he was regarded by liberal senators as a tool of corporate power, and conservative southerners opposed him as a city slicker who stood against states' rights. The Senate rejected John J. Parker on a close vote due in large measure to opposition generated by the American Federation of Labor and the National Association for the Advancement of Colored People. Parker was thought unfriendly to labor, and he was under attack, probably erroneously, as a racist. There would be no other Senate rejection of a presidential Supreme Court nominee for 40 years.

New Deal opposition to the high court was transparently ideological. There was an attempt to disguise the ideological source for the conflict by appealing to another motive. President Roosevelt presented his ill-fated Court-Packing plan as a way to relieve elderly justices from a heavy workload. This obvious attempt by the president to change the decision-making composition of the Court by increasing the number of justices was not lost even among the most casual observers. The plan failed to receive congressional approval not because members revered the Court and wanted to protect it from institutional attack. As Schmidhauser and Berg point out, an ideologically conservative coalition existed in Congress before FDR [Franklin D. Roosevelt] introduced his plan. It coalesced before and functioned after the 1937 Court-Packing congressional vote. The purpose of this coalition was to put the breaks on the New Deal. Though the Court-Packing episode did not involve the confirmation of particular justices, it demonstrates that members of Congress viewed the Court in ideological terms. They did not want to give Roosevelt an opportunity to appoint to the Court a sufficient number of persons who would vote to support New Deal programs and goals. Roosevelt ultimately got his way when the Supreme Court began to uphold New Deal initiatives to save the nation's economy from ruin. The lesson is clear. Ideology has been a prominent factor in inter-branch governmental conflicts.

The Warren Court Era (1952–1969) was another period in this century when the Supreme Court came under severe attack. Decisions concerning such matters as segregation, internal security, school prayer, and criminal justice precipitated hostile reaction in and out of Congress. Many of these issues remain hotly contested into the 1990s and so does the proper role of the Supreme Court.

Warren Court opponents used the occasion of Thurgood Marshall's 1967 nomination to attack its decisions. Southern senators on the Judiciary Committee, including John McClellan, Samuel Ervin, and Strom Thurmond, questioned Marshall, a former solicitor general and then federal appeals court judge, about matters other than his professional qualifications. They also grilled him on his judicial philosophy. For example, Senator McClellan said he could not vote to confirm Marshall's nomination without an answer to his question: "Do you subscribe to the philosophy that the Fifth Amendment right to assistance of counsel requires that counsel be present at a police lineup?" Marshall weathered the storm by employing the now familiar retort that a number of cases were pending before the Court and therefore he should not respond.

About a year later, in 1968, Abe Fortas became the convenient target for those opposed to the Warren Court when President Lyndon Johnson attempted unsuccessfully to promote his old friend and advisor from associate to chief justice. Senator Strom Thurmond vigorously attacked Fortas by harping on the ill-effects of the Court's 1957 decision in *Mallory* v. *United States*. Significantly, Fortas was not on the Court at the time that this decision was handed down. Besides ideology, Fortas was charged with judicial impropriety by advising informally the president on a variety of policy matters, and also for accepting large lecture fees during the summer of 1968. Further, the nomination of Homer Thornberry as associate justice, a Texas crony of the president, to fill the empty seat upon the elevation of Fortas was another negative factor. In the end, the president was forced to withdraw the name of the liberal jurist as chief justice when a motion to invoke cloture failed by a 14-vote margin. Because the 1968 presidential election was near at hand, and since the election of a president from the other political party was thought a distinct possibility, the defeat of Fortas is an outward and visible sign of partisan and ideological politics in the modern battle over the struggle for control of the Supreme Court. Richard Nixon ran on an anti-Warren Court platform, and the selection of justices with "strict constructionist" sentiments was part of his winning strategy.

In politics "what goes around comes around." Nixon's 1968 campaign invited intense scrutiny of judicial nominees who might exhibit any professional or personal weaknesses. As part of his "Southern Strategy" to gain grass-root support for the Republican Party in that region of the nation, Nixon sought to appoint to the Court southerners with a "strict constructionist" perspective. The code words fooled no one. This was not simply a matter of choosing for the Court persons who would exercise judicial self-restraint. Nixon wanted to reverse the liberal trend of the Warren Court. Then, as is the case today, arguments about the proper judicial function and role of justices in interpreting statutes and the Constitution are really debates about judicial outcomes.

Factors involving professional conduct and qualifications played important roles in the defeat of two Nixon nominees. South Carolinian, Judge Clement Haynsworth, was thought by organized labor and its Senate supporters to be anti-labor. Floridian, Judge Harrold Carswell, was painted as a racist. Haynsworth was ostensibly rejected for failing to rescue himself in a few cases involving personal financial gain, and Carswell was portrayed as mediocre. But it is difficult to believe that the underlying causes for their rejections did not involve politics and concerns about the ideological direction of the Court.

Other Nixon and later Reagan appointees were subjected to ideological interrogation of one sort or another. However, the 1987 confirmation hearings on the nomination of Judge Robert Bork to the Supreme Court is the clearest case to date of the Senate concerning itself with the ideological characteristics and probable future judicial behavior of a High Court nominee. Those hearings taught Americans that questioning nominees about their judicial philosophy will not bring down the legal edifice. It is possible to probe nominees' attitudes without exacting promises or compromising judicial neutrality toward present or future litigants. In large measure, learning this lesson took place because the nominee himself wanted his views aired. Ironically, it was the ventilation of his own views that contributed directly to Judge Bork's 42 to 58 vote Senate rejection. Bork felt compelled to present his views and fully answer most questions because he felt that his many published articles on constitutional subjects could be misinterpreted, and therefore, his views may be misrepresented. He did so without invoking the oft-heard disarming refrain that discussion of constitutional matters may prejudice cases coming before the High Court.

Some senators conducted themselves with distinction. Senator Arlen Specter in particular displayed intelligence and courage in defying his president and his party. During and after the Senate hearings, the Pennsylvania Republican asserted that the Supreme Court confirmation hearings will never be the same. Subsequent Senate confirmation hearings held for the nominations of Judges Kennedy and Souter were not as revealing as the Bork hearings. However, in both cases senators attempted to probe, albeit with limited success, the nominees' fundamental values and attitudes toward judicial law making. The hearings for both nominees were relatively brief, lasting only a few days.

Available empirical research indicates that senatorial attitudes are affected by nominees. Controversial nominations stimulate the ideological proclivities of senators, thereby subjecting some nominees to negative votes. The extent to which ideology may adversely affect particular nominee confirmation chances depends upon the direction and intensity of that sentiment. It is little wonder, therefore, why most nominees refrain from a full disclosure of their attitudes and beliefs.

In summary, there is ample evidence supporting the working supposition that the judicial ideology of presidential nominees is a factor that senators probe when deciding whether to confirm or reject candidates. This practice did not start with Robert Bork as has been argued. By the early part of this century, as the Supreme Court became a more visible policy-making institution, the matter of nominee ideology became a more salient concern.

THE ISSUE OF IMPARTIALITY

The oft-heard justification for failing to answer certain questions put by senators during confirmation hearings is that to do so will violate professional norms of impartiality. Nominees protest that to answer particular queries may at the very least lead to the appearance that their minds are closed on specific legal issues, and therefore, litigants may feel they cannot get a fair hearing in court. Sandra Day O'Connor and Antonin Scalia have been the least cooperative. Robert Bork was the most forthcoming, although he refused to answer some questions. Yet nominees before and after Bork have used the impartiality argument to deflect questions. Their reticence has frustrated attempts by senators to obtain pertinent information useful in evaluating nominee suitability. Complicating the matter is the existence of a federal disqualification statute, and ethical standards of conduct gleaned from the American Bar Association Model Code of Judicial Conduct. However, neither constitute sufficient justification for failing to answer queries aimed at ascertaining nominees' general legal and philosophical perspectives.

Section 455 of Title 28 of the United States Code is a revision of a law first enacted in 1911. Section 24 of Title 28, U.S.C., 1940 edition, contains the amended basic law making it applicable to all justices and judges of the United States. The law was amended in 1974 and again in 1978. Most of section 455 applies unambiguously to disqualifications due to personal biases arising out of private financial or fiduciary interests, previous relationships in law practice or government employment, and being a material witness in a case. Section 455(a) raises the most difficulty. It reads: "Any justice, judge, or magistrate of the United States shall disqualify himself in any proceeding in which his impartiality might reasonably be questioned."

Canon 3C(1) of the Model Code of Judicial Conduct adopted by the American Bar Association [ABA] in 1972 recommends a judge's disqualification when impartiality is an issue because of personal bias or prejudice toward a party involved in litigation. However, Canon 4 permits judges to ". . . speak, write, lecture, teach, and participate . . ." in matters impacting the legal system. Jeffrey M. Shaman, Steven Lubet, and James J. Alfini, the authors of a recent treatise on judicial ethics, point out Canon 4 applies to the broader circumstance of quasi-judicial activities where judges speak or write in settings such as public hearings. The normative proscription applies to "*any issue* and not to *pending or impending* judicial proceedings that may come before the judge." The ABA's 1990 version of the Model Code opts for greater expression of opinion. Yet these or any other statutory or ethical provisions do not directly address the matter of nominees revealing their ideological viewpoint. Nor do they require justices to recuse themselves for public comments they might have made prior to their accession to the High Court.

The statutory subject matter found in 28 U.S.C. section 455 deals specifically with appropriate recusal behavior. In the main, the Model Code of Judicial Conduct focuses more broadly upon ethical conduct involving both those situations inviting recusal and those that do not. Although the Code was raised as an issue in recent nomination hearings, no one has invoked any section of it in refusing to answer questions during oral testimony. Sandra Day O'Connor did, however, refuse to answer a *written* question posed by then-Senator Gordon Humphrey of New Hampshire, citing the Code as the basis for her decision. In several other instances the Code was raised as an issue, but the nominees did not rely on it as a basis for refusing to answer questions.

The ABA Code of Judicial Conduct was first approved in 1972, and in August, 1990, the Association's House of Delegates adopted a new revised one. It will take some time before the 1990 version is promulgated in the various jurisdictions. Until then, the 1972 Code remains in effect in 47 states and applies to all judges in those jurisdictions. Within the federal system, the District of Columbia and the Judicial Conference of the United States have approved the 1972 Code, applying its provisions to all judges of the United States district courts, the United States courts of appeals, the Court of Claims, the Court of Customs and Patent Appeals, the Customs Court, and to all bankruptcy judges and United States Magistrates. Significantly, the Code does not apply to justices of the United States Supreme Court. Technically, then, sitting justices do not fall under the Code's ethical prohibitions and mandates. This also applies to nominees who are not sitting on any bench at the time of their confirmation hearings. However, most recent nominees have been sitting federal judges, and one was a state appellate judge at the time of nomination. Since the 1972 issuance, only two nominees, William Rehnquist and Lewis Powell, have not fallen under the purview of the Code.

GROUNDS FOR DISQUALIFICATION

William Rehnquist is the author of the only United States Supreme Court opinion on the subject of recusal. His written opinion was in response to a motion for recusal by the plaintiffs in a class action suit challenging the constitutionality of a program of the federal government for surveillance of civilians. The plaintiffs in *Laird* v. *Tatum* [409 U.S. 1 (1972)], wanted Associate Justice Rehnquist to recuse himself because while he was a deputy attorney general he appeared before the Senate Judiciary Committee in support of a program of civilian surveillance, and he also made comments in another public forum concerning the subject.

Although a reasonable case is made that he should have recused himself in *Laird* v. *Tatum*, Rehnquist's memorandum in defense of his decision not to disqualify himself is instructive. Among other arguments, he points out that other justices have not disqualified themselves in cases involving points of law with which they had expressed an opinion before coming to the High Court. Justices Black, Frankfurter, Jackson, and Hughes are prime examples. However, because other justices may have done the wrong thing does not make it proper for Rehnquist to do the same. Yet the fact that these distinguished jurists did not recuse themselves could mean that they reject the view that because persons don judicial robes they become intellectual and political eunuchs. For these justices, disqualification applies to the more narrow matter of bias toward the litigants, not impartiality toward the great issues of the day. Rehnquist's major point is summarized in one eloquent paragraph. He wrote:

> Since most Justices come to this bench no earlier than their middle years, it would be unusual if they had not by that time formulated at least some tentative notions which would influence them in their interpretation of the sweeping clauses of the Constitution and their interaction with one another. It would be not merely unusual, but extraordinary, if they had not

at least given opinions as to constitutional issues in their previous legal careers. Proof that a Justice's mind at the time he joined the Court was a complete tabula rasa in the area of constitutional adjudication would be evidence of lack of qualification, not lack of bias.

The history of the subject is also revealing. Before the establishment of the court system in the United States, English common law judges were disqualified for only the reason of financial interests. Even finding themselves sitting in cases involving relatives was not a cause for recusal. Personal bias was unacceptable grounds for disqualification. The American practice was broadened by adding relationships and bias to financial interests. Not only are cases involving relatives cause for disqualification, but so are relationships with the attorney or party to the suit. The 1974 amendment to 28 U.S.C. section 455 requires disqualification of any justice or judge who ". . . has been of counsel, is or has been a material witness, or is so related to or connected with any party or his attorney as to render it improper, in his opinion, for him to sit on the trial, appeal, or other proceeding therein."

Modern practice recognizes the possibility that past associations with colleagues in law firms or government agencies may make it difficult for judges to always behave impartially. Sitting in a case involving former clients is such a circumstance. However, it is unclear how much time should pass between serving a client as counsel and sitting on the bench in a case involving that client.

In the past, some justices did not feel restrained to occupy the bench in disputes involving former clients. This is also true for those cases where they were indirect parties, or in cases in which they personally were similarly situated at one time. Both Justices Horace Lurton and Willis Van Devanter heard cases involving former railroad clients. Chief Justice John Marshall was the secretary of state who affixed the seal of the United States to the judicial commission, but failed to deliver the midnight appointment to the intended recipient, John Marbury. Fellow Federalist John Marshall then wrote the opinion declaring that Marbury had a right to the commission, but then went on to deny the remedy sought. Besides the case of *Marbury* v. *Madison* (1803), John Marshall failed to recuse himself in *Fletcher* v. *Peck* (1810), a landmark decision involving the infamous Yazoo land fraud and state confiscation that was similar to a situation where Marshall was likewise a victim. Further, years earlier, as a congressman from Virginia, Marshall voted to compensate those who lost money in the Yazoo land fraud scandal.

Today's standards are considerably higher. Justice Robert Jackson publicly criticized Mr. Justice Hugo Black for participating in *Jewell Ridge Coal Corp.* v. *Local No. 6167* [325 U.S. 161, 897 (1945)]. The case was argued by Crampton Harris, who had practiced law with Hugo Black some 19 years earlier for a brief two-year period. More recently, Justice Byron White felt compelled to disqualify himself from a Denver school desegregation case. Thirteen years earlier his old law firm had once been the bond counsel for the Denver School District. Justice Lewis Powell disqualified himself in a 1972 case involving a court ordered city-suburb merger of the Richmond School District. From 1952 to 1961, he was chairman of the district's school board. Finally, unlike his questionable conduct in *Laird* v. *Tatum,* Mr. Justice Rehnquist's conduct in the Watergate Case, *Nixon* v. *United States* [418 U.S. 683 (1974)], is beyond doubt an example of proper recusal. Rehnquist disqualified himself from the decision in the case because, as a United States Department of Justice official, he worked closely with the president's men in drafting Richard Nixon's original position on executive privilege.

There may be a need for stronger laws requiring recusal in a variety of compromising situations. Nevertheless, it is a mistake to suggest that because candidates for judicial posts have formed attitudes, values, and beliefs about legal and constitutional questions they should be prohibited from rendering judgments. It is reasonable and compelling to expect from jurists a lack of personal favoritism, prejudice or bias toward particular litigants coming before them. Judges can and should be impartial toward the litigants. However, an expectation that they be neutral toward the great issues of the day is an unreasonable one. While attempting to appear more virtuous than Caesar's wife, prospective judges and justices may fall into twin traps. First, they may fail to perform their fundamental responsibility to decide cases once on the bench. As members of a collegial body they should participate in its deliberations, and carry their fair share of the workload. And second, by not answering questions concerning their ideology, nominees withhold important political information from senators. These constitutional office-holders have a duty to discharge reasonably their advice and consent function.

Canon 4 of the 1972 Model Code of Judicial Conduct provides that judges may appear at "a public hearing before an executive or legislative body or official on matters concerning the law, the legal system, and the administration of justice, and he may otherwise consult with an executive or legislative body or official, but only on matters concerning the administration of justice." Thus, in the first instance there is no ethical problem giving testimony before the Senate Judiciary Committee. Why voluntarily appear if one is obliged to remain mute? The answer, of course, is that nominee-judges may speak and exchange ideas with those asking the questions. However, Canon 4 requires that when judges do so they do not raise doubts about their ". . . capacity to decide impartially any issue that may come before . . . them." This creates no insurmountable problem for judicial nominees. They must make it clear that they are open to persuasion on the legal issue, and that the facts of particular cases vary widely and are important in deciding whether general rules might apply. As Professor Sherman and his colleagues rightly conclude, Canon 4 is violated only when nominees display a clear intention to decide a forthcoming case in a certain way without the benefit of hearing the arguments within the controlled setting of the courtroom.

The use of the word *impartiality* found in Canon 3C(1) of the 1972 Code of Judicial Conduct is also a source of confusion. It instructs judges to disqualify themselves in proceedings where their impartiality might be reasonably questioned, but it fails to give a precise definition of the word, "impartiality." However, the term cannot mean the absence of preexisting values, attitudes, and opinions. That we know already from elementary logic. Furthermore, subsections (a), (b), (c), and (d) of 3C(1) all relate to personal knowledge of the parties or third-party relationships. The Canon does not reference preexisting attitudes about issues raised in particular cases.

Canon 3A(6) is a major source of ambiguity. It counsels that a "judge should abstain from public comment about a pending or impending proceeding in any court." Note that 3A(6) does not forbid general analysis and discussion of the great legal issues of the day. Rather, it applies to *pending or impending* proceedings. As legal ethics experts Shaman, Lubet, and Alfini argue, these words must mean pretrial, trial, appellate activity, and litigation poised for litigation. Consequently, Canon 3A(6) applies only to comment on actual cases or controversies in law and in equity and not general issues of law and philosophy. If nominee testimony does not reach actual fact situations that involve real issues begging for a legal resolution, then the Canon is inapplicable.

Months before the Senate confirmation hearings on the Judge David Souter nomination, the American Bar Association revised its Model Code of Judicial Conduct. The August 1990 revision affirms a freedom of speech approach to public comment. The ABA Standing Committee proposed a number of significant changes in the Code. Twenty-five amendments to the committee's document were proposed, but all were defeated. They sought to keep a number of prohibitions, including that dealing with public comment on pending or impending legislation. Canon 3A(6) is now Canon 3B(9) in the 1990 revision and it reads: "A judge shall not, while a proceeding is pending or impending in any court, make any public comment that might reasonably be expected to affect its outcome or impair its fairness or make any nonpublic comment that might substantially interfere with a fair trial or hearing." The addition of the words "reasonably be expected to affect its outcome or impair its fairness" represents an important recognition that not all public comment may make it difficult for judges to render justice impartially.

There can be little doubt that under the terms of the 1990 Model Code judges may comment publicly on court decisions, provided their remarks do not influence the outcome or impair the fairness of litigation currently pending or impending. Michael Franck, a member of the ABA Standing Committee on Ethics and Professional Responsibility, reportedly said: "We ought to allow speech when it serves a legitimate purpose." Further, George Cuhlman, ethics counsel for the ABA's Center for Professional Responsibility, is quoted as saying: "Until a genuine conflict occurs, there's no reason to infringe the first amendment rights a judge should have." Nominee responses to questions of United States senators designed to understand ideological propensities are appropriate if constitutional responsibility and accountability are to have meaning. Consequently, those who argued in the past that the Code of Judicial Ethics constrained nominee behavior before the Senate Judiciary Committee now have even less justification to do so today.

Neither statute nor ethical norms prohibit nominees from discussing the great constitutional questions of the day with United States senators or others.

There are no compelling reasons why, at the very least, nominees' general views should not be known in advance of Court service. Expressing one's view today will not make it impossible or difficult to change that view tomorrow. As the venerable Senator Sam Ervin of North Carolina argued—why should it? After carefully considering the established facts in a case, reviewing the law, reading the briefs, hearing oral arguments, and consulting with colleagues, justices may very well change their minds or at least modify their general views to fit the specific facts before the Court and the desired result. In fact, judges tell us that this happens to them. Good arguments, they insist, can convince them.

A positive feature of the common law tradition is its postulate that we can learn from past lessons. The law is a great laboratory wherein rules and regulations are regarded as testable propositions requiring, from time to time, reexamination. Persons who are ill-disposed to uncertainty make poor judges. Those who are not open to persuasion and do not understand the logic of fact analysis to produce welcome and unwelcome precedents misunderstand the nature of the judicial process, and therefore, should not, in any event, become members of the Supreme Court. Nominees only need to avoid answering questions about identifiable cases that may be extant in the legal process system or are pending in an immediate sense. Otherwise, they have a responsibility to cooperate fully with constitutional officers to answer questions pertinent to the office they seek.

CONCLUSIONS

Senators should feel free to ask questions that may reveal judicial nominees' views on past, present, or future constitutional issues. There is no statutory or ethical justification for secrecy in such matters, save the exception of commenting on pending or impending actual cases or controversies in law and in equity, and then, only when public comment may affect the fairness or outcome of deliberations.

Despite nominee Antonin Scalia's protestations to the contrary, querying nominees about their attitudes concerning past court decisions is consistent with statutory and ethical norms. There is no reason senators may not ask nominees about how they envision the future shape of the law both in general and specific terms. In brief, senators should have a good idea about how future judges and justices will behave. Yet, they should do so with the knowledge that specific facts of particular cases can impact how jurists will behave, and once on the bench the force of argument may persuade the judges and justices to change their minds.

Although asking questions about particular cases and rules of law are pertinent and possess considerable appeal, senators may also gain considerable insight into the minds and possible future behavior of nominees by employing social science knowledge more broadly. Research in political jurisprudence and judicial behavior establishes the explanatory power of inquiries into the social, economic, political, and judicial philosophies of judicial nominees.

Ideology is the summary term describing the set of attitudes and values that are particularly relevant to the performance of the judicial function. The object of the inquiry is to ascertain probable nominee impact upon the policy-making output of the judiciary. Queries may center on the nominees' past political and judicial decision making, and upon their likely short and long term future impact upon the Court's decision making.

Existing knowledge is based on aggregate data and does not hold true in all instances. But, there is solid social science evidence that values and attitudes are stable. This is particularly true of judges and justices. Persons acquire attitudes toward political objects or issues through a lifetime of experience, learning, and interaction. Furthermore, attitudes direct actions. Hence, if past, present, and future situations are sufficiently similar there is every justification to assume that persons will behave in the present and future as they did in the past. It is true that attitudes of adults can change, but it is the exception, not the rule.

Judicial nominees are usually in their middle years of life. Because they often have previous political and judicial experience, there is a record of public decision making. Lawyers as an occupational group have a propensity to write ideas down in the course of conducting their professional activities. This makes the task of gathering attitudinal information less difficult than it otherwise might be.

For instance, senators might ask former criminal prosecutors about the policy of their office toward capital punishment, sentencing policy, the exclusionary rule, or other matters that may help to establish the nominees' past and present attitude toward criminal justice matters. Did a nominee participate in political campaigns as a worker or candidate and what were the ideological positions at stake in those campaigns? If a nominee has had a private law practice, what was the style of that practice? Did the nominee have for clients Fortune 500 corporations or did he or she devote much of his or her professional life to aiding America's poor and underrepresented?

Depending on the number, studying the published opinions of nominees with prior judicial experience may reveal consistent attitude patterns. Wherever possible and practical, Judiciary Committee staff could construct Guttman type scales on a variety of issue dimensions to ascertain ideological consistency and relative scale position of those judges sitting in collegial settings. Asking sitting judges informed questions about particularly controversial cases in which they cast votes and wrote opinions can serve to uncover not only policy views, but also nominees' conceptions of the proper judicial role.

Contrary to what some believe, however, prior judicial experience is not a good predictor of a commitment to *stare decisis*. Finally, culling through and questioning nominees about their publications, including law review and other writings, can serve to reveal a wealth of attitudinal information. Much of the Senate Judiciary Committee's interrogation of Robert Bork centered on his prolific writings. Bork felt compelled to explain his writings and in the process the nation was treated to a splendid constitutional law seminar. Ironically, it may be that President Bush chose David Souter as his first Supreme Court nominee because of the lack of a paper trail, and consequently, senators had one less indicator of nominee ideology.

There was a period when researchers assumed that newly appointed justices take several years before they settle into their new job. The neophytes were said to exhibit signs of bewilderment by their new duties and responsibilities. Being awed by their new surroundings they need several years to become psychologically adjusted. Attempting to ease newly appointed justices into the demands of the job, senior justices do not assign their junior colleagues an equal share of opinion writing. Finally, freshmen fail to align immediately with the Court's existing voting blocs. Recent research findings, however, reject the freshmen effect hypothesis.

Findings for the Reagan appointees indicate the period of bewilderment is short, if it exists at all. Although freshmen justices write fewer opinions during their first term on the Court, by the end of the second term they no longer write the fewest number of opinions. Even so, freshmen author important opinions during their initial terms signifying early integration into the work group. Finally, freshmen are not timid about joining preexisting voting blocs.

The importance of the freshmen effect research is that it highlights the importance of considering the near term consequences newly appointed justices may have on Supreme Court decision making. They can have an immediate impact that senators must consider seriously.

It is untrue that justices today are appointed without considering their immediate impact upon the Court. Particularly during the Reagan Administration, nominees were carefully screened by the president or his advisors for their ideological commitment to a judicial agenda, including a view of the judicial function that in the contemporary context is supportive of conservative ideals. The Reagan appointees did not need time to figure out positions on the great legal and constitutional issues of the day. They were chosen for their ideological correctness. The Bush Administration also carefully chooses judicial nominees with ideology as a central concern. Because today the U.S. Supreme Court deals mostly with matters affecting statutory and constitutional law and because a good number of constitutional law topics are controversial, it makes good political sense to discover nominee attitudes about these subjects.

In summary, senators need not ask the kinds of questions that require nominees to promise how they will vote in future cases. There is no need to do so. Nominee attitudes and values are discernable and may serve as indicators of likely future behavior. The constitutional framers contemplated an inquisitive and active role in confirming presidential appointments. The advice and consent clause of the Constitution justifies an independent scrutiny of nominees by members of the Senate. The historical record reveals that from the beginning of the new republic the Senate has rejected nominees for reasons other than personal and professional qualifications. In one fashion or another, political considerations, including evaluations of the ideological soundness of nominees, influence Senate advice and consent decisions. Properly understood, statutory and ethical norms do not prohibit nominees from revealing their views on the great issues of the day. Nominees may conduct themselves before Senate hearing panels with honor and probity while at the same time providing vital political information.

Briefly stated, nothing in the Constitution, our historical experience, our political practice, ethical norms, nor statutory enactments prohibits senators from asking judicial nominees pertinent ideological questions. Nominees owe an obligation to the nation to be forthcoming if the advice and consent provision of the Constitution is to have real meaning.

☑ N O

Should the Senate Ask Nominees to the Supreme Court Questions about Politics and Ideology?

WILLIAM BRADFORD REYNOLDS

The Confirmation Process: Too Much Advice and Too Little Consent

With the announcement this summer [1991] of Justice Thurgood Marshall's resignation from the United States Supreme Court, the stage is set once again for Senate confirmation hearings to fill a vacancy on the Highest Court. The president nominated an exceptionally well qualified judge on the District of Columbia Circuit Court, Judge Clarence Thomas, to fill the seat.

Almost immediately, the political battle lines were drawn, and interest groups on both sides began their all-too-familiar refrains. Their objective, ultimately, is to convince a majority of senators to support (or oppose) Judge Thomas because he agrees (or disagrees)—or is perceived to agree (or disagree)—with a particular ideology they endorse. The fine art of confirmation-by-litmus-test, as developed and honed during and after the confirmation hearings of Judge Robert Bork for the Supreme Court, seems to be here to stay.

The question of whether the Senate should rise above the fray and exercise its "advice and consent" responsibility untainted by the political haranguing of special interest agitators is no longer seriously asked or answered. Rather, as Professor Melone's heavily footnoted article makes clear, the debate has shifted. [The footnotes of Professor Melone's article were deleted in this reprinting.] The legitimacy of politicizing the confirmation process is no longer open for discussion. That other nominees have been mistreated over the past 200 years—even if only a relatively few—apparently justifies the crudest of tactics in the present environment. The criticism, it is argued, should not be heaped on the senators for seeking politically correct answers, but on the nominee for declining to respond (whatever his or her reason) or, in responding, failing the standard of political correctness.

I continue to be of the school that believes the Senate's "advice and consent" role under Article II, §2, cl. 2 of the U.S. Constitution was understood by the framers in far more modest terms. Professor Melone does an adequate job with the historical compromise that placed in the Executive the power to nominate and in the Senate a check on that power to guard against the president's naming of a justice of "unfit" character, or one without professional "merit."[1]

He stumbles badly, however, in extrapolating (albeit somewhat tentatively) from the framers' debates that the door was unwittingly opened for the Senate to inquire as well into "nominees' ideology." Nor does even that shaky premise sustain the penultimate of the professor's thesis (which we have come to expect from academic circles when the historical analysis fails to produce the desired result), to wit: it is, after all, a "living constitution," which permits the Senate essentially "to use its constitutional authority as it sees fit."

So much for original intent. Not that it makes much practical difference. The argument fashioned by Professor Melone and his like-minded academic colleagues is but an intellectual fig leaf for the senators to hide behind. Senators Biden and Specter wore it rather well to cultivate at least a public perception that their opposition to Judge Bork was reasoned, not political. Senators Heflin and Leahy were far less convincing, while Senators Kennedy and Metzenbaum cast aside all pretexts, seemingly unashamed by the public exposure of their crass political campaign that took not the measure of the man and his credentials, but instead subjected him and the process to a most unforgiving liberal litmus test. Whether one agrees or disagrees with my view that such senatorial gracelessness mocks that body's "advice and consent" responsibility is, I would submit, quite beside the point. The reality is that Professor Melone summed things up about right: the senators will do as they damn well please in the confirmation jousting over a nominee for the Highest Court—even as they pretend to be more deliberative.

Thus, we can expect the inquiry to move sharply away from the topics of judicial qualifications, philosophy, and temperament—all legitimate areas to probe—and, sadly, toward an issues-oriented game of chicken, focused on decisional outcomes, not the methodology a nominee employs to get there. If abortion happens to be the political "hot button" at the time of hearings, whether the candidate is or is not pro-life becomes the litmus test for confirmation. The same holds true for "affirmative action," capital punishment, the exclusionary rule, flag burning, and a host of other issues that make up the grist of the Supreme Court's jurisprudence.

There is, of course, nothing wrong with senators seeking to determine *how* a nominee would approach and go about deciding any or all of these issues. Whether or not historical context is deemed important, what source materials are considered authoritative, the degree of deference (if any) that attaches to Court precedents, and the analytical framework generally followed—these are all appropriate inquiries. But to go beyond methodology and insist on a statement of *what* the nominee's decision will be in any particular case makes political correctness the yardstick for confirmation, not juridicial competence.

THE CORRECT STAND

Refusing to answer the *what* question—except, as with Judge Bork for example, where a thoughtful response had previously been given in writings or opinions—has yet to defeat a nomination. Justice David Souter adopted what seems to me to be the unquestionably correct stand. He demonstrated his general knowledge of competing considerations, identified relevant precedents, even in some instances made reference to learned commentary bearing on the subject raised; he noted that his decision, ultimately, would turn on a careful analysis of the matters he touched upon, the briefs filed by counsel and discussions with his colleagues on the Court. That is, of course, precisely how a Supreme Court justice should approach each issue when first presented to him or her for decision. The demand in confirmation hearings for snap judgments to be offered in response to invariably poorly crafted questions (which all too frequently do not even ask what the senator *thinks* he is asking) encourages highly injudicious behavior. Resisting such pressure is properly judicious.

A case in point involves the law of privacy. Virtually all the senators—with the notable exception of Senator Hatch—have demonstrated repeatedly and emphatically in the last six Supreme Court confirmation hearings—stretching back to Justice Sandra Day O'Connor in 1982—that their grasp of the issue of constitutional privacy is untutored and inexpert. Judge Thomas, too, will soon be subjected to the ordeal of trying, politely, to answer the predictably inept inquiries from Judiciary Committee members about his views on the "law of privacy" (we all know they really mean "abortion"). He would, in my view, be well advised to give the Souter response if, as I suspect, he has not yet had occasion to sort through the constitutional complexities that attend the issue and have divided learned scholars and jurists for years. Such an answer has the virtue of avoiding the litmus test trap set by those senators intent on securing advance commitments on substantive issues—besides which, it happens to be honest.

This does not suggest that Judge Thomas need equivocate on his *personal* views in the pro-life debate *if* he has heretofore shared them publicly with others. Should the question be asked on that level, I would hope the nominee would make the point that his personal views (whatever they may be) are wholly irrelevant to his constitutional analysis; they then should have no bearing on the confirmation deliberations. Nor do I agree with Governor L. Douglas Wilder's misguided observation (later fuzzily recanted) that Judge Thomas' Catholic upbringing serves to disqualify him—any more than the same religious affiliation undid Justice Kennedy or, at the executive level, stood in the way of John F. Kennedy's bid for the presidency.

To be sure, on issues where he has been outspoken, a more intense probe of the nominee's stated positions can be expected, and properly so. Judge Thomas has not been bashful about his views on "affirmative action," for example. The Senate can properly challenge, and the nominee had better be prepared to defend. The search, however, should be not for areas of personal agreement or disagreement, but for the reasoned explanation. Judge Thomas has Supreme Court precedent and Justices William O. Douglas and Lewis Powell among the reasoned advocates on his side of the debate. His open stand against government policies that promote uneven treatment of individuals because of racial, gender, or ethnic differences—oxymoronically labelled "affirmative"— commands the respect of a majority of today's sitting justices, as well as many judges on the federal appellate and district courts. That reality predictably counts for little among the *political* opposition. Among those for whom intellectual honesty still has value, on the other hand, it is the full answer to critics who seek to miscast their nominee as a "radical thinker" or "outside the mainstream."

BASES FOR CONSENT

Will Judge Thomas be confirmed? By any objective measure, he should be— overwhelmingly. The framers nod to the Senate—to give its "advice and consent"—left to the president (and the president alone) the task of nominating. Not surprisingly, George Bush's choices for the Supreme Court are not going to be the same as Michael Dukakis'. So long as the persons proposed are of high moral character, strong legal training and experience, and in good physical health, Senate "consent" should not be withheld because conservative credentials shine through.

Fidelity to the written law and disdain for judicial improvisation is a philosophy of judging that undoubtedly dismays liberal senators weaned on a Warren Court openly disdainful of the written law and known best for judicial improvisations. Yet, it is a philosophy that returns to the legislative branch its constitutional responsibility of framing the law, to the executive branch its constitutional responsibility of administering the law, and to the judicial branch its constitutional responsibility of interpreting the law.

If such conservative thinking is all that stands in the way of confirmation by a liberal Senate—because it is regarded as not politically correct—the worst fears of what mischief could come out of Judge Bork's mishandled confirmation hearings will have been realized. The judiciary will no longer be able to lay claim to independence from the other two branches, having become captive to a highly charged and overly politicized selection process that demands from nominees advance commitments to particular policy results being pressed by a senator or favored "interest group."

The Senate Judiciary Committee's scrutiny of Judge Thomas thus bears close viewing. Not only does the future of the nominee hang in the balance, but so, too, does the very character of the Supreme Court. Regrettably, the fate of both the man and the institution will be determined with little senatorial respect for the constitutional role that assigns that body an "advice and consent" responsibility more modest than it is prepared to wield.

NOTE

1. See Alexander Hamilton, *The Federalist* No. 76.

Questions for Discussion

1. What criteria should be used in selecting a nominee to the Supreme Court? What are the reasons for your answer?
2. Why did nominations to the Supreme Court during the Reagan and Bush administrations produce such stormy hearings?
3. What can be done to remove the controversy surrounding Supreme Court nominations?
4. What effect does the nomination process have on the authority and respect of appointees once they are confirmed by the Senate?
5. What questions are appropriate to ask nominees? What are the reasons for your answer?

Suggested Readings

Abraham, Henry J. *Justices and Presidents: A Political History of Appointments to the Supreme Court.* 3d ed. New York: Oxford Univ. Press, 1992.

Ad Hoc Committee on the Senate Confirmation Process. "Report on the Senate Confirmation Process." *Record of the Association of the Bar of the City of New York*, 47, no. 5 (June 1992), 543–566.

Bronner, Ethan. *Battle for Justice: How the Bork Nomination Shook America.* New York: W. W. Norton, 1989.

Carter, Stephen L. "A Litmus Test for Justices? It Demeans the Court." *New York Times*, April 28, 1993, p. A21.

DeConcini, Dennis. "The Confirmation Process." *St. John's Journal of Legal Commentary*, 7, no. 1 (Fall 1991), 1–13.

Gewirtz, Paul. "A Litmus Test for Justices? Legal Views Do Matter." *New York Times*, April 28, 1993, p. A21.

Gitenstein, Mark. *Matters of Principle: America's Rejection of the Bork Nomination.* New York: Simon & Schuster, 1992.

Kaus, Mickey. "Roe to Ruin." *New Republic*, 208, no. 15 (April 12, 1993), 6.

Kelbley, Charles A. "Bad Judgment on Judges: Why Screening Judges on Single Issues Threatens to Corrupt Our Legal System." *Human Rights*, 15, no. 1 (Fall 1987), 14–19.

Mikva, Abner J. "How Should We Select Judges in a Free Society?" *Southern Illinois Univ. Law Journal*, 16 (Spring 1992), 547–556.

Silverstein, Mark. "The People, the Senate and the Court: The Democratization of the Judicial Confirmation System." *Constitutional Commentary*, 9, no. 1 (Winter 1992), 41–58.

Simon, Paul. *Advice and Consent: Clarence Thomas, Robert Bork and the Intriguing History of the Supreme Court's Nomination Battle*. Washington, D.C.: National Press Books, 1992.

Public Policy

P olitical democracy involves a contest over public policy. An element of that contest includes convincing individuals, private groups, and political leaders that particular policies are wise and just. An underlying theme of democratic rule is that conflicts should be resolved peacefully through discussion, freedom of association, and agreed-upon procedures for determining policy outcomes.

People who choose sides on different issues of public policy do so for many reasons. Sometimes, the choice is based on self-interest, as when a manufacturer or trade union favors protectionism so as to reduce competition from abroad. At other times, the choice is based on a perception of justice, as in issues relating to the elimination of racism or the protection of the environment. Often, choices derive from a combination of self-interested and altruistic impulses.

Part V deals with some contemporary issues in domestic and foreign policy matters of concern to the people of the United States. Specifically, the debate questions consider school choice, immigration, gun control, government support to artists and writers, and the future of U.S. foreign policy.

Chapter 17

Will Choice Produce Better Schools?

Many Americans have become disenchanted with the system of public education. Not a year goes by without a report showing that the education of the country's youth is failing. In some fields of education, such as science and mathematics, most advanced industrial countries do a better job than does the United States.

The problems have been particularly severe in urban areas, where teachers have had to cope with the impact of drugs and violence on physical survival, let alone learning. In inner-city schools the dropout rate is high, particularly for racial minorities. But in public schools throughout the country, good teachers are discouraged not only because so many students do not want to learn but also because public funding for education is so inadequate that teachers cannot do their jobs effectively. Financial problems became particularly severe during the tough economic times of the late 1980s and early 1990s.

In the early years of the Reagan administration, Secretary of Education Terrel H. Bell appointed a blue-ribbon commission to investigate education in the United States. Its report, *A Nation at Risk* (1983), described the system in grim terms and warned of a "rising tide of mediocrity that threatens our very future as a nation and as a people."[1]

The commission made recommendations, including longer school years, tougher curriculums, and stronger teaching programs. Many school systems implemented those recommendations. But ten years later, Bell, then an educational consultant, reported that the results were disappointing.[2]

Although many proposals have been put forward to reform education, there has been little agreement about what will be effective. One controversial approach would allow parents to choose the schools in which their children would be educated.

A principal element of school choice plans is a voucher system. Parents would be given a voucher that allows their children to attend one of many schools. In some plans, vouchers can be used only for private schools; in others, only for public schools.

Advocates of the voucher system say that unless competition is introduced and economic pressure placed on schools, there will be no incentive for school officials and teachers to turn schools into effective educational institutions. Critics of choice say that choice will destroy the public school system and widen the gap between good and bad schools.

The debate is joined in the articles below. Jeanne Allen, former manager of the Center for Educational Policy, argues for choice in an article in the magazine *World and I*. She contends

1. Parents, business leaders, teachers, and public officials want school choice.
2. In their present form, public schools are not the common school of days gone by in which children of all classes and all levels of society could be educated together and learn the fundamentals of democracy.
3. A voucher system provides real equity in educational opportunity.
4. Poor people should be trusted to make intelligent decisions about the education of their children. They will be able to make those decisions in a system of choice.

Jonathan Kozol, a former teacher and now a writer on education, argues against choice in an interview he gave to *Common Cause Magazine*. He contends

1. So-called school choice will further widen the gap between rich and poor in the United States.
2. The voucher system is deeply rooted in racism.
3. The voucher system would still not provide funds for low-income students equal to those available for affluent students.
4. Poor people do not have access to information that will allow them to make a good choice in a choice system.
5. Choice—whether public or private—will result in separate schools for affluent students.
6. Public schools can be made good if they are funded at the level of private schools or public schools in affluent areas.
7. Education can be improved through putting money into school reconstruction, strengthening Head Start (a program to give early educational opportunities to youngsters), a state-by-state drive for school equality, and improvement in teacher education.

NOTES

1. Quoted in William Celis 3d, "Ten Years after a Scathing Report, Schools Show Uneven Progress," *New York Times*, April 28, 1993, p. A19.
2. Ibid.

Will Choice Produce Better Schools?

JEANNE ALLEN

Choice Is Key to Better Schools

As America's public schools remain in deep trouble, more Americans are coming to a simple conclusion: Unless there is a fundamental restructuring of public schools, the nation cannot remain competitive or ensure that students obtain even the basic skills necessary to earn a sound livelihood.

Polls indicate that most Americans see giving parents a choice of schools as the key to school reform. Making parents education consumers forces schools to improve instruction and toughen standards if they want to retain students and the funding that goes with them. It also unleashes the pent-up creativity of educators in response to consumer demand. In fact, more than 55 percent of public school teachers surveyed support school choice even as their unions spend millions to battle it around the country. Educators are becoming increasingly open to the possibility that the monopoly they work for may soon be broken—to their benefit and that of the children.

School choice, whether confined to public schools or expanded to include private and parochial schools, is emerging as the centerpiece in meeting the challenge of failing schools across America. This is due to the simple fact that choice has proven to be the only reform that has brought improvement, while the tinkering of the last 15 years—raising graduation requirements, lowering class sizes, hiking school spending to unprecedented levels—has failed. In fact, while educational spending has risen, student performance continues to go down by every statistical measure.

Last year, for the fourth consecutive year, the Scholastic Aptitude Test (SAT) scores dropped. According to the "Report Card" issued last September by the National Education Goals panel, only 14 percent of American eighth graders can "figure the cost of a meal from a menu" and only a third of eleventh graders can write "a coherent paragraph about themselves."

IRONY FOR LIBERALS

Such dismal statistics have triggered calls for school choice from parents, business leaders, teachers, and public officials. But most smartingly to liberal observers, the strongest backers of choice, for both public and private schools, are minorities and urban residents, by 57 percent. Yet, among public officials, it is the liberals, the professed "best friends" of the urban poor, who are most opposed to choice.

This irony has caused a stir among liberals themselves. Last year, the Democratic Leadership Council scurried at the last minute to adopt a policy on choice in their statement of principles. While agreeing only to back public school choice programs that were supported locally (thereby avoiding criticism of wanting to mandate choice), they nevertheless did adopt a policy toward this ever-popular, albeit still controversial reform.

The same phenomenon has occurred throughout the ranks of the education establishment. Recognizing choice's growing support within the last few years, most of education's special interests have rushed to appease constituents and plead their openness to change. Most straddle the fence and add so many caveats that their ideal choice program would be all but invisible if implemented. But the fact that the National School Boards Association, the Chief State School Officers (state superintendents), and both teachers' unions all publicly express support for choice demonstrates the power of this important reform. Only four years ago, these same organizations declared their opposition and felt no compunction in shouting for more money as the only way to improve public schools.

The unofficial choice "movement" can no longer be written off. Even though, until recently, groups like the National Education Association (NEA) have denounced choice as a right-wing plot to destroy public education, they have not been able to justify the charge. Unfortunately, despite the growing evidence that choice works, and despite its popularity, such myths tend to dominate public discussions about educational choice.

GENUINE EQUITY

Many liberals, in impassioned harangues about what choice will do "to" the schools, invoke "public education" as if it were the name of God. Says Wisconsin Superintendent of Public Instruction Herbert Grover, a foe of the Milwaukee School Choice program, choice is "not a solution but a program that is in conflict with the intent of the common schools established for the common good of our society." Of course, what Grover and so many others like him conveniently ignore is that the original "common school," a place where children of all classes and all levels of society could be educated together and learn about the fundamentals of democracy, is rare among public schools. Public schools, according to such noted researchers as the University of Chicago's James Coleman, are more segregated, less likely to weave together the variegated tapestry of Americans, and not prepared at all to teach about any such thing as democracy. According to Charles Glenn, author of The Myth of the Common School, this ideal cannot be restored without giving parents of all income levels the ability to choose the school they deem most appropriate for their child, thus leveling out the playing field between those that can afford choice and those who cannot.

Parental choice provides real equity in education. Voucher plans require that all eligible participants receive an equal amount to spend at the school of their choice. In some proposals, the voucher would increase as the parents' income level decreased, thus encouraging schools to meet the additional needs of disadvantaged children. These low-income vouchers create a more level playing field by permitting the poor access to the quality private and parochial schools in and near their neighborhoods, which are inaccessible only because of dollars.

In the continuing battle for "civil rights," this is one that liberals conveniently overlook. When the Senate this January debated an administration-backed, low-income voucher proposal, such self-described civil rights leaders as Edward Kennedy (D-Massachusetts) and Howard Metzenbaum (D-Ohio) invoked images of poor children left to Fagin-like characters out to "pick their already empty pockets." There was much hand-wringing over how choice would leave poor kids back in the bad schools, while those from better homes would take advantage of the opportunity to flee. This "creaming argument" asserts that choice would give way to elite academies for the few and dingy schools for the many.

That premise, of course, supposes that poorer and less able children and their parents cannot differentiate between good and bad schools. What they ignore here, too, is that despite the landmark court decision in *Brown* v. *Board of Education*, public schools today are already separate and unequal, failing millions of children who are required by law to attend them, to a degree that Linda Brown and her allies in the real civil rights battles would be loath to see.

Senator Kennedy and his colleagues see no such problem with choice when it comes to abortion. Yet the same so-called right that they argue women should have over their bodies does not extend to children once they are born.

This patronizing attitude is typical of most liberals, who believe that the poor cannot make basic decisions about where to live, how to raise their children, and what schools are best. They dictate to the poor as opposed to providing choices that restore dignity and productivity.

CHOICE SUCCESS STORIES

"Being poor doesn't mean you're stupid," argues Milwaukee lawmaker Annette "Polly" Williams, author of the Milwaukee voucher program that allows up to 1,000 low-income children to attend private nonsectarian schools of their choice, rather than attend the Milwaukee public schools with a 50 percent dropout rate. Williams was a welfare mother of four who raised her children alone in an African-American community where over 70 percent of the residents were on welfare. That did not stop her from working and volunteering at a local private school to be able to send her children there. It also did not stop her from running for, and winning, a key legislative seat that positioned her to help "her people" and landed her before the Wisconsin State Supreme Court and at the focus of national media attention.

Most of the parents of the children who are participating in the Milwaukee choice program are single and on welfare. They relish the opportunity to have a say in their children's lives, especially where education is concerned. In fact, the program has helped children there meet the increased demands of private schools simply because they feel a sense of pride and ownership in the schools they choose to attend.

That sense is also apparent in East Harlem, New York's School District No. 4. Sy Fliegel, who authored and directed the district's acclaimed choice program, says that kids need to share a vision, and they need to feel they are part of something. When teachers are permitted to be in control of their own classrooms, they, too, share that sense of ownership that allows them to be more responsive to their students. Fliegel broke dozens of rules back in 1974 to implement a system of choice among a set of diverse middle schools that the teachers helped design and operate.

Back then, District 4 ranked last among 32 New York City districts. Over the years, the district's graduation rate increased from less than 50 percent to more than 90 percent. Reading and math scores skyrocketed, paralleling the averages of some of New York's best suburban schools. East Harlem District 4 now ranks 16 out of 32 districts and is a place where white parents from the greener side of Manhattan vie to send their children. Fliegel brags that "you won't find any graffiti" in the East Harlem choice schools; people treat better that which they own. The same lessons have been learned from programs that turn public housing management and ownership over to tenants. Suddenly, "the projects" seem to resemble a well-heeled neighborhood more than a public housing zone.

Minnesota boasts America's first statewide open-enrollment plan. The pressures imposed by public school competition prompted a majority of the state's high schools to quadruple the number of advanced placement courses offered to their students. Over 20,000 children have participated in one of the state's four alternative schools or choice programs. In fact, the state's second-chance program, which allows students who have dropped out to return to another school, has brought over 6,000 dropouts back to school.

Minnesota also pioneered the charter schools concept, an idea intended to allow parents and teachers to start their own schools, be "chartered" by the state but freed from all unnecessary rules and regulations. Only a pilot program at present, the charter schools program promises to provide a real boost for teacher autonomy and parental choice.

Another choice-oriented program can be found in Washington State, where for several years, dropout clinics have educated the at-risk child. Students choose to attend the program, which prepares them to either return to the classroom or complete a General Equivalency Degree (GED). Since the program's inception in 1977, participants completing the program are 70 percent less likely to be jailed and 50 percent less likely to be on welfare than before entering the program.

Magnet schools, federally funded programs designed to assist districts that are undergoing court-ordered desegregation, are also schools of choice. Magnets in Prince George's County, Maryland; New Haven, Connecticut; and other cities nationwide are operated as schools of choice; parents vie for slots in these schools, which are assigned either by lottery or on a first-come, first-serve basis. Because magnet schools must compete for students, their educational quality is usually better than that of the public schools. They have also succeeded in creating racial balances through voluntary desegregation. Prince George's County students outperform 65 percent of the students across the state.

Despite the recent defeat in the U.S. Senate of a school choice pilot project for the inner cities, progress is being made. Momentum is building in as many as 20 states for full choice programs that let parents choose the education that is best for their children. Two major impediments stand in the way: One is public ignorance about choice and how it accomplishes school improvement. The public has been brainwashed into believing that the answer to all of education's ills is more money. Many Americans therefore cannot conceive of reform that requires no additional money and may even reduce the spending per student that has increased threefold in the last 10 years.

The other, more damaging obstacle is the public education establishment, or the "blob," as former Education Secretary William Bennett so aptly called it. When the two million-plus member NEA, with its $150 million budget, puts its strength behind maintaining the status quo, and some nearly 50 associations representing everything from "curriculum specialists" to school business officers bond together to oppose choice, it is not an easy task.

The shell is beginning to crack, however. The public is almost weekly treated to stories of abuse and contradictions in public schools. Chicago's establishment, while still in charge, suffered great loss of face when it was revealed that 46 percent of public school teachers there send their children to private schools. These same teachers support unions that want to refuse that opportunity to the less fortunate. It is estimated that nearly 80 percent of the senators who opposed choice in January 1992 send their children to private schools.

It is important and easy for anyone even moderately concerned with schools to understand the real dichotomy in the choice debate. Outside the Washington Beltway, successful choice measures are more often the result of liberal legislators and governors, rather than the right-wing nuts the establishment condemns. The more information that gets out about the perilous public education system, the more likely it is that more liberals will find it difficult to defend the very system that defies their own notions of civil rights.

Will Choice Produce Better Schools?

JONATHAN KOZOL (INTERVIEW BY VICKI KEMPER)
Rebuilding the Schoolhouse

When Bill and Hillary Clinton announced in early January [1992] that their daughter, Chelsea, would be attending an exclusive private school in the nation's capital, they ignited a firestorm of criticism—and rekindled the debate over public vs. private schools and school "choice." There is in Washington a public school good enough for the nation's First Child, many argued.

But such reasoning begs an important question: Even if the Clintons had chosen to send their daughter to one of the District's top-notch public schools, what about all the not-so-good public schools in Washington, and the 80,000 children who have no choice but to attend them—given that the best schools can accept only so many pupils?

It is that question author Jonathan Kozol wants Bill Clinton the president to address, even as Bill Clinton the parent makes other choices for his own child. A former teacher, Kozol is angered and saddened by the increasingly separate and unequal schooling in America, and he calls for a new back-to-basics education movement: public school systems that provide all their students with comfortable classrooms, textbooks, libraries, teachers and—most important—an equal opportunity to learn and succeed.

Kozol's most recent book, *Savage Inequalities,* is a profoundly disturbing look at conditions in the nation's schools, as well as the personal attitudes and political policies that have created them. Kozol spent two years visiting public and private schools in Chicago, New York, East St. Louis, San Antonio, Washington and Camden, N.J. He saw school buildings that had been flooded with sewage, closets serving as classrooms, classes with no teachers and buildings where even the toilets didn't work. He learned of state school-financing formulas that fund affluent districts at a rate 14 times greater than neighboring, low-income districts. He talked with fourth-graders studying logic and high school students who could barely read. He was struck by "the remarkable degree of racial segregation that persisted almost everywhere."

Advocate as well as author, the 56-year-old Kozol insists he will "not accept a rationing of excellence" for the nation's schoolchildren. He encourages elected officials, educators and parents to "stop making new lists [of education goals] and immediately get to work on essentials" such as the expansion of Head Start and reforms in state school-financing systems. He spoke from his home in Massachusetts.

COMMON CAUSE: *What kind of impact does the Clintons' sending Chelsea to private school have on the education reform debate?*
KOZOL: I don't condemn President Clinton for that decision. The daughter of a president is likely to be overwhelmed with press scrutiny, and anything that can afford her some privacy makes sense to me. That's a truly unique situation.

If you're going to condemn President Clinton for that decision, then you'd have to condemn the entire U.S. Senate and House of Representatives, as well as virtually the entire press corps in New York and Washington. Because very few of the journalists I know, certainly very few of the editors and publishers, send their kids to public schools.

I do feel heartsick at the growing inclination of not only the very wealthy but also the upper-middle class to flee. A friend of mine in New York, a woman in one of the publishing houses, when she read the first draft of *Savage Inequalities,* looked at me in tears. She said, "I feel awful. I'm sending my child to a private school. . . . Would it do any good if I were to sacrifice her to public school? What difference would that make?"

The answer I gave is "no." If one person makes that decision, it doesn't really change anything. But if all the editors and publishers of the *Wall Street Journal* and the *New York Times,* CBS, and NBC, and Random House, and Simon and Schuster, if all of them put their kids in the New York City public schools, those schools would change overnight. Because they would not allow their children to be destroyed, and therefore they would work like hell to guarantee that the public schools of New York City were the equal of any top suburban district in the country.

What I'm really getting at here is the increasing tendency of the privileged to secede not simply from public schools, but increasingly from almost all the areas of shared experience in our society. The United States is already a highly stratified society. But at least until recently, there were many areas of what I call "shared democracy," where we met on some kind of common ground and had to negotiate our differences with one another in specific situations.

Nowadays, we see the affluent increasingly refusing to pay the taxes it would take to maintain the public parks, and instead, spending their money to join private health clubs where they get their exercise in company with one another. They're reluctant to pay the money that it takes to provide police protection for the entire city, but increasingly spending a vast amount for private security to guarantee that their condominiums, their office buildings, their apartment houses are well protected.

In the same sense, they're saying that they cannot afford to tax themselves to provide first-rate schools for the children of New York, and then spending $10-, $15-, or $20,000 to send their children to private school. This, as a trend, is alarming. We have always had private schools in the United States. Some of them are wonderful schools, like Exeter. But we are now seeing something new, which is the growing tendency of much larger numbers of people to flee not only to elite schools, but to virtually any school they can get into that will spare their children the obligation, I call it the opportunity, to learn about democracy firsthand, by meeting children of other races and other economic levels. That saddens me very much.

We are already two nations, as far as race is concerned. I worry that we might become 10 or 20 different nations if this continues. I'm concerned about the Balkanization of our society into unique and insulated sectors that will no longer speak even a common language of democracy.

COMMON CAUSE: *President Clinton, the teachers' unions and many others op-pose tuition vouchers that would allow the use of public education funds for private schooling, yet they support the concept of choice within public schools.*

KOZOL: I am relieved that President Clinton has taken a strong stand against vouchers that would permit public funds to be used for private education. No matter what the advocates of vouchers say it is, and no matter how many neo-liberals climb on the bandwagon, vouchers originate in an ideology which is distinctly right-wing. Another historic origin of the voucher concept are the so-called "freedom of choice" schools started in the South by white segregationists after the *Brown [v. Board of Education]* decision. That element, either covert or subtle racism, is deeply rooted in the voucher concept.

The advocates for vouchers nowadays pose the issue in a clever, but I think dishonest, manner. They say something like this: "The rich have always had the opportunity to send their kids to private school. Why shouldn't we give poor people the same opportunity?" But when you ask them what kind of vouchers they have in mind, the amount of money they propose varies from about $1,000 to at most the amount that is spent in an inner-city public school, maybe $5,000. None of them are suggesting the $10- or $15,000 voucher that it would take to send these kids to the prep schools the rich children attend.

So in effect, under the pretense of compassion for the poor, they are simply proposing a privatized caste system in which the rich will continue to go to elite prep schools, and the poor, at very best, would be able to go to another category of private schools, either parochial schools or very poorly funded sort of second-rate private academies.

COMMON CAUSE: *But should there be choice within the public school system?*

KOZOL: First of all, our capacity for historical amnesia sometimes dazzles me. The [desire for "choice" is] exactly what we heard from white people in Missis-sippi after the *Brown* decision in 1954. The fact is the government coerces us to do a great many things for the general good in this society. Our absolute right to the individual pursuit of our own ambitions is curtailed in many areas. And this is another one where it should be.

The myth here of course is that the choices will be equal and that everybody will be equally well-informed about the choices available. But these conditions are, in fact, never met and are virtually impossible to meet. First of all, people can choose only from things they've heard of. Many poor parents are only semi-literate. They have no opportunity to read the materials that school sys-tems distribute, even the announcements calling them to meetings at which these matters might be explained in greater detail.

But even those who can read do not always read aggressively. The poorest people I know are inundated with written materials which they read so pas-sively it is almost impossible for them to overcome the paralysis that over-whelms many aspects of their lives.

The typical conservative answer to this is, "Wait a minute, Mr. Kozol sounds very patronizing. He's telling us that the poor are too stupid to make good choices for their children." The best answer I can give you is that of a black woman in Boston who saw [John] Chubb [a leading proponent of choice] debating with me once on television and said, "We don't need our enemies explaining to our friends that we're not stupid." She said, "Stupidity isn't the issue, access is."

An awful lot of the sophisticated decisions that are made in school choice programs by the middle class tend to be decisions that are arrived at by word of mouth, because they hear very quickly from their brother-in-law, who is the school superintendent, or their sister, who is assistant to the mayor. They hear very quickly about the "boutique" school that's got the terrific principal and the six wonderful young teachers.

In Boston, whenever they discuss school choice—we have a so-called "controlled choice" plan in Boston—the press always points to the same school. I was curious as to why. Then I found as I talked with the few affluent white people I know who still have their kids in public school in Boston, that they all went to the same school. A black woman who lives in Roxbury calls me up every couple of weeks, and she's never heard of school choice, she's never heard of this neat little boutique school.

The reason school choice within a given school district has become so popular, especially with the press, is that it provides the opportunity for people who feel vaguely guilty about fleeing the public system to keep their kids in the public system in what are virtually de facto prep schools.

Now a pragmatic person might reply to me that if we didn't give them those boutique schools, they'd flee the system altogether. And then they wouldn't be there to support the system. But in a sense they've fled the system already, in that they are fighting now only for the school that their child attends, and not for the schools attended by all the other children in the system. They are in a position to raise extra money for that school, to form a real neat local PTA, to volunteer for the library or book fair, do all those things. They can make it into a terrific school, but they have very little incentive to fight for tax support for all the other schools in the system.

There are other problems with intradistrict choice, which has been introduced in Minnesota and in Massachusetts and is being discussed elsewhere. The most obvious one is that virtually none of these plans ever provide transportation money. And that certainly couldn't be an oversight. In general [advocates of intradistrict choice] are people who historically opposed school busing for integration. So it's logical that they would sort of leave that out at this point.

So who is able to take advantage of this plan? The first full year of school choice in Massachusetts roughly 93 percent of those who transferred were white and/or middle class. Twenty-seven percent were poor children. The people who took advantage of it were the people who had your typical two-parent suburban family, with two cars. The poorest parents aren't doing it because they don't have cars.

A classic example, and this doesn't involve race, just economics. Two adjacent towns: Gloucester, Mass., a rather poor school district, a lot of very low-income families, and Manchester-by-the-Sea, one of the wealthiest school districts in Massachusetts, which spends about $2,000 more per pupil than Gloucester does.

What happened when the choice plan was announced? The most affluent people who lived in Gloucester shifted their kids into the Manchester district. Gloucester lost the money that went with those kids. It also lost the advocacy of their parents for the Gloucester public school system. And the kids left behind in Gloucester no longer have the stimulation of some of their most fortunate classmates.

In all respects, Gloucester is the loser. Gloucester has lost several hundred thousand dollars to Manchester. Manchester has in fact been able to hire one of the best Gloucester teachers. They cut a program in Gloucester and added it in Manchester.

I notice that even in some areas, sort of small industrial towns in Massachusetts, where there are a great many black or Hispanic families, virtually the only families that are using the choice option to go to suburban districts are the white middle-class families. It's interesting that here you have white parents, who 20 years ago opposed school busing for desegregation because, as they always told us, it wasn't fair to poor little black children to have to spend an hour on the bus every day to come out to our spectacular school. Now the same people are putting their kids on buses for two hours twice a day in order to flee from black and Hispanic children.

In Massachusetts I don't think there's one family that's transferred from a rich district to a poor district. In virtually every case they transfer from a poor district to a rich one. If you question them further, you usually find they speak of sports facilities. In Minnesota you hear that a lot, kids transferred because it's a better football field or better gym. Convenience is another—because it's easier for the parents, they can drop the kid off on the way to work. Or simply that they are choosing from classmates. That again brings us back to profoundly unsettling racial and class issues.

COMMON CAUSE: *Should we not have magnet schools?*
KOZOL: Magnet schools are different for a number of reasons, the most important one being that they were conceived as levers of desegregation. And they are almost always created with very specific guidelines to guarantee that they cannot become sort of an escape value for the upper-middle class.

COMMON CAUSE: *An undercurrent of the choice movement is the belief that many, if not most, of the public schools in our cities are bad and can't be saved.*
KOZOL: That's a wild exaggeration, a very dangerous one. There are terrific schools in almost every city, and they're not just a few elite schools. Even in poor neighborhoods, you can always find some wonderful schools. And there are remarkable teachers and good administrators in virtually every city.

The fact of the matter is that if these school systems had the same kinds of resources that are available in the wealthiest suburbs, not simply equal funding, but funding that is equal to the relative needs that they face—if New York City, instead of having something like $7,500 per year per pupil, had something like $18,000 per year per pupil as they have in Great Neck, N.Y., there wouldn't just be a couple of dozen terrific schools, there would be several hundred great schools in New York City. And the wealthy would have no reason to flee.

Some critics say, well it's not just money, it's also administration. Frankly, my belief is that the major reason that the inner-city public schools are facing the kind of problems I described in *Savage Inequalities* has very little to do with so-called bureaucratic problems. It has everything to do with inequality and with racial isolation. The fact is that once inner-city kids are racially isolated they get a message. The message is extremely clear, especially when they are in schools, as most of these inner-city schools are now, that are 90 to 99 percent black and Hispanic. The message they get is that they are scorned, they are shunned, that they are viewed as contaminated, that they are viewed as carriers of plague, almost. That's the message they get.

Some people, I believe, misread *Savage Inequalities* to imply I was arguing for separate but equal schools. I was not. The point I was making was that unless there are white and middle-class people in the urban school districts, influential people in the media, lawyers, doctors, all those people, the inner-city school will never get equality. And unless the schools are equal, they won't ever attract white people.

COMMON CAUSE: *Conservatives argue that money is not the answer.*

KOZOL: I've always been amused by those arguments. If money is not the issue, then the people who live in Great Neck, N.Y., must be crazy. If money is not the issue, why are they spending $18,000 a year for the kids in their schools? Obviously, money is the issue. It's bizarre that in this society, where nobody questions the significance of money in any other area of life, these people want us to believe that the laws of economics stop at the schoolhouse door.

Typically they'll say, "Well what are you going to do with more money?" Well, to start with you could cut the classes in many New York City schools from 40 kids in a class down to 19 children in a class. It's still more than they have at Exeter, where they have 13 in a class, but it would be a small blessing.

Then they say sarcastically, "Is a small class going to make a bad teacher into a good teacher?" No, of course not, but a teacher good with 40 kids is dynamite with 20, because she's got twice as much time to spend with every one of them.

COMMON CAUSE: *People fear that when you say equity, you're talking leveling, that all schools are going to become mediocre. Given that there is a limited pot of money, how do you avoid that?*

KOZOL: First of all, that argument is profoundly cynical, because the same people who make that argument are precisely the people who vote against higher taxes. Obviously I don't want to bring the best schools down. But if the people living in the wealthy districts, who also are those who have the most influence on elections and public policy, if these people refuse to contemplate a significant change in the tax structure in this country, which adds new resources, then unfortunately they are right. The only alternative is to take it from their schools.

But it seems to me that that represents a very penurious vision of our society. Listening to those people, you get the feeling that if we give the kids in Camden the beautiful schools that they deserve, the grass is going to turn black in Princeton. I think that this nation is not only wise but wealthy enough to give superb schools to all our children. I'm simply not going to accept what they're proposing, which is virtually a rationing of excellence.

Of course, there is no way to do it without new resources. The most obvious way we're going to get those resources is through more progressive income taxes, which are, for the first time, being discussed in Connecticut. And by significant transfer of federal resources from defense into domestic needs. I don't see any other way this can be done.

COMMON CAUSE: *What can and should President Clinton do to improve the nation's schools?*
KOZOL: First of all, hold fast against the voucher advocates. Second, lend moral and personal support to the parents in over half the states in the United States who are now suing their states for financial equity in their public schools.

Third, I would hope he would at least contemplate the possibility of redirecting large amounts of federal money into educational equity.

He has talked about redirecting some of the military funds into areas of domestic infrastructure. I would propose, instead of bridges and highways, or in addition, that we redirect some of those funds to literally rebuilding the schoolhouses of America. I'm not speaking here of curriculum or testing. I'm speaking of bricks and mortar and technology.

An inspired proposal would be a one-time $50-billion school reconstruction act. Returning soldiers and laid-off employees of military contractors could be put to work building for peace, as it were. That would be an important symbolic victory for equality, and also put to work a lot of unemployed people, many of them the products of segregated and inferior schools 20 years ago.

COMMON CAUSE: *There are so many issues when we talk about improving our schools, everything from national education goals to school restructuring, to teacher testing. What are the greatest needs?*
KOZOL: I think setting goals again, and again, and again, is coming to have a neurotic quality. I've been at this now for 30 years and it seems every five or 10 years we get a new list of goals, but never any talk about the resources it would take to realize them. I would stop making a list and just get to work on a couple of the essentials: Immediately expand Head Start to all three- and four-year olds. I'd like to see it be a full-day Head Start with an additional component for parent education, literacy, and political skills for the parents of these children. So they can be good advocates for their kids.

Number two: A federal reconstruction bill to rebuild the crumbling infrastructure of our schools.

Number three: A state-by-state drive for school equality.

Number four: I would like to see us take a new look at teacher education in this country. That's probably the one area where I agree with some of the conservatives. I think our teachers are frequently denied the kind of full liberal arts education they require, and given a far too mechanistic preparation.

To me the most important priority would be for this nation to reopen the issue of educational apartheid. For many years now I've found it almost impossible even to get people to speak of it. I would come into a school and see not a single white child all day long, and finally I'd say to the black principal, "Hey, would you call this a segregated school?" And he'd smile at me and put his hand on my shoulder, almost sympathetically, and say, "Gee, Jonathan, I haven't been asked that question for 10 years. Of course it is. This is American apartheid."

Is this to continue for another century? Are we at the very most going to try to have site-based ghetto schools? Ghetto schools with more input from ghetto parents? Or are we at last going to question the persistence of the ghetto school—this permanent disfigurement on the horizon of American democracy?

COMMON CAUSE: *What would your model school in a model school system look like?*

KOZOL: A school in the middle of the South Bronx like Exeter. A school with beautiful brick buildings and handsome landscaped lawns, and 13 kids in a class; with teachers who feel so comfortable with that small class size that they don't need to lecture and can enjoy the pleasures of a seminar situation; in which the atmosphere is so comfortable physically and psychologically, for kids and adults alike, that the teachers needn't live and work in a state of psychological siege. I'd like to see the same rich curriculum. I'd like to see a day when we would never dream of asking a black teenage girl to concentrate in cosmetology or food preparation services, a time when we look at those kids from the age of four and five and say, this little girl has the same chance to go to Vassar as the great-granddaughter of John Rockefeller.

The school would have no tracking. We would give the least skilled children the opportunity to learn from the more skilled children, and we'd give the latter a chance to learn something about generosity by helping kids who need the help.

I speak about the physical look of a school a lot because I believe that physical conditions are not just facts in themselves, but they're also metaphors. They tell people how we value them.

COMMON CAUSE: *In all your discussions with children, what did you find are their greatest needs, desires, and goals for their education?*

KOZOL: Well, kids generally, sooner or later, point to most of the things we've just discussed. They'd like to be in a class that's small enough so the teacher has time to give them attention and love. They'd like to be in a building which doesn't insult them by its smell and its crowded atmosphere. They'd like to know from an early age that they can be anything they want, and not have that just be rhetoric, but have that proven by the nature of the curriculum that's offered.

But most of all, the poorest kids want to feel respected. How do you tell kids that we respect them? You prove it to them by putting them in beautiful schools, you prove it to them by giving them the same things they know the richest kids in our country get, because they see it on TV all the time. Most of all, you do it by putting them in the same schools that our children attend, so they know to start with that we do not view them as contaminated human beings. That is a terrible crime that we are still committing in this country.

Questions for Discussion

1. What role does the amount of money devoted to education play in educational achievement?
2. Why are some public schools good and others failures?
3. What are the prerequisites of making a choice system work in a fair and non-discriminatory manner?
4. If racial diversity is required in a choice system, how can it be achieved?
5. What effect would a choice system involving both public and private schools have on the quality of teaching in the public schools?

Suggested Readings

Boaz, David. "The Public School Monopoly. *Vital Speeches of the Day,* 58, no. 161 (June 1, 1992), 507–511.

Celis, William, 3d. "Ten Years after a Scathing Report, Schools Show Uneven Progress." *New York Times,* April 28, 1993, p. A19.

"Choice in Schools: Pro and Con." *Congressional Digest,* 70, no. 12 (December 1991), 289–314.

Doyle, Denis P., Bruce S. Cooper, and Roberta Trachtman. "Education Ideas and Strategies for the 1990s." *American Enterprise,* 2, no. 2 (March/April 1991), 25–32.

Finn, Chester E. "The Ho Hum Revolution." *Wilson Quarterly,* 15, no. 2 (Summer 1991), 63–76.

Fiske, Edward B. "The Report That Shook Up Schools." *Washington Post,* April 25, 1993, p. C7.

Glazer, Nathan. "The Real World of Urban Education." *Public Interest,* no. 106 (Winter 1992), 57–75.

Kirp, David L. "What School Choice Really Means?" *Atlantic,* 270, no. 5 (November 1992), 119–120, 122–124.

Kozol, Jonathan. *Savage Inequalities: Children in America's Schools.* New York: Crown, 1991.

Kristol, William, and Jay P. Lefkowitz. "Our Students, Still at Risk." *New York Times,* May 3, 1993, p. A15.

Steele, Claude M. "Race and the Schooling of Black Americans." *Atlantic,* 269, no. 4 (April 1992), 68–72, 74–78.

U.S. Cong., House of Representatives. *Oversight Hearing on Choice in Schools.* Hearing before the Subcommittee on Elementary, Secondary, and Vocational Education of the Committee on Education and Labor, 102d Cong., 1st Sess., 1991.

Welsh, Patrick. "A Teacher's View." *Wilson Quarterly,* 15, no. 2 (Summer 1991), 77–87.

Chapter 18

Should the United States Reduce the Number of Legal Immigrants?

The United States is a nation of immigrants. The men who wrote the Constitution were either immigrants, like Alexander Hamilton, or were descended from immigrants, like George Washington. Celebrations of U.S. history display reverence for the diverse ethnic and religious groups who came from all regions of the world and contributed to the country's cultural, political, and economic life. Even American Indians who were in North America when European colonists arrived were immigrants, too, as their origins are Asian.

At the time of the adoption of the Constitution, the United States welcomed immigrants. With enormous opportunities in agriculture and industry, the nation continued to need immigrants throughout the nineteenth and beginning of the twentieth century. And with the exception of African Americans, who came here involuntarily as slaves, the people who left their home countries for a life in the New World did so for economic opportunity as well as for religious and political freedom and personal security.

Starting in the nineteenth century, many U.S. citizens, although themselves descended from immigrants, sought to restrict immigration. The motivations behind this campaign differed. At times, anti-immigrant feeling was an expression of racial or ethnic bigotry. At other times, it was generated by economic competition for jobs. In 1882, Congress passed the Chinese Exclusion Act. That act and its extensions virtually ended Chinese emigration to the United States for more than fifty years. Restrictions on other Asian groups were imposed through legislation enacted in 1917.

Congress soon adopted legislation restricting groups other than Asians. In the 1920s it passed laws that not only limited the number of immigrants but restricted particular groups through a quota system based largely on the existing population of the United States.

During World War II, Congress repealed the Chinese exclusion acts. After the war, it passed additional legislation on immigration, most notably the Immigration and Nationality Act of 1952, which kept the quota system to benefit relatives of U.S. citizens but eliminated racial restrictions for naturalization and immigration. President George Bush signed into law the 1990 Immigration Act, which raised quotas of legal immigrants by 40 percent.

Although every year the United States has more legal immigrants than all other countries combined, it also unwillingly receives a large number of illegal immigrants, many from Latin America but some from as far away as China. Like the legal immigrants, the illegal immigrants often come to the United States for the same reasons that people have always come here. Often, they make the journey under perilous conditions, and some die or are victimized by the people they have paid for their transportation.

Congress and private groups have focused on a number of issues involving immigrants. Most of the concern has centered on illegal immigration as well as on foreigners falsely requesting political asylum from political persecution. But a number of U.S. citizens are worried that whether immigrants arrive legally or not, the United States simply must curtail the immigration flow.

In testifying in the House of Representatives before both the Subcommittee on Immigration, Refugees, and International Law of the Committee on the Judiciary and the Immigration Task Force of the Committee on Education, Richard D. Lamm expresses concern about the large number of immigrants. Lamm, a former governor of Colorado and current director at the Center for Public Policy and Contemporary Issues at the University of Denver, contends

1. The United States does not have a labor shortage. Increasing immigration will result in a loss of jobs by U.S. citizens.
2. Increasing immigration exacerbates problems in the country, most notably in education, health care, and environmental protection.

Lamm is not opposed to immigration in principle but he regards the current level as too high.

In an article in the journal *Public Interest*, Julian L. Simon, a professor of management at the University of Maryland, makes the case for an increase in legal immigration. He contends

1. Compared to earlier immigration patterns, the level of immigration to the United States is low.
2. Immigrants supply human capital so necessary to a country's development.
3. Immigrants pay their own share of welfare costs and do not drain welfare payments from U.S. taxpayers.
4. Immigration does not exacerbate unemployment, even among directly competing groups.
5. Immigrants not only take jobs, but they create jobs as well and consequently promote economic growth.
6. Immigrants pay more than their share of taxes.
7. Immigrants have a beneficial impact on productivity.
8. The rate of "investment" return from immigrants to the citizen public is about 20 percent per annum—a good return for any portfolio.

9. The best way for the United States to boost its rate of technological advance, and to raise its standard of living, is simply to take on more immigrants.

☑ YES

Should the United States Reduce the Number of Legal Immigrants?

RICHARD D. LAMM

The Dangers of High Immigration Levels

I am here this morning as a concerned citizen with an interest in immigration policy and its effects on the social, economic and environmental development of our country. My interest in immigration has grown, first out of my involvement in population and environmental issues, and later as a public servant who had to set priorities and make sometimes painful decisions about how to allocate society's limited resources.

During my 12 years as governor of Colorado, I came to recognize that people—regardless of race, religion, ethnicity or national origin—were our state's greatest resource. But I also came to realize that people were an asset that needed careful cultivation if their potential was to be realized. More people do not necessarily make for a better society. Better people do. And you get better people through better education, better health care, better environment, better housing, better public infrastructure and a better sense of community. To support a larger population (if a larger population is our objective), a society must first improve the institutions that make for better, more productive citizens. To do otherwise, is to put the cart before the horse.

Over the years, I have earned the nickname "Governor Gloom" for my public admonitions about the perils facing the United States. In fact, what I have been talking about is our inability to set national priorities and make the hard choices necessary to achieve those objectives. All too often, I believe, those charged with making important national decisions say yes to the demands of a myriad of special interests and say no to the public interest by default. I believe the evidence is empirical: A nation that has amassed $2 trillion in debt in just the past decade is a nation that cannot or will not establish priorities. We are a nation that has been saying yes to every worthy and not so worthy demand of vocal special interests and by default, saying no to the needs and aspirations of future generations who will have to pay the bills.

Thus my assessment of the various bills before this committee is that they are, unfortunately, very much legislation for our times. They set no priorities and make no hard choices. They simply say yes to everyone who has a demand to make on our immigration system. They say yes to:

- more family-based immigration;
- more immigration from those countries that have unfairly dominated the immigration flow;
- more immigration from countries that have been unfairly shut out of the immigration process;
- more temporary workers to satisfy the demands of business interests;
- more long-term workers, who can eventually adjust to permanent status, to satisfy the demands of business interests; and
- more amnesties for illegal aliens.

In saying yes to virtually every interest group with a demand to make on the immigration process, Congress is, by default, cheating the public interest by saying no to:

- better education for America's children;
- better wages and working conditions for American workers;
- better training and retraining programs for displaced or underqualified American workers;
- better health care for America's disadvantaged;
- better and more affordable housing for young and poorer Americans; and
- better environment and more productive use of America's natural resources.

Let me emphasize that I do not believe immigrants are responsible for the social problems that afflict the United States. However, I do believe that population growth is a contributing factor to many of these problems and make their solution more difficult. Immigration now accounts for between one-third and one-half the population growth of the United States, and if this legislation should ever become law, it will account for an even greater share of more rapid population growth. As such, I believe immigration policy is inexorably linked to virtually every aspect of public policy in the United States.

Time does not permit me to address all the aspects of this bill, so I intend to talk about just a few and conclude by offering a few alternative suggestions of my own. Given the distinguished list of witnesses this committee has heard and will hear from, I am confident that all aspects of the proposed legislation will be addressed.

AMERICA DOES NOT HAVE A LABOR SHORTAGE

One of the most perplexing, and quite frankly, ludicrous, assertions I have heard is that the United States is now experiencing or is about to experience a shortage of labor. It is inconceivable to me that a nation of a quarter of a billion people can have a shortage of workers. Undeniably we have a skills and training shortage. Quite clearly we have problems of worker motivation and an erosion of the work ethic. There is also evidence that there is a maldistribution of jobs and workers to fill those jobs. We may lack for a lot of things in this country, but a sufficient supply of workers is not one of them.

At this very moment the United States has more than 6.5 million people who are officially categorized as unemployed. This figure does not even begin to take into account discouraged job-seekers who have given up looking for work, those who have never even entered the legitimate labor market, and those who are involuntarily working part-time. According to economist Robert Kuttner, taken together, America's unemployed, underemployed and those who are presently unemployable, add up to more than 15 million people.

We do not have a labor shortage in the United States! What we have is a frightening social mess—a time bomb that will eventually explode in our midst if we do not take steps to diffuse it. America's growing, disenfranchised underclass is not simply going to disappear because we import foreign workers instead of training and retraining our own. They are going to move further to the fringes of our society and create problems that will ultimately be more costly in both monetary and social terms than bringing them into the economic and social mainstream.

In life, all things are relative which is why we have been hearing complaints from many in the business community of a labor shortage. A quick look at the changing American demography explains why, to some, we appear to have a dearth of workers. Beginning in the mid-1960s through the mid-1980s, the enormous postwar baby boom generation entered the labor force skewing the laws of supply and demand in favor of employers. Ten or 15 years ago businesses did not have to go looking for workers; workers came to them begging for the chance to get a foot in the door. Wages and working conditions were dictated by the laws of supply and demand that existed at that time.

Now times have changed and the tables have turned somewhat, and the business community is understandably not as happy. The baby boom generation was followed by a baby bust generation who are now entering their working years. Instead of applicants beating down their doors, businesses have to go out and recruit workers and even train them themselves. Moreover, today's laws of supply and demand mean that new job force entrants are in a more advantageous position when it comes to setting salaries and working conditions.

Gentlemen, the businessmen and women testifying before your committees and cornering you at cocktail parties, asking for foreign workers, are simply one more special interest requesting a subsidy. Life has suddenly gotten a little tougher for them and rather than finding creative and innovative ways of dealing with a tighter labor market, they and their lobbyists are coming to you asking that you do in committee rooms what the American people failed to do in the bedroom in the late 1960s and 1970s.

There is nothing wrong, per se, with a government stepping in to create an advantageous business climate. That is a legitimate function of government.

However, for the past 20 years we have had exactly the kind of young, abundant labor force that the business community is asking you to recreate through immigration policy. What have been the results? By every yardstick, American competitiveness, wealth, and innovation have declined vis-à-vis our economic competitors. As Charles R. Morris pointed out in a recent article in the *Atlantic Monthly*:

> New workers swelled the American labor force by about 50 percent in the past 20 years, shifting the average age and experience of workers sharply downward. Not surprisingly, with lots of cheap new workers mobbing the doorway, businessmen increased hiring instead of investing in labor-saving machinery—a fancy robot costs about as much as a year's wages for a hundred entry-level workers. Real wages and productivity were stagnant, and the business success stories were companies, like McDonald's, that learned how to pan for gold in that low-wage pool.

Ironically, Germany and Japan, which were experiencing an economic boom during this period, were experiencing exactly the demographic trend that the United States will face in the 1990s. "Personal savings are the ultimate source of all productive investment," writes Morris. "It is the high Japanese saving rate—as much as 18 percent of all personal income—that has financed Japan's global industrial conquest. . . . plausibly enough, an older, more productive work force, with higher real incomes, will save more," he concludes.

Thus, after 20 years of trying to assimilate large numbers of new workers into productive jobs in the economy, a tighter labor market may be exactly what this country needs. During the past two decades we have had the type of rapid work force growth and demographic distribution that this bill would restore through immigration policy—and the results have been less than spectacular. Left alone, the demographic picture of the 1990s would resemble that of Japan and Germany in the 1970s and 1980s and the United States of the 1950s and 1960s. This country was at its most productive during a period when the Depression-era baby bust generation was young and entering the labor force.

What is wrong with returning to a period of population stability, full employment, stable housing costs and rising savings rates? These sound like laudable objectives to me.

There is one more benefit to a tighter labor market that I would like to mention. The growth of this country's underclass, and the breakdown of social values in many communities is partially a result of demographics. We allowed large segments of our society to be relegated to the margins because they simply weren't needed. An economy that had more people entering the work force than jobs available could pick and choose from among the cream of those new workers. There was no need to reach out to those who, for a variety of reasons, did not possess the skills employers sought.

The changing demography of this country has now made these people important. This is the opportunity those who have been left behind have been waiting for. Every able body and mind is once again important. If the excess of new labor force entrants dries up, the American economy will have no choice but to find creative ways of bringing the 15 million Americans who are now outside the economic mainstream into it. By artificially reflooding the labor market, this Congress will be denying those people the opportunities they deserve.

All the well-intentioned, not to mention costly, job training programs you can devise here in Washington cannot replace real employers with real jobs looking for real workers to fill them. Necessity is the mother of invention. And if the only people available are the people asking you for spare change every day on your way to work, then employers will devise ways of turning panhandlers into productive citizens.

This country has had more anti-poverty and job training programs over the past 25 years than anyone can count—and the problems have just gotten worse. How about trying something really novel? Give the free market laws of supply and demand a chance to work!

WORKS AT CROSS-PURPOSES TO OTHER NATIONAL OBJECTIVES

As I mentioned earlier in my testimony, I do not believe immigrants are responsible for the social problems that exist in this country. However, as I also stated, immigration is a population issue and population affects virtually every social and economic issue this nation faces.

There are those who have been making the rounds here on Capitol Hill espousing the "free lunch" theory of immigration—that immigrants are an unmitigated asset who contribute more to society than they use in public benefits. They even come with carefully selected statistics to back up their theories. Well, I am here to tell you that this free lunch theory has about as much merit as all free lunch theories.

As someone who has run a state government I can assure you that whatever small benefits that may be accrued at the federal level are more than offset at the state and local levels. Immigrants are human beings and like all human beings they have needs that must be provided for. Their children need to be educated; they get sick and require health care; they become old and disabled; and they need places to live. The bulk of the burden for providing for these needs is absorbed at the state and local level. Los Angeles, a city with a huge immigrant population, found that it provides an average of $2,245 a year more in services to immigrant families than it collects in taxes.

I will limit myself to just a few examples of how absorbing large numbers of immigrants works to impede other societal goals.

Education

American education is in drastic need of improvement. There isn't anybody who would disagree with that statement—it's kind of like saying the earth is round. We are, by all accounts and all objective standards of measurement, doing an abysmally poor job of educating our children. Yet while another committee is probably meeting across the hall or across the street to devise ways of improving our education system, we are here discussing not how to alleviate some of those problems, but how much greater burden we are going to impose on school systems around the country. Should a nation in which one-quarter of its youngsters fails to graduate high school, in which nearly half of minority students in some cities drop out of school, and in which 20 percent of the population is functionally illiterate, be thinking about new burdens it can place on its education system?

What are our priorities? Should we be spending our precious educational resources on equipping our schools with state-of-the-art computers, or should we be hiring more bilingual education teachers and expanding school lunch programs?

Your colleague, Senator Connie Mack of Florida, has stated that during the 1988–89 school year, Dade County public schools were registering new immigrant children (many of them illegal) "at a rate of 755 per month; that's virtually two new teachers per day and one new school per month." The cost says Senator Mack, "exceeds $27.5 million, or $3,900 per student." Even if the city of Miami had that kind of money to spare, it couldn't build the schools and train the teachers fast enough. The real price is being borne by the school children of Dade County whose already inadequate education is being further devalued.

Just last month, the city of Los Angeles announced that it was going to year-round school sessions because of the overcrowding caused by the enormous influx of immigrants it has been receiving. Has anyone calculated the cost of air conditioning school buildings just so the children can sit in them in the sweltering heat of the San Fernando Valley in July and August?

We know, based on experience, that increasing immigration is going to increase the burdens of those school districts that can least afford to absorb them. It is also going to deny educational opportunities to those in our society who need them most. It's not the kids of Beverly Hills or Pacific Palisades who are going to suffer—they attend protected schools or their parents send them to private schools. It's the kids of Watts and East L.A.—those without options—who will suffer the consequences of large-scale immigration.

Health Care

During my years as governor of Colorado, some of my most difficult and painful decisions involved the closing of health care facilities for the poor. But invariably, the resources we had to work with were insufficient to provide the amount and quality of care we would have liked.

What turned pain into anger and frustration was the knowledge that while I was closing well-baby clinics in one part of the state, Denver General Hospital, the largest public health care facility in the state, was amassing millions of dollars in uncollectible bills for health services rendered to illegal aliens. Later this morning you will hear from representatives of the Los Angeles County Department of Health Services who will tell you that they have had to absorb nearly three-quarters of a billion dollars in unreimbursable services for illegal aliens over the past six years.

Who pays for this? To a degree the taxpayers of those jurisdictions. But the people who pay the greatest price are those who must rely on these public health care facilities for their health needs. This nation, which spends more than half a trillion dollars a year on health care—nearly 12 percent of GNP [gross national product]—does not provide an acceptable level of health care for millions of its poorer citizens. Our health care system is a national disgrace. Yet even as Congress wrestles with the problems of providing better health care to more of our citizens without taking us all to the poor house, we are sitting here this morning trying to decide how much greater burden to load onto our rickety health care system.

Is this how we set national health care priorities?

Environment

As one final example of how immigration-spurred population growth works to thwart other social objectives, I will cite the environment. Again, nobody disagrees that we need to improve the quality of our environment. Moreover, nobody would argue that environmental safeguards, which are inadequate at current population levels, are going to work any better with rapid population growth. I emphasize: immigration is an important component of population growth in the United States.

We are, today, primarily an urban society and the vast majority of new immigrants settle in and around major cities. Anyone who understands how cities develop, knows that they grew up around natural harbors and/or near the most fertile agricultural areas. As these cities have sprawled, they have begun to encroach on the prime agricultural land that was once their life blood. As our population expands and becomes more mobile, we are converting 7,000 acres of farmland for urban uses every day. We may well be on the way to destroying the agricultural capacity that sustains us all.

People often come to Colorado and remark about how much open land there is and conclude that such places have the capacity to sustain millions more people. What is less obvious than the abundance of open land, is the severe shortage of water. In 35 out of the 48 contiguous states today, ground water is being pumped out of the ground faster than nature is replenishing it. In Colorado, a debate has been raging for years over whether to build Two Forks Dam along the South Platte River. Even the dam's proponents concede that it would do significant ecological harm to the entire region. But continued population growth along the Front Range of the Rockies may eventually leave us with no other options.

Again, while we sit here this morning, somewhere else on Capitol Hill your colleagues are wrestling with the problems of air pollution and greenhouse gases, water pollution, toxic waste disposal, solid waste disposal, ground water depletion and probably a dozen other environmental concerns. While they are searching for solutions, we're trying to decide whether we should exacerbate the problems just a little, or a whole lot.

I could sit here all morning and cite examples of how the bills this committee is considering—which would raise immigration levels by anywhere from a few hundred thousand to more than a million people annually—would work to impede progress towards universally agreed upon goals.

The United States does not need large numbers of new immigrants. We are already adding more than 600,000 people—the population of Washington, D.C.—to our population through immigration each year. Some business interests may *want* more immigrants. Ethnic lobby groups may *want* expanded immigration. But I urge you to differentiate between what a few vocal and well-financed interest groups want, and what is in the best interests of the country.

PROPOSALS

I believe, as most proponents of immigration reform do, that immigration, at sensible levels, can be a positive force for the United States. Like anything else that is good and desirable, it [is] best when taken in moderation.

I believe there are a few basic principles to which our immigration policy must adhere:

1. That the levels of immigration do not exceed our capacity to absorb and assimilate them, in a positive sense, into our society.
2. That levels of immigration do not impede our ability to deal with other pressing societal concerns.
3. That immigrants be selected fairly, on the basis of merit and ability to contribute to our society, and without regard to race, religion or ethnicity.
4. That it does not lead to nepotistic, self-perpetuating chains of migration.
5. That it does not impede the ability of those at the bottom of the socio-economic ladder from gaining a foothold on the way up that ladder.

I urge the members of this committee and the Congress to consider the national interest, not the narrow interests of the few, in setting this country's immigration policies.

Should the United States Reduce the Number of Legal Immigrants?

JULIAN L. SIMON
The Case for Greatly Increased Immigration

By increasing somewhat the flow of immigrants—from about 600,000 to about 750,000 admissions per year—the immigration legislation passed by Congress late in 1990 will improve the standard of living of native-born Americans. The bill represents a sea change in public attitude toward immigration; it demonstrates that substantially increasing immigration is politically possible now. That's all good news, and we should celebrate it.

The bad news is that the legislation does not *greatly* increase immigration. The new rate is still quite low by historical standards. A much larger increase in numbers—even to, say, only half the rate relative to population size that the United States accepted around the turn of the century—would surely increase our standard of living even more.

The political problem for advocates of immigration is to avoid the letdown to be expected after the passage of this first major legal-immigration bill in a quarter-century. And since the new law seems to contemplate additional legislation (by providing for a commission to collect information on immigration), it is important to educate the public about how immigration benefits the nation as well as the immigrants.

Increased immigration presents the United States with an opportunity to realize many national goals with a single stroke. It is a safe and sure path—open to no other nation—to achieve all of these benefits: 1) a sharply increased rate of technological advance, spurred by the addition of top scientific talent from all over the world; 2) satisfaction of business's demand for the labor that the baby-bust generation makes scarce; 3) reduction of the burden that retirees impose upon the ever-shrinking cohort of citizens of labor-force age, who must support the Social Security System; 4) rising tax revenues—resulting from the increase in the proportion of workers to retirees—that will provide the only painless way of shrinking and perhaps even eliminating the federal deficit; 5) improvement in our competitive position vis-à-vis Japan, Europe, and the rest of the world; 6) a boost to our image abroad, stemming from immigrants' connections with their relatives back home, and from the remittances that they send back to them; and 7) not least, the opportunity given to additional people to enjoy the blessings of life in the United States.

All the U.S. need do to achieve these benefits is further to relax its barriers against skilled immigrants. Talented and energetic people want to come here. Yet we do not greatly avail ourselves of this golden opportunity, barring the door to many of the most economically productive workers in the world.

If immigration is such an across-the-board winner, why aren't we welcoming skilled and hardworking foreigners with open arms? These are some of the reasons: 1) The public is ignorant of the facts to be presented here; it therefore charges immigrants with increasing unemployment, abusing welfare programs, and lowering the quality of our work force. 2) Various groups fear that immigrants would harm their particular interests; the groups are less concerned with the welfare of the country as a whole. 3) Well-organized lobbies oppose immigration, which receives little organized support. 4) Nativism, which may or may not be the same as racism in any particular case, continues to exert an appeal.

THE DIMENSIONS OF PRESENT-DAY IMMIGRATION

The most important issue is the total number of immigrants allowed into the United States. It is important to keep our eyes fixed on this issue, because it tends to get obscured in emotional discussions of the desirability of reuniting families, the plight of refugees, the geographic origin and racial composition of our immigrant population, the needs of particular industries, the illegality of some immigration, and so on.

The Federation for American Immigration Reform (FAIR)—whose rhetoric I shall use as illustration—says that "[i]mmigration to the United States is at record levels." This claim is simply false: Figure I shows the absolute numbers of legal immigrants over the decades. The recent inflow clearly is far below the inflow around the turn of the century—even though it includes the huge number of immigrants who took advantage of the 1986 amnesty; they are

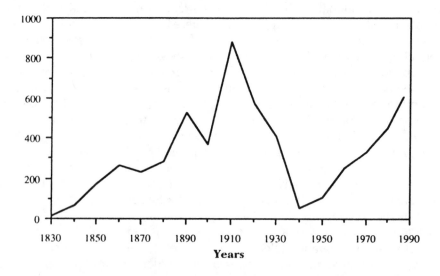

Figure I: Annual Number of U.S. Immigrants (in 1,000s)

classified as having entered in 1989, although most of them actually arrived before 1980. Even the inclusion of illegal immigrants does not alter the fact that there is less immigration now than in the past.

Economically speaking, more relevant than these absolute numbers is the volume of immigration as a proportion of the native population, as shown in Figure II. Between 1901 and 1910 immigrants arrived at the yearly rate of 10.4 per thousand U.S. population, whereas between 1981 and 1987 the rate was only 2.5 percent of the population. So the recent flow is less than a fourth as heavy as it was in that earlier period. Australia and Canada admit three times that many immigrants as a proportion of their populations.

Another way to think about the matter: in 1910, 14.6 percent of the population was born abroad, but in 1980 less than 6 percent of us were. Not only is the present stock of immigrants much smaller proportionally than it was earlier, but it also is a small proportion considered by itself. We tend to think of ourselves as a "nation of immigrants," but less than one out of fifteen people now in the U.S. was born abroad, including those who arrived many years ago. Who would guess that the U.S. has a smaller share of foreign-born residents than many countries that we tend to think have closed homogeneous populations—including Great Britain, Switzerland, France, and Germany? We are a nation not of immigrants, but rather of the descendants of immigrants.

Furthermore, the absorption of immigrants is much easier now than it was in earlier times. One has only to read the history of the Pilgrims in Plymouth colony to realize the enormity of the immediate burden that each new load of immigrants represented. But it is the essence of an advanced society that it can more easily handle material problems than can technically primitive societies. With every year it becomes easier for us to make the material adjustments that

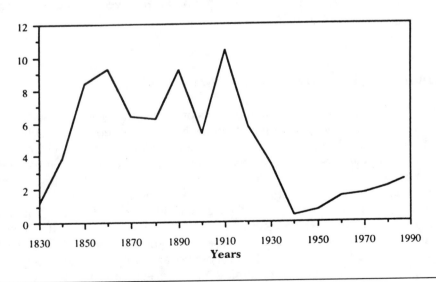

Figure II: Immigrants to the U.S. per 1,000 Inhabitants

an increase in population requires. That is, immigrant assimilation becomes ever less of an economic problem—all the more reason that the proportion of immigrants now seems relatively small, compared with what it was in the past.

Unfortunately, despite recent changes favoring skilled immigrants, our present admissions policy remains largely nepotistic. Most visas are granted to foreigners who have family connections here. Even with the 1990 legislation, the U.S. will admit only about 110,000 people—perhaps 20 percent of all immigrants—on the basis of their job skills. Compare our policy with Australia's, which admits almost 50 percent of its immigrants according to "economic" criteria, and only 30 percent as relatives of citizens. Many of those whom we admit via family preferences also are skilled, of course, but it would be beneficial to us as well as fair to deserving foreigners to admit more people on the basis of merit alone. Indeed, George Borjas of the University of California at Santa Barbara has presented evidence that the economic "quality" of immigrants with given levels of education has declined in recent decades—though the magnitude of the decline remains controversial; the likeliest explanation for the decline is an increase in the proportion of immigrants who are admitted as relatives rather than on their merits alone. On the other hand, Harriet Duleep of the U.S. Civil Rights Commission has recently shown that despite the different admissions policies of the U.S. and Canada (which uses a point system), immigration affects the economies of the two countries similarly—probably because families carefully evaluate the economic potential of relatives before deciding to bring them in.

For years, phony inflated estimates of the stocks and flows of illegal immigrants were bandied about by opponents of immigration in order to muddy the waters. Since the 1986 Simpson-Mazzoli law's amnesty we know that the numbers are actually quite modest, much lower than even the "mainstream" estimates cited in the press. So that scare no longer serves as an effective red herring for opponents of immigration.

MALTHUSIAN AND OTHER OBJECTIONS

Now let us consider the costs and benefits of immigration—even though economic issues may not be the real heart of the matter, often serving only as a smoke screen to conceal the true motives for opposition. Only thus can one explain why the benefits of immigration do not produce more open policies. Because opponents of immigration wield economic arguments to justify their positions, however, we must consider their assertions.

Malthusian objections to immigration begin with "capital dilution." The supposed "law of diminishing returns"—which every economics text explains should not be thought of as a law—causes output per worker to fall. The "law" is so marvelously simple, direct, and commonsensical that it easily seduces thought—especially among academics, for whom such abstractions are bread and butter. Its simplicity also makes the Malthusian notion excellent fare for the family newspaper. In contrast, the arguments that demonstrate the inapplicability of Malthusian capital dilution in the context of immigration are relatively complex and indirect. As a consequence, simple—though incorrect—Malthusianism easily attracts adherents.

Nowadays, however, the most important capital is human capital—education and skills, which people own themselves and carry with them—rather than capitalist-supplied physical capital. The bugaboo of production capital has been laid to rest by the experience of the years since World War II, which taught economists that, aside from the shortest-run considerations, physical capital does not pose a major constraint to economic growth. It is human capital that is far more important in a country's development. And immigrants supply their own human capital.

The main real cost that immigration imposes on natives is the extra capital needed for additional schools and hospitals. But this cost turns out to be small relative to benefits, in considerable part because we finance such construction with bond issues, so that we operate largely on a pay-as-you-go basis. Immigrants therefore pay much of their share.

The supposed cost that most captures the public's imagination, of course, is welfare payments. According to popular belief, no sooner do immigrants arrive than they become public charges, draining welfare money from the American taxpayers, and paying no taxes.

Solid evidence gives the lie to this charge. In an analysis of Census Bureau data I found that, aside from Social Security and Medicare, about as much money is spent on welfare services and schooling for immigrant families as for citizens. When programs for the elderly are included, immigrant families receive far *less* in public services than natives. During the first five years in the U.S. the average immigrant family receives $1,400 in welfare and schooling (in 1975 dollars), compared with the $2,300 received by the average native family. The receipts gradually become equal over several decades. Athur Akhbari of St. Mary's College in Canada has shown that recent Canadian data produce almost identical results. And Duleep's finding that the economic results of Canadian and U.S. immigration are quite similar, despite the different admissions systems, adds weight to the conclusion that U.S. immigrants pay much more in taxes than they receive in benefits.

Of course there must be some systematic abuses of the welfare system by immigrants. But our legislative system is capable of devising adequate remedies. Even now there are provisions in the Immigration and Naturalization Act that deny visas to aliens who are "likely to become public charges" and provide for the deportation of immigrants who have within five years after entry become public charges "from causes not affirmatively shown to have arisen after entry."

As to illegal immigrants and welfare, FAIR typically says that "[t]axpayers are hurt by having to pay more for social services." Ironically, several surveys—for example, one by Sidney Weintraub and Gilberto Cardenas of the University of Texas—show that illegals are even heavier net contributors to the public coffers than legal immigrants; many illegals are in the U.S. only temporarily and are therefore without families, and they are often afraid to apply for services for fear of being apprehended. Illegals do, however, pay taxes.

Some cities and states with disproportionately high immigration do incur significant costs and complications when immigrants first arrive. They deserve sympathy and perhaps federal assistance, though officials should note that immigrants' federal taxes will later effectively pay for such temporary assistance.

THE NON-THREAT OF DISPLACED NATIVE WORKERS

The most dramatic argument against immigration—the bogeyman in the mind of organized labor, which has been its most powerful political opponent since the nineteenth century—has been that foreigners take jobs held by natives and thereby increase native unemployment. The logic is simple: if the number of jobs is fixed, and immigrants occupy some jobs, there must be fewer available jobs for natives.

In the shortest run, the demand for any particular sort of worker is indeed inflexible. Therefore, additional immigrants in a given occupation must to some degree lower wages and/or increase unemployment in that occupation. For example, the large recent influx of foreign physicians increases the competition that U.S. physicians face, lowering their earnings. But because immigrants come with a variety of skills, workers in most occupations feel little impact. And in the longer run, workers in most occupations are not injured at all.

A good-sized body of competent recent research shows that immigration does not exacerbate unemployment, even among directly competing groups; in California, for instance, immigrants have not increased unemployment among blacks and women. And the research, done by several independent scholars from a variety of angles, uses several kinds of data. For example, Stephen Moore and I systematically studied immigration's effects upon overall unemployment, by looking at the changes in unemployment in various U.S. cities that have experienced different levels of unemployment. We found that if there is displacement, it is too little to be observable.

The explanation is that immigrants not only take jobs, but also create them. Their purchases increase the demand for labor, leading to new hires roughly equal in number to the immigrant workers. Immigrants also create jobs directly by opening new businesses. A Canadian government survey of immigrants, which should also describe U.S. experience, found that almost 5 percent—ninety-one of the 1746 males and 291 single females in its panel sample—had started businesses within their first three years in Canada. Not only did they employ themselves, but they also employed others, creating a total of 606 jobs. Thus the total of 2037 immigrants personally created roughly 30 percent as many jobs as they collectively held. Furthermore, these numbers surely rose rapidly after the three-year study period; after one year seventy-one self-employed immigrants had created 264 jobs, compared with the ninety-one immigrant entrepreneurs and 606 jobs observed after three years.

We can interpret this result as follows: even if one native Canadian was pushed out of a preexisting job by every five immigrants—an improbably high number—this effect would be more than made up for by the new jobs, occupied by natives, created by the immigrants' businesses.

The businesses that immigrants start are at first small, of course. But surprisingly, small businesses are the most important source of new jobs. And immigrant entrepreneurs tend to succeed in a dynamic economy, because they are innovative and mobile.

Furthermore, potential immigrants are well aware of labor-market conditions in the U.S., and they tend not to come if there is little demand for their skills. Natives tend not to be harmed even in the few industries—like the restaurant and hotel businesses—in which immigrants concentrate, because natives do not want jobs in these industries. Evidence for this comes from experiments conducted by the Immigration and Naturalization Service and San Diego County. In one case, 2154 illegal aliens were removed from jobs, but the California State Human Resources Agency had almost no success in filling the jobs with U.S. citizens.

Wages are admittedly pushed downward somewhat in industries and localities in which immigrants are concentrated. Barton Smith and Robert Newman of the University of Houston found that adjusted wages are 8 percent lower in the Texas border cities in which the proportion of Mexicans is relatively high. Much of the apparent difference is accounted for by a lower cost of living in the border cities, however. And because immigrants tend to be heterogeneous in their skills, their presence does not disproportionately affect any particular industry; and of course salaries rise in the occupations that few immigrants enter. (Indeed, if immigrants were spread evenly throughout all occupations, wages would not fall in any occupation.) At the same time, immigrants, who consume a wide variety of goods and services, increase the demand for labor across the range of occupations.

TAX PAYMENTS

If immigrants paid relatively little in taxes they might still burden natives, despite using fewer welfare services. But data on family earnings, which allow us to estimate tax payments, show that this is not at all the case.

Immigrants pay more than their share of taxes. Within three to five years, immigrant-family earnings reach and pass those of the average American family. The tax and welfare data together indicate that, on balance, an immigrant family enriches natives by contributing an average of $1,300 or more per year (in 1975 dollars) to the public coffers during its stay in the U.S. Evaluating the future stream of these contributions as one would a dam or harbor, the present value of an immigrant family—discounted at the risk-free interest rate of 3 percent—adds up to almost two years' earnings for a native family head. This means that the economic activities of an average immigrant family reduce the taxes of a native head of household enough to advance his or her possible date of retirement by two years.

Curiously, contemporary welfare-state policies render immigration more beneficial to natives than it was in earlier times when welfare was mainly voluntary. There are two main reasons why today's immigrants make net contributions to the public coffers. First, far from being tired, huddled masses, immigrants tend to come when they are young, strong, and vibrant, at the start of their work lives. For example, perhaps 46 percent of immigrants are in the prime labor-force ages of twenty to thirty-nine, compared with perhaps 26 percent of natives. And only 4 percent of immigrants are aged sixty or over, compared with about 15 percent of natives. Second, many immigrants are well educated and have well-paying skills that produce hefty tax contributions.

Because immigrants arrive in the early prime of their work lives, they ward off a major looming threat to U.S. economic well-being. This threat is the graying of the population, which means that each working native has an increasing burden of retired dependents to support. In 1900, there were five and one-half people aged twenty-five to fifty-four for each person aged sixty and above, whereas the Census Bureau projects that in the year 2000 the ratio will shrink to two and one-half to one—resulting in a burden that will be more than twice as heavy on workers.

Being predominantly youthful adults, immigrants mitigate this looming problem of more retired natives being supported by fewer workers. Indeed, immigration is the only practical way to alleviate the burden of increasing dependency that native workers would otherwise feel.

In the public sphere this means that immigrants immediately lessen the Social Security burden upon native workers. (The same holds for the defense burden, of course.) And if there is a single factor currently complicating the government's economic policies, it is the size of Social Security payments and other assistance to the aged. Immigration—and the resulting increase in tax payments by immigrants—provides the only way to reduce the federal budget deficit without making painful cuts in valued services.

BOOSTING PRODUCTIVITY

Most important in the long run is the boost that immigrants give to productivity. Though hard to pin down statistically, the beneficial impact of immigration upon productivity is likely to dwarf all other effects after these additional workers and consumers have been in the country a few years. Some of the productivity increase comes from immigrants working in industries and laboratories that are at the forefront of world technology. We benefit along with others from the contribution to world productivity in, say, genetic engineering that immigrants could not make in their home countries. More immigrants mean more workers, who will think up productivity-enhancing ideas. As Soichiro Honda (of motorcycle and auto fame) said: "Where 100 people think, there are 100 powers; if 1,000 people think, there are 1,000 powers."

It is well to remember that the development of the atomic bomb hinged on the participation of such immigrants as Enrico Fermi, John von Neumann, and Stan Ulam, among many others. Contemporary newspaper stories continue this historical saga, noting the disproportionate numbers of Vietnamese and other Asian immigrant youths who achieve distinction in competitions such as the Westinghouse Science Talent Search. Ben Wattenberg and Karl Zinsmeister of the American Enterprise Institute write that among the forty 1988 finalists, "22 were foreign-born or children of foreign-born parents: from Taiwan, China, Korea, India, Guyana, Poland, Trinidad, Canada, Peru, Iran, Vietnam and Honduras." They also note that one-fourth of recent valedictorians and salutatorians in San Diego have been Vietnamese, and that thirteen of the seventeen public high school valedictorians in Boston in 1989 were foreign born. Sometimes it seems as if such names as Wang Computers and Steve Chen dominate our most vigorous industry.

THE BOTTOM LINE

An economist always owes the reader a cost-benefit assessment for policy analysis. So I combined the most important elements pertaining to legal immigrants with a simple macroeconomic model, making reasonable assumptions where necessary. The net effect is slightly negative for the early years, but four or five years later the net effect turns positive and large. And when we tote up future costs and benefits, the rate of "investment" return from immigrants to the citizen public is about 20 percent per annum—a good return for any portfolio.

Does all this seem to be a far-out minority view? In 1990, the American Immigration Institute surveyed prominent economists—all the ex-presidents of the American Economic Association, and then-members of the Council of Economic Advisers—about immigration. Economists ought to understand the economic effects of immigration better than others, so their views are of special interest. More than four-fifths of the respondents said that immigration has a very favorable impact on economic growth; none said that its impact is unfavorable. Almost three-fourths said that illegals have a positive economic impact. And almost all agree that recent immigrants have had the same kind of impact as immigrants in the past.

THE REAL REASONS FOR OPPOSITION

I began by citing various reasons for our failure to take in more immigrants, despite the clear-cut benefits of doing so. The first is ignorance of the benefits described above. Second is the opposition by special interests, such as organized labor (which wants to restrict competition for jobs) and ethnic groups (whose members often fear that immigration will cause their proportion of the population to decrease). The third reason is well-organized opposition to immigration and a total lack of organized support for it.

FAIR, for example, has a large budget—it amassed $2,000,000 in revenues in 1989—and a large staff. It supports letter-writing campaigns to newspapers and legislators, gets its representatives onto television and radio, and is in the rolodex of every journalist who writes on the subject. Several other organizations play a similar role. On the other side, until recently no organization advocated more immigration generally. Now at least there is the fledgling American Immigration Institute; and the de Tocqueville Institute did excellent work on immigration in 1989 and 1990, before taking on other issues.

The fourth check to immigration is nativism or racism, a motive that often lies beneath the surface of the opposition's arguments.

Rita Simon of American University, who has studied the history of public opinion toward immigrants, has found that the arguments against immigration have remained eerily identical. In the first half of the nineteenth century, Irish immigrants in New York and Boston were seen as the unassimilable possessors of all bad qualities. One newspaper wrote: "America has become the sewer into which the pollutions of European jails are emptied." Another asked: "Have we not a right to protect ourselves against the ravenous dregs of anarchy and crime, the tainted swarms of pauperism and vice Europe shakes on our shores from her diseased robes?"

The 1884 platform of the Democratic party stated its opposition to the "importation of foreign labor or the admission of servile races unfitted by habit, training, religion or kindred for absorption into the great body of our people or for the citizenship which our laws confer."

Francis Walker, Commissioner General of the Immigration Service, wrote in 1896:

> The question today is . . . protecting the American rate of wages, the American standard of living, and the quality of American citizenship from degradation through the tumultuous access of vast throngs of ignorant and brutalized peasantry from the countries of Eastern and Southern Europe.

In the 1920s the *Saturday Evening Post* also directed fear and hatred at the "new immigrants" from Southern and Eastern Europe: "More than a third of them cannot read and write; generally speaking they have been very difficult to assimilate. . . . They have been hot beds of dissent, unrest, sedition and anarchy."

Although statements like these are no longer acceptable in public, many people still privately sympathize with such views. One can see the traces in nativist codewords that accuse immigrants of "disturbing national homogeneity" and "changing our national culture."

IMPROVING OUR POLICIES

In addition to admitting more immigrants into the United States, we should also consider instituting other desirable changes in policy. Specifically, we must go further to increase the benefits that accrue to the United States from the inflow of highly educated people with high productive potential—especially people with technical skills. To its credit, the 1990 legislation will increase the flow of talented people by increasing the proportion of immigrants who are admitted because of their economic characteristics rather than their familial ties to U.S. citizens. This was worth doing to reduce nepotistic "family connections" admissions, and to treat meritorious applicants without such connections more fairly.

The new system does not greatly increase the flow of highly skilled people, however. An additional 100,000 or so immigrants will be admitted under the new provisions for economic selection; only 40,000 will be skilled people, the other 60,000 being their dependents. The overall increase in numbers admitted will yield perhaps another 30,000 highly skilled people. This is still only a small—though a most valuable—increment to our economy.

The 1990 legislation also contains a beneficial provision allowing entry to people who will invest a million dollars and create employment for ten Americans. Although this provision will not be as profitable for natives as an outright sale of the opportunity to immigrate, as permitted by some other countries, it does move in the right direction. But the new law does not go far enough; it permits entry to a maximum of only 10,000 persons per year under this provision—a piddling number by any standard.

Another policy that the U.S. might employ is simply to give permanent-resident visas to foreigners studying in the U.S. Many foreign students already find ways to remain under the present rules—about half of them students of engineering and science. And even more foreign graduates would remain if they could, which would push up our rate of progress even more.

Furthermore, if young foreigners knew that they could remain in the United States after completing their education here, more would choose to study here. This would provide multiple benefits to the United States. Given assurance that they could remain, these students could pay more realistic tuition rates than are now charged, which would benefit U.S. universities. And these increased rates would enable universities to expand their programs to serve both foreign and native students better. Best of all would be the increased number of highly competent scientific and managerial workers who would be part of the American work force.

In addition, a larger number of students requires a larger number of professors. And a larger number of openings for professors, especially in such fields as engineering and science, would attract more of the world's best scientists from abroad. This would enhance the process that has brought so many foreigners who subsequently won Nobel prizes to the U.S.—to the advantage as well as the honor of this country.

POLITICAL ADVANTAGES

Political power and economic well-being are intimately related; a nation's international standing is heavily influenced by its economic situation. And today the future of any country—especially of a major country that is in the vanguard with respect to production and living standards—depends entirely on its progress in knowledge, skill, and productivity. This is more true now than in the past, because technology changes more rapidly than in earlier times. Even a single invention can speedily alter a country's economic or military future—consider, for example, the atom bomb or the computer—as no invention could in the past, even the invention of the gun. That's why immigration safely, cheaply, and surely provides the U.S. with perhaps the greatest opportunity that a country has ever had to surpass its political rivals.

And the best way for the U.S. to boost its rate of technological advance, and to raise its standard of living, is simply to take in more immigrants. To that end, I would suggest that the number of visas be increased by half a million per year for three years. If no major problems arise with that total (and there is no reason to expect a problem, since even another one or two million immigrants a year would still give us an admissions rate lower than we successfully coped with in earlier times, when assimilation was more difficult), then we should boost the number by another half-million, and so on, until unexpected problems arise.

Immigration policy presents the U.S. with an opportunity like the one that faced the Brooklyn Dodgers in 1947, before blacks played baseball on any major-league team. Signing Jackie Robinson and then Roy Campanella, at the price of antagonizing some players and club owners, put the Dodgers way ahead of the pack. In the case of immigration, unlike baseball, no other "team" can duplicate our feat, because immigrants mainly want to come here. All we need is the vision, guts, and ambition of Dodger general manager Branch Rickey. (A bit of his religious zeal mixed in would do no harm.)

Can we see our national interest clearly enough to reject unfounded beliefs that some groups will lose jobs to immigrants, and to surmount the racism that remains in our society? Or will we pay a heavy price in slower growth and lessened efficiency for maintaining our prejudices and pandering to the supposed interests of groups—organized labor, environmentalists, and others—whose misguided wishes will not benefit even them in the long run?

Questions for Discussion

1. What criteria should be used in determining who should be allowed to immigrate to the United States legally? What are the reasons for your answer?
2. What impact would a higher immigration rate have on employment in the United States?
3. What impact would a higher immigration rate have on environmental protection in the United States?
4. Who are the groups that oppose higher immigration? How valid are their arguments in defense of their position? Explain.

5. What is the impact of increased immigration on relations between ethnic groups in the United States?

Suggested Readings

Bouvier, Leon F. *Peaceful Invasions: Immigration and Changing America.* Lanham, Md.: Univ. Press of America, 1992.

Briggs, Vernon M. *Mass Immigration and the National Interest.* Armonk, N.Y.: M. E. Sharpe, 1992.

Cose, Ellis. *A Nation of Strangers: Prejudice, Politics, and the Populating of America.* New York: Morrow, 1992.

Daniels, Roger. *Coming to America: A History of Immigration and Ethnicity in America.* New York: HarperCollins, 1990.

Harrison, Lawrence E. "America and Its Immigrants." *Public Interest,* no. 28 (Summer 1992), 37–46.

Hoskin, Marilyn B. *New Immigrants and Democratic Society: Minority Integration in Western Democracies.* New York: Praeger, 1991.

Howe, Irving. *World of Our Fathers.* New York: Harcourt Brace Jovanovich, 1976.

Mandel, Michael J., and Christopher Farrell. "The Immigrants: How They're Helping to Revitalize the U.S. Economy." *Business Week,* no. 3274 (July 13, 1992), 114–120, 122.

Portes, Alejandro, and Rubén G. Rumbaut. *Immigrant America: A Portrait.* Berkeley: Univ. of California Press, 1990.

Reimers, David M. *Still the Golden Door: The Third World Comes to America.* 2d ed. New York: Columbia Univ. Press, 1992.

Simon, Julian L. *The Economic Consequences of Immigration.* New York: B. Blackwell, 1989.

Chapter 19

Will Gun Control Laws Reduce Violence?

Firearms take a heavy toll of life and limb in the United States. According to the Federal Bureau of Investigation, firearms were responsible for 14,265 murders in the United States in 1991. Of this number, 11,411 were committed with handguns.[1] Handguns are also responsible for suicides and accidental deaths, and they are used in a multitude of crimes, including theft, assault, and rape.

Young people live in a world of guns. Particularly in the inner cities, children of all ages hear gunshots on their streets; know people who have been threatened, wounded, or killed by guns; and even have guns of their own. Metal detectors have been installed in schools to prevent youngsters from carrying weapons into the classrooms.

National interest has focused on guns as responsible for the increase in violent crime not only from personal experience but also because of incidents that have attracted national attention. To cite a few:

- In 1968, Robert Kennedy, a U.S. senator from New York and brother of the slain president, was assassinated with a firearm.
- In 1981, John Hinckley used a handgun in attempting to assassinate President Ronald Reagan. He wounded the president and caused serious and permanent injury to James Brady, the president's press secretary.
- In January 1991, Patrick Purdy opened fire with a Kalashnikov-type semiautomatic rifle in a Stockton California, schoolyard. He killed five children and wounded nearly thirty others.

The rising number of killings by firearms has led to calls for laws that would regulate their possession or use or even ban them. Already on the books is a 1934 statute, the National Firearms Act, which makes it difficult to obtain types of firearms perceived to be especially lethal or to be the chosen weapons of gangsters. Among these weapons are machine guns and sawed-off shotguns. The 1934 law also provides for a firearm registration system.

Passed in 1968, the Gun Control Act requires all persons dealing in firearms to be federally licensed. It also tightens federal licensing procedures, prohibits the interstate sale of handguns generally, prescribes categories of individuals to whom firearms and ammunition cannot be sold, prohibits the importation of nonsporting firearms or ammunition, requires that dealers maintain records of all commercial gun sales, and contains other regulatory provisions. In 1986, the McClure-Volkmer Amendments (named for Senator James A. McClure, a Republican from Idaho, and Representative Harold L. Volkmer, a Democrat from Missouri) to the Gun Control Act banned the further manufacture of machine guns. They also tightened enforcement of gun control laws at the same time that they modified or eliminated provisions of the existing law that were opposed by gun owners and the gun industry.

On November 30, 1993, President Clinton signed into law the Brady Bill (named after James Brady). The law, which went into effect in 1994, requires a five-day waiting period during which local police are required to conduct a criminal background check of prospective handgun buyers. Some states and localities, moreover, have enacted laws that are more stringent than federal laws, including the banning of all handguns (except for law enforcement officers).

The debate over gun control is a continuing one, involving such matters as social science research and legal issues. Advocates and opponents of gun control differ in their assessment of the facts, especially whether social science data prove that gun control deters violent crime. They also disagree in their interpretations of the Second Amendment to the Constitution, which reads: "A well regulated Militia, being necessary to the security of a free State, the right of the people to keep and bear Arms, shall not be infringed."

The debate is joined in the two articles below. Writing in the journal *Public Welfare*, Senator John H. Chafee, a Republican from Rhode Island, argues for gun control laws. He contends

1. The Second Amendment to the Constitution does not grant citizens an unlimited right to carry firearms.
2. Handguns take a high toll in life through murders and suicides.
3. Handguns are the fourth leading cause of death to children.
4. Children in schools live in danger because of easy access of handguns.
5. Handguns take a terrible toll on health care.
6. It is an illusion to believe that handguns in the home offer protection to the people who live there.

In an article in the conservative journal *Policy Review*, David B. Kopel argues against gun control. Kopel, director of the Second Amendment Project at the Independence Institute in Golden, Colorado, contends:

1. The right to keep and bear arms is guaranteed by the Second Amendment to the Constitution.
2. The best social science scholarship shows that there is no evidence that the country's 20,000 gun control laws have reduced criminal violence.
3. Gun control laws do not deter criminals from obtaining guns.
4. Gun ownership plays an important role in preventing crimes.
5. Attempts to impose restrictions, such as a ban on semiautomatic weapons and the adoption of a waiting period to purchase guns, will have no appreciable effect on criminal violence.

6. A good way to promote gun control is to educate people in the safe and proper use of guns, as the National Rifle Association does regularly.
7. The best way to reduce violence through firearms is by strengthening the criminal justice system so that repeat offenders of violent crimes will not receive lenient sentences.

NOTE

1. U.S. Department of Justice, Federal Bureau of Investigation, *Crime in the United States: 1991* (Washington, D.C.: Federal Bureau of Investigation, 1992), table 2.9.

☑ YES

Will Gun Control Laws Reduce Violence?

JOHN H. CHAFEE

It's Time To Control Handguns

Many Americans believe the United States Constitution gives them the right to bear arms. But, in fact, the Constitution gives them no such right. Shocking? It should not be. State and federal courts over the past half century have ruled consistently that the Second Amendment to the Constitution does not grant citizens an unlimited right to carry firearms. Nevertheless, we pay an enormous price each year because of this "phantom right."

The Senate recently spent an entire day debating whether to mint new coins. By the end of that day, as on every day of the year, 27 children and adults nationwide were murdered by handguns; and another 33 used handguns to take their own lives. Dozens of others were grievously wounded by handguns.

Handguns are responsible for 75 percent of all firearms murders, which, in turn, represent 60 percent of all homicides nationwide. While the number of murders committed with other guns has remained stable, handgun murders have set new records every year since 1988, keeping pace with the skyrocketing national homicide rate. Seventy percent of law enforcement officers killed in the line of duty are shot by handguns. In addition, handguns are an effective and lethal method of suicide. Of the more than 30,000 annual suicides, 18,000—or 60 percent—are related to firearms. Of these, an estimated 70 percent involve handguns.

Perhaps more disgraceful and intolerable is the impact of handguns on children. Last June, two teenagers playing with the popular "Super Soaker" water guns were seriously injured—one in the spine—when an angry bystander who accidentally got wet pulled out a handgun and shot at them.[1] That same month, a Connecticut kindergartner on his way home from school was shot in the head when his school bus inadvertently drove into a gunfight.[2] Released from the hospital in August, the boy has started school. The bullet, however, still is lodged in his skull in that part of the brain that controls speech. He is undergoing speech therapy. His medical fees exceed $20,000.

Gun-related injury is the fourth leading injury cause of death in children, and 40 percent of these are accidental. The risk to children posed by handguns in the home is significant. At least 266 children were accidentally shot by handguns from 1986 to 1988. Nearly 90 percent of these shootings took place in the children's homes or the homes of friends or relatives.[3]

What are we going to do about this slaughter? One suggestion—a good one—is a national waiting period before the purchase of a handgun. The situation we face, however, demands much more than the screening of felons. We need to shut the spigot that, according to the Bureau of Alcohol, Tobacco, and Firearms, is pouring more than two million handguns each year into our society.

Few of us—including myself, until I had the opportunity to study it—realize the extraordinary extent to which handguns play havoc with our best policy efforts. We have a whopping 67 million handguns in the United States, more than twice the 31 million of 20 years ago.[4] Handguns, so easily available and so easily concealed, are pushing our violent-death rate to levels unheard of in this nation, let alone overseas; and each year they are involved in hundreds of thousands of rapes, robberies, and assaults.

There is not a citizen in this nation who is not worried about two critical national needs: improving our education system and reducing the costs of our health care system. But progress on either matter is well-nigh impossible without recognizing the costs placed on each by our current handgun policy. Today, educators and children are distracted by the frightening presence of handguns in our schools. And efforts to hold down health care costs are being shot down by the billions of dollars' worth of damage caused by handgun wounds.

GUNFIGHTS AT SCHOOL

Five years ago, an estimated 270,000 students carried handguns to school at least once; today it is worse. The Centers for Disease Control estimates that 645,000 high school students—1 in 20—have carried a gun at least once in the past month.[5] Handguns have become so numerous in schools that some students are afraid to go to school. A 1991 school crime survey conducted by the Department of Justice revealed that 37 percent of public school students and 27 percent of private school students fear attack at or on the way to school. A 1990 survey of 25,000 eighth-graders from 1,000 public and private schools by the National Center for Education Statistics revealed that one out of every five eighth-graders says that he or she has seen some kind of weapon at school. What do these students do? Many turn to handguns of their own, which feeds the very fear it was meant to assuage.

This horrible ripple effect carries on up to school administrators, who must find monies in meager school budgets to purchase $4,000 metal detectors instead of textbooks. In June, officials of the Los Angeles Unified School District announced that the school system was upgrading school security officers' weapons from .38-caliber revolvers to nine-millimeter automatic pistols in order to match the guns carried by schoolchildren and others on school grounds.[6] These security officers do not patrol city streets, but rather junior and senior high schools.

But what choice do schools have? In years past, a student dispute might mean a fistfight; now, students often settle their quarrels in gunfights on school grounds. Children say they can obtain handguns, and thousands of them do. In the 1987 National Adolescent Student Health Survey, one-third of the students queried said that they could obtain a handgun. Three years later, a Texas A&M University survey found that, even in smaller, rural areas, more than 40 percent of the schoolchildren reported the ability to obtain a handgun. Record-breaking numbers of teenage and preteenage children are taking these handy guns to school every day, often with tragic results. Since 1986, more than 75 students and teachers have been shot and killed and more than 200 have been wounded at school. Another estimated 240 have been held hostage at school.[7] Many schools now keep records of each year's death toll.

Here are some examples from recent headlines: At Brooklyn's Jefferson High School, a student killed one teen and another young innocent bystander, bringing the school's death toll for the 1991–1992 school year to 56.[8] In Crosby, Texas, a 15-year-old honor student shot and killed a 17-year-old star student athlete in the lunchroom for insulting her.[9] In Chicago, a third-grader brought two guns to school from home, selling one to a school bus driver for $20 and showing off the second to his classmates—he shot one of them in the spine.[10] In Obetz, Ohio, at a small school of 531 students, a seventh-grade boy shot a classmate with a revolver.[11] In Potomac, Maryland, a 16-year-old boldly walked into a high school chemistry class and fired his handgun at point-blank range at his intended student victim, who somehow escaped the bullet.[12]

In at least 75 percent of the reported incidents, the gun that showed up at school was a handgun; often, it came from the student's home.[13]

How ironic: we are desperately trying to improve our educational system, yet how can children learn if they are afraid of walking into some fatal dispute? If we cannot guarantee safety in school, innovative ways of improving our education system will be useless. Is this the way our nation wants to prepare for the next century?

A TERRIBLE TOLL ON HEALTH CARE

Health care, another national priority, may suffer even heavier costs. According to the chair of the 1991 Advisory Council on Social Security, firearm injuries cost the U.S. health system more than $4 billion annually. For those injured but not killed by handguns, the probability of requiring medical attention is high: of the 15,000 persons injured each year by a handgun during a crime, virtually all—95.5 percent—require emergency care or hospitalization.[14] Many gunshot wound victims are severely and permanently disabled, requiring intensive medical treatment and rehabilitation. The tens of thousands of bone-shattering, nerve-cutting gunshot wounds place incredible stress on our health care system and are major contributors to its escalating costs. Flooded with gunshot injuries, urban emergency rooms report gridlock weekly. Some physicians report having to disarm their patients before they can treat them. No wonder emergency rooms have earned the nickname, "knife-and-gun clubs." And, despite emergency teams' hard work, weapons technology is outstripping advances in therapeutic skills, as one physician noted.[15]

The fiscal drain caused by this carnage is staggering. In 1984, researchers calculated the per-patient cost of gunshot wounds averaged more than $6,900 and ran as high as $64,000. Recent data collected from 1989 to 1991 at a major New York hospital found costs ranging as high as $274,000 and averaging more than $9,600. One major trauma center found average per-patient costs of $16,700.[16] At Washington (D.C.) Hospital's MedSTAR facility, the cost of treating gunshot patients in 1987 was more than $6 million.[17]

And the costs do not stop upon discharge from the hospital: there are bills for follow-up care, medication, and rehabilitation treatment. Since gunshot wounds can cause severe and permanent injury, rehabilitation can be particularly expensive. Gunshot wounds are the third leading cause of spinal cord injury, behind motor vehicle accidents and falls; altogether, spinal cord injuries cost the United States approximately $6.2 billion annually. According to the Spinal Cord Injury National Model Care Systems in Birmingham, Alabama, acts of violence account for more than one in every seven spinal cord injuries overall and more than one in five spinal cord injuries in young people under age 16. For initial rehabilitation of paraplegics, the per diem cost at a rehabilitation center is $1,500 per patient; the average cost of three months of care totals $135,000. For quadriplegics, the average cost of three months' care in a rehabilitation center is $270,000 per patient. Lifetime costs for outpatient follow-up care for quadriplegics average $570,000.[18]

In addition, hospitals and trauma centers, like school systems, must find the funds for security equipment and armed guards.

Hospitals are closing affiliated trauma centers out of concern that the overwhelming costs of caring for the influx of severely wounded and mostly uninsured victims of street violence will endanger the parent institution. It should come as no surprise that 90 trauma centers have gone under since 1985, victims of the high costs that, in part, are due to gun violence.[19]

Who pays for these colossal health care costs of firearms? The government—read taxpayers—pays approximately 86 percent of the bill.[20]

And the costs do not stop here. In June, New York City announced it was issuing 1,000 new semiautomatic pistols to city police officers to replace their standard .45-caliber service revolvers. Intended to ensure that the police force keeps up with the increasing firepower of handgun-toting street toughs, the cost to the city is $860,000.[21]

A "PHANTOM RIGHT"

In June, I introduced the Public Health and Safety Act of 1992—S. 2913, cosponsored by Senators Alan Cranston (D-Calif.) and Claiborne Pell (D-R.I.)—to ban the sale, manufacture, or possession of handguns and handgun ammunition. The bill makes exceptions for the military, law enforcement agencies and security services, and antique collectors and licensed target clubs. A radical proposal? Hardly. What I would call radical is allowing the terrible status quo to continue.

A number of influential organizations, representing health care professionals, educators, municipalities, children, and the nation's churchgoers, support my legislation. These groups include, among others, the American Academy of Pediatrics, the American Public Health Association, the U.S. Conference of Mayors, the National Urban League, the American Association of School Administrators, the Children's Defense Fund, the National Association of Social Workers, the Presbyterian Church (USA), the United Methodist Church, and the United Church of Christ.

Some will argue that there exists a fundamental constitutional right to bear arms. But if there is one argument that is utter nonsense, this is it. Not only have proponents of this argument not read their Constitution lately—which clearly says, "A well regulated Militia being necessary to the security of a free State, the right of the people to keep and bear arms shall not be infringed"—but they have not followed more than five decades of remarkably unanimous court rulings. Those who speak so eloquently of a "right to keep and bear arms" are clinging to an illusion that the Supreme Court destroyed more than 50 years ago. Never in the history of this country has a so-called right been so loudly trumpeted—and to such good effect: polls show that about 90 percent of Americans do, indeed, believe that individual citizens have a right, guaranteed by our Constitution, to carry a gun.

Yet nothing could be further from the truth. Since the Supreme Court's seminal 1939 ruling in *United States* v. *Miller,* no federal court has ever overturned a gun control law on the grounds that it violates the Second Amendment. In fact, the federal courts have been unwavering in their observance of the high court's 1939 statement:

> In absence of any evidence . . . that possession or use of a (gun) . . . has some reasonable relationship to the preservation or efficiency of a well-regulated militia, we cannot say that the Second Amendment guarantees the right to keep and bear such an instrument. . . . With obvious purpose to assure the continuation and render possible the effectiveness of such forces, the declaration and guarantee of the Second Amendment were made. It must be interpreted and applied with that end in view.

Subsequent state and federal court decisions have reiterated and expanded upon this:

- **Supreme Court of New Jersey,** *Burton* v. *Sills,* **1969:** [The Second Amendment] was not framed with individual rights in mind. . . . It refers to the collective right "of the people" to keep and bear arms in connection with "a well regulated militia." . . . Reasonable gun control legislation is clearly within the police power of the state and must be accepted by the individual though it may impose a restraint or burden on him.
- **U.S. Sixth Circuit Court of Appeals,** *Stevens* v. *United States,* **1971:** Since the Second Amendment right "to keep and bear arms" applies only to the right of the state to maintain a militia and not to the individual's right to bear arms, there can be no serious claim to any express constitutional right of an individual to possess a firearm.
- **U.S. Third Circuit Court of Appeals,** *Eckert* v. *City of Philadelphia,* **1973:** Appellant's theory . . . is that by the Second Amendment to the United States Constitution he is entitled to bear arms. Appellant is completely wrong about that. . . . The right to keep and bear arms is not a right given by the United States Constitution.
- **U.S. Sixth Circuit Court of Appeals,** *United States* v. *Warin,* **1976:** It is clear that the Second Amendment guarantees a collective rather than an individual right. . . . [It is an] erroneous supposition that the Second Amendment is concerned with the rights of individuals rather than those of the states.
- **U.S. Supreme Court,** *Lewis* v. *United States,* **1980:** These legislative restrictions on the use of firearms are neither based upon constitutionally suspect criteria, nor do they trench upon any constitutionally protected liberties. . . . The Second Amendment guarantees no right to keep and bear a firearm that does not have "some reasonable relationship to the preservation or efficiency of a well-regulated militia."
- **U.S. Seventh Circuit Court of Appeals,** *Quilici* v. *Village of Morton Grove,* **1982:** Construing [the language of the Second Amendment] according to its plain meaning, it seems clear that the right to bear arms is inextricably connected to the preservation of a militia. . . . We conclude that the right to keep and bear handguns is not guaranteed by the Second Amendment.

Legal scholars agree with the courts. In November 1990, Erwin Griswold, dean of the Harvard Law School and solicitor general under the Nixon Administration, told the *Washington Post:*

The Second Amendment has never been an impediment to laws limiting private ownership of firearms. . . . Indeed, that the Second Amendment poses no barrier to strong gun laws is perhaps the most well-settled proposition in American constitutional law. Yet the incarnation of this phantom right continues to pervade congressional debate.

Former Supreme Court Chief Justice Warren E. Burger has said:

Few subjects have been as cluttered and confused by calculated disinfor-
mation circulated by special interest groups. . . . The very language of the
Second Amendment refutes any argument that it was intended to guarantee every citizen an unfettered right to any kind of weapon he or she
desires. In referring to "a well regulated militia," the Framers [of the
Constitution] clearly intended to secure the right to bear arms essentially
for military purposes.

During a lecture in 1989 at the University of California, Irvine, former federal
appeals court judge Robert H. Bork said, "[The Second Amendment's] intent
was to guarantee the right of states to form militia, not for individuals to bear
arms." In 1990, Judge Bork told *Time* magazine, "The National Rifle Association is always arguing that the Second Amendment determines the right to bear
arms. But I think it really is people's right to bear arms in a militia."

Finally, former American Bar Association (ABA) President L. Stanley Chauvin,
in a May 1990 editorial in the *ABA Journal,* said:

The U.S. Supreme Court had several occasions to review state regulation
of firearms in the context of the Second Amendment. A review of these
cases reveals the courts have uniformly held that the Second Amendment
relates merely, solely, totally, and only to the unhampered regulation of a
state militia. It does not confer an individual right.

I am amazed that, in spite of this virtually perfect agreement in the courts and
among legal experts, this "phantom right" is so well entrenched in our national
consciousness.

As for those who will argue that handguns in the home are needed for
protection, they have not reviewed the horrific statistics detailing that handguns are far, far more likely to kill a loved one than an intruder. For every case
of self-protection homicide with a gun kept in the home, there are an estimated
43 murders, accidental deaths, and suicides.[22]

Eventually—and I believe it will be sooner rather than later—handgun violence will touch the life of someone in every American family. Handguns,
when introduced into the already volatile mix of conditions that lead to violence, act as a match to dry powder. It is time to act. We cannot go on like this.
Ban them!

NOTES

1. "Water Gunplay Provokes Shooting of 2," *New York Times,* June 10, 1992.

2. "Bullets Fly in Hill: Kindergartner, Hit in Head, Listed Critical," *New Haven Register,* June 11,
1992.

3. Center to Prevent Handgun Violence, *Child's Play: A Study of 266 Unintentional Handgun
Shootings of Children* (Washington, D.C.: Center to Prevent Handgun Violence, 1990).

4. Ibid.

5. Centers for Disease Control, *Weapons Carrying Among High School Students, U.S. 1990*
(Atlanta: Centers for Disease Control, 1991).

6. "LA Schools Arm School Police with Semiautomatic Guns," Associated Press, June 21, 1992.

7. Center to Prevent Handgun Violence, *Caught in the Crossfire: A Report on Gun Violence in Our Nation's Schools* (Washington, D.C.: Center to Prevent Handgun Violence, 1990).

8. "Slain Youth's Poem on Death Is Read at Brooklyn Funeral," "3 Students With Guns Underline Schools' Burden," *New York Times,* March 4, 1992.

9. "Students Mourn Classmate; Girl, 15, Charged in Grid Star's Death," *Houston Chronicle,* Sept. 19, 1991.

10. "School Suspends Boy Charged in Girl's; Shooting," *Chicago Sun-Times,* March 13, 1992; "2 Families Try to Cope with School Shooting," *Chicago Tribune,* March 13, 1992.

11. "Student, 14, Wounded in Cafeteria Shooting," *Columbus Dispatch,* March 6, 1992.

12. "Shots Fired in Pr. George's School; Intended Target Ducks; Three Other Students Sought as Suspects," *Washington Post,* March 14, 1992.

13. *Caught in the Crossfire.*

14. Bureau of Justice Statistics, *Handgun Crime Victims,* special report (Washington, D.C., U.S. Department of Justice: 1990).

15. Senate Committee on the Judiciary, *Murder Rates: Why the Recent Rise?* Hearing #101-1268, 101st Cong., 2nd sess., July 31, 1990.

16. The research data in this paragraph were provided in a conversation between Senator Chafee's staff and researchers at the University of Arizona Medical Research Center, September 1990.

17. "Field Hospitals of the Drug Wars," *Detroit News,* Sept. 16, 1990.

18. Conversation between Senator Chafee's staff and a Los Angeles County rehabilitation center, March 1992, and confirmed in conversations with the Spinal Cord Injury National Model Care Systems, Birmingham, Ala.

19. Letter to Senator Chafee from the American Trauma Society, Upper Marlboro, Md., June 5, 1992.

20. Michael J. Martin, Thomas K. Hunt, and Stephen B. Hulley, "The Cost of Hospitalization for Firearms Injuries," *Journal of the American Medical Association* 260 (Nov. 25, 1988):3048–3050.

21. "More New York Police to Get Semiautomatics in Compromise," *New York Times,* June 16, 1992.

22. Arthur L. Kellermann and Donald T. Reay, "Protection or Peril? An Analysis of Firearms-Related Deaths in the Home," *New England Journal of Medicine* 314 (June 12, 1986): 1557–1560.

Will Gun Control Laws Reduce Violence?

DAVID B. KOPEL

Hold Your Fire: Gun Control Won't Stop Rising Violence

As deaths from rampant gun violence mount, and city-dwellers from Boston to Los Angeles learn to distinguish the pop of a Smith & Wesson pistol from the blast of a Winchester shotgun, Americans insist on action to combat the national crime epidemic.

Although the per-capita murder rate remains below the record set in 1980, the actual number of homicides reached an all-time high of 24,703 in 1991; most of these murders were committed with guns. Most disturbing of all is the rise in violent crimes committed by gun-wielding teenagers. Able to acquire illegal weapons with ease, in spite of a nationwide prohibition on firearms sales to minors, teenage thugs display a disregard for human life that would have shocked the criminals of earlier generations. The latest urban terror, "carjacking," is the seizure at gunpoint of automobiles from their drivers, usually women.

As armed gangs settle turf disputes over drug-selling territory through mortal combat, they kill not only each other, but also innocent bystanders caught in the crossfire. Firearms violence, once thought to be the problem of the inner city, is spreading into the suburbs and beyond. And with depressing frequency, newspapers report stories of children dying in senseless gun accidents. In Louisiana last October, a Japanese exchange student was mistakenly shot when he entered the wrong house on the way to a Halloween party, and, not understanding the warning, continued to advance toward the homeowner despite an order to "Freeze!"

To some well-meaning Americans, the antidote to gun crime is gun control. Senator John Chafee (R-RI) calls for the confiscation of all handguns. Other voices, such as Handgun Control, Inc.'s Sarah Brady, urge a national waiting period on handgun purchases, and a ban on assault weapons. The national media's insistent message is that we must "do something" about guns.

Meanwhile, the National Rifle Association adds tens of thousands of members every month—membership is at a record three million—and continues to stymie gun control at nearly every turn. Although the 99th, 100th, and 101st Congresses passed some minor gun controls, the 102nd Congress went home without enacting any new gun-control measures. The New Jersey legislature is ready to overturn its assault-weapon ban the moment the legislative leadership schedules a vote on the issue.

Critics of gun control believe that it violates the right to keep and bear arms guaranteed by the Second Amendment of the United States Constitution and by 43 state constitutions. In the American political tradition, the right to own a gun is seen as intimately related to the natural right of self-defense, to what John Locke described as the natural right to control and protect one's body and property. Millions of Americans consider an armed citizenry to be one of the principal safeguards against possible tyranny by the state.

The constitutional argument against laws that infringe on gun ownership was strengthened by the 1990 Supreme Court decision in *United States* v. *Verdugo-Urquidez*. There, Chief Justice Rehnquist observed that the phrase "right of the people" occurs several times in the Bill of Rights, specifically the Second Amendment's "right of the people to keep and bear arms," the First Amendment's "right of the people peaceably to assemble," and the Fourth Amendment's "right of the people to be secure in their persons, houses, papers and effects against unreasonable searches and seizures." In all cases, the Court said, the phrase "right of the people" was used as a "term of art" that referred to individual Americans.

But critics of gun control do not base their opposition on political principles alone. They also cite a large body of recent social science research, much of which has been produced by scholars who formerly believed that gun control was an obvious solution to crime.

JIMMY CARTER'S SHOCKER

When gun control first became an important national issue in the 1960s, there was almost no research worth noting on the subject. Partisans on both sides of the debate had hardly more ammunition than intuitions and bumper-sticker slogans.

The man most responsible for the change in the intellectual terms of the gun debate was Jimmy Carter, or, more precisely, the grant-review team that Carter appointed to the National Institute of Justice. Intending to build the case for comprehensive federal gun restrictions, the Carter administration handed out a major gun-control research grant in 1978 to sociology professor James D. Wright and his colleagues Peter Rossi and Kathleen Daly. Wright was already on record as favoring much stricter controls, and he and his colleagues were highly regarded sociologists. Rossi, a University of Massachusetts professor, would later become president of the American Sociology Association. Wright, who formerly served as director of the Social and Demographic Research Institute at the University of Massachusetts, now teaches at Tulane. Daly is now at the University of Michigan.

Wright and his colleagues were asked to survey the state of research regarding the efficacy of gun control, presumably to show that gun control worked and that America needed more of it. But when the researchers produced their report for the National Institute of Justice in 1982, they delivered a document quite different from the one they had expected to write. Carefully reviewing all existing research, the three scholars found no persuasive scholarly evidence that America's 20,000 gun-control laws had reduced criminal violence. For example, the federal Gun Control Act of 1968, which banned most interstate gun sales, had no discernible impact on the criminal acquisition of guns from other states. Washington, D.C.'s ban on the ownership of handguns that had not already been registered in the District was not linked to any reduction in gun crime. Even Detroit's law providing mandatory sentences for felonies committed with a gun was found to have no effect on gun-crime patterns, in part because judges would often reduce the sentence for the underlying offense in order to balance out the mandatory two-year extra sentence for use of a gun.

WHAT CRIMINALS SAY ABOUT GUN CONTROL

The most thorough subsequent study of the efficacy of gun control has been performed by Florida State University's Gary Kleck, who analyzed data for all 170 U.S. cities with a population over 100,000, testing for the impact of 19 different types of gun controls, and looking for the controls' effects on suicides, accidents, and five different crimes. Kleck, a liberal Democrat and ACLU [American Civil Liberties Union] member, found that gun controls did reduce gun suicide, but not the overall suicide rate. The only control that reduced crime was a strict penalty for carrying an illegal gun, which seemed to lower the robbery rate. Waiting periods, various licensing systems, and registration appeared to have no statistically discernible impact. Kleck's analysis was based on data for the years 1979–1981, and is included in his recent book, *Point Blank,* which contains the best single-volume overview of gun-control research.

Wright and Rossi produced another study for the National Institute of Justice, this one involving the habits of America's felons. Interviewing felony prisoners in 10 state correctional systems in 1981, Wright and Rossi found that gun-control laws had no effect on criminals' ability to obtain guns. Only 12 percent of criminals, and only 7 percent of the criminals specializing in handgun crime, had acquired their last crime handgun at a gun store. Of those, about one quarter had stolen the gun from a store; a large number of the rest, Wright and Rossi suggested, had probably procured the gun through a legal surrogate buyer, such as a girlfriend with a clean record. For the few remaining felons who actually did buy their own guns, the purchase might have been lawful because the purchaser as yet had no felony record.

The survey further indicated that 56 percent of the prisoners said that a criminal would not attack a potential victim who was known to be armed. Seventy-four percent agreed with the statement that "One reason burglars avoid houses where people are at home is that they fear being shot during the crime." Thirty-nine percent of the felons had personally decided not to commit a crime because they thought the victim might have a gun, and 8 percent said the experience had occurred "many times." Criminals in states with higher civilian gun-ownership rates worried the most about armed victims.

Since criminals can never be entirely sure which burglary targets may or may not contain a homeowner with a gun, or which potential robbery or rape victims may be carrying a concealed firearm, the ownership of firearms by half of American households provides a general deterrent to crime that benefits the entire population.

HOW GUNS PREVENT CRIME

Consistent with the reports of criminals, ordinary citizens also report that gun ownership plays an important role in preventing crime. Professor Kleck estimates that handguns are used approximately 645,000 times for defense against an attacker every year in the United States.

The figure, ironically, is based on data from a survey conducted on behalf of the pro-control National Alliance Against Violence (NAAV). NAAV hired Peter Hart, a leading Democratic pollster, to survey Americans on guns, asking, among other things: "Within the past five years, have you yourself or another member of your household used a handgun, even if it was not fired, for self-protection or protection of property at home, work, or elsewhere, excluding military service or police work?" Six percent answered "yes." Follow-up questions revealed that 3 percent of the respondents had used the handgun against a person, 2 percent against an animal, and 1 percent against both. That 4 percent said "yes" to defensive gun use against persons meant that about 18 percent of households where a handgun was owned for protection had actually used the handgun for protection.

Kleck's analysis started with the 4-percent "yes" from Hart's data. Kleck made the conservative assumption that each "yes" related to only one gun usage in the last five years—that no household used a firearm for self-defense two or more times in the five years. Thus, 3,224,880 households reported self-defense usage. Kleck then divided by five (since the question had asked about usage in the last five years) to arrive at an estimate for the annual number of uses of a handgun for self-defense: 644,976—or roughly once every 48 seconds.

Since Kleck's estimate is based on responses to a pollster, it should be emphasized that the 645,000 figure is necessarily imprecise. The original question posed by Peter Hart could have elicited a "yes" answer from an insecure gun owner who had perceived a criminal threat that did not in fact exist. Kleck partly controlled self-defense inflation from false "yes" answers by assuming that no "yes" answer related to more than one defensive use. In addition, the 645,000 estimate applies only to handguns; the original question did not ask about defensive use of rifles or shotguns.

In 1990, Professor Gary Mauser, of Canada's Simon Fraser University, asked Americans about use of a handgun or a long gun for self-defense; the responses suggested approximately 691,000 annual defensive uses of guns of all types. Accordingly, we may conclude that guns are used defensively at least half a million times a year.

Of course, the fact that a gun is used for defense does not mean that a shot is fired, or an attacker wounded or killed. About 95 percent of self-defense usage, says Kleck, involves merely the brandishing of a weapon to deter a perceived attack.

While the majority of defensive handgun use is simply brandishing a weapon to frighten away an attacker, Kleck suggests that 1,700 to 3,100 homicides a year are actually justifiable homicides committed by citizens using a firearm to defend themselves or another person against violent attack.

ONE BULLET AT A TIME

While most Americans believe they have a right to own a gun, and believe that guns can be protective, even many gun owners are baffled at the gun lobby's apparent intransigence in its refusal to accept a ban on so-called assault weapons or a waiting period on gun purchases.

The assault-weapon issue, however, turns out to involve much less than meets the eye. First of all, it should be emphasized that most people who own semiautomatics support strong controls on actual machine guns. Ever since the National Firearms Act of 1934, acquisition of real machine guns—guns that continue to fire bullets repeatedly as long as the trigger is held down—has required a difficult-to-obtain federal license. The NRA [National Rifle Association] did not oppose the restrictive machine gun law when it was enacted, and has never indicated any desire to repeal the law.

While machine guns do have a unique capacity for rapid fire, what we know as assault weapons do not. Although most of the public believes that assault weapons are machine guns, the guns in question simply look like military weapons. Appearances notwithstanding, the guns fire just as every other common American gun does: squeezing the trigger fires one, and only one, bullet. According to Martin Fackler, former director of the Letterman Army Institute of Research, assault weapons are actually less lethal than many firearms commonly associated with hunting, such as an old-fashioned 12-gauge Winchester shotgun. The Bureau of Alcohol, Tobacco, and Firearms states that no guns available for sale to the public can be easily converted to fire automatically.

HARD TO CONVERT

The fact that semiautomatic assault weapons differ from other guns only cosmetically is one reason why legislative bodies have had so much trouble defining them. Since the guns do not fire faster than other guns, legislative definitions sometimes focus on extraneous features, such as the presence of a bayonet lug—as if we were suffering from a rash of criminals bayonetting people.

Other definitions are merely a list of particular guns with a military appearance. Among the guns targeted by assault-weapons legislation are the M1 Carbine; the AKS Rifle; the Uzi Pistol and Carbine, the Colt AR-15 H-Bar Rifle; the Springfield Armory 4800 Rifle; the M10 Pistol and Carbine; and the AK-56 rifle. Yet some of these guns are in no way distinguishable from many other guns not on the lists, such as the popular hunting rifles made by Winchester, Remington, and Ruger. As former Attorney General Richard Thornburgh noted, the main characteristic of an assault weapon seems to be that it has a black plastic stock rather than a brown wooden stock.

In practical terms, the legislative definition of assault weapon amounts to "the largest number of guns that a given legislature can be convinced to ban." The New Jersey assault-weapon prohibition even outlaws BB guns.

While assault weapons have been claimed to be the "weapon of choice" of criminals, such guns constitute a very small number of the crime guns seized by the police. The Florida Assault Weapons Commission's 1990 report found that assault weapons were used in 17 of 7,500 gun crimes in the years 1986–

1989. The Washington, D.C. director of the police firearms section stated in early 1989 that not one of the more than 3,000 weapons the Washington police confiscated in 1988 was a semiautomatic assault rifle.

While some gun-prohibition advocates have claimed that a record number of police are being murdered by assault weapons, police-officer deaths in the line of duty are at their lowest level since 1968. The percentage of police homicides perpetrated with assault weapons is about 4 percent, a figure that has stayed constant over the last decade. The FBI's Uniform Crime Reporting Program, which collects extensive data on all murders of police officers, reports no instance of a drug dealer ever killing a police officer with an Uzi.

That assault weapons should appear so rarely as crime guns seized makes sense. Street criminals need concealable weapons, and a Colt or a Kalashnikov rifle is pretty difficult to stick in a pocket. Indeed, rifles of all types constitute a tiny percentage of crime guns. According to the Washington, D.C., Metropolitan Police Department, rifles are used in less than one-tenth of 1 percent of armed robberies in the District. Nationally, only about 4 percent of the weapons used in homicides are rifles.

Occasionally, so-called assault weapons are used in gruesome mass murders. In Stockton, California in January 1991, Patrick Purdy used a Kalashnikov-type semiautomatic rifle to fire 105 shots in about four minutes at a schoolyard full of Cambodian immigrant children. Thirty-five people were wounded, six of whom died. Purdy's rate of fire could have been duplicated by anyone with an old-fashioned bolt-action rifle or simple revolver, and autopsies of the victims showed that the wounds were approximately equal in severity to wounds associated with a medium-sized handgun, which explains why 29 of the 35 people who were shot survived.

Thus, Purdy could have committed the same crime using many other types of guns. But the national media incorrectly told the American public that Purdy had used an automatic AK-47 rifle, and that such guns could be bought over the counter.

Lost in the media frenzy over Purdy's gun was Purdy himself, who committed suicide with a pistol at the end of his spree. Purdy perpetrated his crime after he had told a state mental-health worker that he thought about committing a mass murder with a gun or a bomb, and even though a parole report called him "a danger to himself and others."

Purdy had a lengthy history of crime and arrests, including a robbery in which a 55-year-old woman was seriously injured, receipt of stolen property, criminal conspiracy, possession of illegal weapons, and assault of a police officer, all reduced to misdemeanor charges. His crime career began when he was 14 years old and continued unabated for the next decade, until he killed himself at Stockton. Not one of Purdy's two-dozen encounters with the law ever led to more than a few weeks in prison. The media's hysterical focus on Purdy's gun enabled California's decrepit criminal-justice bureaucracy to escape public censure for allowing Purdy to roam the streets, free to commit his final, horrible crime.

"COOLING OFF"

The waiting period, like the assault-weapon ban, becomes considerably less attractive when examined carefully. While the waiting-period initiative is often called the "Brady Bill," it would not have prevented John Hinckley from shooting Ronald Reagan and Jim Brady. When Hinckley bought two handguns in October 1980, he had no felony record, and no public record of mental illness. The simple police and mental health records check proposed by the Brady Bill would not have turned up anything on him. And since Hinckley bought the guns more than five months in advance, a one-week wait would not have made any difference to him.

Indeed, a "cooling-off" period for handgun purchases requires a number of unlikely assumptions in order to work. First, the potential murderer—denied a handgun immediately—must then decide not to buy a rifle or a shotgun, which the Brady Bill would allow him to do. Then, he must not know how to buy a handgun on the black market, or how to obtain one from friends, relatives, or acquaintances. In addition, the type of murder he intends must not be one for which readily available alternative weapons, such as knives, automobiles, or bare hands will work. Finally, the person who was literally ready to commit a murder on day one of the waiting period must calm down by day seven, and stay calm from that day forward.

This scenario, while implausible, is not impossible; it is at least theoretically imaginable that a waiting period could "save at least one life." But a waiting period can cost lives, too.

"I'LL BE DEAD BY THEN"

Even a short waiting period will inevitably prevent people from protecting themselves against criminal attack during the wait. When Los Angeles citizens went to gun stores to buy firearms to protect life and property during the recent riots, they were told to come back 15 days later, to comply with California's waiting period on all guns.

After Hurricane Andrew, Florida's looters did considerably less damage than their California counterparts, in part because Florida has only a three-day handgun waiting period, and no wait at all on long guns.

Nor are waiting period victimizations confined only to periods of civil disorder. In September 1990, a mail carrier named Catherine Latta of Charlotte, North Carolina, went to the police to obtain permission to buy a handgun. Her ex-boyfriend had previously robbed her, assaulted her several times, and raped her. The clerk at the sheriff's office informed her the gun permit would take two to four weeks. "I told her I'd be dead by then," Latta later recalled. That afternoon, she bought an illegal $20 semiautomatic pistol on the street. Five hours later, her ex-boyfriend attacked her outside her house, and she shot him dead. The county prosecutor decided not to prosecute Latta for either the self-defense homicide or the illegal gun.

A Wisconsin woman, Bonnie Elmasri, was not so lucky. On March 5, 1991 she called a firearms instructor, worried that her husband—who was subject to a restraining order to stay away from her—had been threatening her and her children. When she asked the instructor about getting a handgun, the instructor explained that Wisconsin has a 48-hour waiting period. Elmasri and her two children were murdered by her husband 24 hours later.

Waiting periods that appear reasonable in a legislative chamber may become unreasonable through administrative abuse. Although New Jersey law requires that the authorities act on gun license applications within 30 days, delays of 90 days are routine; some applications are delayed for years for no valid reason. In Maryland, where an appeals process exists, the police are overruled on 78 percent of the denials that are appealed.

INSTANT RECORDS CHECK

If it is determined that the way to keep criminals from getting guns is to impose background checks on retail handgun sales—a questionable determination—a mandatory instant records check makes sense. The same technology that allows a store to receive verification of credit card validity within a few minutes can also allow firearms dealers to dial a state government registry and verify that a gun buyer has no felony record.

Polling data suggests that most Americans prefer the instant check to the waiting period, particularly when presented with the choice of mandatory immediate check (the NRA proposal) versus a waiting period with no requirement that any check be conducted (the Brady Bill). In recent years, many states have made major progress in bringing their criminal-records histories on-line. Thus, an instant check should become feasible in the near future.

And if records are not sufficiently accurate to support an instant check, they are also not sufficient to support a check with a one-week wait. Former Attorney General Thornburgh's task force found that even if there were no improvement in state criminal records, an instant check would be just as accurate as a check that could be completed in one week.

Unfortunately, if adequate safeguards are not in place, the instant check, like the waiting period, can be misused by police departments to create a registry of gun owners. In 1991, California admitted that it had used the state's handgun waiting period to create a list of handgun owners, even though nothing in California law authorizes the compilation of such a list.

Although the federal gun-control debate talks almost exclusively about retail handgun sales and the Brady Bill, the most effective method to deal with criminals obtaining guns might be to focus on the major source of criminal guns: the black market. A sensible first step in dealing with the black market would be to increase penalties for fencing a gun known to be stolen. In some states, theft and sale of a $75 gun amounts only to petty larceny. Selling a "hot" $75 pistol ought to be a more serious offense than selling a "hot" $75 toaster-oven.

NRA'S REFORM PROPOSAL

While Congress has spent most of its gun-control effort debating new restrictions on gun acquisition, the discussion in many state legislatures has shifted to the carrying of firearms. The Second Amendment refers to a right "to keep and bear arms," and if the text is read consistently with original intent and judicial interpretations of the following century, the government cannot require that citizens ask for permission to carry an unconcealed gun in public.

But in many states, the right to carry has been obliterated by laws that require a police license to carry, and by police administrators who give out carry licenses only to the political elite. In New York City, crime victims who will testify at a forthcoming trial, and who are receiving death threats from the criminal's friends, are denied carry permits—while politically powerful citizens are routinely granted them. While New York's abuse of licensing discretion is notorious, the licensing systems in many other cities are also skewed against people without some kind of clout.

Based on a literalist reading of the Constitution, Second-Amendment advocates should lobby for repeal of all laws requiring a license to carry a gun. But instead, the NRA suggests only reform of easily abused gun licensing systems.

The NRA proposal requires that applicants for a permit to carry a protective firearm must undergo safety training and must submit to a police background check. Then, if the applicant passes the safety class and background check, he or she is to be granted a license to carry. The bureaucratic discretion to deny permits to qualified citizens simply because the bureaucrat does not like guns would be removed.

PROGRESS IN THE GUNSHINE STATE

Carry reform was first enacted in Florida in 1987, amidst vociferous cries from gun-control supporters in the legislature that blood would run in the streets as Floridians shot each other while jostling in line at fast-food restaurants. Florida would become the "Gunshine State," it was warned.

Today, those same critics have admitted that they were wrong, and that they regret the harm done to Florida's reputation by the histrionic campaign against carry reform. Indeed, while the murder rate has risen 14 percent nationally from 1986 to 1991, it has fallen 20 percent in Florida. The state's total murder rate was 36 percent higher than the U.S. murder rate in 1986, and is now 4 percent below the national average. In the same period, robbery rose 9 percent in Florida, and 21 percent nationally.

There has been no research proving that Florida's carry reform was part of the reason for Florida's relative improvement in recent years. But the experience of Florida, and of other carry reform states such as Oregon, Montana, Mississippi, and Pennsylvania, demonstrates that people who are already good citizens and who are willing to pass through a licensing process do not suddenly turn into murderous psychopaths when granted a permit to carry a firearm for protection.

INTERRUPTING A MASS MURDER

While tragic mass murders are frequently used by the pro-control lobby to push restrictive laws, evidence suggests that laws prohibiting firearms carrying may be costing innocent lives.

In October 1991 in Killeen, Texas, a psychopath named George Hennard rammed his pickup truck through the plate glass window of a Luby's cafeteria. Using a pair of ordinary pistols, he murdered 23 people in 10 minutes, stopping only when the police arrived.

Dr. Suzanna Gratia, a cafeteria patron, had a gun in her car, but, in conformity to Texas law, she did not carry the gun; Texas, despite its Wild-West image, has the most severe law in the country against carrying firearms. Carry-reform legislation had almost passed the state legislature, but had been stopped in House Rules Committee by the gun-control lobby.

Gratia later testified that if she had been carrying her gun, she could have shot at Hennard: "I know what a lot of people think, they think, 'Oh, my God, then you would have had a gunfight and then more people would have been killed.' Unhunh, no. I was down on the floor; this guy is standing up; everybody else is down on the floor. I had a perfect shot at him. It would have been clear. I had a place to prop my hand. The guy was not even aware of what we were doing. I'm not saying that I could have saved anybody in there, but I would have had a chance." Hennard reloaded five times, and had to throw away one pistol because it jammed, so there was plenty of opportunity for someone to fire at him.

Even if Gratia hadn't killed or wounded Hennard, he would have had to dodge hostile gunfire, and wouldn't have been able methodically to finish off his victims as they lay wounded on the floor. The hypothetical risks of a stray bullet from Gratia would have been rather small compared with the actual risks of Hennard not facing any resistance. But because of the Texas law, Gratia had left her gun in the car and couldn't take a shot at Hennard. Instead, she watched him murder both her parents.

Two months later, a pair of criminals with stolen pistols herded 20 customers and employees into the walk-in refrigerator of a Shoney's restaurant in Anniston, Alabama. Hiding under a table in the restaurant was Thomas Glenn

Terry, armed with the .45 semiautomatic pistol he carried legally under Alabama law. One of the robbers discovered Terry, but Terry killed him with five shots in the chest. The second robber, who had been holding the manager hostage, shot at Terry and grazed him. Terry returned fire, and mortally wounded the robber.

Twenty-three people died in Killeen, where carrying a gun for self-defense was illegal. Twenty lives were saved, and only the two criminals died in Anniston, where self-defense permits are legal. Yet while Anniston never made the network news, Killeen did, and is used to this day as supposed proof of the need for severe gun controls. Precisely because lives are saved, instances of citizens using firearms carried on their persons to defend themselves and others rarely make the national news, even though such defensive acts occur with great frequency, as the research of Professors Kleck and Mauser demonstrates.

EMPHASIS ON GUN SAFETY

Gun control, properly conceived, is not simply a matter of passing laws, or adding to the paperwork involved in retail gun purchases. Gun control needs to involve people control, or more precisely, helping people take control of their own actions. In this regard, the NRA's gun safety programs rank as America's most successful gun-control efforts.

The National Rifle Association was founded in 1871 by Union Army generals dismayed at the poor marksmanship displayed by Union forces during the recent war. The NRA always has placed heavy emphasis on its mission to train American citizens in responsible and effective firearms handling.

Happily, the fatal gun accident rate is now at an all-time low. In 1945, for every million Americans, there were about 350,000 firearms and 18 fatal gun accidents. Today, the per-million rate is 850,000 and 6 accidents. As the gun supply per capita more than doubled, fatal accidents fell by two-thirds.

NRA safety programs implemented by the 32,000 instructors and coaches who have earned NRA Instructor certification have played an important role in the accident drop, and will become even more important in coming years as more and more women choose to own handguns. Since women gun owners are more likely to own for protection, and less likely to have been initiated in sport shooting by an older male relative, safety training for these new gun owners is especially worthwhile, and the NRA has, accordingly, set up a program offering free safety training to women.

The number of fatal firearm accidents for children aged 0–14 has fallen from 550 in 1975 to 250 in 1988. While the NRA always has had junior shooting and hunting programs that emphasize the development of safe sporting gun use under adult supervision, in 1988 the organization launched a safety campaign aimed at the millions of children who never have any exposure to the shooting sports.

The NRA's Eddie Eagle Elementary Gun Safety Education Program is geared for children in pre-school through sixth grade. Using teacher-tested materials such as an animated video, cartoon workbooks, role-playing, and fun safety activities, Eddie Eagle teaches the simple lesson: "If you see a gun: Stop! Don't Touch. Leave the Area. Tell an Adult."

To date, the Eddie Eagle program has reached almost 4 million children and their parents through schools, law-enforcement programs, and a variety of youth programs. Unfortunately, it has been excluded from some urban schools by administrators who refuse to allow pupils to contact anything related to the NRA, even though the Eddie Eagle curriculum does not discuss political issues.

CONTROLLING CRIMINALS, NOT GUNS

The NRA's most controversial recent effort is the organization's CrimeStrike program, which takes aim at aspects of the criminal justice system that the NRA considers too lenient. In pushing for laws allowing greater pretrial detention of violent repeat offenders, the NRA adheres to its conservative roots, to the chagrin of some of its libertarian supporters, who are unwilling to protect the Second Amendment by weakening the Eighth Amendment right to bail.

Other aspects of CrimeStrike, such as support for victims' rights laws, cause no dissent within the pro–Second Amendment coalition, and offer an opportunity to improve a criminal justice bureaucracy that sometimes lets the desire to process cases overshadow the necessity to do justice to the criminal *and* the victim.

NRA CrimeStrike strategies, like NRA lobbying, rely heavily on grassroots pressure. In a recent Texas case, Charles Edward Bruton had been sentenced to two 10-year terms for shooting at a woman and for committing a heinous sexual assault against her 11-year old daughter. Having served only three years, Bruton was up for parole last September. After the shooting victim asked CrimeStrike for assistance, NRA members were notified through NRA magazines destined for Texas; the Texas Board of Pardons and Appeals was flooded with calls and letters; the parole was denied.

CrimeStrike will not single-handedly fix the criminal justice system, nor will safety education eliminate all accidents, nor will carry reform wipe out all street crime. But each of these efforts will improve public safety for all citizens, whether they own guns or not. Everyone benefits from a prison system that keeps violent felons off the streets; everyone benefits from reduced risks of gun accidents; and everyone benefits from street criminals facing increased odds of victims resisting successfully.

Today, rather than merely opposing poorly conceived gun-control legislation, right-to-keep-and-bear-arms supporters are working in positive ways. These efforts will enhance not only the rights of the 50 percent of American families who own guns, but also the safety of the 50 percent who do not.

Questions for Discussion

1. What would be the consequences of a law banning the possession of handguns to (a) criminal violence, (b) accidental injury, and (c) self-defense?
2. How would a ban on handguns be enforced?
3. Would a ban on handguns be more or less effective than the ban on illegal drugs? What are the reasons for your answer?
4. What effect would a waiting period have on the use of handguns by (a) criminals, and (b) innocent people for self-protection?
5. Does the large number of guns available to Americans cause violence, or does violence cause the possession of large numbers of guns? What are the reasons for your answer?

Suggested Readings

Bogus, Carl T. "The Strong Case for Gun Control." *American Prospect*, no. 10 (Summer 1992), 19–28.

"The Brady Handgun Violence Prevention Act: Pros and Cons." *Congressional Digest*, 70, nos. 6 and 7 (June/July 1991), 161–192.

Idelson, Holly. "Gun Rights and Restrictions: The Territory Reconfigured." *Congressional Quarterly Weekly Report*, 51, no. 17 (April 24, 1993), 1021–1026.

Kleck, Gary. *Point Blank: Guns and Violence in America.* New York: Aldine de Gruyter, 1991.

Kriegel, Leonard. "A Loaded Question: What Is It about Americans and Guns?" *Harper's*, 284, no. 1704 (May 1992), 45–51.

Larson, Erik. "The Story of a Gun." *Atlantic*, 271, no. 1 (January 1993), 48–52, 55–57, 60–62, 64–65, 68–69, 72, 74–75, 78.

McClurg, Andrew Jay. "The Rhetoric of Gun Control." *American University Law Review*, 42, no. 1 (Fall 1992), 53–113.

Sugarmann, Josh. *National Rifle Association: Money, Firepower and Fear.* Washington, D.C.: National Press Books, 1992.

"200 Million Guns." *New York Times*, March 8, 1992, sec. I, pp. 1, 30; March 9, 1992, pp. A1, A10; March 10, 1992, pp. A1, A18; March 11, 1992, pp. A1, A20; March 12, 1992, pp. A1, D21; March 20, 1992, p. A20; April 3, 1992, pp. A1, A15.

U.S. Cong., House of Representatives. *Brady Handgun Violence Prevention Act.* Hearing before the Subcommittee on Crime and Criminal Justice of the Committee on the Judiciary, 102d Cong., 1st Sess., 1991.

———, Senate. *Brady Handgun Violence Prevention Act.* Hearing before the Subcommittee on Crime and Criminal Justice of the Committee on the Judiciary, 102d Cong., 1st Sess., 1991.

"Violence." *JAMA: Journal of the American Medical Association*, 267, no. 22 (June 10, 1992), 2985–3108.

Wright, James D., Peter H. Rossi, and Kathleen Daly. *Under the Gun: Weapons, Crime, and Violence in America.* New York: Aldine de Gruyter, 1983.

Chapter 20

Should Government Give Direct Support to Artists and Writers?

In 1989 the Corcoran Gallery of Art in Washington, D.C., prepared to exhibit photographs of Robert Mapplethorpe, a U.S. artist of some renown who had died of AIDS (acquired immune deficiency syndrome). The presentation contained photographs of a homoerotic nature. What made the show controversial was not so much that these pictures would be displayed but that the program was funded by the National Endowment for the Arts (NEA), a federal government unit.

For a quarter of a century, the NEA and its counterpart in the humanities, the National Endowment for the Humanities (NEH), have provided grants for artists, writers, musicians, ballet companies, and museums in the cause of promoting the arts and the humanities. But with the Mapplethorpe exhibition, members of Congress became incensed that taxpayers were funding works deemed offensive by members of Congress as well as by large numbers of taxpayers themselves. Of equal notoriety was federal support to the artist Andres Serrano, who had created a sculpture depicting Christ on the cross submerged in the artist's urine.

Critics of NEA practices, such as Senator Jesse Helms (R-N.C.), introduced legislation to prevent the NEA from funding works that were pornographic. Artists differed with Helms and his supporters about what constitutes pornography. Nevertheless, the NEA soon felt pressure to police itself lest its funding be curtailed and, worse yet, the unit be abolished. A few artists turned down grants by refusing to sign affidavits that the grants would not be used for work that was pornographic. When faced with the prospect of not getting funding, however, most grant recipients complied with the law.

Supporters of the congressional action contended that it was not censorship. The issue, they said, was not the right of artists to exhibit their work no matter how controversial. Some of the opponents of NEA practices even sided with a gallery in Cincinnati when local officials sought to prevent the exhibition of the Mapplethorpe photographs on the grounds that the works were pornography rather than art. That exhibition was not supported by federal money. Cincinnati courts relied on a Supreme Court decision that community standards can be a factor to prevent pornography from being displayed. In a much publicized trial, the director of the gallery was acquitted of the obscenity charges.

The relationship between artist and government is often strained not only in the United States but in other countries as well. Dictators are concerned with what people think and, consequently, persecute writers and artists who do not abide by approved doctrine. In 1989, for example,

349

the Ayatollah Khomeini, the late leader of Iran, put writer Salman Rushdie on a death list, offering a heavenly reward for anyone who killed him because Rushdie's *Satanic Verses* was considered blasphemous. Rushdie, who was living in Great Britain, went into hiding and continued to remain in hiding even after Khomeini's death.

But in democracies, too, there has often been an uneasy relationship between government and the arts. On the one hand, artists are hailed for their accomplishments. On the other hand, their works are sometimes banned. Offensive books and magazines are removed from libraries and bookstores. Laws against obscenity and racism also regulate the creativity of artists and writers.

Criticism of the artists and writers comes from many sources. Fundamentalist religious leaders are sometimes principal advocates of restrictions against the arts. But groups generally associated with liberal views have also favored restrictions. Some feminists, for example, call for city ordinances punishing pornographers. Civil rights advocates have sought to suppress works that they feel depict African Americans in a derogatory manner.

In the following debate, the issue of direct government support to the arts is considered by two prominent U.S. writers: Garrison Keillor and John Updike. In an appearance before a Senate committee considering reauthorization of the NEA, Keillor contends

1. The creation of the NEA helped to promote the arts throughout the United States.
2. The NEA aided him and other writers in achieving professional success at early stages of their careers when they lacked the credentials of popular success.
3. The NEA has contributed mightily to the creative genius of the United States.

Testifying in 1978 before joint congressional committees considering House Joint Resolution 639, which calls for a White House Conference on the Humanities, Updike argues against government support. He contends

1. The essence of government is concern for the widest possible public interest; the essence of the humanities is private study.
2. As an artist, Updike would prefer to please private citizens who purchase his work rather than government officials administering government funds.
3. Better than providing direct grants to artists, government should reduce inflation so artistic enterprises can be self-supporting.
4. "How can legislators, asked to vote tax money away," Updike asks, "not begin to think of guidelines that insidiously edge toward censorship?"

Should Government Give Direct Support to Artists and Writers?

GARRISON KEILLOR
The Case for Government Support

I'm grateful to those who have so ably attacked the [National] Endowment [for the Arts, NEA] over the past year or so for making it necessary to defend it. I enjoy controversy and I recognize the adversary, they are us. My ancestors were Puritans from England. They arrived here in 1648 in the hope of finding greater restrictions than were permissible under English law at that time. But over the years, we Puritans have learned something about repression, and it's as true today as when my people arrived: man's interest in the forbidden is sharp and constant. If Congress doesn't do something about obscene art, we'll have to build galleries twice as big to hold the people who want to see it. And if Congress does do something about obscene art, the galleries will need to be even bigger than that.

All governments have honored artists when they are old and saintly and successful and almost dead, but twenty-five years ago Congress decided to boldly and blindly support the arts—support the act of creation itself—and to encourage artists who are young and dangerous and unknown and very much alive. This courageous legislation has changed American life.

Today, in every city and state, when Americans talk up their home town, when the Chamber of Commerce puts out a brochure, invariably, they mention the arts—a local orchestra or theater or museum or all three. It didn't used to be this way. Forty years ago, if an American man or woman meant to have an artistic career, you got on the train to New York. Today, you can be a violinist in North Carolina, a writer in Iowa, a painter in Utah. This is a small and lovely revolution that the National Endowment has helped to bring about. The Endowment has fostered thousands and thousands of artistic works—many of which will outlive you and me—but even more important, the Endowment has changed how we think about the arts. Today, no American family can be secure against the danger that one of its children may decide to become an artist.

I grew up in a family who never attended concerts or museums, never bought books. I never imagined that a person could be a writer.

Twice in my life, at crucial times, grants from the Endowment made it possible for me to be a writer. The first, in 1969, arrived when I was young, broke, married with a baby, living on very little cash and a big vegetable garden. I was writing for the *New Yorker* at the time but they weren't aware of it. I wrote every morning and every night. I often had fantasies of finding a patron—a beggar would appear at my door one day, I'd give him an egg salad sandwich, and suddenly he'd turn into a man in a pinstripe suit, Prince Bob from the Guggenheim Foundation. But instead of him, I got a letter offering me a job for one month in the Writers in the Schools program in Minneapolis, funded by the

NEA, directed by Molly LaBerge, which sent young writers into the schools to read and teach. In 1969, there were three such programs, in New York, California, and Minnesota; today, there's at least one in every state.

In 1974, a grant from the NEA enabled me and my colleagues at Minnesota Public Radio to start "A Prairie Home Companion." The help of the Endowment was crucial because the show wasn't that great to begin with. For our first broadcast, we had a crowd of twelve persons, and then we made the mistake of having an intermission and we lost half of them. The show wasn't obscene, just slow, and it took us a few years to figure out how to do a live radio show with folk music and comedy and stories about my home town of Lake Wobegon. By the time the show became popular and Lake Wobegon became so well-known that people thought it was real, the Endowment had vanished from the credits, its job done.

When you're starting out, it seems like nobody wants to give you a dime, and then, when you have a big success and have everything you could ever want, people can't do enough for you. The Endowment is there at the beginning, and that's the beauty of it.

When I was a young writer, I looked down on best-sellers as trash, but gradually over the years they improved and then suddenly one of them was mine. First, *Lake Wobegon Days* and then *Leaving Home,* and my desk filled up with offers to speak, to write, to appear, to endorse, which I've thoroughly enjoyed, but I remember very well when nobody else but my mother and the National Endowment was interested, and I'm grateful for this chance to express my thanks.

When I graduated from college, the degrees were given out in reverse order of merit, so I got mine early and had a chance to watch the others, and I remember the last graduate, the summest cum laude, a tall shy boy who walked up the stairs to the platform and en route stepped on the hem of his own gown and walked right up the inside of it. Like him, the Endowment has succeeded in embarrassing itself from time to time—to the considerable entertainment of us all—and like him, the Endowment keeps on going. It has contributed mightily to the creative genius of America—to the art and music and literature and theater and dance which, to my wife and other foreigners, is the most gorgeous aspect of this country. Long may it wave.

Should Government Give Direct Support to Artists and Writers?

JOHN UPDIKE

The Case against Government Support

I am honored to have been asked to testify at this hearing on a bill calling for a White House Conference on the Humanities. This is the first piece of testimony I have to offer. We in the humanities, whether we call ourselves men of letters or men of scholarship, are fascinated and charmed by power and anxious to please it.

The week after I accepted the invitation to speak here for 5 minutes today I received from the National Endowment for the Humanities in a succession of envelopes at least 2 pounds of xeroxed material, ranging from biographies of Chairman [Joseph D.] Duffey to appreciations of the paintings of Paul Cézanne, much of this material duplicatory or even triplicatory, but all of it testifying to the resources of the Secretary of Labor and photocopying equipment.

A freelance writer, working in a corner of his own home, producing his manuscripts on his own manual typewriter works on a Lilliputian scale and must view even this measure of interest in his work with a combination of gratitude and alarm as of a wren whose nest is being appraised by an eagle.

The essence of government is concern for the widest possible public interest. The essence of the humanities, it seems to me, is private study. Publicity is as essential to the one as privacy is to the other. Can these two realms then be joined without distortion? Is it true, as H.J. Res. 639 states, that the development and encouragement of national strength in the humanities is of the utmost importance to the life and heritage of the United States? And is it appropriate to encourage maximum participation by citizens?

I was educated in public schools. When my interests ranged beyond the curriculum there I found material for exploration in the surprisingly well-stocked public library of the nearby city. When I was a young writer I applied for and received a grant given by a private foundation, whose tax-exempt status represented an indirect Government investment in the humanities.

As an older writer I have been blessed with Government-sponsored memberships, invitations and travels. My friendship with writers and critics, including those in Communist and Third World countries, has made me emphatically appreciative of the freedoms and opportunities I enjoyed as an American.

I love my country's Government for its attempt in a precarious world to sustain a peaceful order in which work can be done and happiness can be pursued not for the good of the State but in a State that exists for our good.

I love my Government not least for the extent to which it leaves me alone. My personal ambition has been simply to live by the work of my pen. This is not a very fastidious ambition. If I were aware of large amounts of Federal money available to purveyors of the written words I would attempt to gain access to it and hope to please the administrators of this fund as I hope to please magazine editors and bookbuyers.

But I would rather have as my patron a host of anonymous citizens digging into their own pockets for the price of a book or a magazine than a small body of enlightened and responsible men administering public funds. I would rather chance my personal vision of the truth striking home here and there in the chaos of publication that exists than attempt to filter it through a few sets of official, honorable, public-spirited scrutinizers.

Rather than Government subsidies to ballet companies, I would rather see the Government reduce inflation so that these enterprises could again become self-supporting.

It can be said that the actual achievement of the National Endowment for the Humanities has been to expand the public exposure of privately produced works. When it was decided to dramatize a television series supported by a grant I was of course flattered that one of my stories was presented. But my own television set failed on the night of its screening. The text of the story was unchanged by the experience. But I had not written the story with broadcasting in mind.

The realms of scientific research are now inextricably involved with Government funding. Can we fear that the humanities might become similarly dependent? If I try to think of who in the last century has most brilliantly illuminated our sense of humanity, which I take to be the end purpose of the humanities, I think of Freud and Kafka, of Proust and Joyce, of Whitman, Henry James. I wonder how many of these brave, strange, stubborn spirits would have wanted subsidies from their governments.

How can public salaried men not think in terms of respectability, of social optimism, of broad and uncontroversial appeal? How can legislators, asked to vote tax money away, not begin to think of guidelines that insidiously edge toward censorship?

If Government money becomes an increasingly important presence in the financing of the humanities, is there a danger, I respectfully ask, of humanists becoming politicians?

Questions for Discussion

1. What is pornography? What role should government play with regard to pornography?
2. What role should government play in promoting the arts and the humanities?
3. Should government impose any restrictions on grants to artists and writers? What are the reasons for your answer?
4. Does government aid to the arts inevitably lead to censorship?
5. Should a museum that receives general government support be prevented from exhibiting controversial works? What are the reasons for your answer?

6. Should the same standard for government grants be applied to artists whose works deal with sexually explicit themes as to those whose works promote antisemitism or racism? Justify your answer.

Suggested Readings

Corn-Revere, Robert. "The New Assault on Artistic Freedom." *Student Lawyer*, 18, no. 6 (February 1990), 18–23.

Danto, Arthur C. "Art and the Taxpayers." *Nation*, 249, no. 6 (August 21–28, 1989), 192–193.

Frohnmayer, John. *Leaving Town Alive: Confessions of an Arts Warrior*. Boston: Houghton Mifflin, 1993.

Hughes, Robert. "Whose Art Is It Anyway?" *Time*, 135, no. 23 (June 4, 1990), 46–48.

Kramer, Hilton. "Is Art above the Laws of Decency?" *New York Times*, July 2, 1989, sec. II, pp. 1, 7.

Lipman, Samuel. "Backward and Downward with the Arts." *Commentary*, 89, no. 5 (May 1990), 23–26.

Ryerson, André. "Abolish the NEA: Government Is Incapable of Detecting Artistic Genius." *Policy Review*, no. 54 (Fall 1990), 32–37.

U.S. Cong., House of Representatives. *Hearing on the Rights of Artists and Scholars to Freedom of Expression and the Rights of Taxpayers to Determine the Use of Public Funds*. Hearing before the Subcommittee on Postsecondary Education of the Committee on Education and Labor, 101st Cong., 1st Sess., 1989.

———, Senate. *Reauthorization of the National Foundation on the Arts and Humanities Act: National Endowment for the Arts*. Hearings before the Subcommittee on Education, Arts and Humanities of the Committee on Labor and Human Resources, 101st Cong., 2d Sess., 1990.

Vance, Carole S. "The War on Culture." *Art in America*, 77, no. 9 (September 1989), 39, 41, 43, 45.

Chapter 21

Should the United States Adopt a Policy of Collective Security?

When the United States achieved its independence in the late eighteenth century, it was a small country, with thirteen states along the eastern seaboard. In protecting itself from hostile countries, it benefited from the Atlantic Ocean, which made sustained military operations difficult. At the time, Europe was the most likely candidate to generate serious security threats to North America.

And so U.S. foreign policy was based on isolationism, or noninterference in the kinds of foreign policy concerns that mattered most to European nations. George Washington stated the position squarely in his Farewell Address to the nation as he concluded his second term of office: "It is our true policy to steer clear of permanent alliance with any portion of the foreign world."[1] Until the twentieth century, the United States concerned itself more with its own internal economic and political development than it did with foreign policy. Not only did distance protect the United States, but so, too, did the global political situation and lack of military technology.

The strongest military powers in the world were in Europe, but Europe was not united. Instead it was marked by rivalries and alliances that pitted European nations against each other. The fact that European nations were more concerned with each other than with the United States made it easier for the United States to continue its policy of isolationism.

Lack of military technology, too, served to protect the United States. Air power did not have military application until the twentieth century. For a country to marshal its forces and conquer the United States, moreover, would require much time.

But the twentieth century saw great changes. When World War I broke out in 1914, the United States remained aloof and sought to continue its traditional policy of isolationism. But when German power became too strong, the United States intervened on the side of Great Britain, France, and their allies and helped to bring victory to the Allied Powers.

The United States tried to return to its policy of isolationism. When World War II started in Europe in 1939, the United States again tried to remain aloof. It was not until 1941, when Japan, a new military power in the world, attacked Pearl Harbor, that the United States became directly involved in that war. The United States faced two major enemies—Japan and Germany.

By 1945, Americans accepted the fact that their country could no longer maintain its isolationist position. New technology—air power and atomic bombs—had shown that distance no longer served to protect the nation as it had for more than a century. So now the United States was prepared to play a permanent role as a global power.

Soon after World War II came to an end in 1945, the cold war began. The term, "cold war," describes the conflict between the United States and its allies against the Soviet Union and its allies in which the two blocs regarded each other as mortal foes but sought to achieve advantages for the most part through political, economic, and propaganda means rather than through direct military confrontation. Both sides, moreover, created huge military establishments with nuclear weapons and sought to build global alliances.

World War II had so devastated Europe that the United States and the Soviet Union became the strongest military powers in the world. They were superpowers, and their foreign policies were preoccupied with each other.

The United States built a vast alliance system, with the cornerstone being the North Atlantic Treaty Organization (NATO). That alliance reversed George Washington's view and established a permanent relationship between the United States and other Western nations. As the leader of the Western alliance, the United States sought to protect countries facing domination by the Soviet Union and other communist countries.

A consensus developed in the United States that globalism—a belief that the United States should be involved in countries everywhere—was the correct policy. Although Americans divided on specific foreign policy issues, such as the Korean War and the Vietnam War, for the most part there was an American consensus that the United States could not withdraw from the world.

But toward the end of the 1980s, the Soviet system began to crumble. The Soviet economy was in a shambles. Soviet domestic politics was in disarray as most of the Soviet republics sought independence or greater autonomy. Soviet influence over Eastern Europe diminished, and communist regimes toppled within a year, to be replaced in many cases by democratic governments. Finally, in December 1991, the Soviet Union itself broke apart into fifteen autonomous republics. The cold war was now over.

For more than four decades, the United States based its foreign policy on the Soviet–U.S. relationship. The United States had fought wars, provided economic and military assistance, and given diplomatic support with a primary goal of keeping Soviet power in check. But now the Soviet Union no longer existed. And Russia, the strongest independent country to emerge out of the dissolution of the Soviet Union, became the friend of the United States. The United States gave political and economic support to its new ally.

Even during the cold war, however, the United States also had to wrestle with global problems that had little or nothing to do with Soviet influence or communist ideology. Among these problems were trade relations with its allies, most particularly Japan; the rise of a militarist Iraq;

the proliferation of nuclear, chemical, and biological weapons of mass destruction; and violations of human rights in many of the poor countries in Latin America, Africa, and Asia.

With the end of the cold war, these problems emerged anew. As the U.S. trade deficit with Japan rose, many voices in the United States demanded protectionism. When Iraq invaded Kuwait in 1990, the United States formed a coalition under United Nations auspices. The coalition of U.S. and allied military forces went to war with Iraq in 1991 and liberated Kuwait. Weapons of mass destruction proliferated in countries that had expansionist claims, such as Iran and North Korea. And Americans debated what U.S. foreign policy should be in reaction to the human rights violations in China and Haiti.

Two issues that occupied national attention in 1992–1993 were the grim situation in the African country of Somalia and the breakup of Yugoslavia. In Somalia, thousands of people died in the midst of civil conflict and a collapse of law and order. Bands of thugs prevented food from being distributed to starving people. The United States used its power, including military and economic support, to become part of a United Nations effort to restore order. The politics of starvation came to an end, and gradually order was restored.

Yugoslavia was a far more difficult problem, because ethnic hatred and conflict among its peoples had thrived for centuries. In 1992–1993, television carried reports of atrocities committed against civilians, most notably in the war between the Serbs and Bosnians. The Serbs sought to incorporate Bosnian territory into Serbia. Some commentators and political figures called for the United States to take military action. President George Bush did not take military action. President Bill Clinton was unwilling in 1993 to use military force. But in 1994, he approved the use of U.S. air power in limited circumstances against the Serbs.

The policies of the United States in Somalia and Yugoslavia suggest that the future course of U.S. foreign policy is unclear. With the United States as the only superpower in the world, Americans now debate how to adapt to new global conditions. At the core of the debate is whether the United States should pursue a policy of collective security or collective defense. In a policy of collective security, the United States joins with other countries through regional alliances or through the United Nations to put down aggression everywhere. In a policy of collective defense, the United States organizes its foreign policy to fight to thwart a specific aggressor. The debate is captured in the two articles from the journal *Foreign Policy.*

Edward C. Luck, president of the United Nations Association of the U.S.A., argues for a U.S. foreign policy of collective security. He contends

1. Even without the cold war, the United States remains a global power because of its military, political, and economic assets.
2. Subnational violence may result in international problems involving refugees, national minorities, and weapons proliferation.

3. The strength of the U.S. economy depends on stable conditions in many regions of the world since the United States needs overseas markets.
4. Playing an activist foreign policy role does not mean that the United States has to adopt a reflexive military response to every incident of violence or repression around the world. It does mean that the United States should encourage the use of a variety of measures available under the Charter of the United Nations.
5. The United States would benefit from a strengthening of the collective security resources of the United Nations.

Doug Bandow, a senior fellow at the Cato Institute, argues for collective defense. He contends

1. The foremost duty of the U.S. government is to protect the American people's lives, freedom, property, and constitutional system.
2. It is not in the interest of the United States to eliminate international disorder and instability by preventing aggression and squelching civil conflict, since global disorder per se does not threaten the United States.
3. Even Iraq's intervention in Kuwait did not threaten U.S. security interests. Hence, it should not be used as a model for further intervention.
4. Collective security has practical weaknesses both through regional alliances or through the United Nations.
5. By adopting a policy of strategic independence, the United States need not and should not pursue a policy of political isolation.

NOTE

1. George Washington, "Farewell Address to the People of the United States," first published in *Daily American Advertiser* (Philadelphia), September 19, 1796, reprinted as U.S. Cong., House Document 504, 89th Cong., 2nd Sess., 1966, p. 24.

Should the United States Adopt a Policy of Collective Security?

EDWARD C. LUCK

Making Peace

To intervene or not to intervene has become the critical question in an election year [1992] otherwise devoid of consequential foreign policy debate. Despite graphic scenes of repression, violence, and starvation in Bosnia-Herzegovina, Somalia, and the republics of the former Soviet Union, influential voices are urging America and its allies to look the other way and to forsake additional international responsibilities. But passivity in an era of sweeping changes across the global geopolitical map is myopic and risky, in terms of both America's interests and the lost opportunities to build a stronger system of collective security.

The intervention debate has been conducted less between Republicans and Democrats, conservatives and liberals, hawks and doves, than between competing conceptions of American national interests and responsibilities. Neo-isolationists of the right and left tell us that the demise of the Soviet threat permits a much narrower and more unilateral definition of national security. They would replace collective security with selective security. Tired of the Cold War's burden, they look to others to take the lead in ensuring the subsequent peace. On the other side, largely centrist internationalists see parallels between 1992 and 1936, and they are convinced that the maintenance of our security and our principles is inextricably linked to the course of global events. Neither our security nor our values can long stand if they are not defended collectively when they are seriously challenged.

The debate hinges on three fundamental questions: Does the United States have a significant stake in the way in which the international community handles large-scale violence, wherever it occurs? If American interests are deemed to be involved, when should the U.S. response be unilateral and when as part of a collective international effort, mounted regionally or globally? Finally, are existing collective security mechanisms, chiefly the United Nations, capable of handling such new challenges, and what should be done to strengthen those mechanisms?

Without the moral compass of the struggle against communism, it has admittedly become much harder to distinguish the white hats from the black hats in the localized violence that grips the world. The United States has neither allies nor enemies in most of the conflicts, and hence little stake in who wins or loses. There is no longer need to worry about a local conflict's implications for the broader competition between the superpowers. Based on Washington's new post–Cold War calculus, countries like Mozambique, Somalia, and Yugoslavia that were seen as strategically important only a few years ago now seem more relevant to our humanitarian sensibilities than to our hard-headed national security interests. Events in those areas, we are told, lacked intrinsic significance; it was only their effect on the Soviet-American equation that made them important.

That radical redefinition of American interests suits those on the left who have always resented foreign adventurism and large defense commitments as well as those on the right who have never been comfortable with international entanglements but were motivated to support an activist, containment-oriented foreign policy largely for ideological reasons. At a time of recession at home, moreover, all Americans are tempted to grasp at rationales for turning attention and resources inward.

The difficulty politicians and pundits alike are having in reconstructing a compelling basis for U.S. foreign policy in the wake of the demise of the Soviet Union suggests the degree to which our policies for the past 45 years have been essentially reactive and derivative. Now, without the ambitions of Soviet communism to contain, America lacks a positive strategy for world leadership. There are, however, enduring, nonpartisan reasons for the United States to concern itself with the international community's response to large-scale violence, human suffering, and human rights abuses—even in distant places and among unfamiliar people.

Whether the neo-isolationists like it or not, the United States has been the quintessential global power for almost half a century. Our country possesses a unique combination of military, economic, and political assets acquired over time precisely to protect and nurture our global interests. Some Americans chant that we are number one even as they complain that we cannot afford the costs of leadership; we cannot have it both ways. If we want to retain our status as a world leader, then we cannot walk away from our responsibilities simply because they entail risks and costs. There are also significant and uncertain risks in forfeiting America's leadership position to another country or countries, whether globally or regionally, in a world of such rapid and unpredictable change. Do we really want to encourage other states to fill the void left by an American retreat? Could we then easily and peacefully reassert our preeminence, should our interests be threatened?

Subnational violence may be a much broader threat to international security than it would at first appear. Refugees, national minorities, and weapons proliferation may well trigger a 1990s version of the domino effect. Although it is not inevitable that ethnic, religious, or tribal violence in one country will spread to its neighbors, there are usually significant spill-over effects: The refugee flow from the Balkans and Eastern Europe provides a pretext for the revival of neo-Nazism in Germany and for less-violent unrest elsewhere in Western Europe. Russian nationalists have threatened to upend the Yeltsin government because it has not, in their eyes, been sufficiently militant about the fate of Russian minorities living in the neighboring states of the former Soviet Union. If the multiple conflicts in the former Yugoslavia are allowed to continue, they could provoke a much broader Balkan war. We cannot take for granted that Turkey and Iran will stand by if the Muslim population of Bosnia-Herzegovina faces further slaughter, or that Albania will remain neutral if the violence spreads to

Kosovo, where Serbs govern a population that is 90 percent ethnic Albanian. Local violence in the Balkans and Eastern Europe has already fueled two world wars this century, so unrestrained subnational conflict in the region can hardly be dismissed as a purely European matter.

With the collapse of the Soviet Union and Russia's emergence as a strategic partner of America, the most immediate military threat to the United States is the global proliferation of weapons of mass destruction—nuclear, chemical, and biological—and of the advanced aircraft and missile systems used to deliver them. Two decades of U.S. efforts to advocate non-proliferation, along with multiple layers of international constraints, have helped to slow weapons proliferation. Ultimately, however, it will be necessary to create conditions that reduce the demand for advanced weapons of mass destruction. That effort will entail more decisive and consistent efforts by the international community to enforce a geographically inclusive concept of collective security. A laissez-faire American approach to regional conflicts would have the opposite effect. When the United States and other major powers abdicate their global responsibilities, they tempt would-be regional combatants to fill the void by amassing advanced weaponry. If we do not provide security incentives and disincentives in a given region, we lose much of our influence over local actors and the course of events there. To act only after a local bully has acquired excessive weaponry and, as in the case of Saddam Hussein, has used it against a weaker neighbor is to force an unappetizing choice between a massive military response and a major strategic debacle. Early and collective intervention in such cases may be the stitch that saves nine.

JOBS AND STABILITY

Although the 1992 presidential candidates focused on jobs, not foreign policy, the two issues are connected. In recent years, the fastest growing sector of the U.S. economy has been exports, and the fastest growing markets for American exports have been in the developing regions of the world. In times of recession and stagnant demand at home, foreign trade is doubly important.

Economic rationales for intervention in Kuwait were much stronger than those for intervention in the former Yugoslavia, and they are much less compelling for intervention in Mozambique, Cambodia, or Somalia. But war and instability, wherever they occur, undermine international commerce (except for the arms trade). They impoverish fragile local economies, increase dependence on foreign aid, and reduce demand for the food, services, and goods produced in America. Instability discourages foreign investment and puts existing investment at risk. Local capital is diverted from productive uses to destructive ones, and violence destroys the infrastructure needed to facilitate new trade and investment. War consumes scarce resources and degrades the environment. According to the *Arab Economic Report,* for example, the Persian Gulf war cost Arab countries $620 billion—an extraordinary diversion of productive resources.

Commerce likes stability and predictability; it shuns lawlessness and chaos whether in domestic or international society. As the social and economic structures of whole countries are destroyed by domestic or transnational violence, the character of U.S. economic relations with them tends to shift from private sector initiatives to government-led humanitarian assistance. That kind of dependency relationship creates a global-scale welfare system, rather than the kind of privatization and encouragement of local entrepreneurship that conservative critics say they would like to foster.

More fundamentally, without the unifying theme of the containment of communism, U.S. foreign policy lacks an underlying strategic rationale for the post–Cold War era. While case-by-case pragmatism may be a reasonable tactical approach, it serves neither to integrate the various aspects of U.S. security policy, nor to present a guide for responding to new contingencies, nor to rally domestic opinion and international support for American initiatives. The public is skeptical about American foreign policy because its post–Cold War strategic underpinnings have yet to be explained in a coherent and compelling manner. People can understand our domestic programs, but the rationale for our foreign policy remains murky.

Those misgivings are reinforced by the lack of any clear moral basis for our foreign policy choices. Democratization is said to be important, except in the world's most populous country, China. Likewise, Operation Desert Storm, launched in the name of defending democratic principles, restored a hereditary emir to his throne and left a cruel dictator in power in Baghdad. The Bush administration resists intervention in Bosnia-Herzegovina because it would become a "quagmire," despite graphic evidence of a genocidal campaign of "ethnic cleansing." Millions of Somalis face starvation, yet American and European leaders looked the other way for months because they no longer deemed the country strategically significant. Similarly, the continuing civil war in Afghanistan ceased to be a front-page issue as soon as Soviet forces withdrew. It is small wonder that the American people have lost faith in policies that lack a strategic or moral framework.

As the new administration seeks to recast foreign and security policies for post–Cold War conditions, it should place renewed emphasis on human rights and humanitarian concerns. Respect for international law—including the rights of national minorities, pluralism, and democratic principles—reinforces stability and discourages aggression. Those norms serve American strategic and economic interests. Moreover, administration policies that address the twin concerns of humanitarian and democratic principles would attract broad bipartisan support, rebuilding a durable domestic constituency for U.S. foreign policy.

THE UN MISSION

Neither the American public nor the UN [United Nations] member states are prepared to play the role of world policeman if it entails a reflexive military response to every incident of violence or repression around the world. Rather, they want a strategy that first encourages peaceful conflict resolution and includes intervention criteria that can be applied with a fair degree of consistency. The UN Charter prescribes an often-overlooked continuum of steps for dealing with threats to international peace and security that is as relevant today as in 1945.

According to the Charter, the first responsibility for reaching a peaceful resolution lies with the parties to a dispute, with the international community acting as mediator, observer, fact-finder, arbiter, or guarantor. In those roles, the player with the greatest credibility should take the lead: the United States in the Middle East and South Africa; the UN in Central America, the rest of Africa, and Southeast Asia; the UN and the Europeans together in Eastern Europe. The key is flexibility and a rational division of labor. Threats of sanctions or other enforcement measures may focus the minds of the adversaries and speed negotiations.

Should the parties fail to settle their differences, even with the encouragement of the international community, the Charter then calls on regional organizations to take action under the auspices of the UN Security Council. In most parts of the world, however, regional organizations are weak and their record on peacemaking has been mixed at best. They generally lack the peacekeeping traditions, the resources, and the political unity the council can increasingly muster.

The chief advantage of a regional approach—proximity to the conflict—is often also its most conspicuous disadvantage. Too often local powers have a vested interest in a regional conflict's outcome that the UN, by its very distance, does not. The European Community and NATO [North Atlantic Treaty Organization], which look the most capable on paper, have proven to be divided and ineffectual in dealing with problems in their own backyard—in Eastern Europe and the former Yugoslavia. NATO's traditions, moreover, preclude active out-of-area intervention. So regional organizations, meant to share the peacekeeping burden with the Security Council, have been the weakest link in the chain.

Initial efforts should be preventive. The UN and regional organizations should broadly interpret what constitutes a threat to international peace and security in order to intervene early and peacefully in a wide range of situations with the potential for significant violence. That determination allows diplomats to test the waters and gain a better understanding of the situation before weighing more coercive measures. Only a much smaller percentage of cases should require the international community to move up the ladder and adopt sanctions or use force.

In the foreseeable future, four conditions are most likely to trigger international military intervention: first, a state is threatened or attacked by a powerful neighbor; second, a national government collapses, leaving chaos and widespread domestic violence in its place; third, a government or group commits human rights violations on a genocidal scale; or, fourth, a government engages in rogue behavior, such as sponsoring terrorism or proliferating weapons of mass destruction, in blatant disregard of established international norms. Recent polling by "Americans Talk Issues" suggests that a large majority of Americans would like to see the United States and the UN take military action against dictators in those circumstances. Before undertaking military interventions, however, international bodies should be sure that sufficient political will and financial and military resources are available to see the operation through, even if complications are encountered; that the potential benefits outweigh the likely human and material costs; that the prospects for success are at least relatively good; and, finally, that nonviolent means cannot achieve the same result.

While it is fashionable to dismiss sanctions because they are rarely sufficient to compel a determined aggressor to reverse course, they offer three often-overlooked advantages. First, they pull the international community together, building consensus and allowing it to express common concerns over a country's actions. Second, over time sanctions can stimulate domestic opposition to a regime's behavior and erode support for aggressive or repressive policies. Their effect is slow and subtle, but, if properly enforced, sanctions can make a real difference. Third, as in the case of Iraq, sanctions provide a politically useful stepping stone toward the eventual use of force, even as they give diplomats time to try to convince the aggressor to relent. In fact, the effectiveness of sanctions depends in part on whether the leading countries are perceived to be willing to use force should sanctions fail. For most of its 47-year existence, the UN has had little credibility in enforcing Security Council decisions; its collective security mechanism sits largely unused and untested. While the UN occasionally earned decent marks for its peacemaking and peacekeeping efforts, serious enforcement was accomplished unilaterally and selectively by the major military powers. Multilateralism, to its legion of critics, seemed just another word for doing nothing—an internationalist way of abandoning our foreign responsibilities.

With the end of the Cold War, all that is changing. That there has been no veto on a substantive issue in the Security Council for more than two years has created a presumption of consensus, or at least confidence that none of the veto-wielding powers will block international action. President George Bush and the leaders of countries East and West now regularly invoke the name and authority of the United Nations to lend credibility and legitimacy to their actions, whether undertaken individually or with partners. Even with its pre-eminent military prowess, the United States finds it both financially and politically preferable to enlist other partners, and if possible the UN Security Council, in collective security actions. When the president sought the Senate's blessing for the use of force in the Persian Gulf, he did so in the name of the UN Security Council and of a 28-country coalition, even though the United States and a few allies would do the bulk of the fighting. The UN flag made it easier both to attract partners internationally and to gain popular support at home.

Americans have not turned away from the world—as public opinion polls and the fate of neo-isolationists in this year's primaries attest—but they do not want to bear the cost of policing the world on their own. They understand that other countries are quite capable of sharing the economic costs of collective security, and they recognize that the United States cannot afford to try to do the job alone while our primary economic competitors focus on building their comparative advantage in world trade. The United Nations provides the only generally accepted mechanism for determining the global division of labor, and its burden-sharing formula requires other countries to carry 70 percent of the costs.

In a recent Roper Poll sponsored by the United Nations Association of the U.S.A. (UNA-USA), Americans preferred, by a three-to-one margin, to send the UN's blue helmets rather than U.S. forces to handle regional conflicts, even if it means that the outcome would not necessarily further unilateral U.S. interests. When our allies or enemies are not involved and our objective is to restore peace rather than to gain advantage, it makes good sense to seek a multilateral solution—to choose a collective security over selective security. On the other hand, when the United States has important national interests at stake that are not shared by others on the Security Council, then unilateral action may be the only choice.

Faced with recession at home and the collapse of their chief adversary abroad, some Americans simply want to hand their global responsibilities over to the UN. That, however, is not an option. The UN has no capabilities beyond those its members assign to it. Working through the UN may ease one's burdens by getting others to share them, but it does not eliminate them. The United States, in particular, will be expected to take the lead politically in rallying others to action—and in providing its unique military assets.

A problem arises, however, if the United States and its allies bring to the UN only those issues on which they are unwilling to act but that also garner considerable media attention, leading them to pressure international organizations to assume the burden in a very public fashion. It creates a no-win situation—a strategic Catch-22—for the UN and regional bodies, which cannot be expected to resolve difficult collective security challenges in which the major powers are unwilling to play their part as the eventual enforcers of international will. If the major powers employ international organizations chiefly as public relations vehicles and fail to supply them with the means to get the job done, then the credibility of those organizations, and that of collective norms and decisions, will suffer. Once again, the world will see the UN as a talk shop where performance rarely matches expectations. The world's best chance since 1945 for creating an effective collective security system will be irretrievably lost.

The former Yugoslavia is a good, if sad, case in point. In Croatia, the UN deployed a significant peacekeeping force to police a cease-fire agreement, and it successfully reduced instability and sharply curbed "ethnic cleansing." In neighboring Bosnia-Herzegovina, on the other hand, a modest contingent of UN peacekeepers has been caught in the untenable crossfire with neither the resources nor the mandate to bring the atrocities to an end. Although the nature of events and world public opinion is slowly forcing the leaders of the major powers toward greater engagement, the combatants fight on, unimpressed with the UN's resolve or the slow and reactive character of its policies. Had Security Council members moved quickly and decisively at the time of the Bosnian plebiscite on independence, the story would have been very different.

The other tragic casualty of Security Council caution and indecisiveness is Somalia. Again, the response of the major powers and UN agencies has been too little, too late. Well over 100,000 Somalis have starved to death and all governmental authority has collapsed while the international community has fretted about the risks of humanitarian intervention in such a chaotic, violent environment. Sovereignty was not the question, since no central authority remained in Mogadishu and Somalia had virtually ceased to exist as a state. The problem was instead one of providing sufficient international force to protect food aid and to ensure its safe delivery despite roving gangs armed with machine guns. The risks were real, but the military task was quite limited compared to facing down the Iraqis or even the Serbs. Instead of dispatching the few thousand troops necessary to secure the ports and supply routes, a weary council hesitated and temporized for months, haggling over whether the contribution should be voluntary or assessed. The first UN force did not reach Somalia to help guard the growing flow of humanitarian assistance until September, after tons of food aid had been stolen.

Experiences like those are beginning to give collective security a bad name. Rather than following the military dictum of responding rapidly with a show of force, the United States and others on the Security Council have chosen to move timidly and reactively, allowing others to dictate the course of events. Western governments generally assume that their citizens will oppose participation in international peacekeeping and peace enforcement; yet the opposite is often true. Clinging to outmoded concepts of security, governments resist collective action, treating it as an unusual step rather than as the natural way to handle situations of aggression or massive human suffering beyond the realm of traditional spheres of influence. National governments have not yet accumulated sufficient experience in using the UN and regional organizations to respond to such cases. Situations have had to escalate far out of control, with human costs rising proportionately, before the United States and other leading Western governments have decided to support effective international action. Getting in early improves chances for making a positive difference; waiting often forces an unattractive choice between intervention or passivity late in the game, when the stakes and risks of either option are much higher.

BEGGARING THE UN

The ambivalence of the United States and other major powers toward the United Nations as an instrument of collective security is reflected in the inadequacy of the tools they have given it for the task. The world organization—like its regional counterparts—simply lacks the military capabilities and financial wherewithal to do its job. Only in rare instances have the major military powers been willing to put significant units of their own armed forces at the service of UN operations, and even in those cases their command and control remained outside the UN. Ironically, among the most reluctant have been the five permanent members of the Security Council that possess a veto over that body's decisions and that can hence be assured that their forces would not be used without their approval. If those in control are not ready to put their forces under UN command, then surely those members with little voice in deployment decisions cannot be expected to do so.

Financial constraints and squabbles over how to fund UN operations increasingly impinge on their effectiveness. Member states owe the UN more than $1 billion in dues for the regular budget and peacekeeping, with the United States and Russia, still the world's biggest deadbeats, forcing the organization to look beyond the permanent members to make up the shortfall. There are no reserves to call upon and members greet each proposal for a new mission with time-consuming debate about how to pay for it. While the Security Council has sole power to authorize missions, the General Assembly retains the power of the purse and thus has a controlling voice over the size and cost of new missions. In the case of Namibia, the tug-of-war between major donors in the council and African states in the assembly delayed the deployment of forces so long that it almost undermined the mission. In Bosnia and Somalia, misgivings by the Security Council and key member states—the United States included—over funding helped to postpone UN involvement. Financial uncertainties also seriously delayed dispatch of forces to Cambodia and Croatia.

During the first half of 1992, the number and cost of soldiers wearing the UN's blue helmets quadrupled to 44,000 and $2.8 billion. The steep rise no doubt caught a number of legislatures, including the U.S. Congress, unprepared. Congress granted the Bush administration a two-year $700 million supplemental to help cover the country's 30.4 per cent share of the new peacekeeping costs, but even that money is proving insufficient for the tasks at hand.

A long-term solution to the UN's budget problem will require more than a one-time, band-aid approach. The demand for the UN's peacekeeping and collective security services will continue to grow rapidly, especially during this transitional period in world politics. All the grandiose talk of a new world order will prove premature if the most powerful countries fail to put the collective security machinery of the UN and regional organizations on a secure financial footing. It is ludicrous that the United States, for example, finds it so difficult to contribute the equivalent of less than one-half of 1 percent of its defense budget to pay for UN peacekeeping. The logic of those who call for the continued accumulation of massive military power and yet object to its use in foreign interventions is especially baffling. Apparently they expect the UN, without resources, to perform minor miracles, while the great powers, with huge arsenals and no adversaries to fight or deter, stand by.

The United Nations cannot be an effective instrument for collective security until it has the resources—financial, military, and political—to move quickly, decisively, and forcefully to deal with small conflicts before they develop into big ones. Secretary-General Boutros Boutros-Ghali, in his forward-looking June

1992 report, *An Agenda for Peace,* has modestly called for the creation of a revolving peacekeeping reserve fund of $50 million to match a similar recently established Humanitarian Revolving Fund. Given the growing demand for peacekeeping operations, the sum seems too small. Assuming that the member states' operational assessments replenish the fund, it would be reasonable to put one-fifth of the UN's annual peacekeeping bill, or between $500 and $600 million, into a revolving fund. The fund could be built by a one-time assessment, or by collecting outstanding arrearages.

While anathema in Washington, former secretary-general Javier Pérez de Cuellar's call for interest payments on outstanding dues also makes good sense, though the UN should allow debtor countries a two-year grace period to make up their payments. That delay would give a new administration in Washington, and perhaps the Russians, time to catch up. Those measures should be undertaken in the context of a general review of the regular budget and peacekeeping assessments of all member states. Members of Congress are beginning to ask why the UN assesses the United States, and other permanent members, at a higher rate for peacekeeping than for other UN expenses, and there are a number of larger or relatively affluent developing countries that could do more. With 20 new UN members in little more than a year, and more on the way, the assessment formula needs rethinking. Moreover, as the UN begins to undertake more substantial military operations, the way that member states are reimbursed for their military services should be reviewed as well.

Boutros-Ghali's report also endorses the idea of having states pay their peacekeeping assessments through their defense rather than their foreign ministries, both because of the nature of the task and because it would provide a large pool from which to draw the funds. With the urging of the UNA–USA, Congress has authorized up to $300 million of FY 1993 Defense Department funds for new UN peacekeeping costs, to be released if requested by the president. Senator Paul Simon (D-Illinois) plans to introduce legislation in 1993 to shift peacekeeping funding from the State Department to Defense on a permanent basis. The objective is not just to find a more robust funding source, but to define support for UN peacekeeping and collective security efforts as one of the primary missions of the U.S. military in the post–Cold War era. It is a mission that those in the Pentagon with UN peacekeeping and humanitarian relief experience would welcome.

While the Bush administration has responded cautiously to all of the innovative funding proposals, the two most sensitive issues for Washington—and for many other UN members—involve making forces "available to the Security Council," as called for by Article 43 of the Charter, and bringing the Military Staff Committee, established in Article 47, to life as an international body "to advise and assist" the council on military matters. It has been widely assumed that the American public would strongly oppose sending U.S. troops to fight as part of a UN force or under an international command. However, the UNA–USA's recent Roper Poll suggests that the public is actually evenly divided, perhaps even open-minded, on the point. The public is evenly divided on whether it would be better to make a standing commitment to a UN force or to decide on a case-by-case basis, as well as on whether those U.S. forces should serve under an overall UN command or only under the control of the U.S. president. When pollsters rephrased the question to ask whether forces from the United States and other member countries should be under UN command or that of individual governments, a 50 to 35 percent plurality preferred that the United Nations take charge. It is encouraging to see how well American officers have worked for years under international commands in UN peacekeeping operations in Cambodia, Kuwait, and the Middle East, as well as on a much larger scale in NATO.

The UN probably does not need—and the secretary-general evidently does not want—a large standing military force, a force that would require extensive military installations and outlays for food, clothing, and training. The UN, moreover, certainly could not begin to afford the costs of the vast logistical support or the airlift and sealift capability required to project force around the globe. For that support, it will have to rely on the United States and, to a lesser extent, other major powers. But there is every reason, under current circumstances, to have member states earmark standby forces under Article 43 for rapid call-up by the council and to reactivate the Military Staff Committee to provide planning and coordination.

The UN needs two kinds of standby forces: one for traditional peacekeeping (lightly armed "soldiers without enemies") and the other for peace enforcement under Chapter VII of the Charter (more heavily armed and highly mobile ground forces with air, sea, and intelligence support from the major military powers). A large number of member states currently volunteer forces for peacekeeping missions, so the shortcomings have less to do with quantity or geographical balance than with training, communications, the prepositioning and standardization of equipment, logistics, and, of course, funding. Article 43 forces, on the other hand, should consist of whole units at the brigade or even division level from the land and marine forces of the significant military powers, so that they are as militarily sophisticated as any adversary they might be called on to combat. The total standby force might number between 50,000 and 100,000, which should be adequate to handle a whole range of contingencies short of a Desert Storm.

Such a force would be designed to discourage aggression by serving as a tripwire or deterrent. It would reestablish order in countries where all governmental authority has collapsed, protect the growing number of relatively defenseless ministates from aggressive neighbors, and ensure the delivery of humanitarian relief in extreme circumstances, as in Somalia. If deployed on the border of a state being threatened by a neighboring country—such as Bosnia at the time of its declaration of independence in March 1992, Kuwait in the summer of 1990, or Iran before Iraq's invasion in 1980—UN peace enforcement units could play an important role in forestalling subsequent aggression and the escalation of local hostilities.

This is serious business, of course, and it should not be undertaken lightly. The units should conduct extensive joint exercises and training missions throughout the year, making them a more credible deterrent and a more formidable fighting force. The Military Staff Committee, with representatives of the chiefs of staff of each of the five permanent members and with a network of regional subcommittees, will have to work out a general division of labor, along with effective command and control procedures. Most important, the major powers must be prepared to reinforce the units should their preventive role fail.

Giving the UN significant military and financial resources would be a major step forward, but a complete global collective security system will require other things as well: boosting the capabilities of regional organizations to play their intended role as the first recourse in cases of localized conflict; improving coordination and rationalizing the division of labor between regional and global efforts; persuading the United States and others to share their intelligence findings with the secretary-general and the Security Council on a fuller, prompter, and more regular basis; developing a deeper corps of distinguished global citizens—like former U.S. secretary of state Cyrus Vance—to help the secretary-general carry out his important peacemaking and peacebuilding roles; and, finally, reinforcing international constraints on weapons proliferation, especially in regions with a history of instability and violence.

In the end, however, the problem is not the system of collective security or even its lack of resources. Rather, it is the reluctance of the most influential member states—the United States first among them—to use it. Our thinking has still not adjusted to the realities of the post–Cold War world. If the member states see a UN that looks timid, weak, even anemic, it is in large part because they are looking at a reflection of their own policies. It is also because they are looking through myopic perspectives shaped by the history—not the potential—of internationalism. If we look carefully, we can see the initial stirrings of what could be a far more vigorous and dynamic system of collective security in the years ahead. It is a goal well worth nurturing, for the interests of America as well as the world.

 NO

Should the United States Adopt a Policy of Collective Security?

DOUG BANDOW
Avoiding War

The collapse of the Soviet Union and end of the Cold War are forcing a long-overdue reevaluation of American security policy. Traditional containment is dead, and the search for a replacement is on.

Today, the most discussed alternative is collective security, which, although inherently interventionist, would channel American military activity through a multilateral framework such as regional alliances or the United Nations [UN]. In fact, collective action has long been an important aspect of American foreign policy. The United States created several geographically oriented security organizations, like NATO [North Atlantic Treaty Organization], intended to defend against a particular aggressor. In addition, the United States gained the UN's imprimatur for combat in South Korea and the Persian Gulf. It has also long supported UN peacekeeping efforts elsewhere.

The question today is whether the United States should move from collective defense, which is directed at a specific aggressor, to collective security, which in principle is directed against all unnamed aggressors who violate international norms. Some who favor this step want to update America's Cold War alliances, particularly NATO, for the post–Cold War world. Others would grant the UN more authority to mount military operations against aggressors and perhaps settle civil wars. Since the Persian Gulf crisis, President George Bush has been advancing collective security under the rubric of the "new world order," promising in September 1992 to enhance international peacekeeping through U.S. military participation. But the roots of his approach go back to President Woodrow Wilson's crusade for democracy in World War I.

That experience, however, illustrates the many pitfalls of collective security. Wilson's aspiration to play global peacemaker led the United States into a war with only limited implications for its own security, and led to the sacrifice of nearly 120,000 young American men. Moreover, America's intervention allowed its allies to impose a one-sided peace that spawned a new and far worse war within a generation. Particularly in this new era when the international scene may grow more chaotic even as the threats to the United States decline, it is not in America's interest, nor is it even feasible, for Washington to act as the star player on a collective security team.

The United States emerged from World War II as the only power strong enough to contain what was believed to be an aggressive and dangerous Soviet Union. America instituted its containment policy by ringing the USSR [Union of Soviet Socialist Republics] and China with a network of alliances, bases, and forward deployments including the Rio Pact, NATO, the Australia–New Zealand–United States (ANZUS) agreement, the Southeast Asia Treaty Organization (SEATO), the Baghdad Pact (METO), the Central Treaty Organization (CENTO), and mutual defense treaties with Japan, the Philippines, and South Korea.

Unfortunately, Washington's series of alliances did not come cheap. In the early 1930s, the United States fielded an armed force of about 250,000. By 1945 the military forces had exploded to 12.8 million with $83 billion in expenditures in 1945 (roughly $870 billion in today's dollars). Although American force levels fell rapidly after World War II, the army alone remained larger than the entire military of the 1930s. As the Pentagon proved unable to maintain a force of that size at the wages it was willing to pay, Congress reinstated the draft, beginning 25 years of conscription. With the onset of the Korean War, military expenditures again rose dramatically, and the United States agreed to a "mutual defense" treaty guaranteeing South Korea's security. Never again did the United States reconsider its strategy of global containment.

Most of America's multilateral alliances, like ANZUS, are now moribund. Moreover, the USSR's collapse eliminated the justification for NATO, anchor of the Cold War collective defense system. But even as Russian troops withdraw from Europe, NATO remains in place and the Bush administration sees NATO as essentially permanent. The president has indicated that perhaps in some "utopian day"—a century of so from now—it might be possible to withdraw all U.S. troops.

Yet the mere fact that the Europeans want the United States to stay is not likely to persuade Congress or the American people that roughly 100,000 U.S. soldiers—the number mentioned by the incoming Clinton administration—should remain in Europe. In short, what is the quintessential anti-Soviet alliance to do without the Soviet Union? Embarrassed after the fall of the Berlin Wall, many pro-NATO policymakers and analysts seem to have fastened upon collective security as the alliance's raison d'être. They would, in short, transform NATO into a mini-UN, responsible for maintaining order and adjudicating disputes throughout Europe, among the former Soviet republics, and possibly in neighboring regions.

U.S. defense secretary Richard Cheney said in 1991 that NATO's efforts to recast itself "are clear proof of its ability to adapt creatively to the new security environment." Supporters of NATO argue the same thing. But their efforts probably represent something other than an attempt to further American interests: The rush to turn NATO into a mini-UN demonstrates the tendency of individuals to protect their own interests—in this case their own organization.

Proposals to reconfigure NATO concentrate on extending security guarantees to Eastern Europe against a resurgent Russia, seeking to manage the ethnic and nationalist instability rippling through the Balkans and the former Soviet Union, and creating a rapid deployment force for use in crises inside and outside of Europe.

Security Guarantees to Eastern Europe

Bulgaria, Czechoslovakia, Hungary, Poland, and Russia have all either requested security guarantees from NATO or have indicated an interest in joining what formally remains of the *North Atlantic* Treaty Organization. Former secretary of state Alexander Haig explicitly proposed expanding NATO to encompass all the former non-Soviet Warsaw Pact members, while in June 1991 NATO declared that the alliance would treat any "coercion or intimidation" of the Central or East European states as a matter of "direct and material concern."

Moreover, in November 1991 the NATO members created a North Atlantic Cooperation Council to expand collaboration with Russia, Eastern Europe, and the Baltic states. While the organization does not formally guarantee the security of any country, it opens the way for expanded military ties. Defense coordination and planning are likely to lead to greater Western entanglement in

Central European military affairs and demands for an explicit security commitment.

Seeking To Manage Ethnic and Nationalist Instability

Another potential collective security duty of a new NATO is "managing" change in areas formerly under communist domination. Civil war in Yugoslavia, conflicts between former Soviet republics, tension between Hungary and Romania, and revanchist sentiments fueled by displaced ethnic and nationalist groups across the East are instilling the West Europeans with fear. "We need NATO to protect us against ourselves," one Dutch official told the *Wall Street Journal*.

How far NATO will go to enforce stability is not clear. The North Atlantic Cooperation Council envisions only discussions. But in March 1992 the council considered a possible military role for NATO in Azerbaijan, a region roughly 1,700 miles from Western Europe. While NATO officials rejected any immediate intervention, they indicated they were pleased with the idea of backing up the alliance's peacekeeping efforts with force. Indeed, NATO is preeminently a military alliance and its relative "competitive advantage" compared to other organizations is its ability to intervene with force. Military action is the only way that the alliance can ensure "both security and stability," the benefits cited by then British prime minister Margaret Thatcher in 1989, when she was asked why NATO was still needed.

In fact, many NATO officials seem to favor military intervention for those reasons. Early in 1992, for instance, before the bitterest fighting in Bosnia-Herzegovina, General John Galvin, then the commander of U.S. troops in Europe, identified Yugoslavia as an example of "regional tensions" threatening U.S. interests. He has since been joined by numerous other analysts and officials advocating NATO's intervention in that conflict. Turkey, worried about the possible spread of combat in Azerbaijan, urged NATO involvement there to curb the civil war. Potentially even more far-reaching was the proposal of Dutch foreign minister Hans van den Broeck that NATO troops enforce cease-fires arranged through the 52-member Conference on Security and Cooperation in Europe (CSCE). Then secretary of state James Baker lauded the idea, and NATO secretary-general Manfred Wörner stated that "NATO may well lend material support or even troops to the CSCE if needed and if agreed by our member states."

Rapid Deployment Force For Use In Various Crises

Galvin long advocated creation of a "fire brigade" to respond to emergencies. In late 1990 he stated that "there is pretty good military agreement" among

NATO officers to move in that direction and cited the Persian Gulf war as a model for future NATO actions. Although NATO officials argue that such a force might be needed within Europe to meet threats from states other than Russia, to most advocates of NATO the real issue of responding to unnamed crises lies outside Europe. For instance, the *Economist* pointed to "the explosive Gulf" as a reason to preserve NATO even before Saddam Hussein's invasion of Kuwait. The *San Diego Union* has urged formally "amending the NATO treaty to give NATO the flexibility to intervene militarily outside Europe," a flexibility that the paper argues "could provide the United Nations a valuable adjunct in its efforts to maintain global stability." (In fact, Wörner argues that NATO has already in effect done so by providing important assistance to the UN during the Gulf war.)

NATO traditionally avoided so-called out-of-area activities, but it seems to be moving toward a broader view of its authority. In May 1991, NATO initiated the creation of a rapid reaction force of up to 70,000 soldiers. Six months later the member governments announced a new "strategic concept" that focuses on instability in Eastern Europe and the Mediterranean rather than on a conventional assault from Russia.

So far, NATO's European members have not been ready to extend the alliance's reach to other territory, but in November 1991 the Bush administration argued that without broader responsibilities NATO was likely to suffer reduced political, and hence financial, support in the United States. In part to satisfy Washington, NATO declared that "we reaffirm the continuing importance of consulting together on events outside the treaty area which may have implications for our security." By the summer of 1992, NATO governments were edging closer to the Yugoslavian imbroglio, with Wörner announcing NATO's readiness to provide some 6,000 troops for UN operations to protect aid shipments to besieged Sarajevo. Cooperation with Eastern Europe and Russia also appears to be opening the door for out-of-area intervention. And possible mechanisms to enforce CSCE cease-fires would subtly expand NATO's military jurisdiction to other regions.

COLLECTIVE SECURITY THROUGH THE UN

The United Nations itself offers the second major variant of a collective security strategy. Should NATO and the UN simultaneously enforce a security regime, one or the other is likely to end up with a paramount role. Because NATO commands actual troops, it would probably win any competition with the UN (unless the alliance effectively put its forces at the disposal of the UN Security Council). Only in out-of-area activities far from Europe—which could, however, account for the bulk of future conflicts—does the UN arguably have a comparative advantage over NATO. Further, it is also possible that NATO will not ultimately survive the loss of its longstanding justification with the USSR's collapse, leaving the UN the preeminent collective security forum.

That was, in fact, the original vision for the United Nations. The allied success in World War II encouraged a widespread desire for an international regime that could achieve what Woodrow Wilson had hoped for his ill-fated League of Nations: international order policed collectively by countries. At the Versailles peace talks, Wilson said that "if the moral force of the world will not suffice, the physical force of the world shall." A generation later, America enthusiastically helped establish a global organization, and agreed to a charter that explicitly vests the Security Council with "primary responsibility for the maintenance of international peace and security." The Charter also established procedures for dispute resolution, enforcement activity, and use of armed forces provided by member states. Most of those provisions have never been used, largely because the Cold War disrupted continued allied cooperation, with the Soviet Union using its veto to deadlock the Security Council.

In theory, the UN has enormous authority. Article 42 of the Charter empowers the Security Council to "take such action by air, sea, or land forces as may be necessary to maintain or restore international peace and security." Article 45 orders member states to "hold immediately available national air-force contingents for combined international enforcement action" so that the UN can "take urgent military measures." Plans for military action are to be drafted by a Military Staff Committee. Of particular interest is Article 43, which specifies how the UN can raise a military:

> All Members of the United Nations . . . undertake to make available to the Security Council, on its call and in accordance with a special agreement or agreements, armed forces, assistance, and facilities, including rights of passage, necessary for the purpose of maintaining international peace and security.

The end of the Cold War and Moscow's subsequent cooperation in the Gulf war have led a growing number of observers to embrace the UN's original promise. Secretary-General Boutros Boutros-Ghali, for one, issued a report in June 1992, *An Agenda for Peace,* advocating fulfillment of Article 43. In September 1992 the Security Council established a working group to review his proposals. Similar ideas are swirling around foreign capitals, Washington think tanks, and the conference circuit.

French president François Mitterrand, for instance, has proposed revitalizing the Military Staff Committee, after which his country would place 1,000 soldiers at the UN's disposal on 48-hours notice and another 1,000 troops deployable within a week. Analysts including the former UN under-secretary-general for special political affairs, Brian Urquhart, have promoted the use of Article 43 to give the UN sufficient forces to intervene in civil wars like those in Yugoslavia and Somalia, as well as in other countries where "sovereignty is also dissolving into anarchy." Urquhart envisions "armed police actions" between peacekeeping and large-scale intervention such as that in the Persian Gulf.

Seizing upon Mitterrand's proposal, *New York Times* columnist Flora Lewis urged the UN to acquire "a permanent force in readiness, loyal to its flag and to no state," perhaps made up of Nepalese Gurkhas, which could be supplemented by national contributions. Political scientist Joseph Nye proposed creating a UN "rapid-deployment force" of 60,000 soldiers, with a core of 5,000 troops who would train regularly. In the case of large-scale aggression, as in Kuwait, or a major civil war, as in Yugoslavia, he called for "an American-led coalition."

Washington Post columnist Jim Hoagland envisions a UN operation to suppress the Yugoslavian conflict that is backed, but not led, by the United States. He would give the world body "peacekeeping power," exercised through the Security Council, in order "to turn the UN into an effective agent to restrain regional conflict." Similarly, Senator Joseph Biden (D-Delaware) would use the Security Council to "regularize the kind of multilateral response we assembled for the Gulf War." Since the United Nations lacks its own forces, a multilateral approach is implicit in the council's June 1992 demand that Bosnia's Serbs surrender their heavy weapons or face the consequences. Ostensibly, Americans are coming to support such ideas. Fifty-five per cent of those asked in one recent poll said they are willing to rely on UN forces even in conflicts where U.S. interests are at risk.

The two basic models for expanding UN collective security responsibilities derive, first, from the UN's traditional peacekeeping activities and, second, from its major wars, in Korea and the Gulf. The UN is currently involved in 11 peacekeeping operations, employing 50,220 soldiers, who have been volunteered by individual states. The enterprises vary dramatically in scope, ranging from 40 observers in Kashmir to 22,000 participants planned for Cambodia. The major controversy bedeviling UN peacekeeping today is cost. Under anachronistic postwar rules the United States is to provide 30 per cent of total funding, and the rapid expansion of UN activities over the past year has caused expenses to outstrip contributions rapidly, leaving the United States deeply in arrears for its peacekeeping assessments.

Both large-scale UN conflicts point up a different collective security model. With the Soviet delegate temporarily boycotting the Security Council, that body in 1950 authorized under the Charter's Chapter VII the creation of a multinational force to repel North Korean aggression against the Republic of Korea (ROK). Washington unilaterally made the war's major decisions. General Douglas MacArthur, the American commander of the UN forces, never reported to the Security Council, and his forces were predominantly American. Toward the war's end, in June 1953, U.S. forces had grown to 302,483—89 percent of all non-ROK soldiers. Casualties showed a similar distribution.

The Security Council decided not to create a UN joint command during the Persian Gulf war. The United States formally observed the conditions of the council's resolutions, but enjoyed some latitude in deciding how to implement them. Some 30 years after Korea, America again provided the bulk of UN forces. The UN effort amassed 652,600 combat troops, 78 percent of whom were American. The U.S. death toll, though smaller than feared, also represented the bulk of the allied casualties.

IS COLLECTIVE SECURITY FEASIBLE?

Using regional alliances for collective security has very different practical ramifications from using the UN. But both methods assume it is in America's
interest to eliminate international disorder and instability by preventing aggression and squelching civil conflict. Indeed, stability is the cornerstone of any
collective security policy. Whatever the formal rhetoric of policymakers about
human rights and democracy, the primary goal of collective security is to
prevent invasions or occupations. Secondarily, collective security hopes to
preserve existing internal political arrangements.

Post–Cold War instability should not come as a surprise. For decades the
superpowers suppressed cultural, ethnic, linguistic, nationalistic, and religious
differences within allied states. However tragic their consequences, many of
the disputes surfacing around the world have legitimate causes and could not
be put off forever.

It would be ideal if previous political settlements, however artificial, were
not challenged violently. But the fundamental issue of U.S. policy should be
how to best advance America's security. However appealing the notion of
helping other peoples, the foremost duty of the U.S. government is to protect
the American people's lives, freedom, property, and constitutional system.

Does maintaining the international status quo make America more secure? It
should be obvious that global disorder per se does not threaten the United
States. Various African states, for instance, have suffered grievously for years
without any impact on America, even during the Cold War.

Whatever the value of international stability in this period, Washington paid
a high price for its interventions. It made many a bargain with the devil—or his
surrogates, like Iran's Shah, Nicaragua's Somoza, and Zaire's Mobutu—that
ultimately left the United States less secure. Islamic fundamentalists are now
considered the greatest threat in the Persian Gulf (and the long-term reason the
West backed Saddam Hussein in his aggression against Iran) if not in the rest of
the world. Yet they might never have seized power in Iran had the United States
not meddled in that country for years.

The end of the Cold War terminated the potentially zero-sum nature of
international relations and thereby reduced the value to the United States of
stability in distant lands. The tragic disintegration of Somalia, an American ally,
has few security implications. Washington can even view the Yugoslavian civil
war with detachment. People have advanced lurid scenarios involving the
spread of conflict to Albania, Greece, Turkey, and beyond, but a year and a half
has passed without the bloodshed expanding outside of former Yugoslavia.
Even in 1914, conflict in the Balkans never would have spread to the rest of
Europe, let alone involved America, without the interlocking alliances, worsen-
ing tensions, and widespread popular support for war that characterized all the
major powers before World War I. It is difficult to construct a plausible chain of
events leading to a similar global war today. If the Yugoslavian risk is still
thought to be serious enough to warrant action, then the Europeans, with the
most at stake, should take action. Should they decide the costs of intervention

outweigh the benefits, then Washington certainly has no reason to get involved.

What about the Persian Gulf? Many collective security advocates view it as the exception that proved the rule, the distant conflict between third-rate powers that threatened American security. In fact, relying on the Gulf as an example of the need for collective security demonstrates the weakness, rather than strength, of that case. It is impossible to point to another regional conflict with as potentially far-reaching implications for the United States. At most, Iraq's invasion of Kuwait called for a unique, one-time response.

Several factors now indicate, however, that Iraq's aggression could have been treated as a limited threat best met by other regional powers. First, Saddam Hussein was never positioned to gain a stranglehold over the West's oil supply, and thus its economy. Even if Iraq had conquered the entire Gulf it would have controlled little more than one-fifth of the international petroleum market. That share would have allowed Iraq to increase oil prices only modestly. Second, the protection of Saudi Arabia, not the liberation of Kuwait, was the primary U.S. interest, and that required a thin military tripwire rather than offensive action. Third, Iraq's neighbors, particularly a revenge-minded Iran, were capable of containing Hussein, especially if the objective was limited to guaranteeing Saudi Arabia's security. (Iraq's nuclear program posed a particular challenge to efforts at regional containment, but it did not motivate Washington's intervention. Nor is the very difficult and continuing problem of nuclear proliferation in itself a matter of collective security.)

But a judgment about the necessity of America's intervention in the Gulf is less important than a recognition that Iraq's aggression posed a worst-case scenario for the rest of the world. However compelling the case for action against Hussein, his aggression does not prove the need for some international mechanism, backed by the United States, to maintain order everywhere. In most cases instability poses little danger to America and can be contained by other states, met by more modest steps such as sanctions, or simply ignored.

What if an international incident sufficiently serious to warrant intervention arises? The United States should then help organize an ad hoc force, whether through the UN or among its alliance partners, to meet the specific contingency. The standard for American participation should be the same as that for unilateral military action: that the threat impinges a vital rather than peripheral interest, and therefore warrants the sacrifice of life, potentially huge expense, and other risks inherent to foreign intervention; that no other powers can meet the challenge; and that no peaceful alternatives exist to resolve the issue satisfactorily.

Collective security faces not only theoretical objections but several practical pitfalls as well. Neither regional alliances nor the UN is an attractive vehicle for policing the world. Regional arrangements and organizations can be quite effective in achieving security goals in specific regions. Yet they are less able to promote the broader goal of international stability. In particular, transforming NATO, an alliance constructed to constrain the USSR, into a regional constabulary to keep the peace not only in Europe but elsewhere is no easy task.

The most serious difficulty is reaching a consensus on new out-of-area duties. What long united the fractious European states was fear of Soviet aggression. Questions of Croatian and Slovenian independence, the boundaries between Hungary and Romania, and Islamic fundamentalism in Iran are likely to generate no similar unanimity of opinion.

Indeed, NATO members long had difficulty in agreeing on and implementing policies involving Europe. Persistent unfilled promises by the European members to hike defense spending, for example, demonstrated their tendency to free-ride on the United States. European support for building a natural gas pipeline to the Soviet Union, over strident American objections, showed a different European assessment of the threat from Moscow. And on out-of-area issues, cooperation was often nil. There was no higher priority for the Reagan administration than ousting Nicaragua's Sandinista government, yet several European countries provided aid to Managua. Some European states were equally uncooperative when it came to bombing Libya.

Disagreements among the Europeans on pressing international issues are evident today. Germany quickly recognized the independence of Croatia and Slovenia, over the objections of its neighbors, and it suspended arms sales to Turkey, a NATO member, because of bloody fighting between Turkish soldiers and Kurdish guerrillas. The future will bring more differences, calling into question NATO's ability to act as a peacekeeping organization even if its European members agree to amend its charter to so expand its responsibilities.

The gulf between American and European geopolitical interests is likely to widen, as some issues that worry the Europeans, like civil war in Yugoslavia, have no discernible impact on the United States. Other matters, such as Turkey's Kurdish problem, may be viewed from a broader perspective by Washington, because of U.S. ties to Israel. The likelihood of a transatlantic consensus on many issues in the absence of the Soviet threat is small. In short, NATO, or any other regional alliance, is too flawed to become the new vehicle for collective security.

Is collective security feasible through the UN? To work, collective security requires the cooperation of most major states and an impartial application of common principles. Unfortunately, the UN has never demonstrated a capacity to settle international disputes impartially. Moscow's new willingness to cooperate should not obscure the fact that for 45 years the UN was merely another Cold War battleground. In fact, the failure of the UN collective security system fueled the expansion of regional alliances.

Today, UN policymaking in the Security Council remains at the mercy of the communist rulers in Beijing who, despite a demonstrated willingness to shoot unarmed students and workers, possess a veto in the Security Council. And while many UN member states are moving toward democracy, scores remain dictatorships. Collective security is likely to be ineffective so long as the aggressor is a permanent member of the Security Council, a client state of a permanent member, or a country able to amass eight votes from the Security Council's 15 members, several of whom will be ruled by venal autocrats. Western democracies might choose to shield friendly states from UN censure and enforce-

ment action. Consider what Washington's attitude would be should Israel launch a preemptive attack against Syria, or South Korea against North Korea.

The flip-side risk is that increased peacekeeping authority might shift the UN toward an enforcement role not necessarily related to peacekeeping. That is, it might become a coercive tool of shifting international majorities that control the Security Council from time to time. That shift would be an acute concern if the UN possessed its own military. Although the United States could always veto inappropriate intervention, it would pay a political price for doing so. A recalcitrant Washington could then hardly count on Security Council approval when it wanted UN-backed military action.

The UN seems unsuited to the task of maintaining global order. Neither of the supposed models for UN enforcement of collective security offers much hope. True, traditional UN peacekeeping probably does have some value in helping to prevent small incidents that could spread and in giving responsible officials an excuse to resist domestic political pressure to provoke conflict. In the end, however, UN peacekeeping can only prevent fighting where both parties desire peace for other reasons. For instance, UN peacekeepers arrived in Croatia only after Serbia's Slobodan Milošević decided to redirect his campaign for a greater Serbia. In short, the UN cannot stop war among determined participants.

The major conflicts fought under the UN flag were UN conflicts in name only. The American commitment to intervene, even without allied support, was the most important factor in both Korea and the Gulf. While UN authority was a convenient and politically popular patina, it was not necessary to prosecute the war.

Nevertheless, the United States had to pay a price for the UN imprimatur. Washington's desire for Soviet support in the Security Council forced the administration to ignore the USSR's 1990 crackdown in the Baltic states. China's abstention in the critical council vote authorizing the use of force in the Gulf appears to have been purchased by new World Bank loans, which were approved shortly thereafter, possibly supplemented by reduced pressure on human rights issues. Several of the 10 nonpermanent members who had a voice in shaping Persian Gulf policy were interested in gaining additional Western financial assistance, if nothing else. And the United States was not above using its aid policies to procure votes: Baker responded to Yemen's opposition to the force resolution with a note to Yemen's ambassador stating, "That is the most expensive vote you have ever cast." While such log-rolling might seem unexceptional in a political forum like the United Nations, it hardly augurs well for the creation of an effective collective security system.

In the future other countries might expect not only bribes but also real influence. France's Mitterrand, for instance, apparently advanced his proposal for rejuvenating the Military Staff Committee because it would break America's military monopoly on UN actions. His foreign minister, Roland Dumas, later argued that Europe and the UN should help counter U.S. power. "American might reigns without balancing weight," he complained. Increasingly wealthy and influential, both Germany and Japan have indicated their desire for permanent seats on the Security Council and may also demand a say in future military operations. India, which possesses a potent military, may not be so quiescent in a future action. Among the new nonpermanent members of the Security Council are Cape Verde, Hungary, Morocco, and Venezuela, all of which will bring their own perspectives to Security Council deliberations.

There is nothing intrinsically wrong with the French desire to turn what has been a Potemkin collaborative security enterprise into a real one. But a system subject to the usual vagaries of any international organization, especially the UN, is not likely to either achieve its purpose or advance American interests. Not only might the UN be unduly restrictive where Washington felt intervention was necessary, but more important, a truly effective collective security system could drag the United States into conflicts that have no connection to American interests and that could be solved without Washington's assistance. What if, for instance, France, Germany, Greece, and Italy demand Security Council military action in Yugoslavia? Or if Armenia, Russia, and Turkey propose UN intervention in Azerbaijan? Should America again become the major combatant, perhaps consigning thousands of citizens to their deaths in a potentially interminable conflict with no impact on U.S. security?

Moreover, Washington would have to accept the theoretical possibility of UN action *against* the United States. Granted, it has veto power, but to exercise it in the face of a "world" demand for action would be embarrassing. Put bluntly, to vest the UN with significant military power requires that one trust the 14 other foreign states on the council more than one's own elected government. Past experience does not warrant placing that kind of confidence in the Security Council.

The proposal to give the UN an independent combat force, to be used at the secretary-general's discretion, is even less attractive. Whatever the international body's value as a debating chamber for letting off steam, it has never demonstrated principled leadership unhampered by numerous and arcane political pressures. Today, the UN's potential for abuse is tempered by the role of the Security Council, but if the UN gained the influence flowing from an independent armed force, a coalition of smaller states might attempt to move security power back to the General Assembly. Indeed, the United States itself looked at ways of circumventing the Soviet vetoes during the 1956 Middle East Crisis.

The dramatic international changes of recent years have truly yielded a "new world order," providing America with a unique opportunity to reassess its global role. For nearly five decades the United States has acted more like empire than republic, creating an international network of client states, establishing hundreds of military installations around the world, fighting in distant wars, and spending hundreds of billions of dollars annually on the military. That globalist foreign policy badly distorted the domestic political system, encouraging the growth of an expensive, repressive, secretive, and often out-of-control state.

The justification for interventionist military strategy, so alien to the original American design, was the threat of totalitarian communism. With that threat gone, the United States should return to its roots rather than look for convenient enemies through the mechanism of collective security.

The fundamental question of what is in America's interests remains. Which policy will best preserve American lives and treasure: entangling Washington in a chain of conflicts and civil wars? Or remaining aloof from struggles that affect the United States minimally, if at all?

To advance a unilateral policy of strategic independence, benign detachment, "America First," or even isolationism is not to advocate economic autarky and political isolation. As the world's most important trading state, the United States would be active in the global economy. American culture and ideals would continue shaping countries around the globe. And the United States could still cooperate internationally where collective action was required.

But most foreign security concerns could be handled locally and regionally, rather than globally. Without an orchestrator from Moscow, future acts of aggression are likely to be unique, dictated by the specific circumstances and histories of a region. Thus conflict, and potential conflict, will be best met by the neighboring states that understand the issues and have the most at stake. Peacekeeping is not a new activity; Europe and Latin America have seen many successful efforts to prevent conflict. And as war becomes a decreasingly acceptable tool of statecraft, regional peacemaking efforts are likely to enjoy increasing success.

Such regional arrangements may include a capacity to take military action. Four countries—Gambia, Ghana, Guinea, and Nigeria—dispatched 7,000 soldiers under the aegis of the Economic Community of West African States to police a cease-fire between three competing factions in Liberia's devastating civil war. Last year, Australia, Canada, New Zealand, the Solomon Islands, and Vanuatu created a multinational supervisory team to interrupt Papua New Guinea's blockade of the Pacific island of Bougainville. Russia has joined Georgia in attempting to establish a buffer zone in the territory of South Ossetia. Moreover, the Europeans are slowly rejuvenating, over fierce American resistance, the heretofore moribund Western European Union (WEU), which could organize future European military action.

France and Germany are discussing supplementing their joint force of 5,000 soldiers with an additional 35,000, and have invited other European states to contribute troops. Mitterrand and German chancellor Helmut Kohl proposed breathing new life into the WEU, to which nine of the twelve EC [European Community] countries belong, in order to develop a stronger European voice on defense. Unfortunately, their efforts encountered stiff resistance from the United States, backed by Great Britain, lest a meaningful WEU weaken America's NATO-based ties to the Continent. Nevertheless, at the December 1991 EC summit in Maastricht, the Netherlands, the Europeans agreed to begin channeling more defense resources through the WEU.

Even if one accepts the dubious position that the United States should maintain a residual protective role in Europe, there is no need for NATO to remake itself as a collective security organization. Rather, a separate European force would allow the EC to deal with nearby instability if it wished. NATO's Wörner, in fact, argues that the WEU will be complementary to NATO and will "act where NATO does not act." In such instances NATO-assigned forces could be lent to the WEU. Yugoslavia is one example where the WEU is far better suited to action than is NATO. Indeed, many if not most of Europe's interests in the Balkans and Eurasia will not be shared by the United States, if for no other reason than simple geography.

With no Soviet threat to contain, local and regional quarrels are no longer of vital concern. Those states that once were potential victims of aggression— underdeveloped Korea, defeated Germany and Japan, war-torn France and Britain, and other countries like Australia and New Zealand—have militaries that are now capable of meeting any likely threats to themselves or their neighbors. In the past, collective security was neither desirable nor practical. Today, it has even less appeal.

Questions for Discussion

1. How should the national interest be determined?
2. What is U.S. national interest in the post–cold war world?
3. What are the domestic political consequences of a U.S. policy of collective security?
4. Should the United States intervene in situations in which brutal atrocities and violations of human rights are being committed within a foreign country? What are the reasons for your answer?
5. If the United States and the United Nations had not intervened against Iraq to liberate Kuwait, what would have been the consequences to global stability? What are the reasons for your answer?

Suggested Readings

Abrams, Elliott. "Why America Must Lead." *National Interest*, no. 28 (Summer 1992), 56–62.

Allison, Graham T., Jr., and Robert F. Beschel Jr. "Can the United States Promote Democracy?" *Political Science Quarterly*, 107, no. 1 (Spring 1992), 81–98.

Art, Robert A., and Seyom Brown. *U.S. Foreign Policy: The Search for a New Role*. New York: Macmillan, 1993.

Binder, David, with Barbara Crossette. "As Ethnic Wars Multiply, U.S. Strives for a Policy." *New York Times*, February 7, 1993, pp. 1, 14.

Brzezinski, Zbigniew K. *Out of Control: Global Turmoil on the Eve of the Twenty-first Century*. New York: Scribner's, 1993.

Claude, Inis L. *Power and International Relations*. New York: Random House, 1962.

Cohen, Mitchell. "The Problem of Intervention: What Responses for the Democratic Left?" *Dissent*, 40, no. 1 (Winter 1993), 21–25.

Falk, Richard A. "In Search of a New World Model." *Current History*, 92, no. 573 (April 1993), 145–149.

Goodman, Allan E. *A Brief History of the Future: The United States in a Changing World Order.* Boulder, Colo.: Westview Press, 1993.

Huntington, Samuel P. "Why International Primacy Matters." *International Security*, 17, no. 4 (Spring 1993), 68–83.

Kegley, Charles W., Jr., and Eugene R. Wittkopf, eds. *The Future of American Foreign Policy.* New York: St. Martin's Press, 1992.

Krauthammer, Charles. "The Anti-Superpower Fallacy." *Washington Post*, April 10, 1992, p. A27.

———. "Drawing the Line at Genocide." *Washington Post*, December 11, 1992, p. A27.

Layne, Christopher. "The Unipolar Illusion: Why New Great Powers Will Rise." *International Security*, 17, no. 4 (Spring 1993), 5–51.

Maynes, Charles W. "Containing Ethnic Conflict." *Foreign Policy*, no. 90 (Spring 1993), 3–21.

Scheffer, David J. "Drawing the Line Short of Genocide." *Washington Post*, December 29, 1992, p. A15.

Smith, Gaddis. "What Role for America?" *Current History*, 92, no. 573 (April 1993), 150–154.

Smoler, Frederic (interview with Joseph Nye). "Are We Really Going the Way of the British Empire?" *American Heritage*, 42, no. 3 (May/June 1991), 45–51, 54, 56.

Wallop, Malcolm. "America Needs a Post-Containment Doctrine. *Orbis*, 37, no. 2 (Spring 1993), 187–203.

Acknowledgments (continued from page iv)

Sally Quinn. "Who Killed Feminism?" *Washington Post*, January 19, 1992, pp. C1, C2. Reprinted with permission of the author.

Patricia Ireland. "Feminism Is Not Dead" as it appeared in *Elle* Magazine, June 1993. Reprinted with permission of the author.

Ernest van den Haag. "Pornography and the Law." *The Heritage Lectures* No. 111. Reprinted with permission of The Heritage Foundation.

Michael Gartner. "Panel Discussion—Shaking the Foundations of Free Speech." 61 *Fordham Law Review*, no. 5 (April 1993), pp. 1133–1135. © 1993 Michael G. Gartner. Reprinted with permission.

Linda Fairstein. "Panel Discussion—The Privacy Rights of Rape Victims." 61 *Fordham Law Review*, no. 5 (April 1993), pp. 1137–1140. Reprinted with permission of Fordham Law Review. (*Note:* Footnotes have been deleted.)

Major Melissa Wells-Petry. "Reporters as the Guardians of Freedom." *Military Review*, 73, no. 2 (February 1993), pp. 26–35. Reprinted with permission.

Nadine Strossen. "Blaming the Victim: A Critique of Attacks on Affirmative Action." 77 *Cornell Law Review*. 974 (1992). © 1992 by Cornell University. All Rights Reserved. Reprinted by permission of Cornell University and Fred B. Rothman & Co. (*Note:* Footnotes have been deleted.)

Jay Girotto. "The Mythology of Affirmative Action." Reprinted with the permission of the author.

Daniel P. Franklin. "The President Is Too Powerful in Foreign Affairs." Reprinted with the permission of the author.

Ryan J. Barilleaux. "Understanding the Realities of Presidential Power." Reprinted with the permission of the author.

Paul Calamita and Thomas K. Plofchan, Jr. "Term Limits: Its Time Has Come." *The World & I*, January 1992; Vol. 7 #1. This article appeared in the indicated issue and is reprinted with permission from *The World & I*, a publication of *The Washington Times Corporation*, copyright © 1992.

Timothy S. Prinz. "Term Limitation: A Perilous Panacea." *The World & I*, January 1992; Vol. 7 #1. This article appeared in the indicated issue and is reprinted with permission from *The World & I*, a publication of *The Washington Times Corporation*, copyright © 1992.

Brink Lindsey. "System Overload." *Policy Review*, no. 55 (Winter 1991), pp. 52–56. Reprinted with permission of The Heritage Foundation.

Kenneth F. Warren. "We Have Debated Ad nauseum the Legitimacy of the Administrative State—But Why?" *Public Administration Review*, 53, no. 3 (May/June 1993). Reprinted with permission from Public Administration Review © by the American Society for Public Administration (ASPA), 1120 G Street NW, Suite 700, Washington DC 20005. All rights reserved.

Jeffrey M. Shaman and J. Clifford Wallace. "Interpreting the Constitution." *Judicature: The Journal of the American Judicature Society*, 71, no. 2 (Aug./Sept. 1987), pp. 80–87, 122. Reprinted with permission of the authors.

Albert P. Melone. "The Senate's Confirmation Role in Supreme Court Nominations and the politics of Ideology Versus Impartiality." *Judicature: The Journal of the American Judicature Society*, 75, no. 2 (Aug./Sept. 1991), pp. 68–79. Reprinted with permission of the author. (*Note:* Footnotes have been deleted.)

William Bradford Reynolds. "The Confirmation Process: Too Much Advice and Too Little Consent." *Judicature: The Journal of the American Judicature Society*, 75, no. 2 (Aug./Sept. 1991), pp. 80–82. Reprinted with permission of the author.

Jeanne Allen. "Choice Is Key to Better Schools." *The World & I*, May 1992. This article appeared in the indicated issue and is reprinted with permission from *The World & I*, a publication of *The Washington Times Corporation*, copyright © 1992.

Vicki Kemper. Interview of Jonathan Kozol. "Rebuilding the Schoolhouse." *Common Cause*, 19, no. 1 (Spring 1993). Reprinted with permission from *Common Cause* Magazine, copyright 1993; Washington, DC.

Julian Simon. "The Case for Greatly Increased Immigration." *Public Interest*, no. 102 (Winter 1991), 89–103. Reprinted with permission of the author.

John H. Chafee. "It's Time to Control Handguns." *Public Welfare*, 50, no. 4 (Fall 1992), pp. 18–22. Reprinted with the permission of the author.

David B. Kopel. "Hold Your Fire." *Policy Review*, no. 63 (Winter 1993), pp. 58–65. Reprinted with the permission of The Heritage Foundation.

Edward C. Luck. "Making Peace." Reprinted with permission from *Foreign Policy* 89 (Winter 1992–93). Copyright 1992 by the Carnegie Endowment for International Peace.

Doug Bandow. "Avoiding War." Reprinted with permission from *Foreign Policy* 89 (Winter 1992–93). Copyright 1992 by the Carnegie Endowment for International Peace.

Contributors

HERBERT M. LEVINE *taught political science at the University of Southwestern Louisiana for twenty years. He has written and edited several political science textbooks. He is co-author of* AnimalScam: The Beastly Abuse of Human Rights *(1993). He is currently a writer who lives in Chevy Chase, Maryland.*

JEANNE ALLEN is former manager of the Center for Educational Policy. She is currently executive director of Town Hall and an educational adviser to the Heritage Foundation and several other think tanks in the Washington, D.C. metropolitan area.

AMNESTY INTERNATIONAL USA is a division of Amnesty International, a worldwide human rights organization.

JAMES C. ANDERS is an attorney in the law firm of Fedor, Anders, Massey and Whitlark in Columbia, South Carolina.

DOUG BANDOW, a former special assistant to President Ronald Reagan, is a senior fellow at the Cato Institute in Washington, D.C. He is also a syndicated columnist.

RYAN J. BARILLEAUX is an associate professor of political science at Miami University (Ohio), where he is director of graduate studies. His publications include four books, most recently *Leadership and the Bush Presidency*, and numerous articles on U.S. politics and public policy.

PAUL CALAMITA is the articles editor of the *Journal of Law and Politics*.

JOHN H. CHAFEE is a member of the U.S. Senate from Rhode Island. He is a former governor of Rhode Island and secretary of the navy.

COMMITTEE ON THE CONSTITUTIONAL SYSTEM is a nonpartisan, nonprofit organization devoted to the study and analysis of the U.S. constitutional system.

PETE DU PONT is a former state legislator, U.S. congressman, and governor of Delaware. He is an attorney with Richards, Layton and Finger in Wilmington, Delaware.

LINDA FAIRSTEIN is chief, Sex Crimes Prosecution Unit, New York County District Attorney's Office. She is author of *Sexual Violence: The War against Rape* (1993).

DANIEL P. FRANKLIN is an associate professor of political science at Georgia State University in Atlanta. He is a former American Political Science Association Congressional Fellow and is the author of *Making Ends Meet: Congressional Budgeting in the Age of Deficits* (1993).

MICHAEL GARTNER served as president of NBC News from 1988 to 1993. He is editor and co-owner of the Ames (Iowa) *Daily Tribune.*

JAY R. GIROTTO is a student at Harvard College in Cambridge, Massachusetts, where he studies government and economics. He is the features editor for the *Harvard Political Review* and treasurer of the Harvard-Radcliffe Symphony Orchestra.

PATRICIA IRELAND is president of National Organization for Women.

GARRISON KEILLOR is a humorist. He is author of *Lake Wobegon Days* (1985) and *The Book of Guys* (1993).

MORTON KELLER teaches American political and legal history at Brandeis University in Waltham, Massachusetts. He is the author of *Affairs of State: Public Life in Late Nineteenth Century America* (1977) and *Regulating a New Economy: Public Policy and Economic Change in America, 1900–1933* (1990).

DAVID B. KOPEL is director of the Second Amendment Project at the Independence Institute, a Golden, Colorado, think tank. He is the author of *The Samurai, the Mountie, and the Cowboy: Should America Adopt the Gun Controls of Other Democracies?* (1992).

JONATHAN KOZOL is a former teacher. He is author of *Death at an Early Age: The Destruction of the Hearts and Minds of Negro Children in the Boston Public Schools* (1967) and *Savage Inequalities: Children in America's Schools* (1991).

RICHARD D. LAMM is a former governor of Colorado. He is the author of *The Immigration Time Bomb: The Fragmenting of America* (1985).

BRINK LINDSEY is a trade attorney in the Washington office of Willkie Farr and Gallagher.

EDWARD C. LUCK is president of the United Nations Association of the U.S.A., a nonpartisan national policy research and public membership organization.

BARRY W. LYNN is legislative counsel for the American Civil Liberties Union.

THURGOOD MARSHALL (1908–1993) served as associate justice of the U.S. Supreme Court from 1967 to 1991. As chief counsel for the National Association for the Advancement of Colored People's Legal Defense and Education Fund, he argued and won the 1954 landmark school desegregation case, *Brown v. Board of Education of Topeka, Kansas.*

PAUL McMASTERS is executive director of the Freedom Forum First Amendment Center at Vanderbilt University in Nashville, Tennessee. He is also president of the Society of Professional Journalists.

ALBERT P. MELONE is a professor in the Department of Political Science at Southern Illinois University at Carbondale.

TYE MENSER is a graduate of Harvard College (class of 1993) in Cambridge, Massachusetts. He was a staff writer for the *Harvard Political Review.*

THOMAS K. PLOFCHAN JR. is a research associate at the Center of National Security Law at the University of Virginia School of Law.

TIMOTHY S. PRINZ is assistant professor in the Department of Government and Foreign Affairs at the University of Virginia. He has published articles on congressional elections and congressional careers.

SALLY QUINN is a Washington writer. She is author of *Regrets Only* (1986) and *Happy Endings* (1991).

DIANE REHM is host of the "Diane Rehm Show" on WAMU-FM in Washington, D.C.

WILLIAM BRADFORD REYNOLDS served as counselor to the attorney general and assistant attorney general in the Civil Rights Division of the Justice Department in the Reagan administration. He is an attorney in the law firm of Dickstein, Shapiro and Morin in Washington, D.C.

THOMAS O. SARGENTICH is professor of law at Washington College of Law, American University, Washington, D.C.

JEFFREY M. SHAMAN is senior fellow of the American Judicature Society and a professor of law at DePaul University in Chicago.

BEN SHEFFNER is a graduate of Harvard College (class of 1993) in Cambridge, Massachusetts. He was managing editor of the *Harvard Political Review.*

JULIAN L. SIMON is professor of management at the University of Maryland in College Park. He is the author of *The Economic Consequences of*

Immigration (1989) and *Population Matters: People, Resources, Environment, and Immigration* (1990).

NADINE STROSSEN is president of the American Civil Liberties Union. She is a professor of law at New York Law School.

JOHN UPDIKE is the author of numerous novels, including *Rabbit at Rest* (1990) and *Brazil* (1994).

ERNEST VAN DEN HAAG is the former John M. Olin professor of Jurisprudence and Public Policy at Fordham University in New York City. He is a Distinguished Scholar at the Heritage Foundation in Washington, D.C.

J. CLIFFORD WALLACE is chief judge, U.S. Court of Appeals for the Ninth Circuit.

KENNETH F. WARREN is a professor of political science and public policy at Saint Louis University. He is the author of several articles in administrative law and electoral behavior.

MELISSA WELLS-PETRY, a major in the U.S. Army, is assistant executive officer to the judge advocate general at the Pentagon in Washington, D.C. She is author of *Exclusion: Homosexuals and the Right to Serve* (1993).

JONATHAN YARDLEY is a book critic and columnist for the *Washington Post*. He is the author of *Out of Step: Notes from a Purple Decade* (1991) and *States of Mind: A Personal Journey through the Mid-Atlantic* (1993).